THE
SMITHSONIAN
AND THE
AMERICAN INDIAN

THE
SMITHSONIAN
AND THE
AMERICAN INDIAN

MAKING A MORAL
ANTHROPOLOGY IN
VICTORIAN
AMERICA

CURTIS M. HINSLEY

SMITHSONIAN INSTITUTION PRESS
WASHINGTON AND LONDON

Library of Congress Cataloging-in-Publication Data

Hinsley, Curtis M.
  [Savages and scientists]
  The Smithsonian and the American Indian : making a moral
anthropology in Victorian America / Curtis M. Hinsley.
      p.   cm.
  Originally published: Savages and scientists, 1981. With a new
preface.
  Includes bibliographical references and index.
  ISBN 1-56098-409-0 (pbk.)
  1. Anthropology—United States—History.   2. Smithsonian
Institution. Bureau of American Ethnology—History.   3. Smithsonian
Institution—History.   I. Title.
GN17.3.U6H56   1994
301'.0973—dc20   94-5595
                                                              CIP

British Library Cataloguing-in-Publication Data available
00 99 98 97 96 95 94   5 4 3 2

♾ The paper used in this publication meets the minimum requirements of the
American National Standard for Permanence of Paper for Printed Library
Materials Z39.48-1984.

For permission to reproduce any of the illustrations, correspond directly with
the sources. The Smithsonian Institution Press does not retain reproduction
rights for these illustrations individually or maintain a file of addresses for
photo sources.

Photographic Credits
Department of Anthropology, National Museum of
Natural History, Smithsonian Institution: p. 73
National Anthropological Archives, National Museum of
Natural History, Smithsonian Institution: pp. 90, 96, 124,
144, 163, 165, 173, 176, 191, 198, 209, 241, 269, 288
National Museum of American Art, Smithsonian Institu-
tion: pp. 45, 93, 106, 168, 235, 278

For
Christopher
Sarina
&
Matthew

Contents

Abbreviations Used in the Notes

AES   American Ethnological Association
APS   American Philosophical Society
AR   Annual Report
ASW   Anthropological Society of Washington
BAE-IN   Records of 1903 Investigation of the Bureau of American Ethnology
BAE-LR   Bureau of American Ethnology Letterbooks
BP   Franz Boas Papers, American Philosophical Society
CNAE   Contributions to North American Ethnology
FMA   Field Museum Archives
FWP   Frederick Ward Putnam Papers, Harvard University Archives
GP   Gifford Pinchot Papers, Library of Congress
GPO   Government Printing Office
HUA   Harvard University Archives
LC   Library of Congress
LHM   Lewis Henry Morgan Papers, Rush Rhees Library, University of Rochester
MNCA   Museum of Navaho Ceremonial Art, Santa Fe, New Mexico
MP   W J McGee Papers, Library of Congress
NAA   National Anthropological Archives
OHS   Ohio Historical Society
PMA   Peabody Museum Archives
PSW   Philosophical Society of Washington
SI   Smithsonian Institution
SIA   Smithsonian Institution Archives
SIL   Smithsonian Institution Libraries
SW   Southwest Museum, Los Angeles, California
TASW   Transactions of the Anthropological Society of Washington
USNM   United States National Museum
WDW   William Dwight Whitney Papers, Sterling Library, Yale University
WHH   William Henry Holmes, "Random Records of a Lifetime," Library of the National Museum of American Art, Smithsonian Institution
WSHS   Wisconsin State Historical Society

Unless otherwise indicated, the date of publication for all SI, USNM, and BAE annual reports is the year following the date in the report title. Place of publication is Washington, D.C.

Preface to the Paperback Edition

A few days before Christmas 1882, Frank Hamilton Cushing, on a collecting trip for the Smithsonian Institution's Bureau of Ethnology, reported from the Hopi village of Oraibi that he had encountered implacable resistance from the village elders. Despite his threats and cajolings, Cushing had been unable to persuade the people of Oraibi to part with their belongings for deposit in "Father Washington's" museum of glass boxes in Washington. "They beg for war," he wrote, "and say: 'When the Caciques of the Americans sit on our decapitated heads, then they can dress our bodies in their clothes, feed our bodies with their victuals; then, too, they can have our things to take with them to the houses of their fathers.'" Having concluded that "we can make no collection here, save by force," Cushing hastily retreated from the Third Mesa village on Christmas morning.

In the 111 years since that moment of Oraibi resistance, and remarkably in the past two decades, the dynamics of national power projection and centralization, which so strongly marked and shaped nineteenth-century American culture—and took one form in the anthropological explorations and collections of the Smithsonian—have been countered, both globally and locally, by centrifugal forces of dispersal and return. Within the United States, the passage of the Native American Graves and Repatriation Act, as well as prior legislation directed more specifically to the Smithsonian and its National Museum of Natural History, indicate clearly that the Smithsonian Institution—which from its founding in 1846 promoted North American ethnography, linguistics, and archaeology as promising and important fields of inquiry—has entered a new phase in its relations with Native American peoples. In the last decade, in fact, the small and distant Oraibi voice of resistance has augmented to a chorus of assertion. By the turn of the twenty-first century, "Father Washington's museum" will include the National Museum of the American Indian, premised on survival and continuity rather than nineteenth-century assumptions of discontinuity and demise of Indian peoples.

Since the original publication in 1981 of *Savages and Scientists: The Smithsonian Institution and the Development of American Anthropology, 1846–1910,* the history of anthropology has also undergone considerable growth and transformation. Far from abating, the crises of field access, method, and purpose that overtook the anthropological subdisciplines under the postcolonial conditions of the last third of this century have deepened, calling forth in turn proposals for "reinventing" the discipline, predictions of an "end of anthropology" altogether, and fruitful new perspectives on ethnographic practice as dialogue in the field or literary production at home. Laced throughout the new self-reflections has been an acute consciousness of the embeddedness

11

of anthropology, as both practice and product, in global power relationships. As we now approach the end of the twentieth century, the history of anthropology has grown well beyond issues of "professionalization" to be understood as a promising route toward analyzing the global processes of modernity—specifically the relationships between imperial ideologies, national and global economic domination, and the emergence of disciplinized knowledge forms. Thus, for instance, the painful and immensely complex matter of repatriation of bones and burial goods has become an issue extending beyond proprietorship per se; indeed, the debate is ultimately not over control of bones at all, but over control of narrative: the stories of peoples who went before and how those peoples (and their descendants) are to be currently represented and treated. The heart of the matter, as always, lies in the negotiation between power and respect. Under the current conditions of scrutiny, virtually every institution, tool, and assumption of the anthropologist has come under renewed examination.

In the current context, it seems to me, the history of the relationship between Native Americans, the Bureau of American Ethnology (1879–1965), and its parent institution, the Smithsonian, offers valuable insights into earlier worlds of intention, imagination, theory, and practice—precisely those regions currently under reconsideration and revision. Those insights include the valuable reminder that the history of nineteenth-century anthropology in the United States cannot be separated from deeper cultural quests for understanding, order, and moral balance in a social and political world that seemed to many to border constantly on violent disorder. In this search for moral balance, Native Americans were always more than subjects; they were also active participants as models or resisters, as guides and informants—even, like Francis LaFlesche and William Jones, as anthropologists themselves. In anthropology, as in so many other fields, then and now, the Smithsonian Institution came to express and embody the assumptions, projections, and desires of diverse elements of American society.

New Castle, Delaware
January 1, 1994

Part 1

Anthropology at the
Smithsonian Institution
1846–1880

I

"Magnificent Intentions": Washington, D.C., and American Anthropology in 1846

In the closing years of the nineteenth century, aging, well-traveled American men of letters were fond of looking back, with condescension and nostalgia, to an unformed, innocent antebellum America. Reliving his first visit to Washington in 1849, Henry Adams remembered a sleepy, isolated outpost where "the brooding indolence of a warm climate and a negro population hung in the atmosphere heavier than the catalpas." The early national capital had lacked physical, social, and moral structure: here "the want of barriers, of pavements, of forms; the looseness, the laziness; the indolent Southern drawl; the pigs in the streets; the negro babies and their mothers with bandanas; the freedom, openness, swagger, of nature and man" had lulled and soothed tight Boston nerves. Even twenty years later, amid the chaos and crush of the first Grant administration, Washington still seemed "a mere political camp" to Adams. His fellow Bostonian, Edward Everett Hale, recalled the capital city of the 1840s as a "mud-hole" where "everything had the simplicity and ease, if you please, of a small Virginia town." The capital was so isolated from the larger society that the visitor of the forties seemed to come "out of America into Washington."[1]

Visiting Europeans reserved special spleen for the capital city. Here in "the headquarters of tobacco-tinctured saliva" Charles Dickens noted in 1842 the "spacious avenues, that begin in nothing, and lead nowhere; streets, mile-long, that only want houses, roads, and inhabitants; public buildings that need but a public to be complete; and ornaments of great thoroughfares, which only lack great thoroughfares to ornament." With little trade and a meager permanent population, Washington seemed to Dickens only a "City of Magnificent Intentions." Anthony Trollope, following in the footsteps of his famous mother, commented no less caustically. He arrived in the first, dismal winter of the Civil War to find a pretentious failure of a city, three-fourths of it "wild, trackless, unbridged, uninhabited, and desolate." Trollope saw little nobility of taste in the sparse government structures, still less in the "bastard gothic" architecture of the Smithsonian "Castle." But it was the

sight of the unfinished stump of the Washington Monument on a bleak
Sunday afternoon that evoked a summary judgment of the city and the nation:

> There, on the brown, ugly, undrained field, within easy sight of the
> President's house, stood the useless, shapeless, graceless pile of stones.
> It was as though I were looking on the genius of the city. It was vast,
> pretentious, bold, boastful with a loud voice, already taller by many
> heads than other obelisks, but nevertheless still in its infancy,—ugly,
> unpromising, and false.[2]

Jibes of European and American cosmopolites notwithstanding, antebellum
Washington was not so much a swampy wilderness as a study in American
contrasts. Here the unfinished dreams of civic and national splendor and the
boisterous, brutal realities of American politics, commerce, and racial conflict
coexisted in "a curious combination of sophistication and small-town simplicity."[3] Washington shared in the revival of the national economy following
the panic of 1837, and local business prospered as more government officials
brought their families to live in the capital during the 1840s. But Washington, like other American cities, was also plagued by widespread poverty,
restlessness among low-paid workers, grossly inadequate sanitary facilities,
and a distressing level of lawlessness. Furthermore, despite the general prosperity of the official city, trade remained largely local. By the end of the
thirties it was apparent that the earlier dream of local merchants and investors
of a major commercial metropolis on the Potomac was not to be realized.
With or without the highly touted Chesapeake and Ohio Canal, Washington
would never rival Baltimore or Philadelphia in manufacture or national trade.[4]

In the midst of prosperity, moreover, the capital had a unique racial
situation that produced ambivalent feelings among Whites, northern or southern. Until its abolition in 1850, a lively slave trade existed in the District;
indeed, as James Renwick's Smithsonian building began to rise on the Mall
in the late forties, construction workers could view across the street from its
rear entrance the slave pens of two of the major traders of the District. In
1840, the Black population of the District comprised nearly a third of the
total; over the next decade the general population increased by twenty percent.
The Black population increased somewhat more slowly, dropping to twenty-
seven percent of the District by 1850. But within the Black populace, a
significant change occurred, as the number of free Blacks increased by seventy
percent during the decade; in 1850, the Black free/slave ratio had reached
nearly four to one. The established free Black community of Washington
continued to draw from outside.[5]

The response of Whites in Washington was revealing. As the issue of
slavery extension began to arise in the late forties, the capital was caught
between the sensitive national debate and equally delicate local conditions.
By 1848 the slavery issue was the "all-absorbing topic of the day."[6] But

interest focused chiefly on the District slave trade, and after its abolition two years later, the city relapsed into a strange quiet. By a kind of tacit agreement, Constance Green has suggested, Washingtonians decided to "say nothing, do nothing, that might upset the precarious sectional balance." The capital was "like the stillness at the eye of a hurricane" throughout the prosperous, turbulent 1850s.[7]

Growing scientific and artistic reputation perhaps made it easier to ignore political tempests. If the vision of commercial greatness had evaporated by midcentury, there had always been an older dream, shared by presidents Washington, Jefferson, and John Q. Adams, of "a cultural capital" spreading enlightenment to the nation by roads, canals, and rivers.[8] This vision of Washington as the source and sponsor of internal cultural improvements took several major strides toward realization in the forties, with the firm establishment of the Coast Survey under Alexander Dallas Bache; the Naval Observatory; and the Smithsonian Institution. In 1848 a newspaper correspondent could observe that "if there be one question set at rest in this community, it is that public opinion has decided that the national metropolis shall be distinguished for the cultivation of the mind."[9] Perhaps science and art would bring glory to Washington.

Early efforts provided little ground for optimism. The federal scientific agencies of the early republic did not owe their existence to any commitment to science as such—President Adams's call in 1825 for vigorous support of science met with no positive response in Congress but resulted from either practical needs or the exigencies of exploring and taming the continent. Local scientific societies also fared poorly. William Stanton has observed that, until the 1840s, Washingtonians "had founded a dreary train of institutions—the United States Military Philosophical Society, the Metropolitan Society, the Columbian Institute, the American Historical Society, to name only those of most imposing mien—only to see them crumble through apathy and neglect."[10] The Columbian Institute, founded in 1816, received a charter and five acres of swamp from Congress, but little else. The Institute membership, mainly of local businessmen, civil servants, and military men, managed to limp along through the next two decades, until its records and property were absorbed by the National Institution for the Promotion of Science in 1840.

In its brief burst of activity in the early 1840s, the National Institute (as it was called after 1842) demonstrated both the possibilities and limits of Washington science. The Institute, founded in 1840, resulted directly from two contemporary events: the prolonged public debate over Englishman James Smithson's bequest of $500,000 to the United States to found in Washington an institution "for the increase and diffusion of knowledge among men"; and the United States Exploring Expedition under Charles Wilkes, the country's first such large-scale effort, which began its four-year voyage in 1838. Joel R. Poinsett, who had been secretary of war under Martin Van Buren and was an amateur scientist from South Carolina, had successfully launched the Wilkes Expedition in the face of congressional apathy. Two years later, when the first crates of materials began to arrive in Philadelphia and Washington, Poinsett saw that some organization would be necessary to care for the specimens in order to prevent their dispersal and destruction. But Poinsett also had his eye on the Smithsonian funds. He hoped that the Englishman's money would support a national museum, for which the Wilkes materials, along with the National Institute's own circulars, would provide the basic collections. Between 1840 and 1845, Poinsett, Francis Markoe, and J. J. Abert—all government officials—lobbied to establish the Institute as the heir to the Wilkes collections and the Smithsonian monies. Like its ill-starred predecessor, the Columbian Insitute, the National Institute received a charter but little money from Congress. Ultimately it lost both the collections and the Smithsonian funds, but its failure exposed central issues in the politics of antebellum American science.[11]

The debate over the Smithson bequest revolved around several alternative institutions, including a library, university, observatory, and an agricultural experimental station. Poinsett argued for a "National Museum, with Professors who shall perform the double office of Curators and Lecturers," as an important component of a respectable national culture.[12] After the arrival of the first massive shipment of 50,000 specimens, Congress appropriated $5,000 for their care, and the Institute hired as curator Dr. Henry King, a geologist and mining expert employed in the Ordnance Bureau. The secretary of state made the new Patent Office Building, with its spacious hall, available for display of the treasures. Here King valiantly attempted to organize the swelling Wilkes materials, which soon crowded out the Institute's own growing collections. But when the ships came home in 1842, Wilkes, Charles Pickering, and others of the Expedition's scientific staff, far from showing gratitude for the Institute's labors, complained of the disastrous incompetence of King and the museum-keepers. Wilkes and Pickering argued to a parsimonious Congress that, with the gathering completed, the scientific enterprise was barely under way; preservation, research, and publication now required further public outlay, and these functions must be performed by the scientists familiar with their own collections. They had little patience with the amateurs of the Institute, who saw themselves as a "clearing-house for natural history."[13]

The Wilkes Expedition presented serious issues of private and public interests in science. The Institute men noted, for instance, that the Expedition's zoologist, Titian Peale, had labelled many valuable pieces as his private property, and they suspected that several barrels had been emptied in his Philadelphia museum before coming on to the capital. On the other hand, both Congress and the Expedition scientists expressed concern that the Institute, a private group of "friends of science," should control and possibly damage public collections.[14]

The dispute, furthermore, involved divergent conceptions of "museum." The Institute men clearly envisioned a museum chiefly as an institution of preservation and display, not without a certain element of public entertainment, while the Expedition scientists saw the museum essentially as a locus of study and the collections as a permanent research base, an extension of the Expedition itself. When they ruefully recorded that Dr. King had dismembered their specimens and otherwise violated their collections, behind the charge lay a perception of the museum as an ongoing scientific enterprise. Within such a vision, it is worth noting, lay a significant concept of the specimen as scientific property. Legally, of course, the collections belonged to the government; but, in a second and increasingly important sense, they were peculiarly the property of the collector-scientist, for only he knew them in their entirety and could elicit their full meaning for the public. The problem was both philosophical and proprietary, for it involved the very definition of a scientific object.

The appreciation of the scientist's unique, continuing interest in the objects of his study distinguished the Expedition staff from that of the amateur Institute. Similarly, the clue to the ultimate failure of the National Institute lies in the two chief complaints lodged against it: ignorance and unworthy purposes. Despite King's ineptitude, the second complaint was more crucial. The Institute men showed primary concern for national greatness as exhibited in collections of exotic objects—a kind of scientific and cultural boosterism— but little sympathy for patient, loving understanding of the specimens themselves. Externally oriented showcases could only undermine quiet, internal scientific growth—so the American experience seemed to indicate. In 1829, one John Varden had opened to the public a commercial enterprise, the "Washington Museum of Curiosities," complete with stuffed birds and Egyptian mummies. When the free National Institute drove him out of business, he sold out to it—and promptly became its assistant curator. [15] The Varden case was symbolic and instructive. The Institute men lacked an essential respect for the natural world, a nineteenth-century form of piety that set the true scientist apart from the amateur or the pandering commercial popularizer.

The attitudinal gulf was real and determinative. Through much of the nineteenth century, the number of men who shared serious scientific aspirations exceeded the capacity of the society to provide opportunities for full-time pursuit of those interests. [16] As Alexis deTocqueville perceived at the time, organization for power and promotion of individual and group interest was a central dynamic in American life; but historically this has occurred unevenly. Scientific (like artistic) interests came relatively late to organizational maturity. Consequently, members of the scientific community of mid-century were often forced to rely as much on personal judgments of character as on formal organizational affiliation for identity and mutual recognition.

This was especially true in the disparate collection of studies that comprised anthropology.

In August 1846, the New Confederacy of the Iroquois assembled around the light of their "emblematic council fire" in Rochester, New York, to hear the respected ethnologist Henry Rowe Schoolcraft. In a stirring paean to American distinctiveness, Schoolcraft urged Lewis Henry Morgan and the other young men of Rochester to devote themselves to the study of America's "free, bold, wild, independent, native race." America was unique. Without European patronage, Americans depended exclusively on "personal exertions, springing from the bosom of society" for the pursuit of history, literature, and science. Morgan's New Confederacy was such a voluntary effort, a "brotherhood of letters" to advance historical research, promote antiquarian knowledge, and cultivate polite literature.

The time had come, said Schoolcraft, to develop an American scientific and literary tradition: "No people can bear a true nationality, which does not exfoliate, as it were, from its bosom, something that expresses the peculiarities of its own soil and climate." In constructing its "intellectual edifice" America must draw "from the broad and deep quarries of its own mountains, foundation stones, and columns and capitals, which bear the impress of an indigenous mental geognosy."

The native American Indians had borne this distinctive "mental geognosy," and the present tribes, "walking statues" of their progenitors, were monuments far more worthy of study than the antiquarian remains of the Old World. The White man had superseded the Red in America, which obliged him to preserve the memory of the aborigine. After all, Schoolcraft reminded his audience, "their history is, to some extent, our history," a past full of deep tragic and poetic events. "The tomb that holds a man," he concluded, "derives all its moral interest *from* the man, and would be destitute of it, without him. America is the tomb of the Red man."[17]

Eight days after his address in Rochester, Schoolcraft sent to the Board of Regents of the new Smithsonian Institution a "Plan for the Investigation of American Ethnology," presented at its first meeting in September. In a far less effusive style than the Rochester speech, the veteran ethnologist proposed several major areas of activity for the Institution: support for a "Library of Philology"; archaeological investigation, particularly of the ancient earthworks of the Mississippi Valley; and material collections from living tribes to create a "Museum of Mankind."

Schoolcraft soberly outlined a field of inquiry open for exploitation and ripe for the application of scientific techniques. After a brief, tantalizing reference to the mysteries of the continent, he urged "the scrutiny of exact observation and description . . . under the lights of induction and historical analysis . . . to enable us to appreciate and understand our position on the globe." As investigators applied scientific method to ethnology, the boundaries of mystery and conjecture would certainly recede before established facts. Schoolcraft's optimism embraced various subfields of the science of man: physiology, history, archaeology, geography, and geology. But he stressed language as a "more enduring monument of ancient affinities than the physical type" and called attention to the study of mythology.[18]

Taken together, Schoolcraft's prospectus to the Smithsonian and his Rochester address of the preceding week reflect the undefined state of anthropology in 1846. Inspired in part by a romantic attachment to the natural wonders and vast beauty of America, but embracing a wide range of both established and developing branches of inquiry, the study of man in America stood somewhere between the amateur enthusiasm of Rochester and the scientific standards soon established at the Smithsonian, between a past marked by speculation and an anticipated future of scientific precision.

Created by the conflux of several distinct traditions, mid-century anthropology comprised a series of questions, pursued through methods that cut across various fields and traditions. In Joseph Henry's words, anthropology enjoyed a unique status as a "common ground" for students of the physical sciences, natural history, archaeology, language, history, and literature. All could contribute; all could draw intellectual enlightenment and moral inspiration.[19] Furthermore, if anthropology was institutionally and methodologically fractured, the inquiry nonetheless addressed issues that were crucial to American national and cultural identity.

"Great question has arisen from whence came those aboriginals of America?" Thus Jefferson expressed, in his *Notes on the State of Virginia* of 1784, the central historical question that impelled American anthropology until the Civil War. To be sure, for most Americans the significance of the question was never apparent. John Adams wrote his blunt opinion to Jefferson in 1812:

> Whether Serpents Teeth were sown here and sprung up Men; whether Men and Women dropped from the Clouds upon the Atlantic Island; whether the Almighty created them here, or whether they immigrated from Europe, are questions of no moment to the present or future happiness of Man. Neither Agriculture, Commerce, Manufactures, Fisheries, Science, Literature, Taste, Religion, Morals, nor any other good will be promoted, or any Evil averted, by any discoveries that can be made in answer to those questions.[20]

In part Adams predicted accurately, for anthropologists struggled for decades to find an acceptable utilitarian rationale. But in a more important sense, his skepticism was misplaced. Between the Revolution and the Civil War, Americans groped for an understanding of their republican experiment, their civilization, and their destiny. The creed that gradually emerged from this introspection placed the new nation outside the ravages of human history, freed from the burdens of corrupt European institutions, as a new, perhaps final hope and home for man. Schoolcraft succinctly expressed this providential vision in 1846, when he described America as "a region destined for the human race to develope itself and expand in . . . a seat prepared for the re-union of the different stocks of mankind."[21]

Integral to the national teleology was a picture of the American continent waiting through the ages, pristine and nonhistorical, for the White man's arrival in order to play out a providentially assigned role. The freshness of America lay in the continent's great natural age without historical and moral blemish. It possessed, in other words, no human burdens, since before Columbus the continent had never known civilized institutions.[22] Accordingly, Americans lent no moral significance to Indian "history," which was, as they saw it, not history at all, but the meaningless meanderings of a benighted people. In retrospect it is apparent that the American Indians presented nineteenth-century White Americans with the challenge and opportunity of expanding accepted notions of history so as to embrace radically different human experiences. This proved impossible. Instead, the anthropologist commonly functioned as a variant of the historian, studying and justifying his own history and civilization through the Indian. In the end, few escaped the degradation of denying peoples the integrity of their own histories.

Jefferson's query suggested a second purpose, however, more religious than political in import. George Stocking has identified in British ethnology of the early nineteenth century a central goal: "to show how all the modern tribes and nations of men might have been derived from one family, and so far as possible to trace them back historically to a single source."[23] Like their contemporaries in various fields of natural history, students of anthropology in England and the United States were engaged in a strenuous effort to contain the exploding diversity of the human world within the explanatory framework of the Mosaic account. Defense of monogenism—original human unity in divine creation and descent from a single pair—lay at the religious core of American anthropology into the twentieth century, especially in Washington circles. In service of this goal, Joseph Henry generally excluded from the Smithsonian discussion of physical anthropology as politically explosive and morally repugnant.

For American no less than for British ethnologists, the study of man was a historical and geographical search of deep religious import. Furthermore, as discussed below, while the historical orientation lost ground in succeeding decades to systems of evolutionary classification, beneath these developments the central concern with human unity persisted. In the American context, the significance of Native Americans to White historical identity and national destiny, and the progressive annihilation of these peoples, compounded and complicated the religious impulse in anthropology, lending an urgency to

Indian studies that emerged in Americans' frequent expressions of "salvage ethnology": a unique blend of scientific interest, wistfulness, and guilt.

In their national and religious quest, American investigators at mid-century followed three distinct routes: archaeology, philology, and physical anthropology. The lack of consensus on method, untapped sources of data, and the relative lack of institutional structures and professional criteria created a sense of openness and lively competition that would characterize the subfields of anthropology in this country to the end of the century.

Americans had first encountered the earthworks of the Ohio and Mississippi River valleys in the 1780s, but it was not until after the War of 1812 that Caleb Atwater, of Circleville, Ohio, undertook a systematic investigation.[24] The American Antiquarian Society published his results in 1820. Atwater saw in the earthworks evidence of early occupation by a sedentary, law-abiding people. He hypothesized a migration from northern Asia at a remote period; a long, fixed abode in North America; and movement southward to found the ancient civilizations of Peru and Mexico. A subsequent migration from southern Asia by ancestors of the modern Indians supposedly superseded these original occupants of the American continent.[25]

Less systematic, more speculative observers followed Atwater. Most attempted to account for the differences between the supposed high civilization of the ancient Americans and the more primitive condition of the historical Indians by positing waves of migration and displacement. James H. McCulloh was among the more cautious in arguing against affinities based on the superficial artifacts of the mounds, which might be simply the products of a common human nature. McCulloh's *Researches,* a compilation of the work of others, concluded that ancestors of the present Indians came from the south and built the mounds. Despite disagreements over the identity of the mound-builders, most archaeological investigators agreed that the ancient inhabitants of America had originated elsewhere; and that "physical, moral, and traditionary evidence" pointed to Asia.[26]

Thomas Jefferson provided one of the first accounts of opening a mound, but he predicted that language would ultimately offer "the best proof of the affinity of nations which ever can be referred to." Schoolcraft, too, writing in his diary in 1823, observed that "Philology is one of the keys of knowledge which, I think, admits of its being said that, although it is rather rusty, the rust is, however, a proof of its antiquity. I am inclined to think that more true light is destined to be thrown on the history of the Indians by a study of their languages than of their traditions, or any other feature."[27] As the mounds explorers displayed more imagination than rigor, the predictions of Jefferson and Schoolcraft took on credibility. In the late 1840s, John R. Bartlett expressed a common judgment of archaeological labors when he wrote that "the practical investigations made from time to time by various individuals, have not been sufficiently thorough and extensive, nor have they developed sufficient data to warrant or sustain any definite or satisfactory conclusions."[28] Not until the 1860s would archaeology begin to attain the theoretical respect and academic establishment that philology had enjoyed since the eighteenth century. Faced with the "bewildering visions" of migrations,[29] a number of individuals turned hopefully to philology for the solution to the puzzle of American man.

In 1819 Peter Stephen Duponceau first announced his discovery that all American Indian languages appeared to demonstrate a uniform grammatical structure and underlying plan of thought, which he labeled "polysynthesis."[30] In Duponceau's view, the polysynthetic form permitted expression of many ideas in few words by consolidating the most significant sounds of simple words into compounds rich in meaning, and by combining various parts of speech into verbal forms to express "not only the principal action, but the greatest possible number of the moral ideas and physical objects connected with it."[31] Duponceau seemed to have penetrated to the "vital principle" controlling American Indian languages, a fact which, he hoped, would raise American philology out of the miasma of vocabulary comparisons to a respectable place beside European comparative philology. In America, grammatical structure would become the "true key to the origin and connection of the varieties of human speech."[32]

Duponceau's polysynthesis was more than a description of linguistic connection. He implied as well a single stage of mental development, thus subtly moving the question of Indian identity from the realm of historical affinity to one of developmental stages. The change was further encouraged by the tendency of philologists to borrow the prestige of natural-science method and terminology. Thus, when John Pickering adopted Duponceau's theory a few years later, he stressed the unity of form, noting that the languages exhibited a "uniform system, with such differences only as constitute varieties in natural objects."[33]

Albert Gallatin, Swiss-born statesman and student of Indian languages, similarly accepted polysynthesis as a demonstrated characteristic of American languages, but made allowance for exceptions, such as Basque in Europe, and held out the possibility of undiscovered connections across the oceans. To Gallatin, common structure indicated common origin, while diversity in vocabulary suggested a long time-span since dispersion across the continent—a principle that Jefferson had espoused. Gallatin speculated that the first inhabitants of America arrived at a remote time, "probably not much posterior to that of the dispersion of mankind." As he saw it, American languages showed clear signs of primitive origins; their form derived from "natural causes," indicating that the Native Americans had not degenerated from a higher state, as Schoolcraft and the mounds explorers maintained. Gallatin thus contributed another support to a paradigm of progressive development, though not yet of evolution.[34]

By mid-century the discovery of a single "antique plan of thought" in the structure of aboriginal tongues seemed destined to exert a significant influence on ethnology. With obvious satisfaction, the popular historian George Bancroft announced that a "savage physiognomy" characterized all Indian dialects; each was "almost absolutely free from irregularities, and is pervaded and governed by undeviating laws." The unreflecting American savage, like the bee building geometrically perfect cells, demonstrated "rule, method, and completeness" in his language. Far from indicating degeneration, the aboriginal tongues of America showed unmistakable signs of being "held in bonds of external nature." The Indian thought and spoke in terms of concrete experience, apparently lacking powers of abstract expression. Linguistic evidence showed, said Bancroft, that the American aborigines were still in "that earliest stage of intellectual culture where reflection has not begun."[35]

Bancroft conveyed to a wide audience the optimism (and ethnocentrism) of students of American languages at mid-century. They saw a certainty and regularity lacking in other approaches to anthropology. The precision, it should be noted, did not derive from the fact that language was a human phenomenon. Quite the opposite: linguistic regularities occurred in spite of man's efforts, indicating the operation of general principles of divine origin. Just as men could cultivate and adorn but not fundamentally alter the geology of the earth, so "language, in its earliest period, has a fixed character, which culture, by weeding out superfluities, inventing happy connections . . . and through analysis, perfecting the mastery of the mind over its instruments, may polish, enliven, and improve, but cannot essentially change."[36]

The work of the philologists pointed strongly toward aboriginal American unity and threw into question the ancient civilizations imagined by archaeologists. Both groups agreed, though, that the first inhabitants of America, whoever they were and whenever they had arrived, had migrated from somewhere else; thus they supported the orthodox view of the unity of mankind. As Bancroft summarized their findings, the "indigenous population of America offers no new obstacle to faith in the unity of the human race."[37]

Others were less sure. In the two decades prior to the Civil War, researchers in physical anthropology—notably Samuel George Morton, George Robins Gliddon, and Josiah Clark Nott—aided by the impressive scientific support of Louis Agassiz and the explorations of Ephraim George Squier, demonstrated that Native Americans, with the exception of the Eskimo, possessed a uniform and apparently unique physical type. This "American School" of anthropology directly challenged the Mosaic account by hypothesizing an indigenous, isolated American race, created in and fitted to the climate of America.[38]

Physical anthropology as systematic scientific inquiry in America began with Morton, a Philadelphia physician and anatomist. In the 1830s he began assembling a collection of crania, mainly of North American natives, that was unsurpassed and totaled nearly 1,000 by his death in 1851. In 1839 he published *Crania Americana*, based on his skull collection. This landmark in physical anthropology, the result of a decade of work, exhibited a consistency, precision, and thoroughness that established Morton as the leading American authority in the field.[39]

Morton hoped to determine "whether the American aborigines of all epochs have belonged to one race or to a plurality of races."[40] His conclusion was straightforward: the American Indian peoples, excluding the Eskimo tribes, belonged to a single race. This race Morton divided into two families, the Toltecan and Barbarous (American). The culturally superior Toltecan had built the North American mounds and also established the semi-civilizations of Central America; the historical Indians had descended from the inferior Barbarous (American) branch. In other words, Morton denied racial separation of the mound-builders from the modern American Indians but distinguished between two "families" in terms of cultural development. He emphasized that physically, morally, and intellectually this "separate and peculiar" race of America exhibited no connections with the Old World; even if apparent connections were discovered in the arts and religions, he maintained, the "organic characters" of the Indians would prove them a single, distinct race.[41]

Morton's strength lay in an unprecedented number of cranial measurements; but in fact he relied on only one or two indices, notably the formation of the occipital portion of the skull, in determining an ideal dominant type of American cranium. Repeatedly he noted exceptions and wide variation, but in his conclusions he either ignored them or attributed them to cultural factors.[42] Morton's opinions underwent little modification; he repeated them in his *Inquiry* of 1842, his "Account of a Craniological Collection" in 1848, and his "Physical Type of the American Indians," contributed posthumously to Schoolcraft's *Indian Tribes* in 1852.[43]

Morton's work provided the empirical base for polygenist arguments in the searing slavery-related controversies of the antebellum decade. The polygenist implications of Morton's theories required only time and encouragement to emerge fully. They received both. Louis Agassiz found in Morton important confirmation of his own theories of uniform distribution and local diversity that he found characteristic of the natural history of the New World. Nott and Gliddon drew heavily on Morton in introducing the basics of polygenist doctrine to a popular audience. Their ambitous *Types of Mankind* marshaled the evidence of Morton, the archaeologists, and the philologists to drive their points home. The languages of America, uniform in structure but diverse in vocabulary (as Gallatin had argued), indicated great age and common origin. The mounds similarly suggested long occupation of the continent. But physical anthropology was conclusive: "American crania, antique as well as modern, are unlike those of any other race of ancient or recent times." Other ethnological data—an increasing number of fossil human bones; the apparent lack of alphabet, domestication practices, indigenous agriculture, astronomy, or calendar systems—all seemed to confirm the antiquity, unity, and isolation of the Native Americans.[44]

The work of Nott and Gliddon circulated widely, but it stimulated more vituperation than research and consequently discredited physical anthropology for decades. As Samuel F. Haven, librarian of the American Antiquarian Society, noted in 1856, Morton's theories had become hopelessly enmeshed in "polemical associations."[45] Because of the theological and political complications, physiologists busied themselves in other pursuits, and Morton at his death in 1851 left no disciple to carry on his researches. The Academy of Natural Sciences in Philadelphia inherited his collection of crania.[46]

The National Institute had a "special duty," Joel Poinsett wrote in 1841, to "inquire into the history of the people we have dispossessed." But the structure of the Institute hampered the inquiry: philology was subsumed under the department of geography; physical anthropology fell under natural history; and the department of American history and antiquities embraced all studies of "the Indian races, now fading from the earth; their mounds and pyramids, and temples and ruined cities," as well as questions of their origins and subsequent "degeneration."[47] The fractured anthropology of the Institute epitomized the methodological and disciplinary confusion that both plagued and enriched the inquiry. But within the flux of theory and observation, certain long-term, significant trends emerged. Interwined in the anthropology of the first half of the century were two distinct traditions of reaction to the phenomena of human variety, each a function of individual temperament and intellectual and religious commitment. For pious Christians fully committed to human unity through the biblical account, historical inquiry backward through time promised to reconcile present diversity with single creation. One suspects that classical philology derived much respect as a humanistic discipline from recognition of this potential service. Others, less satisfied with historical connections than with the categories of the powerful natural sciences, sought to order man rather than track men. Indeed, the development of Duponceau's idea of polysynthesis illustrates the ease with which questions of historical affinity transformed themselves into categories of mental and moral development. Whether one followed Morton or the philologists, the North American aborigines emerged as distinct and uniform, due either to "savage physiognomy" of thought and language or to autochthonous creation.

Morton's school, and physical anthropology generally, fell into disrepute in the second half of the century. The reasons were as much political as scientific. As noted earlier, during the 1850s Joseph Henry consistently steered the Smithsonian away from racial debates, even refusing to permit abolitionist lectures at the Institution. Personally he maintained a discreet silence on such matters, and the Smithsonian largely ignored physical anthropology through the rest of the century.[48] The policy was more than a function of local racial conditions, though these may have heightened sensitivity. The polygenist controversy nearly tore apart the American Ethnological Society of New York during the fifties. Ephraim Squier reported that "the question of human unity could not be discussed without offense to some of the members and its casual introduction was made a ground of impassioned protest."[49] Henry could not afford such bickering. His attempt to establish a nationwide scientific network and to bring together in common effort both missionaries and atheistic polygenists like Squier, required absolute neutrality.

With racial categories discounted and even institutionally suppressed, historical speculations of archaeologists suspect for lack of theoretical grounding (and control in the field), and masses of observations and data annually accruing, developmental schemes emerged in the middle decades of the century—independently of Darwinian biology—as a means of meeting both the commitment to unity and the observed diversity. The work of Lewis Henry Morgan, the dean of nineteenth-century American evolutionism, is particularly instructive in this regard. Morgan's career (1851-1881) spanned the decades during which American anthropology moved from primarily historical inquiry into the origins and early relationships of the different peoples of the globe, to "scientific" classifications, or rankings, of humanity in evolutionary stages of social, mental, and moral development. Morgan's own career, from *Ancient Society* (1851) to *Systems of Consanguinity and Affinity of the Human Family* (1871) to *Ancient Society* (1877), marked milestones in this transition from history to stage classification.[50]

While *Ancient Society* has been justly remembered as the full statement of Morgan's three-stage model of social and mental development (savagery, barbarism, civilization), it was *Systems of Consanguinity*, his massive empirical work on kinship published by the Smithsonian, which established Morgan's inquiry as a science and himself as an institution. Morgan conceived *Systems of Consanguinity* as a survey in the tradition of comparative philology but rooted in what he hoped would prove less mutable human phenomena than language: ideas of kinship. Philologists had reduced mankind to a number of linguistic families, but they had been unable to take the final step, to the "vital question" of origins. Ultimately, Morgan hoped, his "new instrument in ethnology" would prove to be "the most simple as well as the compendious method for the classification of nations upon the basis of affinity of blood."[51]

The vitally important truth about *Systems of Consanguinity* is that Morgan did not find the unity he had presumed and sought. Faced with two apparently distinct concepts and systems of kinship, he adopted a developmental explanatory framework in order to preserve a presumed original human unity. In effect, Morgan moved from a vision of man in historical and geographical migration and contact to a comparatively rigid, static construction devoid of historical fluidity.

Morgan's schema of human development, further elaborated in *Ancient Society*, did embrace notions of change and progress, but these were, like Schoolcraft's visions, strongly teleological and bound to a system of unfolding ideas rather than to the immediate historical experiences of peoples. Morgan's legacy to the next generation—Powell and the Bureau of American Ethnology—was the subordination of historical probings to the greater explanatory power and aesthetic satisfaction of ordering man in value-laden stages. Following Morgan's lead, Powell grounded BAE anthropology in the principle that the American Indians must be understood not as a racial type but as representatives of a single stage of human development. In escaping the tyranny and politics of racial typing, and in the name of science, Powell also denied history to the American aborigines. The resulting flatness of historical perspective was costly for all fields of anthropology, but especially so for archaeologists, who did not discard such assumptions and begin to develop concepts of cultural micro-change and methods of tracing cultural forms through space and time until the twentieth century.[52]

The divergent roots of anthropology in the traditions of the humanities and natural sciences, which by 1850 already reached down deeply, produced an inquiry whose unity lay not in method but in subject matter and in purposes that transcended the inquiry itself. With few exceptions, Native Americans constituted the subjects of American anthropology through the nineteenth century. This occasions no surprise, since the natives of the Western Hemisphere, and of the North American continent particularly, posed critical historical and providential questions for White Americans. The central, nagging, political and religious dilemmas were these: Are these people in any sense our brothers? By what right can we claim this land as our own?

Over the middle decades of the century, the various approaches to these problems lost or gained prestige and followers as a result of various factors: new theoretical breakthroughs (especially if originated in Europe); domestic political and racial currents; the growing status of the natural and physical sciences in general in this country; and individual and institutional decisions. Broadly sketched, physical anthropology declined for nearly a half-century as a method; while in archaeology (and to some extent linguistics), the purpose of inquiry shifted away from historical questions to "scientific," formally nonracial classifications of mankind that nonetheless in essence preserved the moral placement system of discredited racial categories. The Smithsonian was a critical institutional focus of these developments, and decisions of Joseph Henry were often determinative. His decision to support ethnology (the general term for anthropological work at the time) as part of his program of providing the experience of science to a wide section of the American citizenry provided tremendous stimulus in numerous directions.

Notes

1. Henry Adams, *The Education of Henry Adams: An Autobiography* (Cambridge, 1961), pp. 44–45, 256; E. E. Hale, *Tarry at Home Travels* (New York, 1906), pp. 377, 381, 387.

2. Charles Dickens, *American Notes* (Philadelphia, n.d.), pp. 111–12, 116; Anthony Trollope, *North America* (New York, 1862), pp. 301–2, 306, 314–15.

3. Constance McLaughlin Green, *Washington: Village and Capital, 1800–1878* (Princeton, 1962), p. 148.

4. Ibid., pp. 152–66.

5. Ibid., pp. 21, 175–80.

6. Ibid., p. 177.

7. Ibid., p. 180.

8. A. Hunter Dupree, *Science in the Federal Government: A History of Policies and Activities to 1940* (Cambridge, 1957), p. 40.

9. Quoted in Green, *Washington*, p. 170.

10. William Stanton, *The Great United States Exploring Expedition of 1838–1842* (Berkeley, 1975), p. 290.

11. For treatment of the National Institute see Stanton, *Exploring Expedition*, pp. 281–304; Sally G. Kohlstedt, "A Step Toward Scientific Self-Identity in the United States: The Failure of the National Institute, 1844," *Isis* 62 (1971); and George Brown Goode, "The Genesis of the U.S. National Museum," USNM, *AR for 1891* (Washington, D.C., 1891), pp. 273–380.

12. Stanton, *Exploring Expedition*, p. 292.

13. Ibid., p. 297.

14. Ibid., pp. 295–96.

15. Ibid.

16. Nathan Reingold, "Definitions and Speculations: The Professionalization of Science in America in the Nineteenth Century," in A. Oleson and S. C. Brown, eds., *The Pursuit of Knowledge in the Early American Republic* (Baltimore, 1976), pp. 33–69.

17. Henry Rowe Schoolcraft, *An Address, Delivered before the Was-Ah Ho-De-No-Son-Ne, or New Confederacy of the Iroquois, at its Third Annual Council, August 14, 1846* (Rochester, 1846), pp. 3–7, 29. For similar but less poetic sentiments, see Schoolcraft's "Incentives to the Study of the Ancient Period of American History," an address to the New-York Historical Society, 17 November 1846 (New York, 1847).

18. Henry Rowe Schoolcraft, *Plan for the Investigation of American Ethnology: to include the facts derived from other parts of the globe, and the eventual formation of a Museum of Antiquities and the peculiar Fabrics of Nations: and also the collection of a library of the Philology of the World, manuscript and printed* (New York, 1846), pp. 5, 12–13. Schoolcraft's *Plan* was reprinted in the SI, *AR for 1885* (pp. 907–14), with the note that although it was never officially adopted by the Institution, "even after the lapse of forty years it possesses sufficient interest and suggestiveness to justify its publication."

19. SI, *AR for 1860,* p. 38.

20. Adams to Jefferson, 28 June 1812, in *The Adams-Jefferson Letters*, ed. Lester J. Cappon (New York, 1959), pp. 308–09.

21. Schoolcraft, *Address*, p. 34.

22. Fred Somkin, *Unquiet Eagle: Memory and Desire in the Idea of American Freedom, 1815–1860* (Ithaca, 1967).

23. George Stocking, "From Chronology to Ethnology: James Cowles Prichard and British Anthropology, 1800–1850," in J. C. Prichard, *Researches in the Physical History of Man*, ed. Stocking (Chicago, 1973), p. XCIV.

24. The history of interest in the earthworks of North America, and of the theories adduced to account for them, has been treated extensively in several works, notably Robert Silverberg, *Mound Builders of Ancient America: The Archaeology of a Myth* (Greenwich, Conn., 1968); and Leo Deuel, *Conquistadores Without Swords: Archaeologists in the Americas* (New York, 1967). A recent regionally oriented survey is James E. Fitting, ed., *The Development of North American Archaeology* (Garden City, 1973). For further background, see Lee Eldridge Huddleston, *Origins of the American Indians: European Concepts, 1492–1729* (Austin, 1967). Gordon Willey and Jeremy Sabloff's *A History of American Archaeology* (San Francisco, 1974) places the archaeology of this period in historical and professional context. The most thorough account of the subject, however, remains unpublished: Thomas C. Tax's "The Development of American Archaeology, 1800–1879," Ph.D. diss. (University of Chicago, 1973). I have relied especially on Samuel F. Haven's valuable historical review, *Archaeology in the United States*, published as part of vol. 8 of Smithsonian Contributions to Knowledge (Washington, D.C., 1856).

25. Caleb Atwater, "Description of the Antiquities of Ohio and Other Historical States," *Transactions and Collections of the American Antiquarian Society* 1 (Worcester, Mass., 1820).

26. James H. McCulloh, *Researches Philosophical and Antiquarian Concerning the Aboriginal History of America* (Baltimore, 1829); see also John Haywood, *The Natural and Aboriginal History of Tennessee, up to the first Settlements by the White People* (1823); Constantine S. Rafinesque, *Ancient History, or Annals of Kentucky: with a Survey of the Ancient Monuments of North America, and a Tabular View of the Principal Languages and Primitive Nations of the Whole Earth* (Frankfort, 1824); John Delafield, Jr., *An Inquiry into the Origin of the Antiquities of America* (New York, 1839); William Henry Harrison, *A Discourse on the Aborigines of the Valley of the Ohio* (1838); and Alexander W. Bradford, *American Antiquities and Researches into the Origin and History of the Red Race* (New York, 1843). Some of these popular expositions enjoyed wide circulation; according to Haven (*Archaeology*, p. 41), one book on the "Moundbuilder Race" (by Joseph Priest) sold 22,000 copies by subscription in thirty months.

27. Thomas Jefferson, *Notes on Virginia*, in *Basic Writings of Thomas Jefferson*, ed. Philip Foner (Garden City, 1944), pp. 116–19; H. R. Schoolcraft, *Personal Memoirs of a Residence of Thirty Years with the Indian Tribes on the American Frontiers* (1851; reprint ed., New York, 1975), p. 176.

28. John R. Bartlett, "The Progress of Ethnology, an Account of Recent Archaeological, Philological, and Geographical Researches in Various Parts of the

Globe, tending to elucidate the Physical History of Man," *Transactions of the American Ethnological Society* 2 (New York, 1848): 4.

29. Haven, *Archaeology,* p. 97.

30. Peter Stephen Duponceau, "Report of the Historical and Literary Committee to the American Philosophical Society, January 9, 1818," *Transactions of the Historical and Literary Committee of the American Philosophical Society* 1 (Philadelphia, 1819): xi–xvi. Quoted in Mary Haas, "Grammar or Lexicon? The American Indian Side of the Question from Duponceau to Powell," *International Journal of Anthropological Linguistics* 35: 239–55. The discussion here is based on Haas's article.

31. Duponceau, "Report," p. xiv; quoted in Haas, "Grammar or Lexicon?" p. 240.

32. Haven, *Archaeology,* pp. 56, 54.

33. John Pickering, "Indian Languages of America," *Encyclopedia Americana* 4 (appendix): 581; quoted in Haas, "Grammar or Lexicon?", p. 241. See also Haas, p. 242; and Regna D. Darnell, "The Powell Classification of American Indian Languages," *Papers in Linguistics* (July 1971), pp. 73–76.

34. Albert Gallatin, "A Synopsis of the Indian Tribes within the United States East of the Rocky Mountains and in the British and Russian Possessions in North America," *Transactions and Collections of the American Antiquarian Society* (Cambridge, 1836), p. 6. Quoted in Haas, "Grammar or Lexicon?", p. 243.

35. George Bancroft, *History of the United States,* 14th ed., vol. 3 (1854), pp. 254–66.

36. Ibid., pp. 256, 264–65, 318. Schoolcraft also found ground for optimism in the slow mutability of language; see his "Incentives," p. 23.

37. Ibid., p. 318

38. The following discussion is based on William Stanton, *The Leopard's Spots* (Chicago, 1960); George M. Fredrickson, *The Black Image in the White Mind: The Debate on Afro-American Character and Destiny, 1817–1914* (New York, 1971), pp. 71–96; Paul A. Erickson, *The Origins of Physical Anthropology,* Ph.D. diss. (University of Connecticut, 1974), p. 66–80; Haven, *Archaeology;* Daniel Wilson, "Lectures on Physical Ethnology," SI, *AR for 1862–63.* pp. 240–302; and Aleš Hrdlička, "Physical Anthropology in America," *American Anthropologist.* n.s. 16 (1914): 508–54.

39. Samuel George Morton, *Crania Americana, or a Comparative View of the Skulls of the Various Aboriginal Nations of North and South America. To Which is Prefixed an Essay on the Varieties of the Human Species* (Philadelphia, 1839).

40. Hrdlička, "Physical Anthropology," p. 515.

41. S. G. Morton, "Account of a Craniological Collection," *Transactions of the American Ethnological Society* 2 (1848): 219.

42. For a critical account of Morton's work and conclusions by a near-contemporary, see Daniel Wilson, "Lectures," pp. 240–65. On reexamination of Morton's collection, Wilson denied the existence of Morton's ideal type—the rounded, brachycephalic "Peruvian" head—among the North American skulls.

43. S. G. Morton, *An Inquiry into the Distinctive Characteristics of the Aboriginal Race of America* (Boston, 1842; Philadelphia, 1844); H. R. Schoolcraft, *Indian Tribes* 2 (Philadelphia, 1852): 316–30. See also, in Schoolcraft, Morton's "Unity of the Human Race," vol. 3, pp. 374–75.

44. J. C. Nott and G. R. Gliddon, *Types of Mankind. or Ethnological Researches, based*

upon the ancient monuments, paintings, sculptures, and crania of races, and upon their natural geographical, philological, and Biblical history (Philadelphia, 1854); quoted in Haven, *Archaeology,* p. 85.

45. Haven, *Archaeology,* p. 81.

46. Hrdlička noted ("Physical Anthropology," pp. 524–26) that Joseph Leidy and J. Aitken Meigs, both of Philadelphia, considered picking up the mantle of the great Morton, but while each contributed in his own way to the advancement of physical anthropology and anatomy, Meigs and Leidy went in other directions. Of Leidy's more than 500 publications in natural science, Hrdlička found only thirteen related directly to anthropology.

47. Joel R. Poinsett, *Discourse on the Objects and Importance of the National Institution for the Promotion of Science, Established at Washington, 1840, Delivered at the First Anniversary* (Washington, D.C., 1841), pp. 19–20, 42–43. On the formation and early activities of the various departments, see the *Bulletins* of the Institute, 1840–42.

48. Green, *Washington,* p. 287.

49. Robert E. Bieder and Thomas G. Tax, "From Ethnologists to Anthropologists: A Brief History of the American Ethnological Society," in John V. Murra, ed., *American Anthropology: The Early Years* (St. Paul, 1976), p. 17.

50. George W. Stocking's essay, "Some Problems in the Understanding of Nineteenth Century Cultural Evolutionism," in Regna Darnell, ed., *Readings in the History of Anthropology,* (New York, 1974), pp. 407–25, has been suggestive for the following discussion.

51. L. H. Morgan, *Systems of Consanguinity and Affinity in the Human Family.* Smithsonian Contributions to Knowledge 17 (Washington, D.C., 1871), pp. 9, 506.

52. Willey and Sabloff, *History of American Archaeology,* p. 88.

II

Promoting Popular Science: Archaeology and Philology at the Smithsonian Institution, 1846–1878

"The most prominent idea in my mind," Joseph Henry wrote in 1847, "is that of stimulating the talent of our country to original research—in which it has been most lamentably difficult [sic]—to pour fresh material on the apex of the pyramid of science, and thus to enlarge its base . . ."[1] Anthropology occupied a prominent place in Henry's vision. In the "Programme of Organization" outlined before his election as first Secretary of the Smithsonian Institution in 1846 and approved by the Regents the following year, Henry proposed to increase knowledge of man in North America through surveys and explorations of mounds and other remains. In addition, the Smithsonian should help diffuse discoveries relating to "particular history, comparative philology, antiquities, etc."[2]

From the beginning, Henry rejected arguments to limit Smithsonian support to fields of science having "immediate application to the practical arts of life." To do so would violate the memory of James Smithson, who had been "fully impressed with the important philosophical fact, that all subjects of human thought relate to one great system of truth." Some fields that held little hope of generalization nonetheless "could hardly fail to produce results of importance in a practical and a theoretic point of view." He specifically mentioned ethnology as one such undeveloped but promising field.[3]

Henry's support for anthropology must be understood as part of a broader scientific promotion. The creation of a national system of scientific correspondents, one of Henry's remarkable achievements as Smithsonian Secretary, accompanied his plans for a continental, even hemispheric coordination of meteorological observations. Both Henry and his assistant secretary, Spencer F. Baird, assumed that their observers would report to the Smithsonian on a variety of scientific topics. He had "long dreamed of some central association or influence," Baird wrote to Henry in 1849, for gathering, digesting, and publishing scientific information in all fields.[4]

Their program was suited to a sparsely populated continent and an early stage of scientific organization. In the middle of the nineteenth century, being a scientist in America was still as much a matter of character and integrity as one of specific academic or laboratory training. A man could be taught to use the latest instruments of physical science, Henry believed, but dedication to the pursuit of truth and willingness to forego the public acclaim that frequently rewarded the fraud or popularizer were qualities that transcended the expertise of separate branches of science. Henry sought to build a system of trustworthy observers whose reports, systematized by instructions and instruments from the Smithsonian, would form the factual basis for scientific knowledge of the American continent.

A physicist without any personal experience in anthropology, Henry was ambivalent about the independence of a field that he always viewed as burdened with unwarranted speculation and consequently in need of purging and guidance. On the one hand, he seems to have turned to anthropological questions as "a kind of middle ground between literature and science, on which men of letters and the investigators of nature may meet with mutual interest," as he advised John Fries Frazer in 1855. On the other hand, Henry recognized degrees of anthropological expertise and warned away interlopers. In the same letter to Frazer cited above, Henry admonished his friend that "however the world may give you credit for knowledge in the line of physical science, you are no authority in the line of ethnology." In the course of his secretariat Henry watched with pride as anthropological studies grew in popularity and, he claimed, in precision. "We have passed," he told one correspondent in 1868, "from the period of pure speculation in regard to [ethnology], into that of the active collection of materials preparatory to the next—that of deduction and generalizations."[5] While some of his colleagues, and perhaps some of the Regents, refused to accept such studies as serious science, Henry saw an opportunity for the Institution to guide the development of a promising field by enlisting the support of a broad network of correspondents and by applying to it the standards of proof of the physical sciences.[6]

Because of its status in 1846 as a field on the fringes of science, anthropology presented an unusual opportunity for making a science, for drawing a clear line between speculative popularization or commercial humbuggery, and the sober search for truth. In this enterprise Henry was a willing and forceful participant; he lost no opportunity to elevate the true investigator and denounce the pretender. To some extent the crusade against amateurism and speculation was simply a matter of giving proper credit. Printing unverified theory, to Henry, was equivalent to "throwing dice for discovery"; only zealous, persevering research deserved recognition.[7]

Henry demonstrated his determination to purge anthropology of speculation with the first volume of the series of Smithsonian Contributions to Knowledge: *Ancient Monuments of the Mississippi Valley*, by Ephraim George

Squier and Edwin H. Davis.[8] Publication in 1848 of this 300-page, lavishly illustrated volume was a landmark in the development of American anthropology, at once symbolizing the commitment of the Smithsonian to the science and reflecting the growing popular interest in America's ancient inhabitants. For Henry the significance of *Ancient Monuments* lay in the rigorous scientific standards it established. He realized his support for ethnological investigations was not altogether expected or shared. He was pleased, he confided to Elias Loomis, to publish an archaeological paper first, "because it will show that I am not inclined to devote the funds entirely to the advance of Physical science."[9]

Squier and Davis submitted their paper to Henry in early 1847. The paper arrived with strong recommendations from the American Ethnological Society of New York, several members of which had been avidly following the Ohio work for some time. Indeed, only financial restrictions had prevented the Society from printing the work itself. Henry responded enthusiastically. Concerned that Squier was considering a commercial outlet, the Secretary urged him to publish with the Smithsonian. Squier's own scientific reputation, he wrote, depended on the appearance of his researches in the transactions of a respectable scientific institution, in which it might receive "that commendation which it is the privilege of only the learned few to grant . . ." Commercial publication, he continued, constituted an appeal to the public that would most certainly "produce a prejudice against the work in the minds of those who are best qualified to appreciate its merits and on whose judgment its character must ultimately depend."[10] Henry convinced the authors. He then formally submitted the work to the Ethnological Society for review and approval. Since the review committee consisted of the same individuals— Edward Robinson, John R. Bartlett, William W. Turner, Samuel G. Morton, and George P. Marsh—who had already expressed a lively interest in the paper, approval was assured.[11]

In the year between acceptance and publication of *Ancient Monuments,* Henry severely edited the memoir, which meant excising what he considered unjustified speculation. Squier added new material, mainly reports and drawings from earlier works and remarks suggesting connections between the moundbuilders of North America and the ancient civilizations of Central America. Henry strongly disapproved and sharply rebuked Squier: "Your labours should be given to the world as free as possible from everything of a speculative nature and . . . your positive addition to the sum of human knowledge should stand in bold relief unmingled with the labours of others," he admonished. Enlisting the impressive scientific support of Morton, Marsh, and Alexander Dallas Bache, the Secretary warned against including any theoretical matter, "except in a very subordinate degree." Full theoretical exposition would have to wait.[12]

By editing, and threatening to withdraw support, Henry imposed his standards on *Ancient Monuments* and established a dominant tone of caution in the memoir. "It has been a constant aim in the preparation of this memoir," the authors announced, "to present facts in a clear and concise form, with such simple deductions and generalizations alone, as may follow from their careful consideration." They had no hypothesis to sustain, but only a desire to arrive at truth, with the result that "everything like mere speculation has been avoided."[13] The result was impressive. *Ancient Monuments* seemed a model of Baconian induction; Squier and Davis had let the facts speak for themselves, John Bartlett observed, and "out of confusion, system began to develope itself, and what seemed accidents, were found to be characteristic." Few disagreed.[14]

Henry's admonitions to Squier and Davis reflected his concern for the reputations of the Smithsonian, the authors, and the science. He realized that if anthropology in America were ever to transcend the realm of hobbyists, students had to forego the lures of public acclaim and subject their methods and results to the scrutiny of the small group of persons—the "learned few"— capable of judging their work in the "regular channels of scientific communication."[15]

But excising unfounded speculation was only half the battle. New rigor and system in data-gathering were badly needed. To this end Henry, a physicist, envisioned applying the methodological system and accurate instrumentation of the physical sciences wherever possible.[16] The Secretary's correspondence with Increase A. Lapham of Wisconsin, one of his most active and enterprising contacts over thirty years, illustrated his efforts to introduce precision in ethnology. In 1850, Lapham requested two barometers for field work on the Indian mounds of Wisconsin, apparently to obtain as complete a picture as possible of the elevations and environments of the mounds. Despite limited funds and the difficulty of shipping the delicate instruments, Henry loaned the barometers. He took the opportunity to remind Lapham that the value of his work depended on "minute accuracy" and strict induction: "We are as yet only collecting the bricks of the temple of American antiquities," he wrote, "which are hereafter to be arranged and fashioned into a durable edifice; it is therefore of the first importance that our materials should be of the proper kind."[17]

It should be emphasized that Henry did not belittle theorizing in itself; he opposed unwarranted, unverified speculation that had no roots in observation and often came from wrong motivations. The insistence on a rigorously inductive ethnology, purged of speculation and based on systematic observation, derived from Henry's perception that diffusion of scientific knowledge had been accompanied by the spread of crank ideas as well, and that Americans were generally unable to discriminate between them. As a result, the fraud often basked in public acclaim, overshadowing the modest, honest scientist. Self-denial and social oblivion were not, of course, necessary elements in Henry's definition of a scientist; but popular recognition was so rare that, as he warned Squier, the scientist who voluntarily sought acclaim soon aroused suspicion among his fellow investigators.

The spread of misleading theory was not necessarily deliberate or malicious; sometimes it merely reflected "defective scientific training" of powerful and original minds. It was, alas, all too easy to stray from "the narrow path . . . to real advance in positive knowledge." But while unwitting detractors saddened Henry, he despised the deliberate deceivers, and the Smithsonian became an important instrument in his lifelong crusade against scientific fraud. Indeed, one of the "germs" of the operations of the Institution, he noted to himself in 1848, was that its reports should "expose popular fallacies and attempt to put down quackery."[18] Above all the Smithsonian must remain free from any taint of excessive speculation or commercial appeal; in 1869 Henry wrote with apparent relief that the Institution had not been touched by the recent Cardiff Giant hoax, and he bitterly reproached the perpetrators of such "unblushing deceptions" for their "bad effect on the morals of the community."[19]

Science was a moral enterprise to Joseph Henry. His enthusiasm for anthropology is fully comprehensible only in the light of his convictions about the mission and needs of science in American society. No country in the world owed more to science than did America, and yet none encouraged and supported it less. "The blindness of the public," Henry admonished a New York audience in 1874, "to the value of abstract science and to the importance of endowments for its advancement is truly remarkable."[20] Americans, he thought, did not recognize or treasure the scientific life because they had not personally experienced the intellectual and spiritual stimulation of contemplating nature.

Not that everyone was capable of becoming a first-rate scientist. Henry was more elitist than egalitarian in his science. He believed that "like the poet, the discoverer is born, not made," and like him must be left to "wait the fitting time of inspiration." Only a few could profitably dedicate their lives to the "high and holy office of penetrating the mysteries of nature."[21] But Henry did not exclude most people from active participation in science. There were many functions and many useful roles, particularly in a young science still gathering its basic materials from remote and unpopulated regions. While only the best scientific minds might perform the ultimate task of synthesis, many could participate in the exciting fact-gathering operations.

Of course, in most scientific activity inductive and deductive processes are not clearly separated; both occur simultaneously, with constant modification of even well-established generalizations in the light of new information. But at mid-century, anthropology appeared overwhelmingly inductive. The young science faced such a formidable task of collecting and classifying the vast materials of the American hemisphere that discovery of laws and regularities receded as a goal into the distant future. Despite his own vigorous speculations, Ephraim Squier appreciated with Henry that "no sciences are so eminently inductive as Archaeology and Ethnology . . . none which require so extensive a range of facts to their elucidation."[22]

The inductive needs of anthropology meshed well with the broader social functions of science in America as Henry perceived them. A wide network of correspondents sending information and specimens to Washington from every region of North America not only increased the factual foundation of ethnology; it also introduced the scientific experience to many persons in whom, "for lack of an awakening word," the love of science had lain dormant.[23] It is imperative to understand that under Henry and Baird the Smithsonian operated to diffuse not only specific knowledge but also the experience of the search for truth and the desire for the serious study of nature.[24] It is difficult to say which function was ultimately more important to the Secretary. Reporting on collections received from explorers in the Northwest Territory in 1867, the Secretary noted with pride that the Smithsonian had served as a stimulating and civilizing force for the inhabitants of the region, "enlivening their isolated and monotonous life by the incitements and facilities it has offered them for the study and observation of the phenomena and objects of nature."[25] Henry originally conceived the Smithsonian's series of Miscellaneous Collections, begun in 1861, as popularly palatable introductory materials on the various sciences, particularly natural history, for persons without access to libraries. However quixotic in retrospect, the blend of scientific erudition with popular enlightenment (beginning with expositions on entomology and conchology) was a serious effort to bridge a perceived social, intellectual, and moral gap in American society. To Henry it was apparent that "the objects of nature, like the specimens of high art, are the luxuries of the cultivated mind, and the awakening of a taste for their study affords an inexhaustible source of pleasure and contentment to the most numerous and the most important classes of the community."[26]

Joseph Henry appreciated the technological advances that accompanied increase in scientific knowledge, but for him the aesthetic and spiritual experience of contemplating order and beauty in the universe was the true, highest reward of science. He sustained a sincere faith in the benevolent influences of science, insisting that "it is not alone the material advantages which the world enjoys from the study of abstract science on which its claims are founded." Science offered "unbounded fields of pleasurable, healthful, and ennobling exercise to the restless intellect of man, expanding his powers and enlarging his conceptions of the wisdom, the energy, and the beneficence of the Great Ruler of the universe."[27] Henry's conviction of the pious, humbling effect of scientific pursuits never failed him, and throughout his life he attempted to spread that exquisite joy to an ever-larger circle.

Between 1848 and 1860, Henry followed Squier and Davis's *Ancient Monuments* with North American archaeological investigations in the Smithsonian Contributions to Knowledge. Henry planned systematic description of the mounds of the eastern United States—a strictly inductive process. The papers at least formally upheld the standard set by *Ancient Monuments*. In the preface to *Antiquities of Wisconsin,* Increase Lapham disclaimed theoretical ambitions; he was a mere surveyor, faithfully observing and recording the facts, "leaving it to others with better opportunities, to compare them, and to establish, in connection with other means of information, such general principles as may be legitimately deduced." Charles Whittlesey, a former member of the Geological Survey of Ohio, displayed even greater humility, claiming only the role of a "common laborer . . . bringing together materials with which some master workman may raise a perfect edifice." A few years later, Brantz Mayer, reviewing Mexican archaeology, warned against speculation in antiquarian studies, in which the "mythic confusion" of the aboriginal past might provide support for wild suppositions. In the present state of archaeology, all labors should form a "mass of testimony" for future researchers. Secretary Henry's hand was firm indeed.[28]

The appearance in 1856 of Samuel F. Haven's review of American archaeology—actually a review of American developments in all branches of anthropology to that time and prepared "by special request of the Institution"— marked the close of this period of broad mound surveys.[29] Under Henry's watchful editing, Haven prepared his synthesis of American archaeology with a judicious, critical eye, rejecting speculative migrations but allowing the possibility of Asiatic connection. He saw no evidence of a race of mound-builders distinct from the historical Indians. Haven appeared "a spokesman for the new era" of factual, descriptive archaeology that Henry promoted.[30]

While observations and data mounted, however, no master craftsman appeared, and clear patterns failed to develop to give broader significance to the archaeology of America. Mayer noted in 1857 that twenty years of archaeological investigations in Mexico had produced no definite historical results.[31] Henry reminded an ambitious correspondent in 1861 that "at present our efforts in this country should be directed to the collection of facts, and the accurate delineation of ancient remains previous to attempting to solve the problem as to the origin of the inhabitants of this continent."[32] In actuality, Henry had begun seriously to doubt that archaeology would ever trace the origins of American man. But at this point he also became aware of recent European archaeological developments.

The decade of the 1860s marked the maturation of Old World archaeology, signified by the publication of John Lubbock's popular *Prehistoric Times* in 1865 and the Paris Anthropological Exposition two years later. The acceptance and adoption of the principles of uniformitarian geology, the establishment of the antiquity of man in Europe through the discoveries of Boucher de Perthes in France, William Pengally in England, and Christian J. Thomsen in Denmark, and the development and wide acceptance of the three-stage technological classification system—Stone, Bronze, and Iron Age—appeared to place Old World prehistory on a new scientific plateau.[33]

Henry immediately saw the relevance of Old World theory to American antiquities, and optimistically introduced them to the United States through the Institution's annual reports, beginning in 1860 with a comprehensive and authoritative report, "General Views on Archaeology" by Adolphe Morlot.[34] Morlot, professor of geology at Lausanne Academy and the man largely responsible for the adoption in Switzerland of the Scandinavian three-age classification, reviewed the latest developments in Old World prehistory and outlined its principles. Just as the geologist used present formations as a guide to past geological changes, so the student of man first examined the different peoples of the earth in their present states in order to understand the different degrees of civilization. Ethnology provided a contemporary scale of development that archaeology then traced in successive stages through time. Adoption of the geological model had resulted in that "great conquest" of the Scandinavian savants, the three-stage analysis of European prehistory. Morlot also reported on Stone Age kitchen-middens* and peat-bogs of Scandinavia, and the ancient lake-dwellings of Switzerland.

Morlot's paper stimulated new interest in collecting Indian relics in America. Henry published four more papers on Swiss archaeology and distributed both a circular requesting recent information relating to ancient mining in the much-discussed Lake Superior region, and George Gibbs's *Instructions for Archaeological Investigations in the United States*. Following the European example, Gibbs encouraged careful excavation of American shell heaps, mounds, caves, and mines, in the hope that "a similar investigation in America may take us back to a very remote period in aboriginal history."[35]

Swiss and Scandinavian researches provided the needed focus for American archaeology, and the tripartite classification of artifacts supplied a fresh framework. They replaced a search for migrations and historical connections that by 1860 had reached a dead end. Henry recognized as much. Americans had been searching in the mounds for the solutions to two distinct problems: the

---

*Piles of shells, bones, and stone implements assumed to be the refuse-heaps of Stone Age peoples.

historical roots of the American Indians and the stages of cultural development that the inhabitants of America had attained. It was critical, Henry believed, to separate the two inquiries in order to distinguish between traits that were attributable to a common humanity and those peculiar to specific peoples.

Even before the discovery of supposedly parallel European phenomena, Henry had gradually come to believe that similarities in material culture could not be accepted as evidence of contact. "That different peoples should make use of the same implements for assisting to effect results of a mechanical kind . . . is no sign that they had intercourse with one another, since these are natural products of the same kind of intellect, or the instinctive productions of man." Men possessed certain common wants and instincts that produced widespread similar products.[36]

The exception to Henry's psychic unity and parallel invention was language, which seemed a possible key to unraveling the histories of individual migrations. "The general structure[s] of distinct and original language," Henry wrote, "may be, and were probably, similar in some respects and identical in others, yet the words are arbitrarily chosen, and therefore are as different as the objects and the relative conditions of different races or tribes are." The study of language was "of the highest importance" in solving historical puzzles.[37]

The important consequences of European discoveries for American archaeology were to stimulate renewed activity but simultaneously to discredit archaeology as a historical tool and redirect the purpose of the work toward classifying artifacts and peoples in categories of material culture. Archaeologists in this country readily embraced the new categories and hastened to place their materials accordingly, leaving to the linguists the nagging problems of aboriginal origin and affinity. The distinction in method and purpose that thus emerged in the sixties proved to be extremely significant for American anthropology in the coming decades.

The career of Charles Rau, Henry's chief archaeological collaborator, illustrated both the personal and professional aspects of archaeology in Washington. Rau's biography reads simply. A lonely, ascetic German immigrant, Rau was born in Belgium in 1826, attended the University of Heidelberg, and in 1848 sailed to New Orleans. For twenty-seven years he taught German to school children in St. Louis, Belleville (Illinois), and New York City. In 1876 he finally obtained a position at the Smithsonian, and five years later became curator of the Department of Antiquities (later Archaeology) in the National Museum. Rau never married, and at his death in July 1887, his valuable personal library and archaeological collection came to the Smithsonian.[38]

Rau's career in this country was not happy. He detested teaching "brutish, half-savage, actually *lousy* Irish boys" in the seventh ward of New York City, a position he held only "by the grace of a few illiterate Irishmen."[39] But Rau consistently failed to obtain the respectable scientific position that he sought in archaeology or ethnology. Prior to the founding of the Bureau of Ethnology in 1879, few institutions in the United States provided employment in anthropology. Most practitioners either relied upon independent wealth or pursued careers that permitted time for anthropological studies as an avocation.[40] For an aspiring investigator like Rau, possessing considerable erudition but neither financial means nor influential friends, the situation in America was acutely frustrating. "For nearly twenty years," he wrote Henry in 1867, "I have been striving to obtain a respectable situation, but in vain." Rau blamed American antipathy to foreigners: "They treat me politely and eulogise me for the interest I take in American ethnology—but their sympathy extends no further."[41]

Rau applied for the few suitable positions that did appear, and each time he asked Henry for support. At the founding of the Peabody Museum in 1866, he eagerly sought Henry's recommendation for the curatorship. "To superintend and to classify on scientific principles a large archaeological collection would be the occupation to which nature, as it were, has destined me," he confided. When Jeffries Wyman received the appointment, Rau was crushed. Wyman was a fine anatomist but no archaeologist, he complained. Henry responded sympathetically: "As in every part of the world called civilized . . . modest merit is frequently overlooked while pushing incompetency is chosen."[42]

Rau continued to teach in New York until 1875, when his position was abolished, leaving him with the "odious" prospect of clerking in an office. Once again he appealed to the Smithsonian for help in realizing "the aim of my life," a major work on the North American Stone Age. Rau assured Baird that he planned a descriptive and comparative rather than theoretical work, dealing in some detail with modern applications of American implements in order to elucidate the uses of ancient specimens. His study would form an interesting Smithsonian publication, "especially at a time when archaeology . . . forms the favorite study of intelligent persons in all civilized countries."[43]

Rau's supplication underscored the humiliating position in which this aspiring student found himself for so many years of his life. He felt that he had much to contribute to the young science but so few opportunities that he had to promote himself as widely as possible. At times his anxiety led to friction with Henry over speed, quality, and distribution of his Smithsonian publications, but Rau had no alternative. "I cannot display my wares behind a window like a mechanic or a merchant," he informed Baird. "I need a field of action for showing what I can do. To whom could I apply for obtaining such a chance, but to men like Professor Henry and yourself?"[44]

Rau finally got his chance in 1875. After some hesitation Henry hired him to study, classify, and prepare the ethnological specimens in the National

Museum for the Centennial Exposition in Philadelphia.[45] It was only a one-year appointment, but Rau managed to stay on as a collaborator and assistant, eventually becoming curator of the Department of Antiquities.

The discoveries and developments in the typological, descriptive classifications of Old World prehistory found an earnest devotee and spokesman in Rau, whose papers in German and American publications provided a trans-atlantic conduit for joining Old and New World observations. Rau hoped to fit the vast quantities of American raw materials into a European theoretical framework. Thus, while his studies and collections were American in subject matter, he looked with admiration to his homeland for guidance.

Rau believed that the search for origins and migrations in the first half of the century had been hopeless and fruitless. Forsaking historical queries, he returned to the model of the eighteenth-century ethnologist William Robertson and the quest for universal patterns of development. Rau contended for "a certain law that regulates the march of civilization, and compels, as it were, the populations of different parts of the world to act, independently of each other, in a similar manner, provided there is a sufficient similarity in their external conditions of life."[46] The search for materials in North America to indicate parallels with European technological stages formed the major theme in Rau's work. In 1864 he published "Artificial Shell-Deposits in New Jersey" in the Smithsonian annual report. The New Jersey shore, he discovered, contained unstratified deposits of oyster, clam, and mollusk shells, bones, implements, and other remains that perfectly matched the European shell-heaps, furnishing "a striking illustration of the similarity in the development of man in both hemispheres."[47] Furthermore, Rau had reports of similar deposits in Long Island, California, Georgia, Massachusetts, and Newfoundland, convincing proof that "the condition of man is everywhere essentially the same, while the rude implements indicate a similarity of wants and identity of mental characteristics by which these wants are supplied."[48]

As early as the mid-sixties, Rau began planning a major work on American antiquities written in German for a European audience.[49] While he continued to contribute short articles to American and European journals, however, he altered this plan in favor of a paper on North America for domestic consumption. American archaeology, Rau observed, had developed into a totally new science in the twenty years since Squier and Davis had published *Ancient Monuments*. European discoveries had shed new light on America, and Rau proposed to "introduce new features by comparing the aborigines of this country with the primeval people of Europe," an undertaking requiring much "moral assistance." The paper, which Rau confidently felt would appear as a volume of the Smithsonian Contributions, would include a synopsis of European archaeological discoveries and systematic comparison of European and American stone, bone, horn, pottery, and metal products.[50]

Charles Rau, the German immigrant who became curator of the Department of Antiquities at the National Museum.

Rau as sketched by Frank Hamilton Cushing, the brilliant young scientist of the Bureau of American Ethnology.

In 1868 Rau made his proposal to Henry. At first the Secretary was enthusiastic, expecting a review of the state of American archaeology similar to Haven's a decade earlier. He suggested that Rau include instructions for archaeological explorers. But when Rau clarified his plans, Henry withdrew and in a shattering letter flatly rejected the project. The time was not ripe, he advised Rau, for an extensive work involving fresh investigations and comparisons. True, archaeology was currently enjoying a lively popular interest; but in 1868 Henry wanted only "sketches of progress, suggestions of hypotheses to direct lines of research, and instructions as to the method of making explorations, and the preservation of relics, etc." Rau could gradually acquire the materials for a summary treatment.[51]

The great treatise never appeared. In 1884 he issued his last and most original contribution to anthropology, *Prehistoric Fishing in Europe and North America*. Undertaken at the suggestion of Baird and ichthyologist George Brown Goode, *Prehistoric Fishing* was Rau's final statement on archaeological matters. He hoped it would "illustrate anew the parallelism in the technical progress of populations totally unknown to each other, and for which only the common bond of humanity can be claimed."[52] The recent discoveries of Charles C. Abbott in the Trenton gravels, described in *Primitive Industry*,[53] had confirmed Rau's belief in the antiquity of man in America. But by 1884 he had to concede that prehistory was considerably more complex in America than in Europe, due largely to the difficulty in discriminating between ancient and recent Indian products. He organized his European fishing utensils according to the traditional categories—Paleolithic, Neolithic, Bronze—but had to arrange the American tools according to function.

Charles Rau enjoyed only a brief career as full-time archaeologist. For fifteen years he struggled to obtain a position in America that would permit him to earn a living in anthropology; then he enjoyed a decade at the Smithsonian. He made no seminal contributions to either theory or field data in anthropology, devoting himself instead to the analysis of museum collections. Consequently, he is remembered today only as an early classifier, if at all. Yet between 1860 and 1880, probably no other man in the United States was more aware of developments in archaeology on both sides of the Atlantic. Drawing heavily on German and English theory, Rau sought order for American antiquities in European theories, and clues to the functions of ancient European relics in the modern uses of American implements. He helped apply European theory in America at the same time that he relayed American discoveries to European scholars. Anonymous and unemployed in his adopted country, Rau achieved some recognition in his native land.[54]

Rau's career reflected the state of archaeology in Washington and the United States in his lifetime. In personal terms, the study of any branch of anthropology provided a livelihood for only a handful; for others it was either an avocation or a struggle. More broadly viewed, anthropology in America, and particularly archaeology, still maintained a colonial relationship to Europe: Americans provided masses of new raw materials but relied heavily on European scholars for direction and organizing principles to fashion them into finished products. As the ambiguity of Rau's last work illustrated, by the 1880s American materials were simply refusing to fit Old World categories. The transatlantic relationship began to change rapidly after the 1876 Centennial, as Washington anthropologists turned their backs on European models to assert a new American independence and uniqueness. Rau died in 1887, just before Powell's Bureau of American Ethnology launched a withering attack on Paleolithic man in America.

The study of language, Schoolcraft advised the Smithsonian Regents in 1846, held the most promise of solving the puzzles of the origins and histories of the American aborigines. While the Regents preferred more tangible collections, Henry agreed with his friend.[55] Unlike the relics of the mounds or the artifacts of living tribes, language was not originally a "thing of man's device" but the "spontaneous production of human instinct" modified by the mental and physical peculiarities of specific peoples and environments. Divinely inspired but humanly altered, language straddled the realms of the universal and the particular. Herein lay its great promise. Eventually, it seemed, knowledge of linguistic principles would permit philologists to distinguish between similarities due to mental structure and those due to historical connection.[56]

Henry promoted American philology primarily through lectures, circulation of instructions, and collection of vocabulary lists. As early as 1849, the Secretary invited Pennsylvania naturalist and linguist Samuel Stedman Haldeman to discuss his views on phonetics, which were advanced for his time; the lectures of the 1857–58 season included a talk on "Comparative philology in some of its bearing upon ethnology" by Joshua H. McIlvaine of Rochester, mentor of Lewis Henry Morgan. Six years later, Yale philologist William Dwight Whitney delivered his "Lectures on the principles of linguistic science" for the first time at the Smithsonian. This landmark series, printed in the 1863 annual report, Whitney subsequently expanded into *Language and the Study of Language*, the first authoritative American textbook on linguistics.[57]

In 1847 and again two years later, Schoolcraft issued a comparative vocabulary list for missionaries, government agents, and soldiers to facilitate his massive information-gathering project. The American Ethnological Society followed Schoolcraft with its own circular in 1852.[58] Henry helped to distribute these, and a few years later the Smithsonian issued its own philological circular. In 1863, George Gibbs, with Whitney's aid, expanded his "Instructions for Archaeological Investigations in the U.S." (1861) to include directions for philological observations, rules for recording sounds, and a short vocabulary list. Simultaneously, Gibbs published a longer comparative vocabulary for the Institution. He improved upon earlier lists by Albert Gallatin and Horatio Hale, chiefly by expanding the number of words from 180 to 211, presented in four languages. Both the instructions and the vocabulary lists received wide dissemination, and after only two years Gibbs prepared a second edition of instructions, with new appendices and blank forms to facilitate "systematic records."[59] Gibbs's circular of 1865 served as the basis for the vocabulary gathering of the next twelve years; Powell used it in his early field work. In 1877, Powell expanded the Gibbs circular into his *Introduction to the Study of American Indian Languages.*[60]

Circulating instructions and vocabulary lists became the Smithsonian's means of connecting linguists established in eastern universities with observers in the western regions—explorers, soldiers, missionaries, and settlers. Whatever their other qualifications, these individuals rarely possessed linguistic training, and they faced formidable obstacles. Linguistic work in North America varied widely in thoroughness, depending on local conditions and the vigor and enthusiasm of the recorder; further, it involved a level of subjectivity that could only be partially reduced by standardizing vocabulary lists and orthography. The resulting frustrations were sometimes acute, as Gibbs indicated to W. D. Whitney in 1861: "I had rather puzzle out the rude spelling of an illiterate man than the over exactness of one correspondent whose work lies before me, every letter overloaded with dots and accents."[61] Whitney appreciated the dilemmas of subjectivity and professional division. "The 'personal equation' as the astronomers call it," he wrote in *Language,* "the allowance for difference of temperament, endowment, and skill, has to be applied, certainly not less rigorously, in estimating the observations and deductions of linguistic scholars than those of the labourers in other sciences." He divided linguists into the "facile and anticipative investigators," who furnished the better explorers; and the less ardent students, who made better critics. Each, he felt, had a legitimate place.[62]

The Smithsonian facilitated the flow of information: instructions and forms went from analysts to explorers, data traveled back from the field. To insure the scientific respectability of materials, Henry submitted them to recognized authorities for review. For this purpose he turned to a small circle of collaborators: in the 1850s, Edward E. Salisbury, the elder Josiah Willard Gibbs (unrelated to George), Cornelius Conway Felton, and, most frequently, William Wadden Turner. After Turner's death in 1859, the Secretary turned to Whitney, George Gibbs, and James Hammond Trumbull. All of the earlier group belonged to an academic tradition and each held a professorship in an established American institution: J. W. Gibbs and Salisbury at Yale, Felton at Harvard, and Turner at Union Theological Seminary. Of the latter group only Whitney held an academic post (at Yale). Henry particularly relied on William Turner and George Gibbs.

William W. Turner (1811–1859) came from England as a child in 1818. Both his parents died within ten years, leaving Turner with the care of two sisters. After first studying printing, he embarked upon a self-education program in Latin, Greek, Hebrew, and Oriental languages, aided by a professor of Hebrew at Columbia. Turner, always as much a bibliographer and bibliophile as an original scholar, worked at the Yale and Columbia libraries for three years before Union offered him a professorship in Oriental languages in 1842. He held this position until 1852, when he moved with his sisters to Washington to organize the Patent Office Library.[63]

In the small intellectual circle of antebellum Washington, the Turners found a congenial home. On Sundays and holidays Turner and his sisters were frequent visitors at the Spencer Baird household, where they were all "privileged inmates," and where Turner, Lucy Baird recalled, was one of the most intimate friends of the family. When Baird asked him to catalog the Smithsonian library in 1858, Turner brought along his sister Jane, who remained with the Institution for thirty years.[64]

Turner joined the American Oriental Society in 1846, and later he became a member of the Historical Society of New York and secretary of the National Institute. While he possessed minimal training and published little, through memberships and contacts Turner attained a position of respect in the thin ranks of American philology. At his premature death in 1859 he was "preeminently distinguished at Washington as the highest authority in all matters appertaining to the knowledge of the languages of the aborigines of America." Turner had "mastered easily and rapidly the principles of comparative philology which have become in the present period the surest guides in tracing the histories and affinities of different races." Henry mourned "a ripe scholar, a profound philosopher, and an honest man."[65]

In 1851 Henry asked Turner to explain his reasons for recommending publication of Stephen Riggs's Dakota dictionary and grammar. Turner's response revealed the motivations of students of North American languages. Scientific study of the aboriginal tongues, he explained, rewarded the comparative philologist by showing not only analogies with other languages of the world but fascinating peculiarities as well, by disclosing "new and curious phases of the human mind." Because every language was the "spontaneous growth" of the mind of the people speaking it, the study of Indian tongues, even without the literature, provided the same kind of "delight and instruction" that the naturalist enjoyed from a new species of plant or animal. Even the rudest forms of speech furnished more reason to admire the work of the "Great Fashioner."

Furthermore, the American languages held clues to pre-Columbian history. While sharing the common opinion that Indian myths and traditions were worthless for historical purposes, Turner thought comparison of vocabularies and grammars of "men without a history" provided the most reliable evidence of contacts. The professor urged that the Smithsonian give to the learned world a complete dictionary and grammar of each American language.[66]

The only group of men "qualified by education and sustained by motives of benevolence" to spend the necessary years studying the "mental idiosyncracies of our rude red brethren," Turner went on, were missionaries like Riggs and his fellow workers at the Dakota mission. The agents of the Bureau of Indian Affairs had shown no interest in ethnological matters. But Turner supposed that there were other competent persons who had simply never had the inducement—Henry's "awakening word"—to undertake such projects.[67]

The missionaries had indeed accomplished major work. Riggs's dictionary/ grammar, jointly sponsored by the Historical Society of Minnesota, the American Board of Missions, and the Smithsonian, represented the collective work of eighteen years among the Indians. The Choctaw dictionary/grammar of Reverend Cyrus Byington, which the good minister rewrote six times while the Smithsonian delayed publishing it for twenty years, represented more than thirty years' labor in evangelical and ethnological vineyards.[68] When he originally accepted the Choctaw work on behalf of the Smithsonian in 1852, Turner took the opportunity to remind Byington of some additional merits of such study. Byington had done the Choctaw people the immense favor, he told the reverend, of explaining their own language to them. This would enhance their own self-esteem and give "vigor and perspicacity" to the thought of future generations of Choctaw. Equally important, it would interest others in their welfare. As Turner sagely observed, "We care only for those about whom we know something."[69]

The last point was important. The familiarizing work of the missionaries advanced the tide of Christian fellowship that Turner saw growing in strength. Where men once looked selfishly to themselves and with hostility at others, Turner wrote eight years before the Civil War, they were now beginning to perceive God's same "wise harmony of plan" among the races of men as among the other natural wonders of nature. Anthropology not only Christianized the heathen Indian but cleansed the White of ignorance and prejudice:

> This science cannot like some others be cultivated as a mere intellectual exercise, nor can any man long pursue it and cherish bitter & contemptuous prejudices against races less fortunately situated than his own; on the contrary a feeling of good will to all men is its necessary result.[70]

The year after Turner's death, George Gibbs IV arrived in Washington and quickly replaced him as Henry's chief linguistic advisor. In training and experience Gibbs and Turner were very different men. Whereas Turner was a product of scholarly cloisters and quiet libraries, Gibbs had spent twelve years in rugged Washington Territory as government official, surveyor, geologist, miner, farmer, and observer of Indians. Turner's knowledge came almost entirely from books; Gibbs's grew from frequent contact with the aborigines. But Gibbs was by no means an uneducated, illiterate mountain man. Like Powell after him, he embodied both the explorer and the scholar. Because his career reflected the peculiar patterns of American linguistic work—because he spoke the language of the explorer and the academic—he served appropriately as Henry's resident collaborator in the Institution's linguistic clearinghouse of the 1860s.

The eldest child of Laura Wolcott and Colonel George Gibbs III, George was born in 1815 into Federalist-Whig elegance on Long Island, New York. He attended George Bancroft's Round Hill School in preparation for West Point, but following a two-year European tour he studied law at Harvard instead.[71] After graduation in 1838 Gibbs practiced law in New York for a decade. But law never became more than a necessary means of livelihood to him, and he spent the greater part of his time collecting minerals and birds and writing the *Memoirs of the Administration of Washington and Adams*.[72]

By 1848 Gibbs had reached a dead end. Thirty-three years old, he had squandered his share of the diminished family estate in high living and liquor, and his legal career was in decline. While his brothers and sisters married, soldiered, and explored, Gibbs remained in New York City with his mother. Desperate to get away, deeply in debt, and infected by gold fever, he escaped New York by joining the "March of the Mounted Rifles" from St. Louis to the gold fields of Oregon.[73]

In the Northwest, Gibbs began to piece together a broken and aimless life. He fell in love with the region and became a close observer of its natural products, including its people. Like the rivers, mountains, and valleys of Washington Territory, which he came to know so well, the Indians were a natural wonder for Gibbs. To be sure, they were a danger and obstacle to settlement, but they were also an important ally in the struggle to survive in the rugged country. Like explorers before and anthropologists after him, Gibbs experienced an unresolved ambivalence toward Native Americans. On the one hand he could write with sincerity that "we too often give a general character to savage races, derived from a few, and those most probably the worst of their nation; forgetting that there may be as great diversity of disposition among them as among ourselves."[74] At the same time he measured the Indians by the only standards he found comfortable. While he watched their steady attrition from White disease and greed, Gibbs served as interpreter to treaty parlays and himself frequently visited young Indian maidens in their villages. Later, with apparently few second thoughts, he attributed the epi-

demic proportions of syphilis among the aborigines to their "erotic temperament," moral laxness, and fish diet.[75]

Gibbs never made a living panning for gold; but between 1854 and 1860,
three survey commissions utilized his firsthand knowledge of the region. Most
significant was his service as geologist, botanist, and naturalist on the Northwest Boundary Survey of 1857, for which he prepared a long report on the
natural history of the Washington Territory. By 1860 Gibbs had erased his
debts and emerged as a respected settler.

He began serious study of the aboriginal Northwest in the late 1850s.
Simple word lists, he realized, served only limited functions; Gibbs emphasized
instead collection of creation myths and other tales. Alone he could accomplish
a restricted amount, but he also became a stimulus to others. When large
numbers of Indians were transferred to local reservations in the mid-1850s,
Gibbs saw potential ethnological treasures, and he enlisted the aid of bored
Army doctors and officers.[76]

In his enthusiasm to broaden the geographical base of his inquiry, Gibbs
even contacted the governor of the Russian colonies in Alaska, providing him
with vocabulary blanks for each of the principal languages of Russian America.
His plans were ambitious: a "complete collection of all languages west of the
Rocky Mountains," including all dialects. His ultimate goal, though, was
to trace migration routes, and thereby determine the geographical origins of
the American Indians. By the end of his years in the West, Gibbs had
established a general theory of westward movement from the Great Plains
along the Columbia and Fraser river valleys to the Pacific. The buffalo country,
he thought, had been the "nursery" of the "countless hordes who have gradually pushed themselves southward & westward." At the same time he believed
firmly in a remoter Asiatic origin. Gibbs never resolved the issue.[77]

In early 1861 Gibbs returned to New York, intending to remain on the
east coast temporarily. After a few weeks he moved to Washington, where
he stayed ten years, first finishing up the Northwest Boundary work, then
serving as secretary to the Hudson Bay Claims Commission, and finally
moving, at Henry's invitation in 1867, into a study in the tower of the
Smithsonian.[78] There he lived for three years. After the death of his mother
in 1870, Gibbs married his cousin, Mary Kane Gibbs, and moved to New
Haven. He died there two years later.

During Gibbs's decade in Washington, he brought his linguistic studies
to partial fruition through his close contacts with Smithsonian officials. He
found the Smithsonian ethnographic collections and linguistic library a vast
new source of materials and enjoyed his near-monopoly of them.[79] At first
he jealously kept his own field notes at his home in New York, but after
1862, when the Boundary employment ended, he sought closer affiliation
with the Institution as an outlet for publication. Eventually his linguistic

materials became the property of the Smithsonian and a major part of Powell's linguistic inventory in the Bureau.

Gibbs had three major projects in mind: an ethnological map of the region west of the Rockies, showing particularly the supposed Indian migration routes; publication of his fifty or more vocabularies and reconstruction of the historical connections they indicated; and a general ethnography, including mythologies and social organizations, of the Northwest Coast aborigines. The third project never got beyond his notebooks. The ethnological map did not become a reality until after his death, in the form of Powell's linguistic map of North America; and only a few vocabularies reached print.[80] Gibbs's failure to realize his dreams led one biographer to accuse him of "frittering away" his years in the Smithsonian tower recopying old vocabulary lists.[81] The judgment fails to appreciate the professional and scientific situation in which Gibbs operated.

Gibbs inherited a scientific tradition exemplified by the cosmography of Alexander von Humboldt: an attempt to treat regions as entities by correlating features of climate with soil, vegetation, and animal and human life. An ethnological map, from this perspective, was only part of a larger enterprise of thorough regional understanding. A synchronic environmental picture had to be the basis for reconstruction of Northwest Coast ethnology, Gibbs believed. This unified, comprehensive approach underlay Gibbs's proposal in 1865 for a "Smithsonian Atlas" of North America. With the close of the Civil War, he urged, the time had arrived to embrace "all departments of natural, physical, and social science" in a grand atlas of the continent, following natural rather than political boundaries. The scientific future of America, he argued, lay in comprehensive undertakings: "If the United States, as we all trust, is now to enter upon a new career of mental as well as physical advancement, it becomes us to anticipate the directions in which scientific inquiry can be pushed."[82]

Gibbs anticipated and encouraged a pan-American perspective in anthropology that would reemerge at the turn of the century under radically changed political conditions. He envisioned close cooperation with Russian and British authorities in the Northwest, and Mexican officials in the Southwest, but also insisted on supervision by an American, possibly an Army engineer with experience in survey work. He hoped for a "continental league of science & art, with its headquarters at Washington" as a "first step to an extended Americanism of which the future is boundless." Gibbs urged that the Smithsonian take the initiative by ignoring language differences and publishing Mexican as well as American work in archaeology.[83]

The blend of investigations that Gibbs called for throughout the hemisphere was possible in the fertile, wide-ranging mind of a single man but impossible to carry out without cooperation of experts in many fields—without organization. Interestingly, over the next fifteen years (the heyday of the western surveys), various individuals operating under government aegis, including Powell, attempted to carry out the kind of regional studies that Gibbs foresaw, but in each case emphasis drifted to one field or another, and the inevitable splintering of disciplines ensued. The unity of the Humboldtian holistic, regional approach broke down.

Problems peculiar to linguistic work also plagued Gibbs. In addition to the tedium of field work, the results were often difficult and expensive to set in type, since they involved designing new characters. This assumed consensus on orthography in the first place, but achieving agreement on a generally useful and yet accurate alphabet preoccupied Gibbs, Whitney, and Powell for years. Gibbs outlined the alphabet problem to Whitney soon after his arrival in Washington, when the experiences of the Northwest were fresh in his mind. What was needed, he told the Yale philologist, was a "field alphabet":

> Could one man of education and leisure visit successively each Indian tribe, or could even a number of such inquirers occupy different portions of the field, taking abundant time to weigh the niceties of sound, a complicated alphabet like that of Lepsius would be practicable . . . But the difficulty is that the men who collect vocabularies in Indian countries are seldom men of philological learning. They are officers of the army, Indian agents, and general explorers, often with very meagre orthographic acquirements, yet sufficiently competent to obtain useful vocabularies, and generally the contributors of the only ones.

To give such men a complicated alphabet would only confuse and dishearten them. A short, simple one was needed, relying on the good sense of the investigator to note unusual sounds. "Different capacities & degrees of training," he confessed, "will estimate these differently."[84]

Whitney did prepare a simplified alphabet for the Smithsonian, but in 1870 Gibbs still complained that most alphabets were "beyond the comprehension of any but their inventors" and presupposed wide knowledge and fine discriminations. He could only conclude that "the explanation, in writing, of unusual sounds is always a hazardous experiment."[85]

Joseph Henry shared only part of Gibbs's vision. Through the 1860s Henry planned for Gibbs to analyze the collected Smithsonian vocabularies, distribute them to others for discussion, and finally derive a linguistic map. But the project dragged on. In 1870, when he had 100 vocabularies, Gibbs proposed that the Smithsonian undertake an ambitious treatise on North American languages, embracing not only its unpublished materials but also earlier vocabularies that were sufficiently reliable and useful for reprinting. Gibbs offered to take responsibility for the Far West, leaving the rest of the continent to half-a-dozen collaborators.[86] Henry reacted cautiously. He favored distributing vocabularies to a small circle of investigators; the vocabularies would then be worked up with new information into a "general system." He referred the question to Whitney and Trumbull, making clear that he preferred to postpone any "treatise." Whitney and Trumbull concurred. Trumbull advised that vocabularies be distributed "to enable all who are interested in the subject to contribute to the work of comparison and discussion for which it might not be easy to find just now any one competent person." The treatise on American linguistics would have to wait for "the coming man."[87]

The caution of Gibbs's coworkers reflected a growing hesitancy to make any summary statement about the languages of America without much more data. Just as he cautioned Squier and Davis against speculation and urged Rau to delay his archaeological masterwork, Henry put off Gibbs's ambitious mapping plans. Whitney still saw confusion in American languages and urged patience. The search for Asian or any other connections was premature and "at variance with all the principles of linguistic science." The conservatism of the academic philologist must have distressed explorer Gibbs:

Sound method [Whitney wrote in *Language*] . . . requires that we study each dialect, group, branch, and family by itself, before we venture to examine and pronounce upon its more distant connections. What we have to do at present, then, is simply to learn all that we possibly can of the Indian languages themselves; to settle their internal relations, elicit their laws of growth, reconstruct their older forms, and ascend toward their original conditions as far as the material within our reach, and the state in which it is presented, will allow. . . .[88]

Whitney, the stern voice of academic linguistics, aimed at very different goals than Gibbs sought. While hailing the "self-prompted study" of "self-denying men" in this "most fertile and important" science, Whitney deplored in the same breath the numerous investigators "with minds crammed with scattering items of historical information, abounding prejudice, and teeming fancies . . ."[89]

James Hammond Trumbull, self-taught Indian language expert from Connecticut, also found fault with the prevailing American linguistic methods. Collecting more Indian vocabularies, he said, was a scientifically useless enterprise. In the days of Gallatin, vocabulary gathering had helped to make sense of a chaotic mass of materials, but the work of Gallatin and the young Horatio Hale had been mere stepping stones. By the 1870s, it seemed to Trumbull, the real work of the linguist began where "the provisional labors of the word-collector" ended. Trumbull realized fully the futility of trying to match word-for-word correspondences between languages that differed fundamentally in their "plans of thought." He insisted instead on thorough knowledge of grammatical structures and analysis of Indian tongues into their basic components. Thus, while he deprecated mere word collecting, he contended that Indian languages could be studied by atomistic analysis. Where Duponceau and Schoolcraft had emphasized the unpredictable whim of the Indian in forming polysynthetic compounds, Trumbull saw order and regularity. The Indian no less than any other man, he insisted, always aimed at "extreme precision" in language. Only this fact made a science of American languages possible.[90]

The criticisms of Whitney and Trumbull exposed the gulf that separated them from Gibbs. The former settler also appreciated the complexity of Indian languages. But Gibbs was also impatient to determine the historical connections of various peoples and their relations to the environment. Whitney and Trumbull searched for the origin and laws, the philosophy, of language; looking to Indo-European models, they desired thorough understanding of speech. As Trumbull expressed his position, "absolute mastery of an Indian tongue is, for one to whom it is not vernacular, the work of a lifetime."[91] Gibbs would have agreed, but he never sought absolute mastery. To him, and to his successor Powell, language study was never more than a means to more important ends.

American Indian linguistics between 1840 and 1870 called forth differing motivations and encountered severe dilemmas. For William Turner, language study was a moral enterprise, closely joined to Christianizing efforts; for Gibbs, aboriginal tongues provided the only reliable key to the profound question of origins; for Whitney, language was a wonder, worthy of scientific study for its own beauty. All saw the need for system in observation and recording, and in the end they agreed that formal training was necessary. Two years before his death, Gibbs finally broke with the Hale/Gallatin tradition by proposing a flexible list of at least 1,500 words and phrases, rather than the 211 of his earlier circulars. Calling for "some new standard" for "an intelligent philology," he deplored the lack of sophisticated grammatical studies and suggested sending out manuals on "How to observe and what to observe" as a "stimulus . . . to the exertions of many who only require to know in what direction to employ their leisure and tastes."[92] Faith in the awakening word lived in George Gibbs as in Henry and Turner. He even proposed college courses to prepare future investigators. But in the end, the strength of Gibbs's salvage ethnology prevailed: in 1871 he advised Henry to halt the analytical and grammatical studies and gather more word lists— before the Indians all died out.[93]

Under Joseph Henry the Smithsonian Institution was a haven of science. The informal, family atmosphere that Henry and Baird created on the Mall contrasted sharply with the brutal political world of Washington in the decades surrounding the Civil War. Here natural scientists and wandering explorers found a temporary home and the leisure to study their collections, and aspiring young men like George Brown Goode and Frank Hamilton Cushing drank in the atmosphere of scientific congeniality. Naturalist Robert Kennicott was not exceptional in finding adjustment to Washington life greatly eased by the cozy circumstances at the Smithsonian during the winter of 1862–63:

> It's all very well to *talk* of the delights of the civilized world, but give me the comfortable north where a man can have some fun, see good dogs and smoke his pipe unmolested—D--n civilization. Not that I see it so much either for I live constantly here at the Smithsonian among a set of naturalists nearly all of whom have spent their lives in the wilderness.[94]

The comfort and informality were destined to be shortlived, because Henry's institution grew from demographic and professional conditions that were rapidly disappearing. In the middle years of the century, the sparsely populated national domain and the drive to diffuse the experience of science widely from Washington produced an enthusiasm for anthropology. The impressive richness of materials; the obvious, rapid, and steady annihilation of Native Americans before the onslaught of civilization; and the strong commitment to "facts" together contributed to making anthropology the Smithsonian's most public science. In 1877, the year before his death, Henry wrote with assurance that anthropology "is at present the most popular branch of science."[95]

Notes

1. Henry to J. B. Varnum [draft], 22 June 1847, SIA.

2. SI, *AR for 1847*, pp. 175–76.

3. Ibid., pp. 179, 181–82.

4. Baird to Henry, 3 November 1849; quoted in William H. Dall, *Spencer Fullerton Baird* (Philadelphia, 1915), p. 191. "Every effort was made to enlist the services of occasional correspondents who wrote to the Smithsonian for information. A letter giving the particulars desired would perhaps have a postscript asking whether there were any Indian remains to be found in the locality . . . In a great many instances these letters bore important fruit . . . ." (T. D. A. Cockerell, "Spencer Fullerton Baird," *Popular Science Monthly* [January 1906], p. 72). Henry and Baird did in fact use the meteorological network for anthropological inquiries. See, for instance, Henry's report (SI, *AR for 1860*, p. 42) on a circular, sent out in conjunction with the Academy of Natural Sciences of Philadelphia, on the physical characteristics of native-born Americans—one of the few instances of Smithsonian activity in physical anthropology in this period.

5. Henry to Frazer, 27 October 1855, Frazer Papers, APS. I am indebted to Nathan Reingold and Arthur Molella for this reference. Henry to Dr. Joseph Jones, 13 August 1868, Joseph Jones Papers.

6. Reaction to the acceptance of Squier and Davis's *Ancient Monuments,* for instance, was not entirely positive. "Those who consider no branch of knowledge of any value but such as relates to the immediate gratification of our physical wants, have objected to the acceptance of this memoir," Henry reported, but it was the first publication to meet his announced standards. "Besides this, it furnishes an addition to a branch of knowledge which is at this time occupying the attention of a large class of minds." (SI, *AR for 1847.* p. 188.) *Scientific American* (5 February 1848) registered disgust that Smithson's bequest was being squandered on "a useless and ambiguous science like Archaeology . . ."

7. Joseph Henry Pocket Notebook, 1848, p. 35, SIA; SI, *AR for 1847,* p. 181.

8. Ephraim G. Squier and Edwin H. Davis, *Ancient Monuments of the Mississippi Valley: Comprising the Results of Extensive Original Surveys and Explorations* (Washington, D.C., 1848).

9. SI, *AR for 1877,* p. 22; Henry to Loomis, 5 June 1847, Loomis Papers.

10. Henry to Squier, 3 April 1847, Squier Papers.

11. Henry to Gallatin, 2 June 1847; Henry to Squier, 23 June 1847; and report of the AES committee, June 1847, all in SI, *AR for 1847.* pp. 185–87. The circumstances of the acceptance of the memoir bothered Henry, since if it became known that the reviewing committee had been chosen by "the author and his friends" rather than by the Secretary of the Smithsonian, it would set a poor precedent for Henry's future operations. Thus he advised "a little management" of the facts, and printed an edited version of his correspondence with the Ethnological Society. Henry to Squier, 23 June 1847, and Henry to Bartlett, 23 June 1847, Squier Papers.

12. Henry to Squier and Davis, 16 February 1848, Squier Papers.

13. Squier and Davis, *Ancient Monuments.* p. xxxviii. Three years later, Squier, in his second Smithsonian publication, again distinguished his own work from past efforts in ethnology: "Men seem to have indulged the belief that here nothing is fixed, nothing certain, and have turned aside into this field as one where the severer rules which elsewhere regulate philosophical research are not enforced . . ." *Aboriginal Monuments of New York* (Washington, D.C., 1851), p. 81.

14. John Russell Bartlett, "The Progress of Ethnology, An Account of Recent Archaeological, Philological, and Geographical Researches in Various Parts of the Globe, tending to elucidate the Physical History of Man," *Transactions of the American Ethnological Society* 2 (New York, 1848): 4. Samuel F. Haven, of the American Antiquarian Society in Worcester, Massachusetts, doubted the soundness of the work, though. Henry, disturbed to learn of Haven's opinion, appealed to him to explain his reservations, noting that "in regard to the character of a memoir on antiquities I must trust to others." Henry to Haven, 19 October 1847, Haven Papers.

15. Henry to Charles Rau, 10 December 1864, SIA.

16. Thomas Coulson, *Joseph Henry: His Life and Work* (Princeton, 1950), pp. 202–03.

17. Lapham to Henry, 12 March 1850 and 1 November 1851, Lapham Papers, OHS; Edward Foreman to Lapham, 29 March 1850, and Henry to Lapham, 22 November 1851, WSHS. In his desire to become "one of the men among whom

knowledge is to be 'increased and diffused' by your Institution," Lapham had written for advice and instruments as early as 1848. Lapham to Henry, 3 April 1848 and 2 March 1849, Lapham Papers, OHS.

18. SI, *AR for 1853*, pp. 20–21; Joseph Henry Pocket Notebook, 24 January 1848, SIA.

19. Henry to Charles Rau, 17 December 1869, SIA.

20. "Address of Prof. Joseph Henry," *Fifth and Sixth Annual Reports of the American Museum of Natural History* (New York, 1874), pp. 44–50 (quotation, p. 47).

21. Ibid., p. 47; cf. SI, *AR for 1847*, p. 181.

22. Ephraim G. Squier, *The Serpent Symbol* (New York, 1851), p. ix.

23. SI, *AR for 1846*, p. 23.

24. This point is central to understanding Henry's operations. I am indebted here to Arthur Molella's suggestions in his unpublished paper, "At the Edge of Science: Visionary Theorizers at the Smithsonian."

25. SI, *AR for 1867*, p. 44.

26. SI, *AR for 1861*, p. 26. In 1856 Henry observed with pleasure that the citizens of Chicago, apparently stimulated by Lapham's work, had founded a historical and antiquarian society. "Man is an imitative animal," he noted to Haven, "and the influence of our successful example sets many in operation." Henry to Haven, 27 October 1856, Haven Papers.

27. SI, *AR for 1859*, p. 17.

28. Increase Lapham, *Antiquities of Wisconsin*, Smithsonian Contributions to Knowledge 7 (Washington, D.C., 1855); Charles Whittlesey, *Ancient Works in Ohio*, Smithsonian Contributions to Knowledge 3 (Washington, D.C. 1852): 6; Brantz Mayer, *Mexican Archaeology and History*, Smithsonian Contributions to Knowledge 9 (Washington, D.C. 1857): 2.

29. Jesse Walter Fewkes, "Anthropology," in George Brown Goode, ed., *The Smithsonian Institution, 1846–1898* (Washington, D.C., 1897), p. 751. Between 1860 and 1872, when Joseph Jones's *Antiquities of Tennessee* appeared as part of vol. 22 of the Contributions, the Institution published countless brief accounts of excavations in its annual reports, but no major works on American archaeology.
    Haven originally intended a "purely historical (not speculative)" introduction to Lapham's memoir, as a "retrospective view" of the factual results of researches on the mound-builders. (Haven to Henry, 4 January, 7 July, and 20 November 1854, Haven Papers.) The project soon expanded, however, to a discussion of developments in philology and physical anthropology as well. Henry advised him to avoid discussion of the "vexed question" of the unity of the race. (Haven to Henry, 10 March 1855; Henry to Haven, 8 December and 17 December 1855; 3 April 1856, Haven Papers.)

30. Gordon R. Willey, "One Hundred Years of American Archaeology," in J. O. Brew, ed., *One Hundred Years of Anthropology* (Cambridge, 1968), pp. 29–53. For a fuller treatment of this period, see Gordon R. Willey and Jeremy A. Sabloff, *A History of American Archaeology* (San Francisco, 1974), pp. 42–87.

31. Mayer, *Mexican Archaeology*, p. 1. Twenty years later, Haven similarly observed that all the empirical advances of two decades in American archaeology had produced little "absolute progress" toward settlement of these "great questions."

(Haven to Henry, 20 January 1876, Haven Papers.)

32. Henry to T. Apoleon Cheny, 11 November 1861, Joseph Henry Collection, Princeton University Library.

33. Glyn E. Daniel has summarized this formative period in "Old World Prehistory," in Brew, *One Hundred Years*. pp. 58–59. For an extensive discussion, see Daniel's *A Hundred Years of Archaeology* (London, 1950).

34. SI, *AR for 1860*. pp. 284–343. Morlot's work enjoyed wide circulation and influence in Europe. See Daniel, *Hundred Years*. p. 79.

35. SI, *AR for 1861*. pp. 34–35, 392–96.

36. Henry, Extracts from Locked Book, 25 April 1862, SIA; SI, *AR for 1865*. p. 46. Such doubts were not original with Henry; see, e.g., E. G. Squier, *Aboriginal Mounds of New York* (Washington, D.C., 1851), p. 84.

    Henry also attributed analogies in social organization to a common human nature. The fact of different races having the same system of sexual promiscuity in remote times, Henry wrote William D. Whitney (in reference to Lewis Henry Morgan's work), "does not prove a unity of origin, but merely a unity of custom, arising from the brutal propensities of the species." (11 May 1869, Whitney Papers.) Henry refused to print an appendix on migrations to Morgan's *Systems of Consanguinity and Affinity in the Human Family* (Washington, D.C., 1871). Henry to Morgan, 8 April 1870, LHM Papers.

37. Henry Locked Book, 25 April 1862, SIA.

38. SI, *AR for 1888*. pp. 27, 91–92; *Dictionary of American Biography* 15 (1935): 388–89 (article by Walter Hough).

39. Rau to Henry, 25 February 1869; 29 November 1867; 6 March 1869, SIA.

40. Regna Darnell, "The Development of American Anthropology, 1879 to 1920: From the Bureau of American Ethnology to Franz Boas," Ph.D. diss. (University of Pennsylvania, 1969), pp. 2–4.

41. Rau to Henry, 29 November 1867, SIA.

42. Henry to Rau, 30 November 1867, SIA. For a recent assessment of Morton's unconscious "finagling" of his data, see Stephen Jay Gould, "Morton's Ranking of Races by Cranial Capacity: Unconscious Manipulation of Data May Be a Scientific Norm," *Science* 200 (5 May 1978): 503–09.

43. Rau to Baird, 1 January 1875, SIA. Henry consistently supported and encouraged Rau, who reported to his friend Carl Herman Berendt in 1876 that while he chafed under the direct supervision of Baird, "der alte Henry hat sich mir genenüber stets als Gentleman gezeigt . . . und wird sich ohne Zweifel in meinem Interesse bemühen." ("Henry has always been a gentleman to me . . . and will undoubtedly exert himself on my behalf.")

44. Rau to Baird, 1 January 1875, SIA.

45. Henry to Rau, 23 April and 10 May 1875, SIA.

46. Charles Rau, "Brooklyn Lecture on Archaeology," unpub. ms., p. 4, NAA; Rau, "On the Parallelism in the Development of Mankind, with Special Reference to the Red Race," unpub. ms., p. 1, NAA. The latter paper is the clearest statement of Rau's concept of parallel invention.

47. SI, *AR for 1864*. p. 374.

48. SI, *AR for 1865* (Washington, D.C., 1872), p. 50.

49. Rau to Henry, 26 October 1863, SIA.

50. Rau to George Gibbs, 30 May 1868, SIA.

51. Henry to Rau, 11 April and 6 June 1868; Rau to Henry, 28 April 1868, SIA.
    In 1875 and again in 1877 Henry asked Haven to prepare a new edition of his 1856 "master work," incorporating the results of the intervening decades. Haven's health did not permit him to accept Henry's offer. Henry to Hayen, 3 March 1875; 26 November 1877; 12 March 1878; Haven to Henry, 20 January 1876, Haven Papers.

52. Smithsonian Contributions to Knowledge 25 (Washington, D.C. 1884): viii.

53. Charles C. Abbott, *Primitive Industry* (Salem, Mass., 1881).

54. See, e.g., reviews of Rau's work in *Archiv für Anthropologie* 13 (1880–81): 150–56, 157–62; also Rau to Henry, 3 February 1875, SIA.

55. The relationship between Henry and Schoolcraft is not entirely clear, but the two natives of upstate New York were apparently close friends for some time. When the Henrys moved to Washington, the Schoolcrafts and Henrys set up housekeeping together, an arrangement that proved most unsatisfactory to the two wives. After Schoolcraft's death in 1864, Henry actively aided his widow in assuring her an adequate income.

56. SI, *AR for 1851,* p. 13. For Henry's belief that languages indicate historical connections, see Henry Locked Book, 25 April 1862, SIA; and SI, *AR for 1865* (Washington, D.C., 1872), p. 46.

57. Henry Pocket Notebook, 1849, p. 14, SIA; SI, *AR for 1851,* p. 27; SI, *AR for 1857,* p. 37; SI, *AR for 1863,* pp. 42, 95–116.

58. Henry Rowe Schoolcraft, *Inquiries, Respecting the history, present condition and future prospects of the Indian tribes of the United States* (Washington, D.C., 1847). Schoolcraft's vocabulary list, reissued in 1849, totaled 350 words. *Indian Languages of North America,* American Ethnological Society Circular No. 1 (June 1852).

59. SI, *AR for 1867,* p. 36; George Gibbs, "Instructions for Archaeological Investigations in the U.S.," SI, *AR for 1861,* pp. 392–96; Gibbs, "Instructions for Research Relative to the Ethnology and Philology of America," SI Miscellaneous Collections 7, no. 160 (Washington, D.C., 1863); Gibbs, "Instructions relative to the Ethnology and Philology of America. Appendix A: Physical Characters of the Indian Races; Appendix B: Numerical Systems," in Smithsonian Contributions to Knowledge 15 (Washington, D.C., 1865). For a useful survey of circulars relating to ethnology, see Don D. Fowler, "Notes on Inquiries in Anthropology—A Bibliographic Essay," in T. H. H. Thoreson, ed., *Toward A Science of Man: Essays in the History of Anthropology* (The Hague, 1976), pp. 15–32.

60. SI, *AR for 1876,* p. 36; SI, *AR for 1877,* p. 24.

61. Gibbs to Whitney, 12 May 1861, Whitney Papers.

62. W.D. Whitney, *Language and the Study of Language* (New York, 1867), p. 324.

63. This account of Turner's career is based on "In Memoriam: Susan Wadden Turner and Jane Wadden Turner" (privately printed, 1898).

64. William H. Dall, *Spencer Fullerton Baird* (Philadelphia, 1915), p. 231; "In Memoriam," p. 9. See also Turner to Baird, 26 August and 23 September 1858, SIA, for evidence of their close personal friendship.

65. Felton to Smithsonian Regents, 4 February 1860, quoted in "In Memoriam," p. 14; Henry to John R. Bartlett, 7 November 1859, Bartlett Papers.

66. "Professor Turner's Letter on Indian Philology" (16 December 1851), SI, *AR for 1851*, pp. 97–98.
67. Ibid., p. 99.
68. J. W. Fewkes, "Anthropology," in G.B. Goode, ed., *The Smithsonian Institution, 1846–1896* (Washington, D.C., 1897), pp. 758–59; "Professor Turner's Letter," p. 97. Byington's Choctaw grammar was published by the American Philosophical Society in 1871; the dictionary, edited by John Swanton, was published by the BAE in 1915. Byington died in 1868.
69. Turner to Byington, 3 December 1852, Rhees Papers, SIA.
70. Ibid.
71. The following account of Gibbs's career is based upon Stephen Dow Beckham, "George Gibbs, 1815–1873: Historian and Ethnologist," Ph.D. diss. (UCLA, 1969); John Austin Stevens, "A Memorial of George Gibbs," SI, *AR for 1873*, pp. 219–25; and *Dictionary of American Biography* 8: 245–46. Stevens and Gibbs were intimate, lifelong friends. Their correspondence of the 1850s and 1860s is in the Gibbs Family Papers, WSHS.
72. George Gibbs, *The Memoirs of the Administration of Washington and Adams, edited from the Papers of Oliver Wolcott, Secretary of the Treasury* (New York, 1846). Gibbs's younger brother, Oliver Wolcott, was also denied admission to West Point, going instead to Columbia University to study chemistry. Alfred, the third son, finally attained West Point, eventually rising to major general. The entire family, including George, followed his career with enthusiasm.
73. Beckham, "George Gibbs," pp. 52–53. On Gibbs's move westward and his early years in the Northwest, see David I. Bushnell, Jr., "Drawings by George Gibbs in the Far Northwest, 1849–1851," Smithsonian Miscellaneous Collections 97, no. 8 (1938). The remarks on Gibbs's financial and personal dilemma derive from references and intimations in his correspondence to his family, 1850–53, in Gibbs Papers, WSHS.
74. Beckham, "George Gibbs," p. 99.
75. Ibid., pp. 102–03, 214; Gibbs, "The Intermixture of Races," SI, *AR for 1864*, p. 377.
76. Ibid., pp. 147, 193–94.
77. Ibid., pp. 194–95, 257.
78. Henry first invited him to take up residence at the Institution in 1861, but Gibbs declined. Beckham, "George Gibbs," p. 246.
79. Gibbs to Laura Wolcott Gibbs, 5 April 1861, Gibbs Family Papers, WSHS.
80. Beckham, "George Gibbs," pp. 232–33. The volumes for Shea were on Yakima, Chinook jargon, and the Lummi and Clallam dialects.
81. Ibid., p. 248.
82. George Gibbs, "A physical atlas of North America," SI, *AR for 1866* (Washington, D.C., 1872), pp. 368–69.
83. Gibbs to Baird, 10 and 22 February and 2 March 1863, SIA.
84. Gibbs to Whitney, 12 May 1861; Henry to Whitney, 1 August 1861 (Whitney Papers), in which the Secretary instructed Whitney to prepare an alphabet "especially adapted to the Indian dialects on this continent." Gibbs had included an alphabet in his 1863 "Instructions for Research Relative to the Ethnology

and Philology of America," SI Miscellaneous Collections 7, no. 160.

85. George Gibbs, "On the language of the aboriginal Indians of America," SI, *AR for 1870*, p. 367.

86. Henry Desk Diary, 8 April and 19 November 1868, and 25 January and 30 January 1870, SIA.

87. Henry to Whitney, 25 January 1870; Trumbull to Whitney, 31 January 1870, Whitney Papers.

88. Whitney, *Language*, p. 351.

89. Ibid., p. 353.

90. J.H. Trumbull, "On the Best Method of Studying the North American Languages," *Transactions of the American Philological Association* (1870): 78.

91. *Transactions of the American Philological Association* 3 (1872): 117.

92. SI, *AR for 1870*, pp. 364–67.

93. Beckham, "George Gibbs," p. 253.

94. Kennicott to Robert MacFarlane, 19 April 1863, Kennicott Papers, SIA.

95. SI, *AR for 1877*, p. 22.

III

An "Omnium Gatherum": Museum Anthropology at the Smithsonian Institution, 1846–1880

Joseph Henry was not a museum man—most of the time. Strictures against museum collections appeared regularly in his annual reports and correspondence, and his battle against museum advocates in Congress and on his own Board of Regents is well known.[1] The first Smithsonian Secretary repeatedly warned that "the formation of a museum of objects of nature and art requires much caution"; he frequently associated museums with gratification of "mere curiosity" rather than serious science.[2] In his last report (1877) Henry made a special effort to distinguish between the secondary, educational functions of the museum and the primary functions of the Smithsonian: support of original investigation and exploration, and publication and distribution of results.[3]

This familiar image of Henry as arch-opponent of the museum involves a chain of historical ironies. Despite his supposed museum antipathy, for assistant secretary Henry chose Spencer F. Baird, who came with his private collections in two railroad boxcars.[4] Henry lived and worked closely with Baird for twenty-five years, during which time the Smithsonian's natural history and anthropology acquisitions grew enormously. In 1857, after years of maneuvering for the proper conditions of transfer, Henry finally accepted the Wilkes materials from the Patent Office Building;.similarly, twenty years later, rather than refuse the vast Centennial Exposition treasures offered to the Institution, at the time of his death Henry was engaged in obtaining from Congress a new museum building to house the objects. These decisions and policies did not arise from weakness or vacillation. As his firing of librarian Charles C. Jewett demonstrated, Henry firmly controlled Smithsonian affairs throughout his tenure; his tolerance for Baird's collecting impulses arose from confidence in his own position.

Henry and the museum thus require reassessment. In actuality, as one historian of science has argued, the view of Henry as a research scientist opposed to museum collections distorts this "very complex, ambiguous person" who actively collected art, books, artifacts, and natural history specimens "while complaining correctly that all these activities would severely hobble the Institution's research role."[5] In reconsidering Henry, it is important to note, first, that his stated resistance never applied to all collections, but only to the kind of "heterogeneous collection of objects of mere curiosity" that comprised most American museums of science and history and plagued the National Institute. He recognized the scientific value of limited collections as bases for research in natural history, and he accordingly accepted "special collections" to demonstrate specific theory. In addition, Henry believed that the Smithsonian could properly concentrate on North American materials, especially ethnological and archaeological materials, which were relatively inexpensive to preserve.[6] In fact, Henry's interests in natural history collections, and in the problem of geographical distribution of plants and animals, dated from his early years in Albany.[7] He recognized, moreover, the scientific integrity and importance of the taxonomic work of Baird and the naturalists, although he did tend to rank them below physical scientists.[8] Henry's position thus did not grow from antipathy toward natural history. Rather, two other factors caused his deep concern: the example of the National Institute and the political vulnerability of museums as institutions.

The act of Congress of 1846 creating the Smithsonian Institution provided for a building to house "objects of natural history, including a geological and mineralogical cabinet." At an early meeting the Regents confirmed these intentions by allotting $1,000 to advise U.S. consuls and other officials about procuring additions to the proposed museum and to encourage the Commissioner of Indian Affairs to collect items "illustrating the natural history of the country, and more especially the physical history, manners, and customs of the American aborigines." Reporting to the Regents in early 1847, the Smithsonian's committee of organization reiterated that "as important as the cabinets of natural history by the charter required to be included in the museum, your committee regard its ethnological portion"; they hoped to enlist the general public in building the anthropological collections.[9]

The shadow of the National Institute lingered over these early deliberations. As discussed earlier, from its inception the leaders of the Institute had placed priority on a national museum as the principal means of promoting "science and the useful arts," and the Institute model had considerable support within the original Smithsonian Board of Regents. Poinsett and his colleagues received tons of specimens from all parts of the continent, but no public funds for their care. As a consequence, the Institute's "National Cabinet" very quickly became a motley collection.

The confused state of the anthropological materials was typical of the Institute's "Cabinet." In 1841 and 1842, donations included such items as an "Indian pipe" (the Institute had many of these); "Bear-skin robe"; "A knife, said to have belonged to Wacousta, a celebrated Indian Chief"; "Skull of John Hicks, a noted Seminole Chief"; "Head-dress worn by Atahualpa, the last of the Incas"; and "39 Indian Arrowheads and White Oak acorns of three varieties." From Egypt, George Gliddon sent boxes of specimens, mainly pieces of stone, trees, shells, and bones. Among Gliddon's numerous gifts was "One piece of the sycamore tree under which tradition says 'Joseph and Mary sat' "—to which the budding Egyptologist and popularizer added: "The tree is old enough." In sum, as one observer noted, the Institute's antiquities amounted to a mixture of "natural science and bold adventure."[10]

Poinsett originally saw the museum as only a means of promoting science, not as a final goal. In the battles over the Wilkes collections and the Smithsonian bequest, though, the museum came to represent the material reason for the Institute's existence, and research programs waited for an indefinite future when the museum would presumably be in full operation. In 1841 John Pickering advised that the Institute encourage efforts by army officers to gather information about Indian languages. Brantz Mayer, secretary of the U.S. legation to Mexico, urged work in Central America. Preoccupation with museum care prevented the Institute from acting on these and other suggestions for research in science. The fresh image of the ill-fated Institute, "crushed to death by the weight of the collections and books" donated to it, surely figured largely in Henry's early conception of the Smithsonian.[11]

Beyond the National Institute precedent, however, Henry's resistance to museums was primarily political. His constant admonition that a large building and care for collections would bankrupt Smithson's bequest arose from his desire to keep Smithsonian science independent of political influence. He knew that a large museum would eventually require government funds, which meant annual trips to Capitol Hill and entrapment in Washington politics. "But now comes the danger," he wrote in 1877. Entering the political sphere, the Institution might "fall under political dominium." Henry had always recognized the danger. "Will [the Smithsonian] not be subject to party influences, and to the harassing questions of coarse and incompetent men?" his Princeton friend Charles Hodge had queried Henry in 1846. Knowing the risk, Henry nonetheless took it in the hope of establishing, against great odds, an independent scientific organization, free from the charlatanry and quackery of American politics and popular science. To be sure, the powers of Capitol Hill, of the "coarse and incompetent men" who ruled America, were awesome—"it will probably be found necessary to make a few oblations to Buncombe," Henry confessed—but these could be best resisted, he hoped, by minimizing financial dependence.[12] As the museum developed, it pushed Henry into the dependence he had feared, leaving his successors, Baird and Langley, without the luxury of a choice. Even before the end of the century, the oblations had become obligatory.

The Smithsonian did not actively encourage anthropological collecting before the Civil War. During the fifties, Baird amassed large numbers of mammals, birds, reptiles, fish, shells, and minerals from the exploring and surveying expeditions of federal departments, as well as from state govern-

ments, local scientific societies, and individuals.[13] Few anthropological specimens appeared among these acquisitions. In 1850 Ephraim Squier shipped
five large "stone idols" and other items from Nicaragua to Washington,
offering them as the nucleus of a "National Archaeological Museum." Henry
agreed on the importance of such a museum but cautioned that it should be
of "special objects and not an omnium gatherum of the ods & end[s] of
creation."[14] For the next seven years Baird recorded only occasional Indian
relics and artifacts.

Acquisition of the government (including Wilkes's) materials in 1857
augmented total Smithsonian collections by about twenty-five percent, and
a considerable portion of the new treasures were anthropological.[15] William
J. Rhees's *Guide to the Smithsonian Institution* (1859) claimed that the Institution
possessed "one of the most extensive and curious ethnological collections in
the world." The cases occupied the entire upper west gallery of the museum
hall, one-fourth of total museum space. In contrast to the Secretary's emphasis
on North American natural history, the anthropology drew from regions
outside North America visited by Wilkes and other explorers, chiefly islands
of the South Pacific. In fact, of fifteen display cases, only one featured North
American groups. The contents of each display unit were determined by
whatever items happened to have been collected, with haphazard results.[16]

By the time of the Civil War, then, if the Smithsonian's museum anthropology still displayed little scientific system, it at least showed sober intentions, particularly in comparison to the National Institute's "Cabinet." Portions of the latter still existed in the Patent Office in 1859, when Alfred
Hunter published a *Popular Catalogue* to these collections.[17] Comparison of
the guides to the two museums is instructive. Both, for instance, featured
calumets, or peace pipes. But while Rhees's pamphlet briefly explained the
supposed material and construction of the pipes, Hunter took the opportunity
to lecture the public on Indian character:

> The disappearance of the original inhabitants of the Western continent
> is not the result of destruction, but a decaying atrophy, which nothing
> can avert, except the cataclysm of the Caucasian strain. The Indian
> . . . is a brute and bully to his women, a blackguard when in liquor,
> and more cruel and ruthless than all the bloodquaffing demons of Scan-
> dinavia when fortune gives him the upper hand.[18]

Hunter's prose reflected the confusion and arbitrariness in the Institute's
museum. The display case adjacent to the Indian pipes contained the lower
jaw of a sperm whale, insects from British Guiana, "remains of a Megeth-
erium," coral, fossils, and crystal. In contrast to the chaos over at the Patent
Office, the Smithsonian, while still far from systematic classification, had
come some distance.

During the 1860s, and especially after the distractions of the Civil War, the Smithsonian's anthropological acquisitions increased rapidly for two reasons: European developments in archaeology, and trans-Mississippi expansion. The developments in Old World archaeology discussed in the previous chapter inspired Henry to a vigorous search for American antiquities, which he encouraged through circulars, correspondence, and his annual reports. Material results were gratifying: "Every state in the union," reported Baird in 1873, "has been represented to a greater or less extent in the form of stone-axes, pipes, pottery, etc." Henry was sanguine about the prospects of the archaeological specimens; no longer merely curiosities for "the wonder of the illiterate," by 1868 they promised to provide a basis for reconstructing the human history of North America. [19]

While collections from the eastern half of the continent came from shell heaps, mounds, and ploughed fields, explorers and agents in the western territories divested living tribes of clothing, implements, ornaments, and anything else they could be persuaded to sell or give away. The various territorial surveying parties of the post-war decade—under Hayden, Wheeler, King, and Powell—deposited their considerable ethnological treasures with Baird. [20] In addition, the assistant secretary combined efforts with other government agencies, such as the Department of Agriculture and the Bureau of Indian Affairs, to make maximum use of travelers, explorers, and agents in the West. Smithsonian archaeology, in other words, centered geographically east of the Mississippi (the shift to the Southwest would occur in Powell's Bureau during the 1880s); ethnological study and collection usually focused on the disappearing tribes from the Plains to the Pacific, with special attention to those already removed or settling in the Indian Territory. Geographically, institutionally, and paradigmatically, ethnology and archaeology in North America continued to suffer a debilitating separation. The absence or advanced decline of living cultures in the Northeast, Southeast, or Mississippi Valley, together with the general orientation of American archaeologists toward classification by technological stages, effectively removed the possibility of establishing historical depth and continuity in their studies. West of the Mississippi, the brutal, constant warfare against the dying tribes of the northern Plains, the Rocky Mountains, and the Southwest served strongly to confirm the popular image of the Indians as a nomadic, warlike race without proper home or history.

Within the quiet world of the Smithsonian, museum anthropology flowed with these broad cultural currents. Before 1880 all materials relating to Native Americans, whether archaeological or ethnological, came to the "ethnological division"; later the reorganization of the early eighties created departments of ethnology (Otis Mason), antiquities (Rau; later, Thomas Wilson), and arts and industries of civilization (George B. Goode), thereby formalizing the distinct purposes and conceptual divisions that had come to characterize the science of man in the museum. The museum thus confirmed in its structure the longstanding line between America's prehistory and the cultural status of the Indian, as well as the presumed wide gulf between the Indian and Anglo-Saxon civilizations. From the beginning, the logic was difficult to maintain, and almost immediately, in the eighties, the influx of large amounts of pottery, ancient and modern, from the sedentary, historical Pueblo peoples of the Southwest challenged the validity of the separation between archaeology and ethnology. To which division did the pottery belong? Significantly, Smithsonian officials postponed the dilemma by creating, under William Henry Holmes, a separate "Section of Aboriginal American Pottery."

The methods and personnel of this period, both in museum and field, emphasized broad coverage and freedom of movement, physically and intellectually. The men who built the early collections were naturalists and explorers, not ethnologists. Edward Palmer (1831–1911), listed regularly in the annual reports of the 1860s and 1870s as a major contributor to ethnology, exemplified the pattern. Palmer was primarily a botanical collector—"Plant Explorer of the West," his biographer has aptly suggested[21]—who spent the better part of almost every year of his adult life, between 1857 and 1910, roaming the western regions of North America. He collected for friends, patrons, and institutions in the East, largely leaving to them the work of classifying, labeling, studying, and exchanging the specimens he provided. The same was true of his auxiliary work in anthropology. Throughout his life Palmer revealed a consistent pattern of dependence: "anxious for opportunities to travel and collect, but without organizing ability to direct his own expeditions; sincere in his devotion to the prosecution of science, but not realizing his own limitations; willing to let his work as a collector speak for itself, and proud of his work, without understanding that the collections in themselves were not enough to make him the intellectual equal of such men as Henry and Baird."[22]

Abrasive and insensitive in personal affairs, Palmer established early a pattern of constant movement. He emigrated from England in 1849, and three years later attached himself as hospital steward to the La Plata exploring expedition to South America under Thomas Jefferson Page. Following his return in 1855, Palmer moved to Cleveland, back to England (where he briefly married), returned to New York and Cleveland, where for a short time he attended medical lectures, then proceeded on to Kansas in 1857. By 1860 Palmer was in Colorado, as always collecting plants and animals with every opportunity. On the basis of his meager medical experience, he served in the Union Army as an assistant surgeon in the campaigns in the Indian Territory, and due to his military connections he spent the years 1865–67 in Arizona as a surgeon at the various military posts recently established to control Apache outbreaks. He devoted most of his time here, however, to gathering and shipping eastward specimens of plants and seeds. The following year he moved again to the Indian Territory as agency doctor among the Kiowas and

Comanches, but his preoccupation with collecting and excessive disregard for his Indian patients caused his removal to the nearby Wichita agency, where presumably he indulged his collecting impulses without the burden of medical duties.[23]

Palmer made his first ethnological collections for Baird in 1867 in Arizona and continued this side interest during the next year in the Indian Territory. The Smithsonian ethnology catalogs list items from the Apache, Pima, Papago, and Comanche peoples, and Henry noted that Palmer's collections formed "very complete illustrations of the manners and customs of the tribes."[24] Palmer's methods among the harassed tribes of the region reflected his detached view of the Indians themselves, as shown in his account of one incident. An Apache child, wounded in an Army raid, had died. "The females of the camp," Palmer recounted, "laid it out after their custom & covered it with wild flowers and carried it to a grave. . . . They hid it so completely that its' body could not be found, as I had a wish to have it for a specimen . . . no persuasion could induce them to tell the secret, so I did not get the specimen."[25]

After a year of strenuous traveling through Utah, Arizona, and northern Mexico under the joint auspices of the Department of Agriculture, the Army Medical Museum, and the Smithsonian, Palmer settled for three winters in Washington (1871–73), spending the summers with Baird at Woods Hole, Massachusetts. Here he collected and prepared marine specimens at $60 (later $100) a month for Baird's U.S. Fish Commission; during the winter he performed similar curatorial work in the Smithsonian museum.[26]

Palmer's peripatetic services for the Smithsonian, the Peabody Museum of American Archaeology and Ethnology, and government agencies continued through the seventies and eighties—indeed, for the rest of his life. The year 1874 found him collecting for private patrons in Florida and the Bahamas. Between 1875 and 1877 he made botanical and ethnobotanical collections (and nearly starved) on Guadalupe Island, off the lower California coast; then, working for both Baird and the Peabody Museum in preparation for the 1876 Centennial, he undertook archaeological work in Utah and Arizona and collected on the Mohave Reservation and along the Gila and Colorado Rivers in southwestern Arizona.[27] After three more years of combined botany and archaeology, in 1880 Baird secured him a position in Powell's Bureau of American Ethnology, working under Cyrus Thomas's mounds survey.

Though the pay was sufficient ($125 a month), Palmer's three years in the BAE were unhappy ones. He was constantly in the Southeast, traveling among mounds between Tennessee and Arkansas, at the same time collecting artifacts for the National Museum and the New Orleans Exposition of 1884–85. Thomas and Powell gave him no formal credit for his work, and Palmer left the Bureau and the mounds with relief in 1885 to collect for three years in the more appealing region of Mexico.

Movement was the key to Palmer and his science. Placing himself at the service of sponsors—the Army, Smithsonian, Peabody, and private patrons—whose needs and interests matched or complemented his own, Palmer salvaged frenetically among Native Americans and among plants. He thus typified the scientist-explorers of post-Civil War anthropology, who collected materials with which others might build a science. The scientific results, however, followed the structure of the pursuit: Palmer's ethnological and archaeological collections (unlike his botanical work) were spotty and unsystematic: good, perhaps, for exciting public interest in museums, but unsatisfactory for scientific purposes, despite Henry's hopes. Furthermore, Palmer himself was opportunistic, but he was also powerless and dependent. From one perspective, he cut his own paths across North America, and certainly the sensations of physical freedom must have been very real and important to him. In a larger sense, though, he followed the well-worn cultural tracks of Army desolation and settler exploitation, contributing in his own way to both knowledge and annihilation.

From Palmer and others, the Smithsonian received massive amounts of material. As early as 1865 Baird began noting the backlog of anthropological materials, uncataloged and unarranged for lack of time and labor. Over the next decade the situation worsened as the anthropological specimens began to dominate the accession books. According to Baird's annual reports, in 1868 twenty percent of new materials were anthropological; by 1874 they had increased to one third.[28] The accessioning work—preparing, studying, drawing, classifying, and labeling—fell to a handful of individuals with more enthusiasm than training. Donors of large collections frequently stayed over the winter months in Washington, living in the Smithsonian quarters and organizing their materials. Robert Kennicott, for example, spent the winters of 1858–59 and 1862–63, following his trips to the Northwest and the Arctic, preparing his materials at the Smithsonian; as we have seen, Palmer similarly busied himself with museum tasks during the winters of his collecting years.

Baird's chief aide in anthropology in these years was, however, no explorer. Edward Foreman (1808–1885), in contrast to Palmer, spent his entire life near the city of his birth, Baltimore.[29] After receiving a medical degree in 1830, Foreman spent nearly twenty years as a professor at Washington University of Baltimore (1835–1853), in the same years avidly studying and collecting in local geology, paleontology, botany, conchology, and archaeology. He became an active corresponding member of the National Institute of the 1840s, to which he sent a collection of shells and advice on specimen exchange. Between 1849 and 1853, he served as Henry's and Baird's "General Assistant," in charge of the Smithsonian's correspondence and collections. He left the Smithsonian for a position in the Patent Office, where he stayed until the outbreak of the Civil War.

The years of war and its aftermath were scientifically barren ones for Foreman. A Confederate sympathizer, he moved out of Washington to Catonsville, Maryland, but prudently kept up contact with his close friend Baird. "Being deep in the cultivation of vulgar vegetables," he wrote to Baird in 1864, "I neglect all scientific pursuits, the more so, as there is not a soul within attainable distance who sympathizes with such avocations . . . the cursed war absorbs and brutalizes everything." At the close of the war Foreman found himself "in a state of literary and scientific destitution" (as he told Baird) and in 1867 announced himself ready to return to the Smithsonian in order to "proceed with the arrangement of the Smithsonian Ethnological Collections this winter ensuing . . ."[30]

Between 1867 and 1884, when he resigned in ill health, Foreman made entries for approximately 45,000 ethnological specimens in the Smithsonian accession catalogs (of an estimated total of 75,000 received in this period).[31] But Foreman was not satisfied with brief verbal descriptions, as he explained to Baird in 1878: "I have never, as intimated, in any instance omitted making sketches of objects received, knowing too well that they give the only certain data for making a proper return to owners;—the only safeguard against meddlesome and purblind officials."[32] Even if the motivation were less scientific than proprietary, Foreman's tiny, meticulous drawings—some 5,000 of them altogether—still provide valuable clues to artifact identity for students of the collections today.

Foreman's sketches are silent, poignant reminders of both his relevance and his irrelevance for modern museum anthropology. Foreman belonged to antebellum America: he was a Baltimore gentleman, a medical man, a naturalist—the kind of man who actively participated in the local scientific societies of nineteenth-century America. He, too, believed in Henry's "awakening word," and he happily bore testimony to "the great liberality and promptitude which I have invariably found to actuate naturalists, though personally strangers to each other. I have attributed these noble qualities as much to the gentle influences exercised by their quiet pursuits as [to] the wish to extend the humanizing results which always attend the cultivation of science."[33] But Foreman belonged among the fortunate few who established long-term institutional connections; the many who did not had to rest contented with tenuous ties. Not that Foreman's own Smithsonian situation was ever secure, even in the last years. On one occasion at the end of 1879, when Foreman was seventy-one years old, Baird informed him that due to museum overexpenditures he and several other assistants must be dispensed with for six months. "I hope this will not be any serious inconvenience to you," Baird commiserated, "as the step is absolutely necessary under the circumstances. Of course we will be obligated to get alone [sic] the best way we can, in regard to labeling the ethnological specimens . . ."[34]

A sample page of Edward Foreman's drawings from the U.S.
National Museum Ethnology Accession Books, 1879.

The approach of the 1876 Centennial Exposition accelerated the trend, already strong, toward government support of the Smithsonian museum. Since the transfer of the government collections in 1857, Congress had annually appropriated $4,000 for their maintenance. In 1870, faced with ever-growing collections, Henry lobbied successfully for an increase to $10,000 for museum maintenance, and another $10,000 for construction of new facilities in the Smithsonian Building. Further increase of the maintenance allotment to $20,000 in 1872 signaled an important shift in congressional attitude toward the museum, as well as considerable financial relief for Henry and Baird.

The increased funding of the early seventies ushered in a decade of dynamics between the growing collections, financial support, organizational complexity, and specialization. In anthropology the unprecedented Centennial preparations included much collecting, in which Palmer, Foreman, and dozens of others participated, and which absorbed thousands of government dollars. The resulting acquisitions required, in turn, thousands more for new facilities and permanent museum workers. By 1877 the "division of ethnology" boasted three paid assistants: Rau, Foreman, and a young protégé of Baird's, Frank Hamilton Cushing. Equally important, the larger collections required and the larger staff permitted new distinctions: "After the arrival of the [Exposition] materials at Washington, 1876–1877, there appears to have been made a more marked division between archeological and ethnological material than had previously obtained, and the title of Dr. Rau was changed to 'Assistant, Archeology'," an early department history stated. More changes ensued. Rau and others who had previously served as assistants in 1880 became "curators," receiving for the first time specific letters of appointment defining their duties.[35]

By 1881, the final consequence of these rapid developments was a more efficient, formal, specialized "National Museum" for the education and enlightenment of the American people. Mass education had become primary during the seventies. In a sense, of course, Henry had always intended Smithsonian science as moral uplift, but in his final years he seemed increasingly to value the museum as an educational instrument. Here the visitor effortlessly received valuable impressions that served as the basis for further mental development. "It is truly surprising," he observed, "how tastes may be formed, how objects before disregarded may, when viewed as a part of a natural family, be invested with attractions which shall ever after render them sources of refined pleasure and unalloyed enjoyment." While the Smithsonian Institution should continue its scientific researches, Henry suggested, the "public museum" should "largely partake of the popular element." Supported by the U.S. government, the museum would appeal to Americans visiting their capital. Moreover, while adding to the attractions of Washington, the museum would draw to itself isolated private collections, "especially of anthropology."[36]

Henry's vision of the future National Museum included a major role for anthropology. He was especially proud of the archaeological series of North American implements amassed during his long tenure, supplemented by important collections from European excavations; and he was particularly anxious to see them arranged in good order, as a model of the developmental sequences that could be discovered in the history of any of the civilized arts of man. After years of patient, cautious accumulation, Henry finally felt that the archaeology of North America was sufficiently complete for preliminary description and exhibition. He devoted an entire new room to anthropology, "the branch of science attracting perhaps at the present time more attention than almost any other . . ." To his old friend Asa Gray, Henry confided, "I shall make a grand display."[37]

In 1880, more than twenty years after his first guidebook, William J. Rhees published a *Visitor's Guide to the Smithsonian Institution and National Museum*. Because all the collections were about to be transferred to the new museum building (paid for by Congress), the guide was only temporary, and, as in 1859, "no attempt [was] made at a scientific classification or description of the specimens." But Rhees described well the scope of the collections. True to Henry's vision, "Anthropology Hall" occupied the entire second story of the central building—more than 150 display cases. Only Rau's archaeological series appeared in a systematic manner, while many ethnological items— baskets, bows, arrows, and dance masks—were simply shoved under display cases, where presumably visitors could examine them.[38]

Rau's classification of prehistoric archaeological specimens separated North American objects by materials; remaining anthropological exhibits, while somewhat disorganized, appeared geographically, and in some instances, according to specific tribes. Many cases, however, still retained vestiges of the chaos of National Institute days: Case 80 contained, among other oddments, a "tomahawk presented to Davy Crockett by the young men of Philadelphia," "Fragments of one of the bolts to which Columbus was chained in San Domingo," and an old English battle axe from Windsor Castle.[39] As Rhees's catalog illustrated, even after Henry's death the National Museum's anthropological collections were still in great part a congeries of archaeological relics, ethnological curiosities, and historical Americana badly in need of definition.

In evaluating anthropological activity in the early Smithsonian museum, it is possible to dismiss the period, the conditions, and the men as "amateur" or "preprofessional" and let it go at that; alternatively, there is strong temptation to romanticize the fluid structure, the personal freedom, and the absence of bureaucracy under Henry and Baird. To be sure, operations were highly personal, in part due to lack of funds for hiring a permanent staff—volunteers, temporary help, and personal friends do not conform readily to bureaucratic rigor—and in part because museum specialists were often not available. While the Smithsonian served as the repository for enormous, ever-accruing government collections, Baird could initiate and underwrite no anthropology projects of his own before the founding of the BAE in 1879 created a new source of funds for research and (in Baird's opinion, at least) collecting. As a consequence, in field or museum, Baird's anthropology went forward as a "Nebenfach"—a side or auxiliary activity by individuals with broader interests. In some cases those interests were defined geographically, in others by lines of specialty, in still others by various combinations of the two, for these were simultaneously the final decades of a vigorous American surveying tradition and the early stages of a new, university-bred era of specialization.

The careers of men like Palmer and Foreman (and Charles Rau) point to the double edge that the Smithsonian Institution, and government agencies generally, presented to nineteenth-century Americans. The dilemmas lay not with the Smithsonian but with the inherent limitations of certain institutional structures, in particular with the difficulties of superimposing national horizons and networks upon a nation of predominantly local communities and loyalties. As Powell soon discovered in both his BAE and the U. S. Geological Survey, it was impossible to pursue national programs without treading on local toes.[40] Edward Foreman got a brief taste of American parochialism in anthropology on a trip to Cincinnati in 1875. Acting as representative of Baird and Henry, Foreman's objective was to review the private archaeological cabinets of prominent Cincinnati gentlemen and persuade them to loan choice specimens to the Smithsonian for its Exposition exhibits in Philadelphia. The Cincinnati men got over their disappointment at not seeing Henry or Baird, but Foreman could not overcome their jealous possessiveness: "All of the collectors freeze hard to their specimens and are unwilling to let them go out of their sight," Foreman reported. "Some were exhibited at the recent Cincinnati Exposition but the owners conveyed them to the Hall in person and brought them away when the show was over. They know & feel that Ohio has great claims to consideration on account of her antiquities, and are indignant at any instance of valuable specimens being carried out of the state and probably to foreign lands."[41]

Personal desire and expectation complicated formal institutional relationships. The Smithsonian unquestionably provided scientific stimulus and opportunity for thousands of Americans, as Henry hoped and intended. But merely by creating visions of possibilities that could not, under the circumstances, find more than partial fulfillment, Henry's institution set in motion across the country complex personal and professional dynamics of aroused interest, hopeful ambition, frustration, and resentment—as well as much gratitude.[42] The Smithsonian could not at the same time promote democratic participation and also discriminate among enthusiastic participants without dampening ardor. Even for those, like Palmer and Foreman, who attached themselves (however tenuously), the line between opportunity and exploitation is still difficult to draw, as it must have been for them at times. They were fortunate, but they were also used. The early Smithsonian—the institution and the science—in this as in many respects was riddled with ambivalence, leaving us finally with only rich images to ponder. Palmer, fifty years old, after thirty years in the field, digging unnoticed in the mounds of Tennessee and Arkansas; Foreman, in his seventies, meticulously recording entry after entry with an artist's hand: these are some of the lasting, haunting images of Smithsonian museum anthropology a hundred years ago.

Notes

1. See, e.g., Wilcomb E. Washburn, "Joseph Henry's Conception of the Purpose of the Smithsonian Institution," in Whitfield J. Bell, ed., *A Cabinet of Curiosities: Five Episodes in the Evolution of American Museums* (Charlottesville, Va., 1967), pp. 106–66.
2. SI, *AR for 1849* (Washington, D.C., 1854), p. 173.
3. Washburn, "Joseph Henry," pp. 143–44.
4. William H. Dall, *Spencer Fullerton Baird: A Biography* (Philadelphia, 1915), p. 220.
5. Nathan Reingold, "The New York State Roots of Joseph Henry's National Career," *New York History* 54 (1973): 143. Reingold's article is a persuasive presentation of Henry's consistent positions on science, research, and museums. For reappraisal of Henry in the cultural environment of early nineteenth-century America, see Arthur P. Molella and Nathan Reingold, "Theorists and Ingenious Mechanics: Joseph Henry Defines Science," *Science Studies* 3 (1973): 323–51.
6. SI, *AR for 1850* (Washington, D.C., 1854), p. 194; Henry to Louis Agassiz, 10 June 1865 (from Mary Henry typescript), SIA; Henry to Alexander Dallas Bache, 6 September 1846, SIA.
7. Reingold, "New York State Roots," p. 140; SI, *AR for 1856*, pp. 41–42.
8. See, e.g., Henry to Bache, 15 August 1864, quoted in Washburn, "Joseph Henry," p. 152. The entire letter is reproduced in Nathan Reingold, ed., *Science in Nineteenth-Century America: A Documentary History* (New York, 1964), pp. 216–217.
9. SI, *AR for 1846*, pp. 11–13, 19.
10. *Second Bulletin of the National Institute* (Washington, D.C., 1842); contributions are listed throughout; for Gliddon, see p. 232. See also Francis Markoe and J. J. Abert to George P. Marsh, 8 April 1844, with appended description of the Institute collections, in George Brown Goode, "The Genesis of the U.S. National Museum," USNM, *AR for 1891*, pp. 322–25. The observer was H. T. Tuckerman writing in the *Southern Literary Messenger* in 1849, quoted in Goode, "The Genesis," p. 236.
11. Pickering to Markoe, 1 September 1841; Mayer to Markoe, 11 September 1841, in *Proceedings of the National Institute* (Washington, D.C. 1841), pp. 107, 112–13; Goode, "The Genesis," p. 335.

12. Henry to J. P. Lesley, 12 January 1877; Hodge to Henry, 5 December 1846; Henry to J. B. Varnum, 22 June 1847; all quoted in Washburn, "Joseph Henry," pp. 145, 113, 112.

13. A. Hunter Dupree, *Science in the Federal Government: A History of Policies and Activities to 1940* (New York, 1957), p. 99.

14. SI, *AR for 1856,* pp. 22–23; Squier to Henry, 2 December 1850, in SI, *AR for 1850,* appendix II, pp. 78–80; Henry to Squier, 5 December 1850, Squier Papers.

15. Baird's list of the major new acquisitions appeared in SI, *AR for 1858,* pp. 52–53.

16. William J. Rhees, *Guide to the Smithsonian Institution and National Museum* (Washington, D.C., 1859), pp. 69–75.

17. Alfred Hunter, *A Popular Catalogue of the Extraordinary Curiosities in the National Institute Arranged in the Building Belonging to the Patent Office* (Washington, D.C., 1859).

18. Ibid., p. 23.

19. SI, *AR for 1873,* p. 45; SI, *AR for 1868,* p. 33.

20. For the western surveys, see William H. Goetzmann, *Exploration and Empire: The Explorer and the Scientist in the Winning of the American West* (New York, 1966); Dupree, *Science in the Federal Government;* William Culp Darrah, *Powell of the Colorado* (Princeton, 1951); Wallace Stegner, *Beyond the Hundredth Meridian: John Wesley Powell and the Second Opening of the West* (Boston, 1954).

21. Rogers McVaugh, *Edward Palmer: Plant Explorer of the American West* (Norman, Okla., 1956). The following discussion of Palmer is based largely on McVaugh's careful tracing of Palmer's career.

22. Ibid., pp. 11–12.

23. Ibid., pp. 15–40.

24. Ibid., pp. 34, 38; SI, *AR for 1867,* p. 45; SI, *AR for 1868,* p. 30.

25. Ibid., p. 30.

26. Palmer's position as "curator" in the SI, *AR for 1871* (Washington, D.C., 1873), p. 30, referred apparently to these routine labors.

27. McVaugh, *Edward Palmer,* pp. 60–71.

28. SI, *AR for 1868,* p. 54; SI, *AR for 1874,* p. 49.

29. The following discussion of Foreman's career derives from personal correspondence with Charles E. Ellis, a descendant of Foreman who has painstakingly reconstructed Foreman's life and work at the Smithsonian. I am indebted to Mr. Ellis for permission to utilize his materials and findings.

30. Quoted in Ellis to Robert Elder, 29 November 1973, copy in author's possession.

31. Estimated by Ellis, who has examined most of the surviving ethnology catalogs in the Anthropology Department Processing Laboratory, Smithsonian Institution.

32. Quoted in Ellis to Elder, 29 November 1973.

33. Quoted in Ellis to the author, personal correspondence, 16 March 1974.

34. Ibid. As General Assistant between 1849 and 1853, Foreman had received $100 a month, about a third less than Baird. His salary for the later period has not been determined; catalog records indicate that he continued to work after Baird's memorandum.

35. "Historical Sketch of the Division of Prehistoric Archeology" (ca. 1906), pp. 4–5, OTM Papers, NAA; the title of Rau's department, originally Archeology, changed to Antiquities in the mid-eighties, to Prehistoric Anthropology in 1888, and again to Prehistoric Archeology in 1897—changes that reflected the unclear status and function of American archaeology in this period.

36. SI, *AR for 1870*, pp. 33–36.

37. SI, *AR for 1873*, p. 35; Henry to Gray, 4 March 1874, Gray Papers.

38. William J. Rhees, *Visitor's Guide to the Smithsonian Institution and National Museum* (Washington, D.C., 1880), pp. 69–75.

39. Ibid., p. 59.

40. An outstanding and complex instance of jealousy and conflict in the 1880s between Powell's BAE and the Davenport (Iowa) Academy of Sciences is recounted in Marshall McKusick, *The Davenport Conspiracy* (Iowa City, 1970).

41. Foreman to Baird, November 1875, NAA.

42. From this viewpoint, the Smithsonian fire in 1865, which destroyed most of the records and correspondence of the Institution, could be viewed with mixed feelings, as William H. Dall *(Spencer Fullerton Baird*, pp. 234–35) noted:

    Professor Henry had invariably replied to all his correspondents with extreme courtesy, no matter how absurd the proposition advanced or question asked. When the inventor of a scheme for perpetual motion sent his manuscript, he was politely informed of its receipt and that it would be carefully 'filed with the archives of the Institution.' This was usually sufficient for the vanity of the inventor. But later on someone, irritated at the non-appearance in print of his lucubrations, would write an angry letter inquiring the reasons therefor, and would be politely informed that all the valuable archives of the Institution had perished in the flames. The Professor once declared that the relief of mind thus afforded was almost worth the cost of the fire.

Part 2

Anthropology as
Government Science
1879–1910

IV

From Culture History to Culture Areas: Anthropology in the U.S. National Museum, 1881–1908

Chaos was a major social and intellectual concern of Victorian Americans. It took many forms: the personal threats of a precarious, seemingly whimsical economic system that distributed rewards without regard to individual merit; the social disruptions attendant upon mass immigration, disorderly urban growth, and the emerging class antagonisms of unregulated industrial capitalism; the cosmic chaos of a secular universe without guiding hand or final purpose. Historians have long pointed to reaction to Charles Darwin's biological evolutionism—specifically to his hypothesis of natural selection, which seemed to replace a world of design with one of chance occurrence—as a measure of commitment to the orderly, understandable cosmos of antebellum America. But for most people the personal and social chaos of unsettled daily life was more immediate and tangible than the chance variation and selection of the biological world. Responses to dislocation were weighty and deliberate: massive architecture and machinery, comprehensive philosophical systems, even oppressive clothing—all facets of the culture seemed to express a heavy-handed materialism aimed at concreteness and assurance, as if the culture, lacking a central mass, would fly apart. Assertion of control bespoke deep fear of fragmentation.[1]

The museum as an institution embodies imposed order. Not surprisingly, during its "golden years" between the Civil War and the First World War, American museum anthropology served anthropologists and their public as a bastion of certainties, as an important defense against racing change, social turmoil, and a world of more human variety than was previously imagined or, one suspects, desired. After the Civil War, museums, along with public schools, began to assume the moral and political functions of educating and socializing the mass public of an emerging industrial order. At the same time, museum focus shifted noticeably from the natural wonders of God to the artificial inventions of man, especially the material achievements of the Anglo-Saxon. While industrial museums and expositions displayed the superiority of civilization, museum anthropology made the same point by exhibiting the inferiority of other peoples. It contributed to the celebration of America's coming of industrial age by demonstrating relative racial and national accomplishment.[2]

American anthropologists belonged to a society caught in the paradoxes of its own progress. The celebration of civilized power that characterized American public expositions and museums between 1876 and 1917 could not completely hide a sense of loss and fear: loss of innocence and natural vigor, and fear that civilized man was also losing control over the products of his own genius. To some, indeed, mankind seemed to be "dragged on by an attractive power in advance, which even the leaders obeyed without understanding, as the planets obeyed gravity, or the trees obeyed heat and light."[3] Caught between a fading human past and an uncertain technological future, anthropologists in the nation's capital felt a particular responsibility to retrieve that past in order to take a hand in determining and shaping man's fate. The task seemed monumental and absolutely crucial to them. As Otis T. Mason, first curator of ethnology in the National Museum, explained in 1883, the anthropologist enjoyed a sense of involvement in vital affairs, for he or she participated in the universal quest for the "secrets of man's origin, progress, and destiny."[4]

Still, the secularization implicit in the shift from cabinets of natural wonders to museums of man's works was far from complete. The men who established anthropology in the National Museum saw their enterprise as a pious endeavor in an age of science and religious doubt; they called themselves scientists, but theirs was as often an aesthetic and religious exercise, and always a moral service to the nation. By displaying order in the tangible works of man through all ages and places, they would confirm cosmic purpose. The consequence of this stance was an anthropology that was constraining rather than expansive, classificatory rather than exploratory. The anthropologists of the early National Museum sought to contain the world within walls and categories; they sought old verities, not new truths.

The life of science, Joseph Henry had believed, at once humbled and ennobled the individual, instilling piety before the beauty of God's creation and raising the student of nature to spiritual heights. Otis T. Mason found such fulfillment. Mason approached the science of man with wonder, and his joy grew with time. The plenitude of the human mind endlessly enthralled him. Rooted in the animal but approaching the Creator with an inventive faculty, humankind required the methods of natural science but necessarily inspired religious awe. As the first curator of ethnology in the National Museum (1884–1908), Mason attempted throughout his life to find compatibility between the two.

Mason came from humble beginnings. He was eleven when his family arrived in 1849 in northern Virginia, leaving behind a trail of financial difficulties from Maine to New Jersey. Here he tended cows and studied surveying with a neighbor, but young Mason most admired the seminarians who came to preach on Sundays, and he dreamed of college. In 1856 his grandfather sent him to Columbian College (now George Washington University) in Washington, D.C. At Columbian he received the standard education in Scottish moral philosophy from the president of the college, Reverend George W. Samson, became interested in biblical and classical studies, participated in the college literary societies, and delivered the salutatory address at his graduation in 1861.[5]

Mason stayed on as the principal of Columbian Academy, the preparatory department of the college. Over the next twenty-three years he became a fixture at the school, teaching natural history, classics, history, English, mathematics, and geography to the boys who came to the nation's capital to be educated, and helping to introduce to the school the "general principles of Natural Science." The department was informal, even intimate; for many years the boarding students lived in the Mason household. Apparently in exchange for his loyal services to the college, Mason acquired additional academic credentials—A.M. and Ph.D.—from Columbian. By 1880 he was instructor of English and history in the college; four years later, when he left Columbian for the National Museum, Mason was listed as "Professor of Anthropology" in the prospectus for the Corcoran School of Science and Arts of Columbian University.[6]

Mason's life, Walter Hough wrote in 1909, was completely "bound up" with the Smithsonian Institution. In the early 1850s he had seen Henry perform a brief experiment at the Institution, an event he still recalled vividly half a century later.[7] But his interest in the eastern Mediterranean region drew him permanently into the Smithsonian and indirectly into American anthropology. Arriving at the Institution one day in 1869 to examine some Semitic inscriptions, Mason explained them as well as he could to Baird and Henry. But when he finished Baird recommended that he "give all this up. If you devote your life to such a subject as this, you will have to take the leavings of European workers. It will not be possible for you here in America to obtain the material for important researches; but—I give you the two Americas!" Mason later recalled that he was "born again that day."[8] The chance meeting had "opened the Western Hemisphere to my mind and changed the current of my life."[9]

Mason soon joined Baird's corps of "resident collaborators," devoting all spare time to North American ethnology. His forte and joy was classification: patient, careful search for similarities and distinctions among objects. As he handled and examined each specimen minutely and lovingly, his impelling motive was always his "ardent desire to say the last word" on specimens, leading him "to so thoroughly examine their structure and function that he was as familiar with them as were their original makers . . ." Baird directed

Mason's activities closely, and the younger man responded dutifully: "My sole object is to put the collection completely under *your* thumb. And every word I write, every object I put in a tray is to that end."[10]

Mason worked conscientiously at his avocation. During his twelve years as collaborator, he absorbed the fundamentals of natural science taxonomy from Baird, applied them to the ethnological collections, and soon emerged as the Museum's anthropology expert. He began his own card catalog of North American Indian tribes, which he expanded in collaboration with Powell into an early synonymy, the "nest egg" of the BAE's *Handbook of American Indians North of Mexico* (1907–10).[11] In addition he edited the archaeological reports from correspondents that appeared in the annual reports between 1874 and 1883; by 1878 Baird considered him the Smithsonian's expert on such matters.[12] Finally, between 1873 and 1877, at Baird's request, Mason submitted monthly reports on anthropology to *Harper's Record of Science and Industry,* and later to *American Naturalist;* between 1879 and 1892, again at Baird's urging, he contributed comprehensive annual reviews of work in anthropology to the Smithsonian reports.

Mason was impressed with the great strides anthropology had taken in a few decades. Emerging from a recent past of speculation and drawing on the latest discoveries in the physical and natural sciences, anthropologists were assembling a complete, sophisticated view of man in nature and society. This maturation, Mason reasoned, resulted from significant changes in social and professional structure. Anthropology had become an open science. Previously its various branches had been dominated by individuals working for selfish, partial ends and generalizing from incomplete, private collections. "There are times in the settlement of a new country," Mason allowed, "when every man is his own carpenter, smith, and physician." But by the 1880s the day of the tyros had passed; the period of organization in American science was at hand, but it was to be an open organization.[13]

In part, Mason only expressed the fascination with centralization that was increasingly evident at the nation's capital in the closing decades of the nineteenth century. But he went further. The marvelous thing about the study of man, Mason observed, was that it offered something for everybody to investigate. Every person was a specialist, because there was an anthropological aspect to every walk of life, from mothers and schoolteachers to musicians and legislators. "Who may be an anthropologist?" Mason asked, and answered: "Every man, woman, and child that has sense and patience to observe, and that can honestly record the thing observed." Each had only to look into the historical and scientific aspects of his or her specialty to become a student of humanity and contribute to the growing science. Here there was "no priesthood and no laity, no sacred language . . . [here] you are all both the investigator and the investigated . . ."[14] Mason envisioned an open science embracing thousands, nurtured by the spirit of voluntarism and service that marked his own early years with the Smithsonian. Like many of his contemporaries, he assumed that anyone undertaking anthropology did so out of love. He reminded one correspondent that "we are working for the pleasure of it," and to another he urged patience and hard work:

> Very few of us walked a bee line into our present work. We just fell in love with it and by and by the doors opened . . . If you have a living income, stick to it, watch, and pray. I will have you in mind. Maybe the train will be delayed, but don't miss it when it does arrive. Write for the papers. Be seen about the societies. Take a hand in the drudgery. If Doctor [Roland B.] Dixon asks you to go a mile, go with him twain. When I was young and strong I served and result came."[15]

Mason realized, however, that broad participation and specialization led nowhere without coordination. Within Washington, Mason argued, the Bureau of American Ethnology, the National Museum, the Army Medical Museum, and the Anthropological Society of Washington had begun to centralize resources, making it possible for all to contribute. These central organizations, which characterized "modern anthropology," were accomplishing a "wonderful reformation" by turning the "rambling and disorganized labor" of previous years into "systematic and rational employment." With pride he noted the number of professions represented in the proceedings of the Anthropological Society and he appealed to all workers, even soldiers going to war zones, to collect items in their line.[16]

The goal of organized science was to coordinate disparate observations and distill generalizations. Mason approved heartily of local scientific societies as vehicles for joining the energies of many individuals with widely varying interests and a common desire to participate in science. Aside from the obvious social benefits, the presentation of a paper for criticism aided the author in grasping the subject.[17] More importantly, the voluntary society could guide local exploration that would otherwise be wasted. Just as Henry in the middle years of the century had looked to individuals like Increase Lapham for local scientific leadership and information in newly settled territories, Mason relied a few decades later on the young societies as "essential to a correct exploration of our entire country."[18] As in social, economic, and political affairs, in science all individuals were servants of one another, members in "a universal combine for mutual helpfulness."[19]

In 1873 Mason introduced culture history to Washington. Mason's principles of museum classification derived directly from the system of Gustav Klemm at the Museum of Ethnology in Leipzig. Walter Hough later observed that this "epochal synthesis" appeared at a "psychological moment" in the history of American anthropology; certainly the Klemm model did promise to give meaning and order for the first time to the Smithsonian's ethnology collections.[20] Klemm, like Mason, was concerned to replace local, partial collections with central repositories in order to facilitate comparative study. This was no simple matter of convenience, however. The only legitimate study of man, Klemm argued, was a composite history of human development through the familiar stages of savagery, barbarism, and enlightenment (or civilization). Beyond all "geographical, isothermal, chronological, tribal, linguistic and religious" divisions lay a single, continuous historical growth. This continuum was the ethnologist's proper, ultimate focus of study.[21] Klemm thus reformulated for students of material culture the beliefs in unity and teleological movement that, in various forms, had been staples of anthropological thought for more than a century.

At the same time, Klemm hastened to embrace the most recent teachings of natural science, and he incorporated into his "Kulturgeschichte" an important appreciation of physical environment. "Nature was the foundation of culture," Klemm and Mason agreed; man's dependence on nature and his progressive subjugation of it must both be recognized in a complete science of man. According to Klemm's prescription, the ethnologist must follow the lead of the naturalist and analyze his subject in all its geographical and developmental variety, then put all his observations together to present the larger historical picture. Nowhere were anthropology's distinct roots in natural science and moral philosophy more visible than in Klemm's attempt to combine the two traditions. In effect he presented to the ethnologist two functions, which he viewed as complementary: to examine minutely into the conditions of human need, creativity, and use in particular contexts; and to "study and seek to comprehend and exhibit the human race, in all its members, as a totality, in its origin, development, present condition, and future prospects, in all its tendencies and relations." The ethnologist must be naturalist first, philosopher second.[22]

Mason's career elaborated Klemm's theories. The central concept in Mason's version of culture history was invention. Man was the inventing or "artificializing" animal; ultimately, Mason wrote, the identity of the human species lay in this characteristic. Certain animals possessed inventive capacity in embryonic form, and some had possibly seen "the dawn of culture" in constructing habitations and storing food. To an extent they had begun the war on nature, but without fully awakened minds. But "the human animal has mastered all," Mason explained to Charles F. Lummis in 1906. "That is why I love, admire, and study him." Only restless, unsatisfied man translated needs into desires, then responded with inventions to fulfill them. Man's "superabundant brain" had always "held in trust the possibilities of the future, and stamped upon man the divine likeness."[23]

Mason defined invention broadly: as changes in materials and processes; as modifications in structure and function of artifacts; as changes in the inventor or society. The concept referred, in fact, not merely to mechanical devices but to cultural processes.[24] In the broadest sense, invention could be any series of actions toward some new end; social change might be defined, in fact, simply as a highly complex chain of inventions. In sum, the categories of invention encompassed all human activities. While Powell's Bureau of American Ethnology concentrated on language, religion, and folklore, Mason turned to the works of the hands for insight into the mind. The difference was one of approach, not purpose. "It has been the ruling thought of my life," he reflected in 1906, "that the people of the world have left their history most fully recorded in the works of their hands."[25] His "great idea," as he called it, was that "the true history of our race is written in things . . . the material expressions of the human mind." Culture history enabled the ethnologist to trace modern industries and institutions to their sources, to "put handles on stone implements, men and women into ancient ruins, and thoughts into empty crania."[26]

All people invented, but primitive man saw dimly and thought imperfectly. In his mind lay the germs of inventions that civilized man would elaborate more fully. Like most of his contemporaries, Mason saw the mind of primitive man as undeveloped, imperfect, and inefficient. This vision produced an ambivalent judgment in which such peoples received credit as human participants, but clearly inferior ones. Mason sought out and recognized early signs of aesthetic taste or ingenuity, and he insisted that those "in possession of our family records" deserved sympathetic understanding. But the "unbroken kinship of minds, savage and civilized, from first to last" did not imply equal valuation.[27] Among other distinctions, primitive man invented less spontaneously and playfully than his civilized brethren. Walter Hough explained:

> It is too easy to dream. The poets get weaving from the spider and fire from branches waving in the wind, but early man was not an Edison to seize the salient points of nature replete with what was to be. It is nearer to the earth to find that man got his knowledge of wood friction by a series of more or less conscious observations during a long period in working wood and vegetable fibres. This is conceived to have been a long process devoid of brilliant and analogical deductions, but advancing at times quite rapidly toward the goal.[28]

Mason and Hough, like Lewis Henry Morgan, were less interested in particular histories than in the "series of ever perfecting thoughts" for which the human mind was in fact no more than a constantly evolving agent of expression, and which had led man inexorably to a condition approaching "most nearly to the mind and life of the Creator."[29] On occasion Mason came close to bestowing divinity on nineteenth-century civilization. Fittingly, though, the exalted status was struggled for, the diadem had to be deserved.

Methodologically, continuity was critical. Like geology, a scientific an-

Walter J. Hoffman, posing as a Crow painter.

Frank Hamilton Cushing demonstrating pottery-making technique.

thropology could not admit discontinuities and cataclysms in the record. There were no wide gulfs between naturalism and the world of artifice, as shown by the fact that even in the nineties, "the crowning decade of the crowning century" (as Mason reflected on it), traces of "ancient ingenuity" still lingered among the civilized.[30] The continuous mental connection provided a one-way path to the primitive world, enabling the imaginative and dexterous ethnologist to relive, rethink, and reproduce the acts and artifacts of his untutored ancestors—in effect, to surpass the savage in his own pastimes. For Mason and his assistant Hough, meticulous attention to artifact structure and material was only the first, necessary step to rediscovery of the methods of manufacture. Mason's classic work on basketry exemplified the approach, but most of his shorter museum studies had the same purpose. For some— Frank Cushing comes to mind—the fascination with reproducing Indian life went a step further, to the dangerous presumption of showing skill by "improving upon" the aboriginal. Mason never went so far, but his logic was the same: a logic of superiority by virtue of evolutionary transcendence.

It is not difficult to see in Mason's insistence on continuity yet another instance of his debts to the natural sciences. In 1883 he referred to anthropology as "the application of the instrumentalities and methods of natural history to the study of man"; Franz Boas recognized a few years later that biological analogy was the "leading idea" in Mason's work.[31] In part this was a deliberate attempt to insure scientific respectability. "The older ethnologists," Mason recalled late in his life, "have had a struggle to get recognized as students of science," and so he took "a little grim comfort" in adopting acceptable terminology.[32] His attention to Klemm and long apprenticeship to Baird could only have confirmed the orientation.[33] "Culture history," he once proposed, "takes up the thread of human social groupings where biology drops it and traces its further weavings."[34] Like biological species, every tool, building, or garment had passed through a series of traceable transformations. For this reason Mason valued highly Hough's natural science training, and in his own "measuring, counting, and dissecting," Mason's first step with a specimen was to identify its geographic and ethnographic provenance, shape, structure, purpose, and unique properties, "just as a naturalist would [with] a plant or an animal . . ."[35] In the end, though, Mason's essential piety required that the implications of Darwinian biology, as he understood them, be closely restricted. The unfolding of culture, he insisted, was neither haphazard nor chaotic, but a gradual working out by human minds and hands, guided by "some pilot with his hand upon the helm in the industrial history of the globe . . . steering toward a light with which he was perfectly familiar."[36]

In establishing culture history in the Smithsonian's National Museum, Mason enjoyed the strong support of another young protégé of Spencer Baird, George

Brown Goode.[37] Like Mason, Goode came to the Smithsonian in the early seventies. He organized and invigorated the new National Museum in the eighties, and as assistant secretary of the Smithsonian under Baird and Samuel Langley, he oversaw museum operations until his premature death, at forty-five, in 1896. Scion of old-stock Virginians and New Englanders ("singularly free from foreign mixture," Samuel Langley noted), Goode was born in 1851 in Indiana, received private tutoring as a boy, and at fifteen entered Wesleyan College in Connecticut. After graduation he studied briefly under Louis Agassiz at Harvard in 1870. The following year he met Baird, and the meeting was the "turning point of his professional life." Baird immediately chose the young man as his "chief pupil, his intimate friend, his confidential adviser, and his assistant" in natural history. In 1873 Goode moved to Washington, where he lived in the Smithsonian building with the Henry family and a dozen other staff members. He never left.[38]

Apostle of scientific knowledge and public-spirited naturalist, Goode became an eloquent spokesman for the museum as a cultural instrument and index of civilization. He shared Henry's concern over the low esteem of science in America, but Goode blamed the scientists. They had become so involved in their own pursuits that they had lost sight of the higher obligation of science to the nation: to promote physical, mental, and moral welfare. In the United States more than elsewhere it seemed critical that "accurate knowledge and a scientific manner of thought" exist among the people. To George Goode, science seemed destined to save the world. Through the unfolding of his intellectual powers, man was gradually but surely approaching a God-like destiny; and men of science above all had to assume the heavy responsibility, as "the natural custodians of the treasured knowledge of the world," to share that knowledge with the people.[39]

The ideal national museum, according to Goode, had three roles: to preserve the "material foundations" of scientific knowledge; to encourage research; and to educate the "popular mind."[40] Until 1876 the National Museum had performed the first two and ignored the third, and Goode prepared to reorganize it along educational lines. Whereas in the past museums had been the private preserves of the fortunate few, limited in scope and interests, Goode envisioned new functions. His "museum idea" foresaw a system of public museums and libraries enriching the life of every community in the nation. In democratic America these facilities would be adapted to "the needs of the mechanic, the factory operator, the day-laborer, the salesman, and the clerk, as much as to those of the professional man and the man of leisure." A network of museums across the country would provide continuing adult education, civilizing the masses and assuring America's front rank among the enlightened nations of the world. It was an unabashedly patriotic and politically conservative endeavor, part of an effort to use museums, parks, and libraries as "passionless reformers" with positive moral influence.[41]

Man in nature and society was the center of Goode's museums. The National

George Brown Goode, Samuel Langley, and Otis Tufton Mason
installing Eastern Island images in the National Museum, 1888.

Museum, wrote one visitor of the early eighties, "takes man as its central pivot, and around this is to revolve everything that man has done in the past or in the present in the world he lives in."[42] But while the natural history departments presented little problem in exhibition technique, no satisfactory models existed among ethnological museums. Anthropology seemed to fall somewhere between science and art, a field not to be arranged according to either humanistic or strict natural science principles.[43] Ultimately Goode and Mason agreed upon a combination of methods for display: geographical, Klemm's developmental (also called synoptic or genetic), and according to materials. Looking to Leipzig and to the Pitt Rivers Museum of weaponry in Oxford, Goode and Mason organized their anthropology mainly along developmental lines, stressing the unity underlying apparent diversity of human phenomena throughout the world. Significant lessons could be taught, they believed, by placing all weapons, hats, boats, fire-making apparatus, or whatever, of all ages and all peoples, together in a single series in order to show the "natural history" of a particular idea from its earliest manifestations among primitive peoples to its fullest flowering among the advanced industrialized nations of the world. In Goode's words, "the series should begin with the simplest types and close with the most perfect and elaborate objects of the same class which human effort has produced."[44]

On July 1, 1884, after twelve years of unpaid service, Mason became curator of the Division of Ethnology in the reorganized National Museum. He had no idea how many specimens belonged to his division. In the first place, the Museum had recorded all ethnology and archaeology acquisitions together until 1881. The ethnology estimate had been 200,000 in 1882, but after personally examining the collections Mason revised it to 500,000. The figure was only a guess, but he started counting from there anyway.[45] Secondly, the boundaries between departments were unclear. Arts and industries was supposed to include "civilized" industries; ethnology contained the artifacts of "primitive" peoples. In practice the line was impossible to draw. On his first day as curator, Mason complained that his division received all the materials not wanted by Rau in archaeology or the curators of arts and industries; ethnology was squeezed between the prehistoric and the historic. For his part, Goode lamented that his arts and industries consisted of "all materials possessing anthropological significance, which are not elsewhere assigned." His heterogeneous collections were so intimately tied with ethnology, he confessed, "that it is impossible to make a definite division between them."[46]

Beginning with only one assistant, Mason worked steadily at the chaotic collections, but the huge backlog of uncataloged and unprepared materials prevented visible progress. In 1886 Walter Hough joined Mason, and the following year Lucien Turner came. But the ethnology force, never more than four or five, was severely hampered by the constant flow of new accessions, lack of space and funds, and the distractions of unending expositions. Some of the collections were in deplorable condition. "Between breakage and the moths," Mason told James C. Pilling, "things are fallen on evil times." Cushing's Zuñi materials were especially damaged and salvageable only by an expert, "such as Mr. Cushing himself."[47] In these circumstances volunteers provided a precious service. In every division the small salaried staff was supplemented by a corps of unpaid workers, students, military men, and collectors, assigned or invited to organize collections with which they had some familiarity. Furthermore, ties with other government bureaus continued to aid the curatorial staff in the 1880s. Half of the National Museum's twenty-seven curators and assistant curators in 1888 were detailed from the Geological Survey, the BAE, the Fish Commission, the Army, and the Navy.

Honorary curatorships (successor to Henry's resident collaborators) brought more help but also more collections. The Museum accepted private collections and in return made the donor an honorary curator or custodian for life, giving him access to the collections. Joseph D. McGuire was a case in point. McGuire, a local lawyer active in the Anthropological Society (and later in a semi-official capacity in the BAE as well), donated his archaeological collection and joined the Division of Prehistoric Anthropology. He received no salary but enjoyed "delightful standing and social attachment," stationery and mailing privileges, and an occasional opportunity to make money through lecturing or publishing—"in addition to his dignity."[48]

By 1900 all this was rapidly changing. The volunteer system flourished in the fluid milieu of a formative period, and that era was closing in the Museum. In 1897 Charles D. Walcott, succeeding Goode as Museum director, announced a new regime. The new director was astonished to discover that the Museum actually paid the salaries of only twenty-six of sixty-three scientific staff members. The system of unpaid workers had gone too far, Walcott thought; it lowered morale because volunteers were not sufficiently under the control of the regular staff. Worst of all, there were few young people in training to succeed senior officers.[49]

In the early years Mason needed all the help he could get, paid or gratis. He took every available moment for his own museum studies, which he considered preliminary to public display. Because he never went afield himself, Mason depended on the collections for his work, and they accordingly determined its focus and orientation. His first two museum studies, "Throwing-Sticks in the National Museum" and "Basket-Work of the North American Aborigines," both published in 1884, were intended as models for a monograph series to cover the collections of all primitive inventions. The articles mixed geographical and developmental approaches. On the basis of detailed examination of the structures of the throwing-sticks of the Arctic region, Mason distinguished thirteen regional types and attempted to correlate func-

Offices of the Department of Ethnology at the National Museum, c. 1890.

tions with structures. The study confirmed, he said, that the peoples of the Arctic were "driven" to modify this weapon with change of environment. But Mason also placed his artifacts on a developmental continuum, from the simple Anderson River model to the "most perfect" Norton Sound instrument, which appeared to incorporate all the features of the others.[50] The life histories of the Eskimo peoples, it appeared, were closely connected to the fauna of the region, for within the broad "generic similarities" of the Arctic, Mason found extreme differentiation in cultural phenomena. The study of basketry, which eventually grew into Mason's classic *Aboriginal American Basketry* (1902), exhibited his talent for studying the minutest techniques in the manual industry that he called "the savage art par excellence." Through detailed drawings of weaves and ornamentation and close attention to materials, shapes, structures, and presumed uses, Mason worked out typologies of form and technique. In many cases the types and terminology of his ethnological "comparative anatomy" are still considered useful.[51] In *American Basketry* he also outlined about a dozen regional varieties, defined by geography or tribe (depending on the precision and extent of Mason's collection).[52] As he continued his museum studies of primitive basketry, cradles, knives, bows and arrows, traps, and domestication of animals and plants, the unity theme gave way increasingly to the mystery of varieties and the influence of environment on their shaping.

The practical problem with ethnographic displays was lack of sufficient description for many of the Museum's older collections. When such "desultory" material did not portray the "total life history" of a tribe, the curator could best use it, Mason thought, in synoptic series illustrating the progress of the race, at least until the imperfect material could be "ennobled" with life and meaning by new artifacts from reliable sources. This the early BAE provided, along with firsthand observers to explain the functions of their pieces. Before 1880 the only regions of North America represented in the Museum in any depth were parts of the Northwest Coast and Alaska. The Bureau collections, reflecting Powell's interests and activities, came chiefly from three other regions: the Pueblos of the Southwest; the Southeast; and the Ohio Valley. In 1906 Hough estimated that the BAE had contributed a third of the Museum's ethnology, concentrated in these areas.[53]

Mason's first attempt at an "ethnic idea" in exhibits in 1886 involved Eskimo collections, which he had been studying for some time. The display was awkward. Mason tried to join rigid natural science categories with a dawning understanding of the fluidity and complexity of human phenomena. He set up a checkerboard arrangement of exhibits, dominated by the concept of the ethnographic region. While he defined fifteen regional or ethnographic areas, he cautioned that "it must be distinctly understood that these areas are wholly secondary to types and material." By walking along one axis of the checkerboard the visitor viewed a single cultural region in all its inventional variety; moving at right angles he could follow a single invention. Mason thought the educational advantages were obvious, for "with all the objects in the Eskimo collection being placed in their appropriate boxes," the visitor could easily learn that the people of a given area do or do not use a specific device.[54] The checkerboard plan had the merit of preserving at once the dignity and order that Goode insisted upon, the supposed rigor and clarity of natural science taxonomy, and the integrity of the ethnographic unit as Mason understood it. He hoped eventually to apply his scheme to other peoples and regions, and in 1888 he began serious work on his "ethnic series."[55]

Franz Boas first visited Mason's Eskimo collections in 1885, and he came away deeply disturbed.[56] Despite Goode's assurances that articles that belonged together "in a monographic way" would never be disturbed, Boas felt that the Museum's strongly developmental arrangements severely hampered study. In 1887 he addressed the issue in *Science*. The belief that connection exists between similar phenomena occurring among widely separated peoples, Boas began, lay at the heart of Mason's natural science model of ethnology. Mason offered three explanations for such similarities: migration of peoples; migration of inventions through passing contact; and the axiom (among Washington anthropologists) that like causes produce like effects, or that the human mind everywhere produces the same products "under the same stress and resources." To these principles, however, Boas added a fourth: unlike causes also produce like effects. Outside of a vague sense in which it could be said that all men act "suitably" to their environments, mental unity possessed no explanatory power because of the complexity of human mental processes. Occurrence of similar phenomena from unlike causes in fact appeared more likely to Boas.[57]

Boas's disagreements went deeper still. The attempt to classify human works into biological categories missed the whole point of post-Darwinian natural science. The focus of investigation should be the individual phenomenon "in its history and in its medium," not abstraction into a synthetic grouping determined by the special interests of the scientist. "By regarding a single phenomenon outside of its surroundings, outside of other inventions of the people to whom it belongs, and outside of other phenomena affecting that people and its productions," Boas lectured Mason, "we cannot understand its meaning." Mason's system taught only that man in different parts of the world has made similar inventions; it promoted no deeper understanding. The productions and individual styles of specific peoples must be studied as a whole—an impossible task when artifacts were distributed about the museum. "Classification is not explanation" in biology or ethnology, Boas concluded.[58]

From his established Washington post, Mason responded graciously to the young German immigrant. Dismissing the suggestion of unlike causes as ingenious but mistaken, he affirmed his commitment to the methods and instruments of biology as "an immovable foundation" for the science of man. Of course in ethnology as in biology there were "polyorganic units" that belonged together—the artifacts from a single burial mound, for example. But a museum curator drew on people with diverse interests in establishing his collections, and the exhibits had to reflect and appeal to those different minds.[59] The true value of synoptic exhibits, Mason later observed, lay in their appeal to unlearned men and women in all walks of life, who found "charming food for thought" therein.[60] Mason also took the opportunity to reaffirm the wisdom of his comparative approach, and he reminded Boas that every ethnologist going to study a specific people in depth should keep comparisons with other groups constantly in mind. In short, Mason conceded nothing.[61]

Boas again attempted to explain his position. The true nature of biological or ethnological phenomena lay in their full historical and social contexts, not in present appearances. In this light the tribal arrangement seemed to Boas the only useful system for museum study. "In ethnology," he remarked pointedly, "all is individuality." Taking aim squarely at Mason's entire structure, Boas confessed his deep conviction that the museum must demonstrate, through ethnically arranged exhibits, the all-important fact that "civilization is not something absolute, but that it is relative, and that our ideas and conceptions are true only so far as our civilization goes."[62]

At this point Mason turned to Powell for help. Powell's candid response included a surprising confession of ignorance. Addressing only the question of museum classification, the powerful head of Washington anthropology defended Mason's assumptions. Tribal organization in the museum was impossible because of the constant migrations, absorptions, and redivisions of the North American tribes through the historical period. Under modern conditions there were no stable, permanent tribal units to be represented, the Major argued. Nor could the archaeological artifacts of North America yet be safely assigned to specific tribes. But more than this, no classification of the peoples of North America could ever succeed. Physical anthropology had only established general varieties; all the work of the Bureau on language had provided only "imperfect" distinctions. Arts, institutions, opinions, religions, material products—these could be grouped, but not peoples. Powell did leave open the possibility of delineating "art regions" as potentially meaningful units, but the Bureau was only beginning to elaborate this concept in 1887. After nearly a decade in the Bureau, Powell had concluded that "there is no science of ethnology, for the attempt to classify mankind in groups has failed on every hand." "The unity of mankind," he answered Boas, "is the greatest induction of anthropology."[63]

The gap between Boas and the Washington scientists was unbridgeable in 1887. Mason and Powell stressed system and unity; Boas saw uniqueness and individuality. Though they all realized the potential of museums as educational facilities, Boas showed primary concern for the serious student of collections, while the Washington men served the mass public. But beyond this they differed on the very lessons to be taught: while Mason preached the unity of human cultural development in all its varieties, Boas was already implying cultural relativism and pluralism. The historicism and attention to cultures as complex, discrete phenomena that Boas urged seemed grossly unscientific to those who celebrated man's "ever increasing comprehensiveness," his ability to coordinate and systematize, as his "crowning glory."[64] And Boas's reproach to taxonomy would never impress a museum curator whose first thought after preparing a specimen was always "where to put it."[65] And yet over the next decade, as Mason approached the zenith of his influence in American anthropology, he began to focus on ethnographic regions, or culture areas, as he called them. Indeed, Mason had already begun to incorporate such schemes into his exhibits by 1887, as we have seen. His cultural history had always recognized regional variation in inventions as a problem for study. During the nineties, in response to a number of experiences and influences, he turned enthusiastically to ethnic "life-groups" as the central exhibit form for museum anthropology, supplanting the boring comparative cabinets of artifacts arranged row on row. But he did not do so singlehandedly. In order to grasp the complex background and the significance of this change in museum method, it is first necessary to consider the career of William Henry Holmes, the artist-anthropologist who designed and implemented the new life-group form in Washington.

William Henry Holmes (1846–1933) was an artist all his life. On his appointment at age seventy-five as the director of the National Gallery of Art, a student whom he had taught in his native Ohio a half-century before congratulated his former schoolmaster: "I have the feeling," he wrote, "that you have now reached the position for which nature intended you. For we always thought of our 'Teacher' as an artist."[66] The road to the National Gallery had been long and winding. It traversed geology, ethnology, and archaeology, and it passed through a series of prominent scientific institutions: the Hayden Survey, the National Museum, Chicago's Field Museum, and the Bureau of American Ethnology. But the meanderings and detours of Holmes's "lifetime devoted to science and art" nonetheless pointed finally in a single direction. The source of artistic creativity was the focus of Holmes's life. How do men define beauty? How do innate principles, social forces, or environmental factors combine to produce art as an individual and social phenomenon? These questions impelled and defined Holmes's anthropology, from the early surveys of the San Juan cliff-dwellers through the prolonged, bitter struggle over Paleolithic man in North America. Following Mason's prescription, Holmes probed the "anthropological aspect" of his own vocation; in so doing he inquired into the wellsprings of his own artistic soul.

Born in 1846, Holmes came to view himself as "an original predestined member of the [Smithsonian] family."[67] Fierce familial loyalty was not uncommon among the Institution's early scientific corps. But Holmes originally came to Washington in 1871 to study art, not science. At the art school of Theodore Kauffman he met Mary Henry, daughter of the Smithsonian Secretary, and in April he visited the Institution. While sketching a bird on this first visit, Holmes came to the attention of a visiting naturalist, and he soon found himself employed to draw fossil and mollusk shells for Fielding B. Meek and William H. Dall.[68] This led, in turn, the following year, to a position as artist on Ferdinand V. Hayden's U.S. Geological Survey of the Territories. Holmes remained with Hayden for six years as artist and geologist, exploring the Yellowstone region, the mountains of central Colorado, and the San Juan Valley in New Mexico and Arizona. During the 1875 season he took personal charge of the San Juan expedition; it was here, among the remains of the mysterious "cliff-dwellers" of the Southwest, that he first confronted the fascinations of North American archaeology.

Holmes's San Juan report (1876) gave early indications of his future style and emphasis in archaeology.[69] Like his pen-and-ink landscapes of the Colorado plateau country, that style was marked by precise observation, remarkable visual clarity, and close attention to form and process. Still, through the pages of the brief, fully illustrated report, Holmes's recently acquired geological sobriety contended with imaginative, romantic responses to the allures of the cliff-dwellers. For Holmes the 1870s were formative, unforgettable years of freedom and rapid growth; he loved the trans-Mississippi West. But emotion required restraint to yield scientific results. He fought that battle for years, resolving the issue only by harnessing his imagination to the service of a strongly inductive science. In 1876 he could barely control his wonder, and his struggle marks a significant personal milestone in the transition to a chastened, disciplined exploration of the Southwest. Approaching the ruins at Rio Mancos, Holmes found himself "led to wonder if they are not the ruins of some ancient castle, behind whose mouldering walls are hidden the dread secrets of a long-forgotten people; but a nearer approach quickly dispels such fancies, for the windows prove to be only the doorways to shallow and irregular apartments, hardly sufficiently commodious for a race of pygmies."[70] His journal reveals more explicitly that, just as they collected geological specimens, Holmes and his men sought precious archaeological booty. The result was an enterprise that combined serious observation, imaginative speculation, and something of the treasure hunt:

In one of the recesses and·just by the side of the entrance-way, Dick (who was with me) came upon an object that made him shout with excitement and expectation. In scratching among the debris he came suddenly upon the top of a large earthen jar, tightly closed by a stone lid. 'Harry, I've got it' he cried, 'I have found it at last, here is their treasure. Here are the gold dubloons at last, buried in the wall. Ah! Ye don't believe it, just come and see.' Excitedly we cleared away the sand and raised the lid. The opening was deep and dark and to our chagrin, empty; only a little dirt, 'bah.' Well there must be others and they may be full. So to work we went and for an hour the dust flew and the loosened rocks rattled down the steep cliff and plunged into the deep gulches. Another large jar was brought to light, also empty of rubies and [of] gold dubloons and gorgeous trinkets there was not a sign. Besides large jars there was nothing but a bit of cane plaiting [,] fragments of what must have been very neat work. We left many of the rooms and recesses unexplored; for we had no implements and our fingers were already blistered.[71]

The public never saw Holmes's notebooks, but his San Juan report and W. H. Jackson's model of cliff-dwellings at the government exhibition in Philadelphia announced their discovery to the world. While he found neither gold nor rubies, Holmes came away from the canyon with something far more precious: an aroused imagination already pondering the secrets of America's human past:

From the top of the wall we looked out and down; there was the deep Canoma Valley. The cliffs above the trees slope below, and the winding thread of the Mancos in the green strip [at] the bottom. How secure; how impregnate [sic]; one man with loose rocks at his command could keep off the world. I had the feeling of being in an eagle's nest and was tempted to take wing and fly, but only screamed and then started at the perplexing echoes. We admired the skill with which these fortresses were built and the hardihood, and were amazed that such means of defense could have been conceived and carried out with the nearest water far below, and only these great jars to contain a supply. With their fields and flocks and the supply of water within the hands of an enemy . . . [they] must have perished or have crept down the cliffs to fight or yield to the foe. They are gone now indeed and have been for centuries and now like vandals we invade their homes and sack their cities. We, at least, carry off their earthen jars and reprimand them for not having left us more gold and jewels.[72]

Holmes's language in notebooks and final report is suggestive. That the "nearer approach" of clear-eyed science must supersede the distant visions of the romantic or the treasure-hunter would soon become an article of faith among government anthropologists. If science replaced the superior ancient races of earlier speculators with a race of physical or cultural "pygmies," if it forced attention from gold and rubies to the mundane treasures of ethnology—rush matting, stick bundles, potsherds—the adjustment was only a necessary step. Sober deflation prepared the ground for new standards of cultural evaluation.

As Holmes's San Juan report showed, the archaeology and ethnology of the Southwest, like the geology of the region, permitted and invited historical inquiry, and the area offered valuable clues to the processes of cultural change. The puzzle of relationships between past and present inhabitants confronted and fascinated every student of the Southwest, including Matilda and James Stevenson, Frank Cushing, John G. Bourke, Washington Matthews, Lewis H. Morgan, and Adolphe F. Bandelier. But in the context of Washington anthropology, ethnohistorical inquiry seemed to hold limited value. While it promised insight into past migration, contact, and affinity among specific peoples, scientific classification of mankind on the Morgan/Powell model required more permanent, universal standards and patterns than those provided by observing historical flux. To become a science, anthropology had to transcend history—so Powell believed. The problem permeated the Bureau of American Ethnology, but the resulting tension between developmental classification and attention to historical context seems to have been especially severe among students of the Southwest.

With the dissolution of the Hayden Survey in 1879, Holmes studied art in Europe for a year. On his return he joined Powell's Geological Survey, where he remained until 1889, when he moved over to the BAE. By then he had for several years been a museum anthropologist and a recognized expert on the evolution of decorative art. His studies of pottery of the eighties displayed the tension between historical questions and evolutionary classification. Specific intellectual influences are impossible to pinpoint, but it is apparent that by the early eighties Holmes had thoroughly absorbed the evolutionism of Morgan and Powell, and he framed his studies of primitive art accordingly. Holmes hoped to discover the origins of art: not particular historical precedents or influences on specific forms of cultural expression, but the general laws of aesthetic development. He explained change as development or growth, rejecting, in normal evidential circumstance, diffusion through borrowing or contact.[73] He firmly believed that degree of aesthetic progress, when correlated with like evidence from other fields of human activity, could serve as a reliable index of cultural status.

The debate over the origins of primitive art was widespread and prolonged in the second half of the nineteenth century. In the Washington context it took on special significance, for it touched on virtually all subfields of inquiry, from Cyrus Thomas's mounds survey to the issue that would embroil Holmes after 1889, the antiquity of man in North America.[74] Holmes emphasized technique and material as sources of decorative forms; he accordingly minimized the role of aesthetic ideas or simple spontaneity in the "early stages" of art. Geometric designs were originally suggested to the primitive artist by, for example, the imprint of a woven design on wet clay, or were transferred from one technical art to another, e.g., basketry to pottery. In explaining the appearance of ideographic forms, he hypothesized various series of stages—three stages for Pueblo pottery, a more complex series for Chiriqui work—moving, with mental and cultural growth, from purely nonideographic to pictorial designs. He also allowed for the possibility of degeneration from the higher delineative stage back into geometric design. In either case, Holmes agreed with Powell that such art forms had expressed tribal philosophy at a certain stage of development, and as such were useful in tracing the mental development of mankind. But a universal conjectural history, not specific tribal histories, was always Holmes's objective. As T.H.H. Thoreson has observed, "Holmes never contended that he was depicting the evolution of any particular design; his series were instead illustrative of what he called 'general tendencies' and 'general laws.' Empirical research was aimed toward filling in the gaps in the evolutionary sequence, while the only serious question (the core of the art question) lay in explaining how such a series did or could have come about."[75] In Holmes's words, "Investigations relating to the history of culture proceed on the theory that from the simplest possible beginnings in the manual arts advance was made until the highest round of the ladder was reached and that a study of the entire series must reveal the steps, the processes, and the laws of advancement."[76]

The emphasis on material and technique derived from the assumption that men in stages of savagery were highly vulnerable to the influences and suggestions of environment. Because they were more closely tied than barbarous or civilized peoples to their material world, there was little room for play, imagination, or free creativity in art or other activities. The life of primitive man as portrayed by Holmes and his colleagues was restricted and grim, to be sure. But more importantly, the vision led to a methodology that prescribed narrow treatment of artifacts. The approach might be called "reconstruction" or "reenactment" of the material conditions and techniques of invention. The first step in reconstruction, as described above, involved minute examination of artifacts to determine material and process of manufacture. Having analyzed the product, the anthropologist then proceeded to reenact the process (see illustrations of Hoffman and Cushing).

Reconstruction was the heart of Mason's museum work, and his best museum taxonomies, notably his work on North American basketry, emerged from this method. Hough, Hoffman, Cushing, and Holmes shared the basic assumption, which emerged in various forms in their work. On the positive side, the method produced the delineation of areal types that would eventuate in Mason's concept of culture areas. At the same time, though, it is clear that the men in the National Museum were "playing Indian" in a presumptuous manner. The danger and limitation in the method lay in assuming that demonstration of supposed conditions and techniques of invention constitutes a sufficient anthropology; that knowledge of structure or technical process is, in fact, knowledge of invention or creativity. But the Washington men saw only driven savages, not independently creative agents, in primitive art.

In two unpublished papers toward the end of his life, Holmes set forth his views on the evolution of aesthetics. He distinguished between two fundamental drives (exigencies of survival, desire for betterment) and the "major factors" in cultural advancement: religious beliefs and "the struggle for advantage through the increase of personal attractiveness." In early stages, he still believed, "religion has been a chief factor in shaping and advancing culture"; throughout North American aboriginal life the anthropologist finds that "every beautiful article is there because religion demanded it." Only in later stages does love of beauty emerge as a major creative factor: "In early art development the dynamic force was religion, but clinging to it, like a slender vine, was the esthetic impulse—the love of beauty for its own sake."[77]

Beneath Holmes's malleable personal exterior lay a set of rock-hard convictions about the progressive evolution of art—from geometric, nonideographic to delineative forms, from motives of religious superstition to refined sense of beauty, from imitation to spontaneity—that remained rigid and undisturbed for fifty years. (Not surprisingly, he held very conservative views of painting. A great admirer of Thomas Moran, he once noted that Moran's panorama of the Grand Canyon would someday be fully recognized, after "the lunacy of impressionism" had passed, as the greatest landscape in American painting.)[78] Having established as much, Holmes gave his attention only to the conditioning elements—physical environment and materials— that determined the rate of cultural progress and shaped specific styles. It is in this context that development of his museum life-groups in the 1890s must be understood.

Holmes's pottery studies made him central to Powell's organization of anthropology, but he achieved wide recognition in scientific circles as a result of his role in the debate over North American Paleolithic man during the 1890s.[79] To this bitter wrangle, which embroiled the major anthropological institutions of Boston and Washington in a test of scientific respectability, Holmes contributed a simple notion that rapidly achieved the status of scientific proof. The insight derived directly from the "reenactment" method of the Washington men. In accord with the growing orthodoxy among government investigators, Holmes rejected the effort to establish New World archaeological periods of technology to parallel those of western Europe. He thus began by assuming that Paleolithic man had never existed in North America, thereby placing the burden of proof on the proponents. Faced with

A realistic lay-figure group set up along Piney Branch in
Washington, D.C., by W. H. Holmes.

W. H. Holmes in "an ocean of paleoliths," which he demonstrated
to be "refuse of Indian implement making."

claims by Charles C. Abbott, George F. Wright, and others, from 1872 onward, of Paleolithic finds in the glacial gravels of New Jersey, in Minnesota, and elsewhere, Holmes in 1889 took to the field himself. At the Piney Branch site on Rock Creek, just outside the capital city, Holmes discovered a quarry site with thousands of "paleoliths" strewn over the ground. Reconstructing the scene in his mind and experimenting with the rude stone implements and products himself, he realized that the so-called paleoliths were the unfinished products and rejects of the primitive manufacturing process. In his published articles he not only presented the theory but demonstrated the step-by-step manufacturing process and the products at each stage.

For men who despised mystery and lauded simple, common-sense explanations, Holmes's breakthrough established him fully. Clarence Dutton, with whom he had worked in the early Geological Survey, spoke for his Washington admirers: "I have just been reading your article in 'Science' of Nov. 25th, on Modern Quarry Refuse and the Paleolithic Theory. It strikes me as about the most level headed article in the anthropologic 'racket' I have seen for many a year. Your simple statement of the facts is such as to carry conviction with it by the sheer force of good sense and to resist it looks like 'biting a file.' I wonder I never thought of that view of the situation before. We always do wonder when a simple sensible explanation comes forward to take the place of a complex overloaded hypothesis [,] and no better evidence is wanted of the strength of a hypothesis than its perfect simplicity and naturalness."[80] Over the years Holmes marshalled additional criteria for challenging every claim for Paleolithic man—uprooted trees, mud slides, the integrity of the investigator—but his simple demonstration and reconstruction at Piney Branch established his reputation as a man of scientific caution and perception.

Holmes was indeed formidable by the early nineties. His published reviews of Paleolithic finds were masterpieces of cautious, apparently open-minded treatment that nonetheless systematically destroyed every claim. Drawing on accepted geological and archaeological practice, he excused ignorant, misled discoverers while unmercifully castigating his serious opponents, such as George Wright and Charles Abbott. His paper on "Primitive Man in the Delaware Valley," read at the meetings of the American Association for the Advancement of Science and published in *Science* in 1897, demonstrates his style and tactics.[81] Granting that "pioneer investigators [are] struggling through a difficult period of inquiry," Holmes put forward the maxim of uniformitarian geology that the first step in knowing the past is understanding the present. He observed that the historic peoples of the Delaware Valley, the Algonkian stock, were Neolithic peoples who produced among their stoneware many unfinished objects. These could have intruded below the surface into "glacial gravels" through a variety of natural and human means:

"Every bank that crumbled, every grave dug, every palisade planted, every burrow made, every root that penetrated and every storm that raged took part in the work of intermingling and burial . . ." The student must consider these processes of past and present before "conjuring up shadowy images of other races." Blind adherence to European theories of a "uniform race on both sides of the Atlantic" and a desire to "establish a peculiar theoretic culture for America," as well as excessive attention to similarities of form, had interfered with respectable archaeological practice. But now, Holmes concluded, "It may be regarded as substantially proved that the glacial gravels proper contain no relics of art, and it would appear that now very few persons, indeed, expect them to yield any evidence whatever on the subject of human occupation."[82] The verdict was premature, but Holmes's reputation became firmly established in the process.

Holmes's museum orientation grew in part from such scientific debate. The antiquity issue impressed upon him again the importance of re-creating the conditions and techniques of invention and art. At the same time he was quick to recognize the desirable effects of drama, plot, action, and emotional involvement in the life-group approach to popular museum anthropology. Reflecting perhaps the growing influence of photography in anthropological field work at the time, Holmes's displays were intended as snapshots of primitive life long vanished.

The Smithsonian had experimented with life-size wax figures from the early seventies, and the government displays at Philadelphia had included figures of Swedish peasants, but the approach was still decidedly subordinate to the extensive showcases of primitive implements arranged by Rau and Mason. The Louisville and New Orleans fairs of 1884 and 1885 for the first time made serious attempts to portray specific peoples in an environmental situation. These exhibits showed the social life and industries of the Alaskan and Eskimo groups (at the time the strongest regional collections in the Museum). But the "ethnic series" still shared space with archaeological artifacts and models of American ship-building.

Chicago marked the critical change in technique and arrangement. Under Holmes's direction, the Smithsonian exhibits displayed an impressive number of life-size, realistic groups of North American aborigines working in pristine, pre-Columbian surroundings. The theme was environment, but the new element was the group, and the concept changed the displays from pieces of sculpture to "pictures from life." In a professionally important departure, ethnologists Cushing, Mooney, and Hoffman, along with Holmes, supervised the construction of the exhibits personally, contributing their invaluable direct field experiences. Though the lay groups would not supplant the more traditional showcases, Goode assured himself, they did possess certain limited and valuable functions. His only concern was to maintain "dignified, systematic order" in the exhibits.[83]

After Chicago virtually every government anthropology exhibit featured primitive peoples working and playing in appropriately naturalistic environments. At Nashville, people learned about the strong contrasts between Eskimo and Pueblo surroundings and life styles, and also saw a Kiowa camping circle. The Pan-American Exposition of 1901 displayed twelve groups of aboriginal folks of the entire Western hemisphere (along with thirteen series of inventions). At the St. Louis Exposition in 1904, W J McGee, outdoing them all, imported half-a-dozen groups of live "savages" from all over the world to set up housekeeping on fair grounds in the middle of America.[84]

Otis Mason never joined the debate over Paleolithic man, but between 1887 and 1896 logic and personal experience also pushed him steadily toward ethnographic exhibit techniques. Two events were particularly formative: his tour of European museums in 1889 and the publication of Powell's linguistic map and classification in 1891. The immediate purposes of the European tour were to study museum methods and to attend the Paris Exposition, but for Mason the journey answered the prayers of a lifetime. At Paris he reveled in meeting the great European savants of his day: Adolphe B. Meyer, Sir John Evans, Adolf Bastian, and Paul Broca. Meyer, director of the Dresden Museum of Zoology and Anthropology, so impressed the American visitor that he wanted to "grapple him to [his] soul with hooks of steel." Alfred H. Keane, his host in London, Mason considered a "great godsend" to anthropology as well as "the jolliest Englishman I ever saw . . ." The whole experience humbled Mason. "How my heart rejoices when I see the men whose thoughts have moved the world," he confided to his wife. "I ought to have taken this trip thirty years ago. My intellectual life has been in a bag."[85]

Exhibits even more than intellects overwhelmed him. In the Pitt Rivers collections at Oxford, Mason studied the developmental scheme, "the only one in which every piece has a raison d'être." Unlike the British Museum, where "they have a pen for each country and when they get a new specimen they turn it into the pen," at Oxford every specimen had its place. At the Musée Guimet in Paris and with Meyer in Dresden, Mason received further confirmation of his own methods, but he also began to appreciate ethnographic approaches. The British Museum's Polynesian collection, Mason reported, "made my mouth water"; and at the India Museum he was struck with the wax figures of working groups.[86]

Paris was a revelation. The entire exposition, which he thought the "most thoroughly anthropological" to that time, taught the history of human culture by means of models of habitations and working scenes displayed along the Seine. Mason reported enthusiastically on the twelve African villages with real villagers and the Tonkinese temple with Buddhist priests performing rites. The crowds thronged like children to the working scenes. Although the French showed "no caution" in displaying anthropological science in such groups, Mason had to admit their popular success. "It was an exposition," he wrote home, "whose presiding Genius was a teacher, a professor of history, whose scholars were the whole world."[87]

Mason returned convinced that "all that Europe will ever know of [the American Indian] will be what we tell her."[88] With this thought and renewed energy he began preparing the government exhibits for the Chicago World's Fair. Here he saw an opportunity to display fifty years of North American anthropology by the Smithsonian and government agencies.[89] Powell's map, the culmination of that work opportunely published in 1891, furnished the stimulus and organizing principle for his efforts. Mason's goal at Chicago was to honor Powell, the map, and American anthropology.[90] The linguistic map, Mason thought, focused the critical questions of American anthropology in 1893: To what extent does language coordinate with industries and other activities as a sign of kinship or race? What are the effects of climate and natural resources on arts and industries? He attempted to elucidate these problems by hanging an enlarged copy of the map (sixteen by twelve feet) in the center of his Chicago exhibits. Of Powell's fifty-seven stocks Mason chose sixteen "great families" and arranged the costumes and arts of each group in separate alcoves. He hoped thereby to present a "practical solution" to the central question of the connection between race, language, material culture, and systems of thought.[91]

In Chicago, Mason first expressed unambiguously an awareness of the complexity of cultural phenomena, particularly of the role of the physical environment in influencing cultural behavior. Environment promised to explain the vast diversity of human activities and social systems that the researches of the 1880s had unexpectedly discovered in North America. By 1893, BAE ethnologists had already begun to learn at firsthand of the "intimate connection between the practical activities of the people, their artistic productions, their philosophies, and their myths."[92] Consequently the analyses of phenomena into classes of activities that had organized research in 1879 were steadily yielding to a deepening sense of complexity and interdependence—and much confusion. The physical environment, stressed by Gibbs in the 1860s and by Boas again in 1887, became a critical tool that explained ethnographic diversity, gave coherence to the various activities common to an ethnic or regional unit (or in Mason's scheme at Chicago, a linguistic unit), and yet preserved the presumed racial and cultural unity of aboriginal North America.

Mason presented his case for environment at the International Congress of Anthropology during the Exposition. It was now clear, he argued, that the American aborigines were "practically" a single race, dispersed in the precontact era into many culture areas, which had developed hundreds of separate languages, social systems, mythologies, and philosophies. Each human product, as Mason analyzed it, contained "an element of intellectuality and an element of materiality," something of the people and something of the environment. This was as true of language and religions as of pottery and clothing, for just as ideas inhered in the works of the hands, so "there is solid material with the intellectual culture concepts . . ." Beliefs no less than arrows were influenced by environment. The distinctive features of all human products could only be understood in terms of the "patronage and directorship of the region."[93] In the spirit of the Congress of 1893, the slogan of which was "Men Not Things," Mason seemed to be moving slowly from his earlier concern with materials to environments, from the study of man to studying men, from culture to distinct cultures.

The following year Mason elaborated his culture-area concept further in his presidential address to the Anthropological Society of Washington. Drawing liberally on the earlier geographical and environmental studies of Karl Ritter, Arnold Guyot, and George P. Marsh, Mason turned from his preoccupation with man's conquest of nature to view human activities as shaped and modified by the forces of the earth. Taken as a whole, the earth, he said, was the mother of all men, the storehouse of material resources, the reservoir of tremendous potential forces, and man's first teacher. But the earth consisted of many "great isolated parts or patches," which Aristotle had called *Oikoumenai,* Adolf Bastian labeled geographical provinces, and Mason termed inventional or culture areas. Each region possessed a unique set of conditions shaping a certain kind of human life. Despite the mixings and migrations of North American aborigines in historical times, Mason felt certain that many of these separate culture areas could still be traced. Since distinct zoological and botanical regions produced distinct arts, the anthropologist encountering a people with unique industries must search the region for the resources that "endowed and patronized" those arts.[94]

Mason then outlined in greater detail eighteen culture areas of the Western Hemisphere, but with one significant addition: he reminded his audience that the emphasis on environment should not obscure the crucial fact that human ingenuity produced all art, for which environment provided only the occasion, the mold.[95] Furthermore, Mason was careful to point out that the establishment of ethnic units belonged to the "centrifugal period" of human history, during which small groups of men had spun out from major centers to develop their own cultural patterns in various degrees of isolation from one another. (Powell's vision of linguistic differentiation was analogous.) Mason went on to postulate a second, centripetal stage of industrial history, well under way in the 1890s, in which all men moved gradually from discrete, independent cultural units to an all-embracing world community, a single cosmopolitan cultural area. Already man had replaced the natural cultural regions of many parts of the world with his own artificial political boundaries. Eventually these unnatural boundaries would be swept away, too, and all arts and industries developed in isolation would mingle and blend into "the proper flow of true culture." As Mason saw the future, "non-progressive races [would be] extinguished or driven to the suburbs, the play of worldwide action left unincumbered [*sic*], the flow of world-embracing commerce unimpeded, and every desire of man will be gratified."[96]

In evaluating the development of an ethnographic and environmental orientation in the life-group exhibits of the National Museum, it is useful to recall Boas's axiom: unlike causes often produce like effects. Boas's arguments had probably convinced nobody in Washington in 1887. The new exhibit style derived not from Boasian philosophy but from currents within the Washington anthropological community, including sensitivity to positive public response. What did Goode, Mason, and Holmes intend to teach the public with the new techniques? Essentially the same lessons of the earlier taxonomic exhibits: the fundamental unity beneath the diversity of human experience, a unity demonstrated in man's psychic activity—his inventions— and a unity to be achieved finally in the approaching coalescence into a single racial, linguistic, and cultural community. Beginning as one, man would end as one. Nothing less could instill the public piety toward man's Creator and the belief in American destiny that were their ultimate concerns. Although Mason to some extent transcended the bald evolutionism of the Klemm model of "Kulturgeschichte," the life-group orientation that he and Holmes pioneered in Washington served rather than questioned the superiority of Victorian American culture. As Frederick W. Putnam learned in Chicago in the nineties, there was always a strong element of the midway and the sideshow in exposition anthropology, even with the highest scientific intentions.[97] The need to attract and entertain in order to educate the American populace decisively influenced museum anthropology. One historian has remarked that "without the proper control of scholarly texts subject to 'professional' standards, an exhibit could in fact feed the taste for racist exoticism that it was meant to curb."[98] But even with such controls the outcome would have been uncertain. Visitors might discover Mason's "charming food for thought," but they would hardly rise to Boas's central insight that "civilization is not something absolute, but . . . is relative, and . . . our ideas and conceptions are true only so far as our civilization goes."

Mason and Holmes freely admitted that "there are two ways to study a large museum, both excellent and each necessary to the full development of the other: one is ethnical, the other technical."[99] But here the similarity with Boas ended. Boas was steadily building in these years toward a concept of cultures as historical, accidental accretions, at the same time approaching the principle of divorce between race and culture that his immigrant head-form studies and subsequent work would confirm. The Washington museum men were moving in the opposite direction; or perhaps had stopped moving. In the nineties they embraced environmental concepts and exhibition techniques essentially to explain and apologize for the underdevelopment of most peoples of the world. Still seeking the unity of their science and of man in the face of an explosion of new observations and data, they celebrated variety in order to contain it and ultimately deny its import. Thus Holmes in 1903 explained recent developments in anthropology: "It is customary with anthropologists to regard the physical and cultural phenomena as constituting a single unit, *the correlation between race and culture being intimate and vital,* and it is a cherished idea to present this unit with the completeness and effectiveness that its importance warrants."[100] It is abundantly clear that Holmes's environmentalism supplemented and modified but never supplanted strong categories of race and evolution. The moral lesson could not help but emerge clearly in exhibits as well as writings, and it must have come through to the museum-going public:

> In the inevitable course of human history the individual races will probably fade out and disappear, and the world will be filled to overflowing with a generalized race in which the dominating blood will be that of the race that today has the strongest claim, physically and intellectually, to take possession of all the resources of the land and sea. The resultant race will not have of the native American blood even this one three-hundredth part, because they are decadent as a result of conditions imposed by civilization. As diagrammed by the ethnologist of the far future the career of the Indian will appear as a lenticular figure—beginning in nothing, ending in nothing—a figure of perhaps universal application by the historian of mundane things.[101]

In 1898 Mason suffered a stroke that paralyzed his right side and forced him into semiretirement. He continued in the Museum, but his public and social life otherwise stopped. For six years he attended no meeting of the Anthropological Society, and it was nine years before Hough read Mason's "Comparison of Malaysian and American Indian Basketwork" before the Society that he had cofounded twenty-eight years before. Further tragedy befell the aging curator with the deaths of his wife and, in 1904, of one of his three daughters. The latter event broke up his house in Washington, and he distributed his large anthropological library to the Smithsonian and elsewhere. His fragile health forced him to spend several weeks of each year recuperating from fatigue and conserving his remaining strength at a seminary, a sanitarium, or at the home of a surviving daughter.[102]

With characteristic optimism and enthusiasm, however, Mason persevered. Practicing a "rhythmic life," he immersed himself more than ever in his work. Unable to use his right hand for more than a few minutes at a time, he taught himself to write with his left to the beating of a clock. He arose regularly at four in the morning to write, and except for rest periods away from Washington he rarely missed a day at the Museum.[103] During the last years of his life, Mason closely regulated his extra-official life in order to give all his strength to his job at the Museum. It kept him busy. In 1902 Langley asked Mason to serve as acting head curator of the Department of Anthropology as well as curator of ethnology.[104] Despite doubts about his strength, Mason agreed; in May 1905, he became permanent head curator, retaining his divisional position. He kept both jobs until his death in 1908.

In the last decade of his life Mason abandoned North American anthropology for the greener fields of East Asia. In moving beyond the continental boundaries of the Western Hemisphere, he conformed to larger tendencies in the Museum, the BAE, and government science generally in the first decade of the new century. The American war in the Pacific and Caribbean opened the eyes of government scientists to the rich fields of exploration in these areas, and the Russo-Japanese War of 1904 focused attention on Northeast Asia as a territory promising rich harvests for science.[105] These themes all appeared in Mason's work at the time. He reminded Smithsonian officials of the possibilities for ethnology and physical anthropology in the Panama Canal work, in archaeological finds and the mixture of races among the workers.[106] The war in Manchuria inspired him to explain Japanese and Russian expansionism in terms of biology rather than politics. Although his effort here was a mélange of cultural, racial, and linguistic evidence, it represented a sincere attempt to apply anthropology to a current problem. He encouraged Americans sojourning in this "meeting-ground of the two great ruling types of mankind in Asia" to collect for the Museum.[107] The eastern Mediterranean, the "backbone of Asia" and Mason's original focus of study, caught his attention once again after thirty years. He also became interested in the question of ancient migration routes across the Pacific.[108]

But his heart, he told George Grant MacCurdy in 1907, was "now in Malaysia, with my proto-Americans."[109] Mason's new fascination with Southeast Asia grew from the collections that arrived regularly from world traveler William L. Abbott. Independently wealthy and violently allergic to civilization, Abbott had been combing the islands of southern Asia, as well as central Asia and the east coast of Africa, since 1890. His collecting ventures on the *Terrapin* lasted for months at a time, and on his brief returns to Singapore he shipped tons of materials to Washington. Until 1903 these consisted chiefly of natural history collections, but over the next five years he sent Mason large ethnological shipments.

The two men enjoyed a mutually satisfying relationship reminiscent of early Smithsonian days. Mason, never a field man and now confined to his office, took deep, vicarious pleasure and excitement in Abbott's adventures. North America was becoming too crowded with young, enthusiastic investigators anyway, and the old man welcomed the opportunity to explore virgin fields: "A lot of young men, God bless them, are rummaging the Western Hemisphere for ethnic fame," he wrote Abbott. "If I can quietly steal aboard the *Terrapin* in spirit and let them rage, that will suit my 72 pulse better. I would follow you anywhere," Mason offered, "but give me a night to think it over."[110]

Abbott loathed civilization as much as Mason rejoiced in it. "I never feel as if life were worth living in Europe," he wrote to Hough, "until the scorching wind from the desert strikes the ship in the Red Sea, east bound." Abbott delayed as long as possible returning from his "happy land" to the bad air and overheated houses of America and England. Even twenty-five days in "rotten" Singapore, with its hotels full of American women with shrill "catlike drawls," left him feverish and "crazy to get away and smell the water and the coral beaches again." After so many years in the East, the West seemed strange to him, and he avoided contact with any people, "black, white, or brown, except the jungle people or wild tribes."[111]

Abbott was a collector who "worked" his region, not an ethnographer. He considered himself a poor observer of men, and he refused to write up his travels or permit Mason to discuss them in describing the collections.[112] The ethnographical map of Southeast Asia showed thousands of isolated cul-de-sacs with little apparent intermixture. Abbott and Mason agreed that a mere passerby could not make scientific comments on ethnology. Abbott estimated that ten years' work would be required for a "decently thorough" investigation, and he had neither the time nor patience for it. Like Mason, he preferred to move on to untapped and untouched regions. The long fingers of Western culture were reaching, via Singapore, to even the remotest peoples. Abbott was determined to get to them first.

On the basis of Abbott's work, Mason became convinced that the indigenous "brown race" of southern Asia represented a stage of industrial development midway between the savages of North America and the early civilized societies of the West. The basketry and other arts indicated in complexity and refinement a high stage of manual industry, beyond those of aboriginal America. In every art and industry, Abbott's gifts seemed to fill gaping holes in Mason's culture history. Still, Mason recognized among the Malaysian pieces some specimens "touching the very bottom of primitive culture."[113] He halfheartedly pursued the idea of a Malaysian source for American Indians, or perhaps a common source for both peoples; at other times he wondered if Captain James Cook had introduced certain arts to the region. But Mason reached no firm answers, and published only a detailed examination and glossary of Malaysian basketry. *The Vocabulary of Malaysian Basketwork,* issued in 1908 on the day of his funeral, was impressively detailed and lavishly illustrated, like Mason's *Aboriginal American Basketry* four years previously. But once again Mason lost himself in the details of specimens.[114]

The significance of Mason's infatuation with Abbott and Malaysia lies in the fact that after thirty years he turned his back on American anthropology and on the promising concept of cultural areas. Mason was bored and dissatisfied with North American work. Boas had analyzed the reason back in 1887, when he observed that the historical scientist or cosmographer absorbed himself intently in the phenomena of a region, while the impatient, law-formulating scientist constantly extended the range of his study over new areas.[115] Mason fitted the latter description precisely. In 1904, encouraging Jesse Fewkes to pursue a thorough ethnological research of the Caribbean, Mason remarked revealingly that the region would open "a new and rich field as a relief from the overthrashed straw of our own native tribes."[116] Mason was suffering from intellectual malaise. The experience and reflections of his first ten years as curator had borne fruit in more sophisticated concepts of culture areas superimposed upon a strong sense of cultural development. But here Mason had stopped.

Perhaps it was the stroke; or perhaps the powerful impact of political and military events diverted him. More likely, though, Mason set his own limits. Recognition of the shaping influence of environment collided with Mason's deep convictions of man's God-like, independent creativity. Mason's college training in the certitudes of Scottish moral philosophy warred constantly with the evolutionary naturalism dominant in America in his mature years. The result was tension between undeniable environmental influence on the vast array of human products, on the one hand, and Mason's strongly teleological notion of human unity, on the other. Most of the Washington anthropologists shared the dilemma. Mason's compromise was a constant search for specimens and data to fill up the rows of boxes that constituted his vision of human culture. Having begun his career in anthropology relying on constant acquisition of new material, after 1900 he turned with relief to fresh fields and vast raw materials, leaving America to younger scholars. His exhausting scientific pilgrimage was over.

The anthropology that Goode, Mason, and Holmes established in the National Museum in the last quarter of the century answered deep artistic and religious needs. Goode carried forward in his museum Joseph Henry's profound commitment to public moral education, although in the process he helped drive the Museum permanently into the very political dependence that Henry had so feared. Holmes and Mason devised the exhibit form for the lessons of that education. For Holmes the development of life-group exhibits provided an outlet for strong artistic and imaginative drives, at the same time permitting demonstration of the life of the primitive artist and inventor. The stress on naturalistic setting, material environment, and, in most cases, the immediate family as the relevant social group, fitted the purposes of men who as scientists recognized the varieties of human life, past and present, but who as moralists of their age insisted on original unity, purpose, and progress in history, and at least the reflection of divinity in man. They adopted the rhetoric of evolutionary naturalism, but their purposes were deeply pious.

In the beginning, Mason wrote in a poem of his youth, the Angel of Beauty had created the world and the soul of man in intimate compatibility. At first there had been only a "shadowy forecast" of God's purpose. When He spoke, "each material and ethereal thing/Became a word; the form articulate/Of his intention and predestining." Mason never deserted that vision of God's design, and he carried his own natural theology over into a secular, scientific twentieth century. To those in the industrial age who claimed that science had eclipsed art, that great aesthetic triumphs belonged to the past, the men of the National Museum responded with a strong affirmation of the indissoluble link between science and art, and of man's undying, God-implanted love of beauty:

Take knowledge, culture, every hot desire;
Give us of soul-stirred sorrow no surcease;
Try us till tried in the refining fire,
But give, oh! give us Beauty's smiling face.[117]

Notes

1. The general orientation presented here owes debts to Robert H. Wiebe, *The Search for Order, 1877–1920* (New York, 1967); Paul F. Boller, Jr., *American Thought in Transition: The Impact of Evolutionary Naturalism, 1865–1900* (Chicago, 1969); and Paul A. Carter, *The Spiritual Crisis of the Gilded Age* (DeKalb, 1971).

2. On American museum anthropology between 1860 and 1920, see Donald Collier and Harry Tschopik, Jr., "The Role of Museums in American Anthropology," *American Anthropologist* 56 (1954): 768–79; William C. Sturtevant, "Does Anthropology Need Museums?" *Proceedings of the Biological Society of Washington* 82 (1969): 619–50. I am grateful to Ira Jacknis for permission to consult his unpublished study, "Franz Boas and Museums of Anthropology in America, 1880–1920," which has influenced my analysis.

3. Henry Adams, *The Education of Henry Adams: An Autobiography* (Boston, 1961), pp. 338, 343–45.

4. Otis T. Mason, "What is Anthropology?" (Washington, D.C., 1883), p. 5.

5. For Mason's early years, see Walter Hough, "Otis Tufton Mason," *American Anthropologist* 10 (1908): 661–67; Mason to William J. Rhees, 1 November 1904, Rhees Papers, Huntington Library; Mason to Charles Hallock, 28 July 1899, in Hallock, "Smithsonian Gleanings: Scientific Work and Professional Correspondence, 1860 to 1912," SIL Manuscripts; Mason to Sallie Mason (daughter), 27 September 1889, in "Letters from Europe," SIA.

6. For Mason's career at Columbia, see Elmer Louis Kayser, "Columbian Academy, 1821–1897: The Preparatory Department of Columbian College in the District of Columbia," *Records of the Columbia Historical Society* (1971), pp. 150–63. See also the catalogs of Columbian College (after 1873, Columbian University) and the catalogs and prospectuses of Columbian College Preparatory School, 1861–84, in George Washington University *Bulletins,* GWU Archives. Quotation from GWU *Bulletin* 51 (1871): 45. The Corcoran prospectus appears in *Bulletin* 64 (1884). As early as 1873, the new university had planned to include in its new school of sciences a course in "Ethnology, Archaeology, and Anthropology." In 1884, the catalog listed a course in anthropology for the first term of the fourth year, but there is no evidence that the course was ever offered, or that Mason taught anthropology at Columbian.

7. USNM, *AR for 1909,* p. 62; Mason to Dr. Willis Moore, 18 February 1906, Mason Papers, NAA.

8. The story of Mason's conversion to American studies appears in T.D.A. Cockerell, "Spencer Fullerton Baird," *Popular Science Monthly* 68 (1906): 79–80. Mason made frequent reference to this critical meeting, usually assigning it to the early 1870s. See also Mason to G. T. Emmons, 9 May 1908, Mason Papers, NAA.

9. USNM, *AR for 1902,* p. 32. The statement comes from Mason's "autobiography," according to this necrology. I have been unable to find any trace of an autobiography, or any reference to it in Mason's papers.

10. Hough, "Otis Tufton Mason," p. 663; Mason to Baird, 26 August 1874; Baird to Mason, 14 July and 23 July 1874; Mason to Baird, 31 July 1874 and 18 July 1878, SIA. Although Baird took a personal interest in the ethnological collections, he apparently made little headway in classification. He reported in 1874 that the Institution had distributed 2,069 ethnological specimens, of 1,950 different "species."

11. Mason to John G. Henderson, 8 June 1907; Mason to F. W. Hodge, 31 January 1907, Hodge-Cushing Papers, Southwest Museum, Los Angeles.

12. Some of the original letters, with Mason's editorial comments, are in NAA (Series 2431, Archeology); Baird to Leslie Bessett, 22 July 1878, SIA.

13. O. T. Mason, "The Scope and Value of Anthropological Studies," *Proceedings of the American Association for the Advancement of Science* (1883), pp. 370, 378–79.

14. Mason, "What is Anthropology?" pp. 3–4, 13, 20.

15. Mason to W. F. Sands, 7 October 1905; Mason to Arthur P. Rice, 18 May 1906, NAA.

16. Mason, "What is Anthropology?" p. 5; "Scope and Value," pp. 376, 379; Mason to William V. Judson, 4 March 1904, and to Richard Rathbun, 16 March 1904, NAA.

17. Mason to Rathbun, 28 October 1905, NAA. Others who shared Mason's opinion were Lester Ward, who presented early drafts of *Dynamic Sociology* to early meetings of the Anthropological Society of Washington, and Powell, who first tried out virtually all his major works on the Society members.

18. Mason to E. W. Hensinger, 24 March 1905; Mason to Daniel G. Gillette, 10 March 1905, NAA. His advice included the suggestion that the ASW found a school of anthropology by upgrading the old Saturday Lectures at the

Smithsonian and inviting public school teachers. Mason to W J McGee, 9 February 1893, McGee Papers, LC.

19. O. T. Mason, "The Birth of Invention," in SI, *AR for 1892*, p. 610.

20. O. T. Mason, "The Leipsic Museum of Ethnology," SI, *AR for 1873*, pp. 390–409; Walter Hough, "Historical Sketch of the Division, Ethnology," ms., pp. 33–34, NAA. Mason's discussion of Klemm's system was condensed from "Extra-Beilage zu No. 104 der wissenschaftlichen Beilage der Leipziger Zeitung" and "Erster Bericht des Museums für Völkerkunde in Leipzig, 1873."

21. Mason, "Leipsic Museum," pp. 392–96, 401.

22. Ibid.

23. Mason, "Birth of Invention," p. 604; Mason to Charles Lummis, 4 June 1906, NAA.

24. Walter Hough, "Otis Tufton Mason," *Encyclopedia of the Social Sciences* 5 (1930).

25. Mason to J. S. Warmbath, 4 June 1906, NAA. Mason encouraged folklore and linguistic work by local societies like the ASW: "If it is possible . . . to reconstruct the material history of a region by means of its monuments and relics, so from its lore we may by patient study reconstruct its intellectual history." (Minutes of ASW meeting, 2 February 1886, ASW Papers, NAA.)

26. Mason to "Mr. Willard-French," 21 September 1904; to Albert G. Bauersfeld, 14 June 1904; to R. D. Cambiaso, 1 November 1906, NAA.

27. O. T. Mason, "Culture History" ms., NAA, unnumbered and "Not Assigned" notes; untitled paper in "Evolution of Inventions" notebook, pp. 10–11, NAA; "Scope and Value," p. 381; "Birth of Invention," p. 605; Mason to Blanche Nevin, 11 February 1906, NAA.

28. Hough to J. W. Fewkes, 5 January 1920, USNM Papers, NAA.

29. Mason, "Culture History" ms. notes.

30. Ibid; see also his notebooks on "Evolution of Inventions," NAA.

31. Mason, "Scope and Value," p. 367; *Science* 9, no. 224 (20 May 1887), p. 485.

32. Mason to M. L. Kissell, 13 February 1908, NAA.

33. Mason's clearest statement of his debts to Klemm and natural history appears in "The Educational Aspect of the United States National Museum," *Johns Hopkins University Studies in Historical and Political Science* (1890), pp. 505–19.

34. Mason, "Culture History" notes.

35. Mason, "What is Anthropology?" p. 13; Mason to Edgar A. Mearns, 1 November 1907 and to W. L. Abbott, 6 March 1907, NAA; "Educational Aspect," p. 505; USNM, *AR for 1884*, p. 57; Mason to Constance Goddard Davis, 13 April 1904, NAA.

36. Mason, unnumbered notes in "Culture History" notebooks.

37. Discussion of Goode's career is based on Henry Fairchild Osborn, "Goode as a Naturalist," *Science*, n.s. 5, no. 114 (5 March 1897), pp. 374–79; Samuel P. Langley, "Memoir of George Brown Goode, 1851–1896" (Washington, D.C., 1897), a thorough and touching memoir read before the National Academy of Sciences, 21 April 1897; "Goode Memorial Meeting," *Science*, n.s., vol. 5, no. 114 (5 March 1897), pp. 365–72; William Van Zandt Cox, "George Brown Goode: A Memorial Sketch," *American Monthly Magazine* (January 1897), pp. 1–11; and Paul H. Oehser, *Sons of Science: The Story of the Smithsonian Institution and its Leaders* (New York, 1949), pp. 92–105.

38. Langley, "Memoir," pp. 4, 6–7.

39. Osborn, "Goode," pp. 375, 378–79.

40. George Brown Goode, "The Organization and Objects of the National Museum" (USNM Circular 15), in *USNM Proceedings* 4 (1881), appendix 4. Goode presented his organizational scheme for the first time in this and two other circulars (Nos. 1 and 13), all appearing in the appendix to this volume of the *Proceedings*.

41. George Brown Goode, "Museum-History and Museums of History," *Papers of the American Historical Association* 3 (1887): 261–63; Goode, "The Principles of Museum Administration," in *Annual Report of the Museums Association of Great Britain* (1895), p. 71.

42. Barnet Phillips, "Two Letters on the Work of the National Museum" (reprinted from *New York Times*), USNM, *AR for 1884,* appendix 2.

43. Goode, "Museum-History," p. 512.

44. USNM, *AR for 1884,* p. 54. The Pitt Rivers Museum opened in Oxford in 1884; from 1874 to 1878 it was located in the Bethnal Green Branch of the South Kensington Museum. (Beatrice Blackwood, "The Origin and Development of the Pitt Rivers Museum," in *The Classification of Artifacts in the Pitt Rivers Museum, Oxford.* Pitt Rivers Museum Occasional Papers on Technology 11 [Oxford, 1970].)

45. The 500,000 figure was inflated. Twenty years later, Hough estimated the ethnology specimens at about 193,000. (Hough, "Historical Sketch of the Division of Ethnology," ms., NAA.)

46. "Diary of O. T. Mason in the National Museum, 7/1/84—5/23/91," NAA, entry for 1 July 1884; USNM, *AR for 1884,* p. 53.

47. Mason to Pilling, 27 August 1884; to Powell, 27 September 1884, BAE-LR, NAA.

48. Mason to Edward Lovett, 23 April 1904, NAA.

49. USNM, *AR for 1897,* p. 10.

50. O. T. Mason, "Throwing-Sticks in the National Museum," USNM, *AR for 1884,* part 2, pp. 279–91.

51. O. T. Mason, "The Eskimo of Point Barrow," *American Naturalist* 20 (1886): 197–98. Personal communication from W. C. Sturtevant.

52. O. T. Mason, "Basket-Work of the North American Aborigines," USNM, *AR for 1884,* part 2, pp. 291–316; cf. Mason, *Aboriginal American Basketry: Studies in a Textile Art Without Machinery,* USNM, *AR for 1902,* pp. 171–548.

53. Walter Hough, "History of the Division of Ethnology," handwritten ms., unnumbered pages, NAA.

54. USNM, *AR for 1886,* pp. 89–90.

55. Mason, "Diary," 21 September 1888. Mason's elaborations of his checkerboard scheme underscored order. To William DeC. Ravenal, assistant to Langley, he explained it with detailed drawings: "Supposing there are six great divisions of men and six ways of supplying wants. You will then have 36 exhibits, and if they were laid out in a vast room checker fashion you could study the ethnology of mankind by going from north to south, or activities of all mankind by moving east to west. This would represent any epoch of the world. And

if you had a building of several stories, each one would represent a grade of culture and these would constitute the synoptic series of *all activities* of *all peoples* in *all ages,* 216 exhibits in all." (Mason to Ravenal, 13 May 1905, NAA.) It is interesting to note that in the 1960s, Bernard Fagg planned a new building for the Pitt Rivers Museum, a circular structure with concentric bands devoted to major artifact types, and wedge-shaped sections for major cultural and geographical areas. Exhibition areas and underground storage areas were both to be so arranged. (Personal communication from W. C. Sturtevant.)

56. The Mason-Boas debate described below has been discussed from a somewhat different viewpoint in John Buettner-Janusch, "Boas and Mason: Particularism versus Generalization," *American Anthropologist* 59 (1957): 318–24. For an incisive and suggestive treatment of the event, however, see George W. Stocking, Jr., ed., *The Shaping of American Anthropology, 1883–1911: A Franz Boas Reader* (New York, 1974), pp. 1–20. According to Mason's diary, Boas visited the Museum on December 3–5, 1884, and January 7–13, 1885.

57. Franz Boas, "The Occurrence of Similar Inventions in Areas Widely Separated," *Science* 9, no. 224 (20 May 1887), pp. 485–86.

58. Ibid.

59. O. T. Mason, "The Occurrence of Similar Inventions in Areas Widely Apart," *Science* 9, no. 226 (3 June 1887), p. 534.

60. Mason to William DeC. Ravenal, 13 May 1905, NAA.

61. Mason, "Occurrence," p. 534.

62. Franz Boas, "Museums of Ethnology and their Classification," *Science* 9, no. 228 (17 June 1887), pp. 587–89.

63. J. W. Powell, "Museums of Ethnology and their Classification," *Science* 9, no. 229 (24 June 1887), pp. 612–14.

64. Mason, "The Birth of Invention," p. 603.

65. Mason, "Educational Aspect," p. 515.

66. Melvin Grove Kyle to Holmes, 9 August 1920, in WHH 14: 167.

67. Ibid., 1:8.

68. John R. Swanton, "William Henry Holmes," *National Academy of Sciences Biographical Memoirs* 17 (Washington, D.C., 1937): 224.

69. W. H. Holmes, "Report on the Ancient Ruins of Southwestern Colorado, Examined During the Summers of 1875 and 1876," in *Tenth Annual Report of the United States Geological and Geographical Survey of the Territories* (Washington, D.C., 1878), pp. 381–408.

70. Ibid., p. 390.

71. "Field Notes of W. H. Holmes in Charge of the San Juan Division of the Geological Survey of the Territories, 1875," in WHH 4: 23–24.

72. Ibid., p. 30.

73. Powell had set forth the appropriate guidelines in "On the Limitations to the Use of Some Anthropologic Data," in BAE, *AR for 1879–80,* pp. 71–86.

74. Timothy H. H. Thoreson, "Art, Evolution, and History: A Case Study of Paradigm Change in Anthropology," *Journal of the History of the Behavioral Sciences* 13 (1977): 109.

75. Ibid., pp. 112, 113.

76. W. H. Holmes, "The American Man and His Culture," ms., n.d., series 4695, p. 4, NAA.

77. Ibid., p. 5; W. H. Holmes, "The Story of the Human Race. Notes for Lecture by Dr. Holmes, Dec. 5, 1916,"Series 4695, pp. 5–6, NAA.

78. WHH 2: 97–98.

79. The complex story of the debate over Paleolithic man between 1875 and 1900 has never been told in depth. For a brief account of Holmes's fieldwork and theoretical position, see Virginia H. Noelke, "The Origin and Early History of the Bureau of American Ethnology, 1879–1910," Ph.D. diss. (University of Texas at Austin, 1974), pp. 126–33.

80. Dutton to Holmes, 10 December 1892, in WHH 6: 51.

81. W. H. Holmes, "Primitive Man in the Delaware Valley," Science, n.s. 6, no. 153 (3 December 1897), pp. 824–29.

82. Ibid., pp. 824–26, 828.

83. USNM, AR for 1884, pp. 51–52.

84. USNM, AR for 1893, pp. 52–56. Importation of natives and use of model villages as outdoor exhibitions at international expositions are discussed and illustrated in P. H. Pott, Naar wijder horizon: Kaleidscoop op ons beeld van de Buitenwereld (The Hague, Mouton & Co., 1962).

85. Mason to Sallie Mason (daughter), 3 August 1889; to Goode, 3 August, 16 August, and 5 September 1889; to Sallie (wife), 7 September 1889; to New York Examiner, 26 August 1889; all in "Letters from Europe. Written by O. T. Mason to Dr. Goode and the Mason Family, July 17–Oct. 7, 1889," SIA.

86. Mason to Goode, 31 July, 1 August, 3 August, 8 August, 31 August, and 5 September 1889; "Letters from Europe."

87. Mason to Goode, 31 July, 3 August, and 16 August 1889; Mason to New York Examiner, 26 August 1889; "Letters from Europe." Mason, "Anthropology in Paris," American Anthropologist, o.s. 3 (1890): 34.

88. Mason to Goode, 31 August 1889; "Letters from Europe."

89. USNM, AR for 1891, p. 139: O. T. Mason, "Ethnological Exhibit of the Smithsonian Institution at the World's Columbia Exposition," Memoirs of the International Congress of Anthropology (Chicago, 1894), p. 211.

90. Mason to McGee, 21 May 1893, NAA. An untitled ms. in Mason's papers, NAA, discusses the history of American anthropology and the critical questions of the early 1890s and presents an outline of ethnogeographic units of North America. This ms. expresses more clearly than his published statements Mason's sense of accomplishment that the Powell classification provided, e.g.: "Only those who have for themselves undertaken to bring order out of this chaos realize the importance of this achievement." (Page 9 of unnumbered pages)

91. USNM, AR for 1892, pp. 101–02; Mason, "Ethnological Exhibit," p. 211.

92. Ibid., p. 210.

93. Ibid., pp. 214–15.

94. O. T. Mason, "Technogeography, or the Relation of the Earth to the Industries of Mankind," American Anthropologist, o.s. 7 (1894): 137–53.

95. O. T. Mason, "Influence of Environment Upon Human Industries or Arts," SI, AR for 1895, pp. 639–65, esp. 662–63.

96. Mason, "Technogeography," pp. 153–61.

97. Ralph W. Dexter, "Putnam's Problems Popularizing Anthropology," *American Scientist* 54 (1966): 315–32.

98. Jacknis, "Franz Boas," p. 4.

99. O. T. Mason, review of Stewart Culin's *Korean Games*, in *American Anthropologist*, o.s. 9 (1896): 22–23.

100. Holmes to Richard Rathbun, 7 October 1903, Holmes letterbooks, NAA. Emphasis added.

101. WHH 9: 157–59.

102. Mason's personal life is gleaned from casual comments throughout his correspondence, in USNM Letterbooks, NAA. See, e.g., Mason to Ella F. Hubby, 28 September 1904; to C. H. Robinson, 16 December 1904; and to A. L. Kroeber, undated but presumably early 1906. Holmes's later career is treated in Chapter. IX.

103. Mason to Alice M. Earle, 2 October 1906; to David M. Ritchie, 23 January 1906, NAA.

104. Walcott's museum plan, instituted in 1897, reversed earlier terminology, creating three "departments"—anthropology, geology, and biology—each of which consisted of several "divisions."

105. See, for instance, Holmes and Mason's "Instructions to Collectors of Historical and Anthropological Specimens," *USNM Bulletin* 39, part Q (Washington, D.C., 1902), "especially designed for collectors in the insular possessions of the United States."

106. Mason to Richard Rathbun, 7 August 1904, NAA.

107. Mason, "The Races at War in the Far East," notebook and unpublished ms.; Mason to William V. Judson, 4 March 1904; and to Rathbun, 16 March 1904, NAA.

108. Mason to Frederick W. True, 1 October 1904; to Raphael Pumpelly, 4 October 1904; to the consul general to Ecuador, 8 December 1903; and to Zelia Nuttall, 4 June 1906, NAA.

109. Mason to George Grant MacCurdy, 12 January 1907, NAA.

110. Mason to Abbott, 27 June and 25 October 1904; 29 April 1905, NAA. Correspondence to Abbott is in the Mason Letterbooks, NAA; correspondence from Abbott to Mason and other Smithsonian officials is in the William L. Abbott Papers, NAA.

111. Abbott to Mason, 15 May 1903; 30 March, 14 May, and 28 September 1904; Abbott to Hough, 4 October 1907, NAA.

112. Abbott to Mason, 30 March 1904; 14 April 1907, NAA.

113. Mason to Abbott, 29 April 1905; to Rathbun, 17 January 1905, NAA.

114. Mason to Abbott, 23 September 1907, NAA; O. T. Mason, "Vocabulary of Malaysia Basketwork: A Study in the W. L. Abbott Collections," *USNM Proceedings* 35 (Washington, D.C., 1908): 1–51.

115. Boas, "The Study of Geography," p. 137.

116. Mason to Fewkes, 1 July 1904, NAA.

117. O. T. Mason, "The Spirit of the Beautiful," delivered before the Enosinian Society of Columbian College, 22 June 1863 (Washington, D.C., 1863), pp. 9, 10, 17–18.

John Wesley Powell in his final years, c. 1900.

V

Spencer, Morgan, and Powell:
The Intellectual Framework of the
Bureau of American Ethnology

"For the young men whose lives were cast in the generation between 1867 and 1900, Law should be Evolution from lower to higher, aggregation of the atom in the mass, concentration of multiplicity in unity, compulsion of anarchy in order . . ."[1] Thus Henry Adams summarized the intellectual tenets of the tumultuous decades of the late nineteenth century. John Wesley Powell would have found little to disagree with in Adams's statement. Like many others of the generation that fought as young men in the Civil War, Powell struggled all his life to compose a philosophy that at once embraced the powerful truths of evolutionary science, preserved unity and purpose in a changing cosmos, and bolstered the faith in human dignity and autonomy that he inherited from an antebellum Methodist childhood. His anthropology is understandable only by recognizing the force of these commitments. Throughout his scientific career, Powell sought a single causal principle, a scientific God, to explain all phenomena. The monistic tendency had two consequences for his programs. First, it tended to blur distinctions between the subject matter of diverse sciences; his anthropology was laced with borrowings from biology, physics, anatomy, and elsewhere. Secondly, the inclination to stress a general "scientific method" of thought rather than expertise in a specific discipline explains the temerity with which Powell borrowed men from all walks of life and applied their talents in the Bureau.

The unifying, reductionist proclivity was very strong in Powell. But he also revealed a contrary tendency, partially in reaction to Charles Darwin and Herbert Spencer (as he understood them), to set man apart from the rest of the world as a separate, qualitatively different object of study. The assertion of human uniqueness within universal evolution was an attempt to free man from the determinism Powell perceived in Darwin and from the passivity he saw as man's lot in Spencer's cosmic evolutionism. Powell may have been mistaken in both perceptions. Still, in establishing the "New Ethnology" in Washington he specifically rejected biological analogy as a false guide to the human world, and he discounted physical anthropology as a means to a useful classification of peoples.

Like Otis Mason, Powell celebrated the human mind; it was always the primary focus of his inquiry. Mind became for him the generative force in man's evolution, the process behind the human products and activities that anthropologists studied. Man's mind set him above the rest of the universe. Powell intended to trace the development of mind from the most primitive savages to Washington scientists. Material culture, kinship systems, languages, folklore—all were inherently interesting, but they were ultimately only the data of the science, the outward manifestations that revealed the operations of an underlying agency.

Herbert Spencer exerted a profound influence on Powell. Though he rarely cited Spencer or anyone else in his writings, Powell always had the English philosopher before him as a model and challenge. Spencer's massive *Synthetic Philosophy*, which began to appear in the 1860s and to receive critical attention in the United States in the next decade, attempted to embrace all existence in a single framework. He hoped to subordinate all knowledge to a supreme, cosmic law of evolution, positing a single, unknowable force behind all phenomena. Drawing especially on the powerful axioms of nineteenth-century physics—the persistence of force, the indestructibility of matter—Spencer sought a law applicable to every field of scientific investigation.[2]

The universe, Spencer claimed, was in constant change, leading at any one time in one of two directions: toward integration of matter (evolution) or disintegration of matter (dissolution). Evolution involved not only the integration of matter but, equally important, increasing heterogeneity and differentiation of parts and functions. This was a single process of the whole universe and its parts, determining at once geological change, biological evolution, the development of human society, and the growth of the mind.

Spencer defined progress simply as increasing differentiation from homogeneous to heterogeneous structures. Progress so defined was apparent, for example, in the development of the solar system from a nebular mass to an ordered planetary system; in the gradual differentiation of the parts of the earth; in races of men diverging from a common ancestry; in the accelerating divisions of labor and other functions in human societies; and in the historical development of dialects and languages from a few mother tongues.

At the outset Spencer conceded that the ultimate cause of universal evolution was unknown and unknowable, although men would always compose theories about it. Such conjecture belonged to the realm of religion, which unlike science possessed no substantive knowledge but was merely a healthy and necessary awareness of the boundaries of human cognition. By positing the existence of an Unknowable beyond the limits of cognition, and by arguing for the compatible, complementary nature of science and religion, Spencer disarmed potential clerical critics and imposed a certain humility on those who applauded positive human knowledge.

Biological interpretation of human society became a distinctive feature of Spencerian thought. Social forms developed according to natural laws, not by man's design. Social structures revealed the same patterns of growth, specialization of functions, and interdependence of parts that plants and animals displayed. Spencer's profound respect for the laws governing man, and his disenchantment with social reform efforts in England, led him to discount attempts at social guidance based on partial knowledge or special interest. He saw only arrogant foolishness in the panaceas of those who would use government to shape society according to their visions. The purpose of social science, as he explained in *The Study of Sociology* (1872), was not to aid in calculating needs and remedies but to teach the futility of ill-considered plans. Schemes that ignored the complexity of society brought only disaster and retrogression. Sociology must remind men of their limitations and fit them to their fates. In this sense the presumptuousness of the *Synthetic Philosophy* was illusory; Spencer's work, read carefully, is a monument to humility in an age of arrogance.

Powell knew Spencer's work well, and he grew to dislike the Englishman intensely. They shared the desire to synthesize knowledge, to be sure. But Spencer's Unknowable was, to Powell, an abomination, an insult to the human mind, and a throwback to the metaphysical speculations that had plagued mankind for most of its history. Powell was fond of repeating the well-worn axiom that research proceeds from the known to the unknown. To contend that the unknown is ultimately unknowable, that the human mind faces final limits to its penetration into the secrets of the universe, seemed only the "despondency of unrewarded mental toil." Spencer's metaphysics, said Powell, amounted to no more than the "spectral imaginings that haunt the minds of introverted thinkers as devils possess the imaginations of the depraved."[3]

Powell both judged Spencer severely and often caricatured him. In Spencer's "intoxication of illusion facts seem cold and colorless," and like a "wrapt dreamer" the philosopher "imagines that he dwells in a realm above science" where "feverish dreams are supposed to be glimpses of the unknown and unknowable." Writing from his easy chair, wrapped warmly in his own imaginings, Spencer threatened the empirical science that Powell saw as America's glory. The Spencerian philosophy was a prime example of what happens when hypotheses dominate inquiry. "When an hypothesis gains such control over the mind that phenomena are subjectively discerned, that they are seen only in the light of the preconceived idea," Powell wrote in a thinly disguised attack on Spencer, "research but adds to vain speculation. A mind controlled by an hypothesis is to that extent insane; the rational mind is controlled only by the facts, and contradicted hypotheses vanish in their light."[4]

Hypothesis was a necessity in scientific inquiry, of course. Progress was impossible without it. "Men do not go about the earth indiscriminately discerning and grouping," Powell observed.[5] Proper discernment involved seeing phenomena in relation to other objects, and this required direction. Generations of philologists, for instance, had recorded linguistic data—sounds and words—with considerable precision, resulting in masses of unorganized data. But scientific research, Powell insisted, "is not random observation and comparison, but designed discernment and classification; it is research for a purpose, and the purpose is the explanation of imperfectly discerned phenomena."[6]

Darwin had taught that pure induction and pure deduction were equally fruitless.[7] Some facts possessed value for some purposes; some did not. While the fool collects facts, the wise man selects them, suggested Powell: "The true scientific man walks not at random throughout the world making notes of what he sees," but chooses a narrow field of specialization, using and discarding hypotheses as required. Both deductive and inductive methods had been superseded by the method of working hypotheses.[8]

Powell's call for an improved inductive science was hardly new. Even in the early nineteenth century, the supposed heyday of "pure Baconianism" in America, it is doubtful that scientists ever rigorously denied selecting among data. As Nathan Reingold has observed, neither the supposed anti-intellectualism nor the emphasis on taxonomy of early American science necessarily implied data-grubbing without theory.[9] The terms "Baconianism" and "pure Baconian induction," as employed by the Washington scientists, assumed the use of hypotheses. The critical distinction for them was that hypotheses be discarded readily, willingly, in the face of contrary facts.

Powell maintained that Spencer's fundamental mistake lay in his notion of force. Force was Spencer's term for the unconditioned, unknowable reality. Although man could never comprehend this reality, he did experience its effects as matter and motion. By "intrinsic force" a body manifests its existence; by "extrinsic force" it moves. Both manifestations, said Spencer, are received in human consciousness, which necessarily posits from them the existence of an Unknowable.[10]

This was dangerous nonsense to Powell. It was an unfortunate fact of life that men loved mystery over scientific truth, he recognized sadly; "in the revelry developed by the hashish of mystery, the pure water of truth is insipid." The "intellectual intoxication" of metaphysics apparently held far greater attraction than the simple truths of science, yet Powell claimed to find a "spirit of sanity" in the true and simple.[11] The steady progress of science, he answered Spencer, had gradually resolved all the mysterious "forces" of metaphysics into understandable antecedent motions. Only gravity, chemical "affinity," and magnetism remained unexplained, and Powell felt certain that these too would eventually prove to be merely other modes of motion.[12] Powell thus resolved Spencer's mysterious forces into forms of motion and believed he had removed a major metaphysical obstacle from science. In actuality, his own concept of "motion," if not unknowable, was remarkably obscure.[13]

At the very foundation of Spencer's philosophy Powell saw unacceptable passivity and vulnerability to inscrutable forces. Spencer contended that homogeneous phenomena, from stars to societies, are inherently unstable and soon develop heterogeneous features. It was the agency of change in this scheme that marked the attitudinal gap between the two men. Spencer contended that outside forces acted upon certain parts of the homogeneous mass to cause differentiation. The agency thus seemed to lay with outside forces, not within organisms.

Spencer's unknowable forces and his derivative social theories equally sickened Powell. The first reeked of metaphysics and the second belittled man. The point of Powell's philosophical excursions was to show that the generative mechanism of evolution came not from without but from within. Motion, he was fond of saying, was the first and only property of matter.[14] Applied to man, this meant that the motivating force in evolution was the human mind, the highest organization of motion. Spencer's false philosophy taught that man, subject to forces beyond his control, could do nothing. Such doctrines, Powell told a meeting of the Anthropological Society of Washington in 1881, would "neutralize nine-tenths of the legislation of the world."[15] The hero of the Grand Canyon feared that if such an attitude became prevalent, "modern civilization would lapse into a condition no whit superior to that of the millions of India. . . . When man loses faith in himself, and worships nature, and subjects himself to the government of the laws of physical nature," Powell exhorted, "he lapses into stagnation, where mental and moral miasm [sic] is bred."[16]

Powell never questioned the validity of biological science itself. Biology under the genius of Darwin and Thomas Henry Huxley accounted for the highest attainment of the century. It was thus hardly surprising that the best scientific minds of the time were engaged in biological research, he noted, for evolutionary biology had provided an attractive vision of the future. "The philosophy of biology," Powell found, "satisfies the reason." Had scientists discovered either degeneration or endless cyclical movement in life, "the gift of science to man would have been worthless." But biology had instead discovered steady progress to a higher life, and Powell rejoiced that "science has discovered hope."[17] Furthermore, the biologists themselves did not misapply their principles; rather it was those on "the verge of science" who spread pernicious errors through the press. Consequently, Powell lamented, " 'The Survival of the Fittest' is inscribed on the banner of every man who opposes any endeavor to ameliorate the condition of mankind."[18]

Darwin must not be misread, Powell insisted.[19] The explorer of the Colorado knew from first hand that the natural world teemed with abundant life; he had been studying the flora and fauna along with the geology of the trans-Mississippi region since before the Civil War. But Darwin and Wallace had clarified the nature of competition among plants and animals. Powell fully concurred with their observation that the life of the few was secured at the cost of the many. The "wanton superfluity" of nature introduced plants and animals to a world of fierce competition where only the lucky and the well-adapted—the "favorites of surrounding circumstances"—survived.[20] Results were mixed. Graceful, perfumed flowers proliferated and became even more beautiful through the agencies of insects and birds; but at the same time noxious and thorny plants also prospered. Progress of the few by the death of many resulted in "hardness, bitterness, piercing cruelty, and deadly poison . . ." And if the floral realm created such products, animal evolution by claw and fang, Powell showed, "has cost the world a hell of misery."[21]

Powell readily translated the observations of nature into moral lessons. Tender and hard fruits growing on the same hillside, the beautiful and the ugly coexisting in the same forest—all demonstrated that, by his standards of taste at least, "good and evil flourish in the same soil." Competition among animals gave rise to anger, hatred, ferocity, fear, and pain, as well as the delicate and lovely marvels of the faunal world: "So good and evil dwell together."[22] The world of nature was a wasteful, extravagant process unworthy of man.

Man had irrevocably altered the mechanism of evolution. Powell and his colleagues in Washington science argued strenuously that the population theories of English clergyman and mathematician Thomas Malthus, which Darwin had employed so brilliantly, had application solely to the biological realm; their original application to man, in Malthus's *Essay on the Principles of Population,* had actually been quite wrong.[23] In rejection of Malthus lay a statement of the physical and attitudinal gulf separating the Old and New Worlds. Certainly the English theoretician, writing at the close of the eighteenth century in a rapidly industrializing island nation, and the explorer of the wide expanses of North America saw very different human futures. Where Malthus projected population pressures on relatively dwindling food supplies, Powell anticipated no lack of food, only possible maldistribution.

Wallace Stegner suggested that Powell's broadest philosophical positions must be seen in terms of "ultimately regional roots," a midwestern boosterism and optimism that saw bounteous nature and open spaces.[24] This is an important insight. To be sure, Powell's *Report on the Lands of the Arid Region of the United States* (1878) and his subsequent fight for the Irrigation Survey and a rational land-use policy in the West fully demonstrated his prescient doubts that portions of the continent could sustain unplanned settlement.[25] But in more sanguine moments, and for different audiences, he could express a confidence that emerged from the heart of North America:

Men are not crowded against plants, men are not crowded against beasts, and men are not crowded against one another. The land is yet broad enough for all. The valleys are not all filled, the hillsides are not all covered. The portion of the earth that is actually cultivated and utilized to supply the wants of man is very small; it compares with all the land as a garden to a plain, an orchard to a forest, a meadow to a prairie. Nature is prodigal of her gifts. The sweet air as it sweeps from zone to zone is enough to fan every cheek; the pure water that falls from the heavens and refreshes the earth and is again carried to the heavens on chariots of light is more than enough to refresh all mankind; the boun-teous earth spread out in great continents is more than enough to furnish every man a home; and the illimitable sea has wealth for man that has not yet been touched.[26]

Vestiges of brutal competition did linger among civilized men as degrading crime, or in organized form as warfare. But far from improving the race, argued the Civil War veteran, crime on the individual level and warfare as a collective activity selected out the best and healthiest for destruction, leaving behind the deformed and weak to propagate. To the extent that man fell individually or collectively under the laws of biological evolution, he degraded himself to the level of the beast.[27]

Fortunately, throughout the centuries man had increasingly freed himself from the despotism of biology and transferred the struggle for existence from himself to the products of his genius. In the process he had changed the cruel law of evolution into an agency of human improvement. The key was man's inventive mind. Invention, as Washington anthropologists employed the term, embraced all products of man's mind.[28] Every invention of civilized man, from the reaper to representative government, stood as the culminating product in a long series of predecessors. In each line of invention there had been a few successful efforts—ideas, institutions, or technological improve-ments that served man adequately for a time—but far more failures. This occurred because man, like nature, created abundantly:

Man invents more devices than he can use; of the many only the few are selected consciously and intelligently because they are the best. And all these inventions are made not because men struggle with nature for existence, but because men endeavor to secure happiness, to improve their condition; it is a conscious and intelligent effort for improvement. Human progress is by human endeavor.[29]

In all times and places men invented rival concepts and instruments, which competed with one another for adoption. Man picked the most useful, dis-carding the rest. Human evolution resulted solely from this process of human selection, Powell insisted; natural selection played no role beyond the animal stage.

Perhaps it was the proximity to the Patent Office that made man's inventive capacities so enthralling to Powell and his Washington colleagues.[30] Powell had a tentative explanation for human inventiveness. He observed that with evolution from lower to higher organisms, plants and animals produced fewer offspring, until, at the highest civilization, reproduction reached a minimal rate. At the same time inventive capacity increased enormously through the various grades of higher animals and races of man. Spencer had argued similarly in *Principles of Biology* that as the race progresses, fewer offspring will be produced; in his words, "individuation and reproduction are antagonistic." This led Powell to conjecture that "the marvelous powers of reproduction are transferred from the body of man to the soul of man, and he multiplies his intellectual creations at an amazing rate."[31]

Powell put theory to practice. As numerous contemporaries recalled, he gave freely of the "offspring" of his mind, merely stating his thoughts for the world to accept or reject. Grove Karl Gilbert, geologist in the Survey, recalled that "the fruits of his study were cast forth as simple seeds, to germinate or perish, according to their worthiness or unworthiness, or as the accident of their environment might determine."[32]

Chance variation and survival by struggle resulted in the proliferation of varieties and species of plant and animal. According to Powell's scheme, primitive man, originating at a single locus, or possibly a small number of centers, had also followed biotic laws, differentiating into varieties characterized by skull, skeletal, skin, hair, and other physical peculiarities. Races of men had formed early. Had the trend continued, distinct species would have resulted. But at some critical point in human history, differentiation was checked and man assumed control of his evolution. From this point, which occurred at different times for different peoples, man began the long, slow return to homogeneity through cultural evolution.

Both polygenists and monogenists had a place in Powell's conjectural history. He conceded the possibility of a common biological origin but posited a multitude of cultural origins. From a condition of dispersal and variety (Spencer's heterogeneity), man had steadily moved back toward the interdependence and solidarity of his "pristine homogeneity."[33] The return to unity came about in various ways. Useful arts and inventions spread rapidly to appropriate peoples, thereby creating common bonds; through conquest and in other ways, social institutions also dispersed. More difficult was the spread of dominant languages, opinions, and higher methods of reasoning, but Powell claimed to perceive in his lifetime a tendency toward "homogeneity of tongue" and the global spread of scientific philosophy. Equally promising, men all over the world were intermarrying, as the American experience exemplified. While the "synthetic chemistry of social life" was bleaching black Americans, the American Indian was rapidly fading as a distinct race as well. Powell predicted that within three generations there would be no pure Indian or Negro blood in North America: "Civilization overwhelms Savagery, not so much by spilling blood as by mixing blood, but whether spilled or mixed, a greater homogeneity is secured."[34]

I have many facts which fit perfectly into the system which you have laid out: the bearing of these facts I did not understand before. Had I more fully appreciated your system, I believe I could have given you much additional data . . . After reading your book, I believe you have discovered the true system of social and governmental organization among the Indians.[35]

Powell never stated his debt to Lewis Henry Morgan more explicitly than in the above passage of 1877, but he envisioned BAE anthropology as the fulfillment of the work begun so promisingly with *Ancient Society*. Morgan's famous three-stage scheme of social development—through savagery, barbarism, and civilization—was handy, current, and authoritative when Powell founded the Bureau in 1879. Above all it was a system, and as many observers have noted, Powell owed a large intellectual debt to the Rochester sage.

Morgan, like so many others, had accepted Darwinian natural selection on his own terms. Man, he agreed, began at the bottom of the scale and slowly worked his way up, but Morgan's scale was quite different from Darwin's. Men and animals, according to Morgan, began as separate creations of God, endowed with all the same faculties but to different degrees, so that man subsequently progressed more rapidly. Thus, when Morgan used his favorite phrase, "Man works himself up," or when he discussed mental similarities between man and the "mutes," as in his classic study of *The American Beaver and His Works* (1868), he never intended to lower man to original identity with animals. Morgan's evolutionism was actually tied closely to eighteenth-century models that embraced an idea of material progress but not change in mental structures. For Morgan it was ideas, not mind itself, which grew and developed over time. Furthermore, as discussed previously, his work on the development of human society originally grew from strongly historical interests, and he moved to theories of developmental stages only under great pressure to organize his data.[36]

Morgan saw human history as the product of "unrecognized social processes and conscious decision," in which the growth of ideas, especially concepts of property, played a critical role.[37] "Historians, out of a certain necessity," he wrote in *Ancient Society* (1877), "give to individuals great prominence in the production of events; thus placing persons, who are transient, in the place of principles, which are enduring. . . . It will be recognized generally that the substance of human history is bound up in the growth of ideas, which are wrought out by the people and expressed in their institutions, usages, inventions, and discoveries."[38] The emphasis on the elaboration of ideas marked a strong teleological strain in Morgan. Indeed, he claimed to see "unconscious reformations" toward a future social ideal that humanity was approaching. For Morgan, history ultimately "was enacted *through people* with a common 'principle of intelligence' seeking ideal standards invariably the same."[39] The history of society was, in short, all part of the grand plan of the "Supreme Intelligence."[40]

Ancient Society traced that plan. Morgan followed man's cultural growth through savagery and barbarism (each subdivided into lower, middle, and upper planes) to civilization. The divisions were neither new nor unique, but he also proposed an explanation of the mechanics of human progress. The "real epochs of progress," he advised Joseph Henry in 1873, "are connected with the arts of subsistence which includes the Darwinian idea of the 'struggle for existence.' "[41] Without enlarging the basis of subsistence, man could not have propagated and dominated the globe; it followed that "great epochs of human progress have been identified, more or less directly, with the enlargement of the sources of subsistence."[42]

Morgan defined his "ethnical periods" through subsistence arts, then correlated social and political institutions to the fundamental classification. In lowest savagery, man had lived for centuries by digging roots and gathering berries; eventually he acquired fire, and in upper savagery he invented the bow and arrow and hunting. Domestication of animals, cultivation of grains, and pottery-making marked the beginning of lower barbarism; iron smelting closed upper barbarism and ushered in civilization.

Each level possessed its characteristic forms of government, family, and property—the three institutions treated in *Ancient Society*. Human government, he said, had followed two successive plans: kinship organization, based on gentes, phratries, and tribes; and later, political organization, founded upon territory and property relationships. Under the first, government was personal; under the latter it became territorial. Without a concept of individual property, the earlier arrangements had no class distinctions—they were essentially democratic. But with progress in subsistence arts and consequent acquisition of land and personal property, the communal arrangements of this early "gentile society" gave way to political relationships based on property and territorial rights.

Concomitant changes had occurred in family structures. Drawing on his extensive kinship work, Morgan outlined five stages of family organization, from consanguine (group marriage between brothers and sisters) to monogamous (insured paternity and exclusive inheritance of property). Since in the earlier stages of promiscuity descent could be reckoned only through the mother, he reasoned, the family was everywhere originally matriarchal.

The growth of ideas of property from their origins in savage minds caused and accompanied changes in inventions and social institutions. Morgan meant by "property" a single, growing force among all men, a divinely implanted principle that took various forms. Consequently, Morgan did not distinguish the nuances beneath the general term. It is clear, however, that he deplored the vast accumulations of private wealth, in individual and corporate forms, that alienated man from man and threatened social harmony. He called for return to the communal ownership pattern that had supposedly characterized savage society. With their meager belongings, common lands, and houses, the men of savagery barely knew individual property. But by the upper status of barbarism the various improvements in inventions gave rise to enough individually owned property to require laws regulating ownership, and what had been only "a feeble impulse" among savages grew to a "tremendous passion." The foundations of the economic inequalities of civilization—personal wealth, family inheritance, aristocracy—had been laid.[43]

He observed the results in American civilization with deep uneasiness. During his career as lawyer and land investor he had watched lumbering and mining interests ravish the upper Michigan forests, and he came to deplore the brutal Indian wars and the growing rapacity of American economic enterprise.[44] Although he believed the United States had largely abolished class distinctions, Morgan never saw his own society as the apex of evolution. Here lay his hope, for surely society would continue to change in the future as in the past. That change, Morgan predicted, would involve a return to democratic, communal principles and a rejection of individual property as a basis for social relationships. Democracy, "once universal in a rudimentary form," would return in a fuller and more perfect flowering.[45] Toward the end of *Ancient Society* Morgan delivered an inspiring declaration of faith in man's ability to transcend the thralldom of individual property. Property, he pronounced, has become "an unmanageable power," and "the human mind stands bewildered in the presence of its own creation." But human intelligence would surely master property and usher in a glorious future of peace and harmony:

A mere property career is not the final destiny of mankind, if progress is to be the law of the future as it has been of the past. The time which has passed away since civilization began is but a fragment of the past duration of man's existence; and but a fragment of the ages yet to come. The dissolution of society bids fair to become the termination of a career of which property is the end and aim; because such a career contains the elements of self-destruction. Democracy in government, brotherhood in society, equality in rights and privileges, and universal education, foreshadow the next higher plane of society to which experience, intelligence and knowledge are steadily tending. It will be a revival, in a higher form, of the liberty, equality, and fraternity of the ancient gentes.[46]

By the middle of the 1870s, when Powell was doing his field work, Morgan was the recognized dean of American anthropology. *Ancient Society,* his enduring theoretical contribution to the science, confirmed his eminent position. "It is not one of the least results accomplished by Mr. Morgan," Powell wrote in 1880, a year before Morgan's death, "that he has gathered about him living disciples who are reaping harvests from fields planted by himself." Powell stood foremost among those followers. Morgan had "laid the foundation for the science of government as it is finally to be erected by the philosophy of evolution," Powell announced.[47] Without accepting all his assumptions, Powell found a kindred spirit in Morgan. Morgan's critical views on private property and his optimistic vision of future social organization matched Powell's own concerns about western land development. Perhaps Morgan's most important lesson for statesmen, wrote Powell, was that "government by the people is the normal condition of mankind"; despite occasional lapses and setbacks, democracy would prevail by natural selection. "Hope for the future of society," Powell concluded happily, "is the best-loved daughter of Evolution."[48] For his part, Morgan enjoyed Powell's comments and agreed that his book was "a tremendous thrust at privileged classes . . ."[49]

The two ethnologists shared as well a respect for the primitive peoples they studied, which, while not free of ethnocentrism, did encourage sympathetic treatment. Morgan's humanism lay partly in his belief that relative progress among men was largely accidental. Environmental conditions and chance inventions played major roles in advancing one people rather than another. *Ancient Society,* in fact, closed not with the ringing declaration for the future cited above, but with the peculiarly diffident reminder that civilization, while probably inevitable in God's plan, was at least in its timing the consequence of "a series of fortuitous circumstances." Civilized man owed his present condition, Morgan lectured the public, to "the struggles, the sufferings, the heroic exertions, and the patient toil of our barbarous, and more remotely, of our savage ancestors."[50]

Morgan's emphasis on the central role of human intelligence in conquering nature struck a sympathetic chord in Powell, and he was fascinated with the way in which Morgan correlated social institutions with notions of property and subsistence arts. "In the lower stages of culture," Powell later wrote, "all progress rests upon the arts of life." To discover the "efficient agency" in human development from one stage to the next, the anthropologist must look to man's "art-inventions," particularly those of subsistence.[51] Here lay the cornerstone of a scientific anthropology.

Powell wanted to do for the science of man what Darwin had done for biology: formulate a powerful guiding theory of (human) evolution buttressed by an unassailable mountain of empiricism. Morgan made a critical contribution with his development stages marked by characteristic, correlated forms of inventions in material goods, ideas, and institutions. Here the student could see the unity of the human mind in its full clarity, as it created essentially similar products across the spectrum of human needs at each point in evolution. Methodologically, this was a breakthrough for Powell. If Morgan's scheme could be expanded from arts of subsistence, family, government, and property to include the full range of man's creations, the anthropologist operating with only the remnants of a given tribe could rebuild its life entirely, like the paleontological reconstructions of Georges Cuvier. Further, with the full panoply of man's inventions at each stage spread before him, the student of man could then proceed to examine by inference the development of the magnificent agency that had created them: mind. This was Powell's final destination, to which Morgan opened a way.

Correlating the different categories of human activities thus became a prime feature of the New Ethnology, as Powell termed Bureau anthropology. Past investigators had examined languages, material arts, kinship, and social institutions without seeing them in relation to each other. But study of any single field of human activity without discovering relations to all others amounted merely to collecting curiosities:

> All the grand classes of human activities are inter-related in such a manner that one presupposes another, and no one can exist without all the others. Arts are impossible without institutions, languages, opinions, and reasoning; and in like manner every one is developed by aid of the others. If, then, all of the grand classes of human activities are interdependent, any great change in one must effect corresponding changes in the others. The five classes of activities must progress together. Art-stages must have corresponding institutional, linguistic, philosophic, and psychic stages.[52]

Morgan had taken the first step by connecting certain institutions and economic factors in a causal sequence. But his work was imperfect, Powell found, because he never explained the interdependence satisfactorily, and because he largely ignored language and mythology, Powell's personal areas of interest.[53]

Powell's stress on man as a subject with multiple aspects requiring simultaneous, coordinated study came partly in reaction to the unsatisfactory racial classifications of physical anthropologists. Beyond the primary division into four or five races, physical features had been found useless in distinguishing tribes, so that the student of man had to go beyond biological criteria in order to investigate men in groups. As Powell never tired of saying, the study of man is demotic, not biotic. This became, in McGee's words, "the germ of a rejuvenated ethnology, i.e., a science of races based on human rather than animal attributes."[54] Both primitive and civilized peoples were to be most profitably studied as groups, "in which each individual reflects and is molded by the characteristics of his associates . . ."[55]

By extending Morgan's initiative and attempting to raise the "New Ethnology" above the methods of biology, Powell took American anthropology

one important step toward a holistic approach to human society. In a rudimentary way he saw that the material arts, social institutions, customs, beliefs,
and languages of groups of people are interconnected in various complex ways,
and to some extent he permitted Bureau ethnologists to explore these interconnections. But the advance should not be overestimated. Powell operated
within specific intellectual confines. The correlations and interconnections
referred to stages of culture, not to specific cultures. The goal was to discover,
for example, how savage subsistence arts are related to savage linguistic
behavior in general, without application to a given tribe. The experiences of
particular societies constituted only the data of Powell's anthropology, not
the final scientific object. Consequently, Powell had no compunctions about
dismantling an ethnographic study into components and reassembling them
with data in the same "lines" of activity from other peoples. At heart, Powell
remained always comparative.

The dichotomy between ethnographic completeness and "lines" of study
appeared in Powell's own early field work of the 1870s. While he emphasized
language and mythology, Powell's interests extended to most aspects of social
life: kinship terminology, ceremonialism, curing practices, material culture;
he even noted treatment of children, the aged, and the insane.[56] But Powell
took great liberties with his data, abstracting, for example, the stylized songs
and chants from his Southern Paiute tales.[57] And while he apparently intended
to write up his notes on the various tribes of the Numic peoples into an
ethnographic summary, over the years he actually used his field notes, particularly his observations on psychology, in a highly selective manner.[58] The
burdens of administering two agencies explain in part his failure to produce
integrated studies, but full ethnographies were simply less important to
Powell than applying the data to a larger developmental picture.

Powell's evolutionary anthropology, as he imposed it on the Bureau of
American Ethnology, envisioned lines of human activity running from savagery to civilization (he later added "enlightenment" as a fourth stage). The
intention was, first, to draw correspondences across categories at each stage
of development. Secondly, since the "culture-grades" in fact represented stages
of mental growth, the array of inventions at each level would presumably
provide sufficient data for inferring the nature of mental operations at that
point. For instance, a brief summary of Powell's vision of savagery was as
follows: The savage has extremely rude tools and methods for obtaining food,
shelter, and clothing; kinship is vague, determined in the female line; he has
spoken language, gesture speech, and picture-writing, but no hieroglyphic
or alphabetic writing; he attributes animal characteristics to inanimate objects,
and deifies animals. Lack of conventional characters in writing, and inability
to perform simple arithmetic without counting on the fingers, provided firm
evidence for Powell's general conclusion: the savage mind had only "slightly

developed" capacities for "perception" (defined as instantaneous trains of inductive reasoning). But during barbarism the gradual accumulation of wealth, stimulated by improved arts of subsistence, led to an ability to perceive simple numerical relations. And the development of arithmetic issued, Powell theorized, in "a nicer discrimination of phenomena" generally and new systems for grouping them.[59] At the same time, as man domesticated animals the mysteries of animal life were dispelled and zootheism faded; conversely, with the growth of agriculture, meteorological factors became all important to man's survival, and he became increasingly physitheistic (worshipping natural phenomena). By such reasoning Powell developed a close causal chain across the fields of culture and mind, without any mysterious gaps, running from animal-like existence to civilized society. It was, McGee summarized, a "comprehensive anthropology, broad enough to touch every human ideal and passion and law and motive . . . ."[60]

Powell's views were well established by the early 1880s; subsequent statements merely elaborated them. From his geological studies of the seventies he had carried over a fertile idea: that phenomena must be analyzed in terms of the agency or process that produced them, not in terms of apparent similarities. This principle was the "keynote" of both his geology and his anthropology.[61] When he turned to primitive peoples, he saw that the multitude of human products "are best interpreted in terms of agency, the agency in this case being human thought."[62] Mental power was the driving force in human affairs. Fully appreciating the analogy, linguist Frederick Max Müller once referred to BAE anthropology as "intellectual geology."[63]

It is difficult to recapture the sense of empirical chaos in both geology and anthropology by the end of the 1870s in the United States. A long apprenticeship to European savants was ending, but the search for organizing principles was almost desperate. This partly accounts for the contemporary impact of Morgan and the feeling of revelation in Powell's discussions of mind as the agent in human evolution. The overarching principles and the confidence and direction that Powell instilled in the Bureau provided at least the appearance of scientific unity in a young, politically vulnerable organization. But as following chapters illustrate, the Bureau was a collection of individual personalities, not a disciplined school of believers; if the intellectual framework was formally adopted, it was not always privately absorbed. The freedom provided by Bureau salary and support was more determinative than Powell's evolutionary designs. Of course each case was distinct: James Mooney paid little attention to Powell's philosophical musings, while W J McGee carried them to an extreme degree that warped his own field observations and in the long run exposed fallacious assumptions. In every instance, though, Powell offered patronage and protection for anthropology that could not be found elsewhere in nineteenth-century America. Institutional support required a clear statement of purpose and a systematic, comprehensive framework for the science of man. Powell provided both.

Notes

1. Henry Adams, *The Education of Henry Adams: An Autobiography* (Boston, 1961), p. 232.
2. Herbert Spencer should be experienced firsthand. The account presented here is based chiefly on *First Principles* (New York, 1880 [reprinted from 5th London edition]).
3. J.W. Powell, "The Three Methods of Evolution," *Bulletin of the Philosophical Society of Washington* 6 (Washington, D.C., 1883): xxxiv.
4. J. W. Powell, *Truth and Error* (Chicago, 1898), p. 8; Powell, "Three Methods," p. xxxiv.
5. J.W. Powell, "Human Evolution," *TASW* 3 (Washington, D.C., 1883): 203.
6. Powell, "Three Methods," p. xxxiv.
7. J. W. Powell, "Darwin's Contributions of Philosophy," *Darwin Memorial Meeting of Biological Society of Washington* (Washington, D.C., 1882), pp. 60–70.
8. Ibid., pp. 67–69. For a similar discussion, see Powell, "Human Evolution," pp. 203–05. The classic contemporary statement on the use of hypothesis, respected by Powell and his Washington circle, was Thomas C. Chamberlin's "The Method of Multiple Working Hypotheses," *Science*, o.s. 15 (1890): 92–96; later expanded in *Journal of Geology* 5 (1897): 837–48.
9. Nathan Reingold, "American Indifference to Basic Research: A Reappraisal," in George H. Daniels, ed., *Nineteenth-Century American Science: A Reappraisal* (Evanston, Ill., 1972), p. 47.
10. Spencer emphasized that the two major manifestations of force—matter and motion—were received by human consciousness in terms of effort (muscle strain), reflecting his own early interest in psycho-physics (*First Principles*, pp. 159–61). Spencer was not always certain that the distinction between the two modes of force could be rigidly maintained, but "the forms of our experience" justified the separation (*First Principles*, pp. 162–64). Spencer revealed finer sensitivity to the subjectivity of human observation than his critic Powell. Indeed, awareness of cultural and personal idiosyncrasy was a powerful motivation in Spencer's attempt to build a philosophy that would transcend such considerations. His personal isolation and estrangement from society, to a great extent self-imposed, might be seen as part of Spencer's attempt at cultural transcendence.
11. Powell, *Truth and Error*, pp. 4–5.
12. Powell, "Three Methods," pp. xxviii–xxix.
13. If Spencer's notion of force was not recognizable to physicists, neither was Powell's concept of motion, nor other terms he lightly borrowed from the physical sciences. When confronted by physicists and pressured for explicit definitions, the Major came off badly. See, e.g., the series of exchanges in 1896

between Powell and "M" in *Science*, n.s. 3: 426–33, 513–14; 595–96; 631; 743–45. "M," apparently a physicist, gave up in exasperation.

14. Powell, "Three Methods," p. x1.

15. Smithsonian Institution Miscellaneous Collections 25 (Washington, D.C., 1883), p. 42.

16. Ibid., pp. 1i–1ii.

17. Powell, "Darwin's Contributions," p. 66.

18. Powell, "Human Evolution," pp. 207–08.

19. Powell's most complete statements on the nature of biological and human evolution appear in "Three Methods" (1883), "Human Evolution" (1883), and "Competition as a Factor in Human Evolution" (*American Anthropologist*, o.s. 1 [Washington, D.C., 1888]: 297–321). The following discussion is based chiefly on "Competition," Powell's most vigorously anti-Spencerian statement of the period. The major themes can be found throughout Powell's writings in the 1880s.

20. Powell, "Competition," pp. 298–99.

21. Ibid., pp. 300, 304.

22. Ibid., pp. 300–01.

23. This discussion leaves aside the question to what extent Darwin was indebted to Malthus (as opposed to William Paley or Charles Lyell) in the development of his idea of struggle. After 1859 both Darwin and A. R. Wallace credited Malthus with the original insight into population pressures, and the Washington men of the 1880s saw that they must address Malthus. See Loren Eiseley, *Darwin's Century: Evolution and the Men Who Discovered It* (Garden City, 1958), pp. 178–82.

    The Anthropological Society of Washington was a hot-bed of anti-Malthusian and anti-Spencerian forces, led by Powell, Lester Frank Ward, and James C. Welling. Here Ward first tried out chapters of his *Dynamic Sociology* amid general agreement that Spencerian evolution amounted to "a green sickness or mental chlorosis." (*TASW*, meeting of 9 May 1882, p. 13. See also Welling's "The Turning Point of Modern Sociological Science" and discussion, ibid., 7 November 1882, pp. 15–33; and his "The Law of Malthus Inductively Investigated," 1 February 1887, after which Powell repeated his conviction that "Population has hitherto been limited through ignorance and injustice.") At the ASW meeting of 21 December 1886, geologist Clarence Dutton presented a Malthusian analysis of Henry George's *Progress and Poverty* and was sharply attacked by Ward.

24. Wallace Stegner, *Beyond the Hundredth Meridian: John Wesley Powell and the Second Opening of the West* (Boston, 1954), pp. 8–21.

25. Ibid., pp. 202–38, 294–350.

26. Powell, "Competition," pp. 301–02.

27. Ibid., pp. 302–03.

28. Powell sometimes used the term "human arts" synonymously with "activities" and "inventions."

29. Powell, "Competition," p. 308.

30. The Patent Office was well represented in the ASW membership, and several papers focused on man's material inventions.

31. Powell, "Competition," p. 53. It is impossible to say if the Washington scientists took seriously this inverse correlation between biological and mental progeny. Two points are certain, however: the widely held fascination and admiration for invention, and the growing concern over low production among the "Aryan stock." In this context Powell's explanation, backed by Spencer's earlier statements, was plausible and flattering.

32. Quoted in "John Wesley Powell Commemorative Meeting," *Proceedings of Washington Academy of Sciences* 5 (1903): 116.

33. J. W. Powell, "From Savagery to Barbarism," *TASW* 3 (Washington, D.C., 1885): 193.

34. Ibid., pp. 193–94.

35. Powell to Lewis Henry Morgan, 23 May 1877; as quoted in Virginia Noelke, "The Origin and Early History of the Bureau of American Ethnology, 1879–1910," Ph.D. diss. (University of Texas at Austin, 1974), p. 52.

36. George W. Stocking, Jr., "Some Problems in the Understanding of Nineteenth Century Evolutionism," in Regna D. Darnell, *Readings in the History of Anthropology* (New York, 1973), pp. 420–23; L. H. Morgan, *Ancient Society: or Researches in the Lines of Human Progress from Savagery through Barbarism to Civilization*, ed. Eleanor Burke Leacock (Cleveland, 1963), p. IViii.

37. Morgan, *Ancient Society*, p. IIxvi.

38. Ibid., p. 311.

39. Ibid., p. IViii. Emphasis added.

40. Ibid., p. 563.

41. Quoted in Carl Resek, *Lewis Henry Morgan: American Scholar* (Chicago, 1960), pp. 136–37.

42. Morgan, *Ancient Society*, p. 19.

43. The preceding summary is based on Resek, *Lewis Henry Morgan*, pp. 137–40.

44. Ibid., pp. 144–45.

45. Morgan, *Ancient Society*, p. 351.

46. Ibid., pp. 561–62.

47. J. W. Powell, "Sketch of Lewis H. Morgan," *Popular Science Monthly* (November 1880), pp. 120–21.

48. Ibid., p. 121.

49. Quoted in Resek, *Lewis Henry Morgan*, p. 143.

50. Morgan, *Ancient Society*, p. 563.

51. Powell, "Savagery to Barbarism," p. 184.

52. BAE, *AR for 1881*, p. iii; Powell, "Savagery to Barbarism," pp. 175–76. The emphasis on viewing objects or phenomena in relation to others became an obsessive concern in Powell's later philosophical ruminations; in his eyes one of the most important lessons of his philosophy of science was the insistence that true understanding of phenomena lay in seeing their relations to others. In *Truth and Error* he expressed the idea in terms of physics—motion, speed, position—but it originally grew from his early disenchantment with biological taxonomies. He was not consistent regarding the number of categories, usually but not always referring to five areas of human "activities" or "humanities."

53. Powell, "Savagery to Barbarism," p. 174.

54. Quoted in "Powell Commemorative Meeting," p. 120.
55. BAE, *AR for 1894*, p. xviii.
56. Powell's collections, in the U.S. National Museum, have been examined in Don D. Fowler and John Matley, "Material Culture of the Numa: The Powell Collection, 1868-1876," Smithsonian Contributions to Anthropology (Washington, D.C., 1975).
57. Don D. Fowler and Catherine S. Fowler, "Anthropology of the Numa: John Wesley Powell's Manuscripts on the Numic Peoples of Western North America, 1868–1880," Smithsonian Contributions to Anthropology 14 (Washington, D.C., 1971): 17, 19.
58. See, for instance, the first chapter of *Truth and Error*.
59. Powell, "Savagery to Barbarism," pp. 190–91.
60. Quoted in "Powell Commemorative Meeting," p. 121.
61. Ibid.
62. Ibid., p. 122.
63. *Journal of the Royal Anthropological Institute* 21 (1891–92): 211.

The BAE insignia, designed by W. H. Holmes in 1879,
showing cliff dwelling, pictographs, and cloud-and-rain symbol in the sky.

VI

Toward an Anthropological Survey: The Early Years of the BAE, 1879–1893

Inequality was an inescapable social fact in post-Civil War America. The discovery of defeated, impoverished, excluded multitudes, immigrant or aboriginal, within an increasingly rigid, differentially prosperous class society came as shock to a nation that still held to a creed of open opportunity. For most, the answer lay where it always had, in exhortation to self-mastery—from the novels of Horatio Alger to the Dawes Act of 1887—even as this steadily faded as a realistic option for masses of people. For some concerned middle-class Americans, however, the experiences of war and the disorganized postwar condition of the country, North and South, gave additional impetus to systematic, institutional study and treatment of social problems. The embryonic forms of political science, economics, and sociology that emerged in these decades came partially as response to concern over the dispossessed. They were at once a political threat, an economic failure, and a moral disgrace.[1]

Perhaps because anthropology arrived late to academic respectability, its history has seemed unique and complex among the early social sciences.[2] But study of the North American Indian shared with political economy and sociology a common source in both the recognition of less fortunate, possibly doomed peoples, and interest in their political and moral meaning for the nation. Language is indicative in such matters. Arguing in 1862 to establish the Massachusetts State Board of Charities for the care of Irish-American poor, Samuel Gridley Howe set forth the alternatives: "We have here this foreign element among us; we cannot get rid of it if we would; and we should strive to fuse it into our common nationality as fast as possible. We strengthen our state by homogeneity; we weaken it by the contrary course."[3] Howe expressed the dawning awareness of ethnic heterogeneity and social and economic inequality that not only spurred the growth of the social sciences as promising academic disciplines, but underlay the drive for scientific understanding of the American Indian as a domestic social problem as well. Lot M. Morrill, Republican senator from Maine, reminded his colleagues in 1867 that "we have come to this point in the history of the country that there is no place beyond population to which you can remove the Indian . . . and the precise question [now] is, will you exterminate him, or will you fix an abiding place for him?"[4] Seven years later, reporting to Congress on the destitution of the Indians of the Colorado and Utah territories, John Wesley Powell employed strikingly similar terms: "There is now no great uninhabited and unknown region to which the Indian can be sent. He is among us, and we must either protect him or destroy him."[5]

Between 1860 and 1890, American demography and identity embraced the entire continent. As a consequence, in these years the Indian ceased being a subject of foreign policy and became a focus of domestic concern for the United States. The gradual shift of responsibility for Indian affairs from the War Department to the Department of Interior at once symbolized and institutionalized this critical alteration in perception. At the same time, one senses, observers and policy-makers of Powell's generation suffered a loss of alternatives as the immense industrial might of American civilization proceeded westward. The phrases of Howe, Morrill, and Powell were echoed endlessly in public statements of the postwar decades, but they amounted to a litany of limited options. In the aftermath of the slavery controversy and the distractions of war, it seems, the Indian question had finally been reduced to a bare choice: civilization or extermination.[6] These were the polar points of a debate carried forward with all the rigid clarity of Victorian certainty.

The mobilization for war and the permanently altered political balance in Washington of the 1860s released irresistible dynamics of expansive economic power that flowed through the following years. These unchallenged forces determined the deep currents of American history for the rest of the century. For the Indian cultures of the trans-Mississippi West, the result was final, massive tragedy; but it was tragic for others, too. Strong military presence and territorial scientific explorations in the West during the seventies served to provide the necessary preconditions for settlement and exploitation: familiarity with the land and a measure of peace and security. To be sure, the men who, like William Henry Holmes, served under Wheeler, King, Hayden, and Powell in the Survey years breathed deeply the invigorating airs of freedom and power, certain that "they held under their hammers a thousand miles of mineral country with all its riddles to solve, and its stores of possible wealth to mark. They felt the future in their hands."[7] But the future lay in other hands, as Powell subsequently discovered in the fights over his Irrigation Survey. Scientific pathfinders like Powell achieved the dubious stature of the explorer and pioneer. Latter-day Leatherstockings, they were themselves doomed to pass away before the destructive progress they heralded, enjoying only an ephemeral heroism.

By the last third of the nineteenth century, the basic directions of American growth were no longer open to question, and they spelled destruction for aboriginal cultures. Social evolutionism was one way of dealing with discrete, unequal human fates. Evolutionary modes of thought imbued the economically inevitable with a veneer of moral grace as Americans turned to science to assure the rightness and acceptance of current trends. Understandably, identity as a scientist in Victorian America provided not only desirable status but the illusion of individual power to shape human affairs. The fascination with science and the scientist may be seen, in fact, as an important part of an effort to discover motivation and cause other than economics to justify the vulgar prosperity and hidden misery of American society: if the transcendent Yankee was still alive in Gilded Age America, then the task of the social scientists was to uncover proof of his existence. This need was as old as the Puritan settlements; only the language was new.

The choice between extermination and civilization of the Indian was, from this viewpoint, merely one outgrowth of a driven, unilinear society. It was of course a choice only for the White man—the Indian no longer enjoyed choice—between barbaric power and various milder forms of domination. That is precisely the point: the parameters were established and unalterable after the Civil War, leaving only issues of style and procedure open to discussion. Powell's Bureau of American Ethnology was originally founded to address such questions.

In March 1879, Congress passed the civil sundry bill for the next year, which consolidated the Wheeler, Hayden, King, and Powell surveys into the United States Geological Survey. As a result of Powell's personal lobbying, and almost as an afterthought, the bill also established the Bureau of American Ethnology (BAE), with an initial appropriation of $20,000 "for completing and preparing for publication the *Contributions to North American Ethnology*, under the Smithsonian Institution."[8] The BAE was Powell's personal creation, the culmination of his experiences in science, politics, and exploration during the 1870s; it emerged from the Survey tradition and in every important respect continued the patterns of structure, procedure, and purpose of the Survey years. The BAE was to be a permanent anthropological survey.

The roots of the Bureau lay in the seventies, when Powell did his only extended anthropological fieldwork, gradually realized the need for a government-sponsored bureau for anthropology, and formulated the general research plans that dominated the BAE until his death in 1902. The story of Powell's early exploits in geology has been told from various perspectives; it is sufficient here merely to present the background relevant to the Bureau and to clarify Powell's arguments for its existence.[9]

In 1870, following his successful first descent of the Colorado, Powell's Geographical and Topographical Survey of the Colorado River of the West and its Tributaries was commissioned with an appropriation of $12,000. A clerical error may have sent the Survey to the Smithsonian rather than the Interior Department, but Powell worked well with Joseph Henry, as he acknowledged in the first volume of *Contributions to North American Ethnology:*

> For the last ten years I have habitually laid before Professor Henry all
> of my scientific work, and have during that time received the benefit
> of his judgment on these matters, and to a great extent I am indebted
> to him for advice, encouragement, and influence.[10]

In 1874 Powell's survey, now renamed the Geographical and Geological
Survey of the Rocky Mountain Region, went back to the Interior Department,
where it remained until 1879. During these years Powell was deeply involved
in geology, but his personal interests shifted steadily to anthropology, and
the Rocky Mountain Survey began to gather together the corps that would
constitute the original BAE. Powell had time for only sporadic work among
the Numa, but even when he could not go to the field, as in 1876, he worked
on materials in Washington. At one point he brought Richard Komas, a
Northern Ute, to attend school at Lincoln University in Pennslyvania, and
employed him as a clerk in the Washington office.[11]

Between 1873 and 1878 Powell developed his essential argument for a
government-supported scientific bureau of anthropology. In 1873 he was appointed Special Commissioner of Indian Affairs to investigate the condition
of the Numic peoples of the Great Basin territory.[12] On arrival in Salt Lake
City he heard rumors of an impending Indian uprising but soon discovered
that the Indians were far more terrified than the White settlers. Whites had
spoiled former hunting areas and occupied all the best land, forcing the
Indians to scatter into small groups and eke out subsistence through nut and
berry gathering, root digging, and begging. The settlers had nothing to
anticipate but annoyance from such demoralized creatures, Powell concluded:
"Nothing then remains but to remove them from the country, or let them
stay in their present condition, to be finally extinguished by want, loathsome
disease, and the dissent consequent upon incessant conflict with white men."[13]

It was an old story, repeated with each wave of settlement westward; George
Gibbs had experienced similar, sad progress in the Northwest in the 1850s.
But in the canyon country there was so little arable land in the first place,
and already so many Whites, that the Indians' situation was critical. Powell
recommended sending them away to established reservations, totaling 10,000
square miles, of which "only a small portion . . . is fit for agricultural
purposes, much of it being sandy desert and mountain wastes." The Numa
would relinquish in exchange 410,000 square miles of homeland.[14]

The trade was worth it, Powell thought, if the reservation arrangements
were handled in the proper spirit. He reported that the Indians fully appreciated the hopelessness of their situation and desired only the necessary tools,
training, and cattle to become self-sufficient farmers. At the same time that
he banished the Numa to already crowded reservations of sand and rock,
Powell clung to past dreams and made careful recommendations for their

education to civilization. His "Suggestions on the Management of these Reservations" expressed a sympathetic but firm attitude toward childlike folk. Above all the Indians must be taught self-sufficiency and work, receiving goods only in compensation for labor. Powell advised giving fabrics rather than ready-made clothing and teaching the women to sew; discouraging nomadic behavior by providing houses rather than tents; and giving each family a cow as a first personal possession, for "as soon as an Indian acquires property, he more thoroughly appreciates the rights of property, and becomes an advocate of law and order."[15]

Powell's concern was sincere. He gave close attention to reservation conditions because he viewed them as the only hope for Indian survival in the White world. Transition to agrarianism seemed the sole alternative to total dependence on government goods, once the environmental base of old patterns was gone. But when he turned to the central question of inquiry: "What division of the roaming tribes do their linguistic and other affinities dictate?" Powell had to admit ignorance.[16] The names by which tribes were known to Whites were not the same as those used by tribes for each other, and they gave no indication of historical relationships. The point was highly practical, for if hostile tribes were settled together they would merely fight and scatter again, at great expense to the government. Efficiency and humaneness demanded a system based on intelligence and scientific knowledge.

The bitter Indian wars of the mid-seventies confirmed Powell's fears. At the same time, the appearance of Lewis Henry Morgan's *Ancient Society* in 1877 gave both renewed hope and a usable framework for a scientific ethnology. In his 1878 report to the Secretary of the Interior, Powell expressed a new sense of urgency. The rapid destruction of the North American aboriginal population meant that habits, customs, and languages were disappearing at an alarming rate. "In a few years," he warned, "it will be impossible to study our North American Indians in their primitive condition, except from recorded history." He urged "utmost vigor."[17] Drawing from Morgan's scheme, Powell lectured on the attributes of savage society, focusing on the distinction between communal and private property. The personal rights of property recognized in civilization, he instructed the politicians, were "intensely obnoxious" to the Indian, who saw them as an evil for which the White would eventually be punished by the gods. The point was simple: savagery was a distinct stage of social development, with its own complete system of institutions, customs, and beliefs. The studies of the 1870s had already revealed the "fundamental fact" that the aboriginal peoples of America, while organized in distinct groups, shared a common cultural stage, "so that the tribes of any district can not be successfully studied without observation among the tribes of other districts . . ." The complex of savagery had to be understood and overthrown before one could introduce civilized notions and habits. In summary, Powell urged, we must either deal with the Indian as he is, looking to the slow but irresistible influence of civilization . . . to effect a change, or we must reduce him to abject slavery. The attempt to transform a savage into a civilized man by a law, a policy, an administration, or a great conversion . . . in a few months or in a few years, is an impossibility clearly appreciated by scientific ethnologists who understand the institutions and social conditions of the Indians.[18]

Powell's report of 1878 presented the logic of the early BAE. In the first place, Morgan had demonstrated that the American Indian must be understood not as a racial category but as a savage stage of human culture. Understanding of the Indian thus required total comprehension of savagery, which could only be accomplished through centralized, systematic study of aboriginal populations. At the same time, however, Powell aimed at a second, distinct goal: tracing of historical migrations and contacts between tribes and stocks. Thus at the founding Powell blended the historical and classificatory orientations that had coexisted for decades within American anthropology. He thereby built into the Bureau a dichotomy of purpose that would both enrich and plague its operations for the rest of the century.

Furthermore, to the politicians Powell stressed the potential utility of anthropology:

In pursuing these ethnographic investigations [he reported in 1878] it has been the endeavor as far as possible to produce results that would be of practical value in the administration of Indian affairs, and for this purpose especial attention has been paid to vital statistics, to the discovery of linguistic affinities, the progress made by the Indians toward civilization, and the causes and remedies for the inevitable conflict that arises from the spread of civilization over a region previously inhabited by savages. I may be allowed to express the hope that our labors in this direction will not be void of such useful results.[19]

But he also emphasized that there were no panaceas in Indian policy; permanent solutions must await the scientists.[20] Not that Powell urged passivity. On the contrary, through the BAE and as director of the U. S. Geological Survey from 1881 to 1894, he fought two of the most powerful, complementary dynamics in American culture: unplanned settlement, with its destructive impact on Indian peoples and the natural environment; and well-intentioned but ignorant efforts to "save" the Indian through conversion to Christianity and civilization. He questioned both the ruinous expansion and the belief in quick solutions that only eased consciences. Powell revolted against a world of easy solutions. Man must act, he preached; he must take control, but only on the basis of full, final scientific knowledge.

Under the circumstances it was probably inevitable that when Powell announced his intention to "organize anthropologic research in America," the statement contained divergent purposes. On the one hand, he would vigorously pursue the search for historical connections and the mapping of aboriginal America as aids to informed policy. This more than any other single purpose was the focus of BAE activities until the publication of the Powell linguistic map and classification of 1891, when the survey impulse finally expired. From that point the Bureau began to lose direction and to drift. On the other hand, Powell intimated at the founding even more grandiose plans: nothing less than a complete science of man. Deeply influenced by Morgan's model and Spencer's comprehensive approach, Powell foresaw a central organization that would found a "New Ethnology" of final, positive knowledge to explain and justify the wide disparities in human conditions, past, present, and future. Science was still a deeply moral enterprise. In 1878 the Secretary of the Interior had announced that "The 'Indian frontier' has virtually disappeared."[11] A year later Powell's new Bureau began to explore the political and moral import of that event.

The founding of the BAE profoundly altered the context, force, and direction of nineteenth-century American anthropology, but the precise nature of those alterations has never been specified. After the Boasian "school" of cultural anthropology rose to dominance in the 1920s and '30s, Robert H. Lowie and others established their own professional and tribal identity in part by drawing a clear line between the amateur proponents of unilinear evolutionism of the late nineteenth century, and the wave of Boas-trained students that formed the profession of anthropology after the turn of the century. The division was presumed to be at once institutional, attitudinal, and theoretical; the break seemed complete. Recent studies, often employing the insights and terminology of Thomas Kuhn, still emphasize major institutional and intellectual paradigm changes from the Bureau to Boas, but with awareness that such metamorphoses are fuzzy, gradual, and partial. Indeed, the stress now lies on continuities.[22] In order to address the issue of the Bureau's status in the professionalization of anthropology, the question must be rephrased so as to place the institution in historical context: In what ways did the BAE mark the culmination of certain trends in nineteenth-century science, including anthropology? On the other hand, in what ways did Powell's organization, by intention or otherwise, foster patterns of research, communication, personal identity, or institutional growth that are recognizably "professional" in a modern sense? The final judgment here is that Powell's organization was root-and-branch a nineteenth-century institution—the product of conditions and assumptions of another age—and that to view it as an early form or precursor of modern professional social science ignores Powell's deeply held commitments to the contrary. Powell never intended to "professionalize" anthropology, though he did hope to organize and systematize research. Powell drew simultaneously on two anthropological traditions, one from the natural sciences, the other deriving from the broad realm of eighteenth- and early-nineteenth-century moral philosophy. The first of these—the natural-history exploring, surveying tradition that came to him through such men as Humboldt and Gibbs—dominated American natural science to the Civil War and reached its peak in the western territorial surveys of the seventies. The scientific premium of the survey lay on discovery and description. Within this tradition there was a further division between those who, like George Gibbs, stressed holistic understanding of a region, and those who spread their nets more widely but selectively, such as Edward Palmer, botanist and ethnologist. In other words, the tradition embraced a broad continuum: from areal concentration to expertise in a specific line of work. While local scientific societies sustained (as they still do) the tradition of holistic inquiry defined by locality, by the end of the century powerful economic and cultural forces were determining its demise. One signal of the trend on the national level was the emergence of the BAE from the territorially defined Powell Survey.

The survey tradition centered on the individual for initiative and execution. In fact the American mythology of the lone trailblazer probably found more correspondence with reality among naturalists than among, say, commercial entrepreneurs. But the limits of this structure became apparent with the swelling ambitions of men like Gibbs and Powell. For a time the Smithsonian of mid-century provided one institutional solution to men whose visions exceeded their personal powers: Joseph Henry's distribution of circular questionnaires brought information more systematically while stimulating new exertions among the growing circle of correspondents. The intention, and effect, was to increase rather than limit participation in a guided scientific endeavor. But circulars provided, it turned out, insufficient control over personal idiosyncrasy, and in retrospect the next developments seem obvious and inevitable: first, the personally led expedition with hand-picked men; following that, the permanent bureau of research filled with tested and trustworthy companions. The developments follow logically: frustration with unsystematic data led to increasingly elaborate circulars with detailed instructions; similarly, desire for personal influence in molding the scientific results created ever-more-rigid organizational structures. Finally, the sheer vastness of the undertakings induced a new appreciation of team effort.

But that is less than half the picture. Powell's commitments to individual freedom and autonomy warred constantly with the very structures he was creating. Here lay a deep paradox for Powell: system in science threatened to destroy individual genius. It was more generally the dilemma of a society that placed ever-greater value on efficiency and coordination in production, whether scientific or industrial—never mind the costs to the quality of the scientific (or industrial) experience. But Powell did mind, for like Joseph Henry he remembered and treasured his own scientific and spiritual awakening, and he wished the same for as many others as possible.

To Powell the individual was always prior to the organization, for only the individual perceived new needs and initiated new programs. Organizations, because they were no more than the extensions of the individual, were inherently limited. W J McGee best expressed this viewpoint in 1888 to Eugene W. Hilgard, an agricultural chemist. Agricultural geology, he predicted, would be the geology of the coming generation, but first the prophet of the science must arise and awake the people from torpor; until then, nothing could be expected from organized science. McGee reminded Hilgard that neither the state nor the federal surveys could "give inspiration or furnish brains to employees; the inspiration and the brain must precede the organization and give character to it; and the organization can only furnish means to ends already clearly perceived." It was necessary first to have "the genius of a born leader among thinking men" directed to clear goals.[23] In the Bureau this vision created loose arrangements in which individual personalities sometimes determined whole projects, and it led to accusations of poor planning. But the organized science of Powell and McGee was to be a conscious extension rather than a harnessing of nineteenth-century independence and individual effort.

It was not always perceived that way. The first generation of Americans to work in large, relatively impersonal structures (whether industrial, academic, or governmental) sometimes experienced severe problems of adjustment. The slow spiritual decay of the white-collar clerk world of Victorian America has yet to be examined by historians, though the Bartleby figures were legion by 1900. From the outside, such organizations appeared cold, unappreciative, and exclusive; from the inside, they could seem cold, unappreciative, and expropriative. Powell struggled for a balance between necessary bureaucracy and individual recognition and visibility, and he generally succeeded. For instance, both the BAE and his Geological Survey issued separate monograph series of lavishly illustrated papers by individuals. Additionally, the annual reports contained long monograph appendices, and the body of each report was organized around individual work. Administrators took care to outline the field and office work of each subordinate month by month. In the BAE reports it is sometimes possible to follow the monthly movements of individual personnel over stretches of years.

Still, Powell's structure of science was no simple democracy of discoverers. The legacy of Lewis Henry Morgan, which Powell self-consciously inherited, placed him clearly in the second anthropological tradition referred to above, one with very different implications for the purpose and structure of the science. Morgan's science of man, like that of contemporaries Herbert Spencer,

Edward B. Tylor, and Henry Maine, stood in the tradition of conjectural, reasoned histories of mankind, which had recent (though disrupted) roots among the French and Scottish moral philosophers of the eighteenth century. In contrast to the believer in the natural-science survey, the conjectural historian sought an all-embracing account of man's mental, social, and moral evolution based on comparative observations and organized in various series of stages. Where the naturalist/explorer emphasized descriptive taxonomy and (some of them) regional holism, the goal of the comparative method was boundless, overarching synthesis—universal laws of human development.

The nineteenth-century moral philosophers (including Morgan and Powell) who built grand conjectural structures of human development aimed in the end at a predictive science of man; they looked to the past mainly for clues to the future. The relevant point for present purposes is that in the scientific structure of this tradition, the generalizing savant stood apart from the mass of data-collectors, whose labors constituted only the essential first stage of science. The scientific enterprise was consequently divided into two classes of functions: the lower, preliminary work of exploration, observation, and collection; and the higher tasks of synthesis. Every man had a potential role as a scientist of some order, but some individuals were more complete scientists than others. When Otis T. Mason claimed that "every man, woman, and child" could be an anthropologist, he tacitly assumed a hierarchical, deferential community.

There were, in short, degrees of individual completeness in Bureau science. Furthermore, these degrees were determined not by depth of training in a specific field, but by character, integrity, and breadth of exposure across the sciences—precisely the subjective, loose criteria against which proponents of university training would do battle. "Worthy has been the work of specialists in the extension of knowledge, during the past half-century," McGee observed, "but nobler still have been the tasks of the fewer searchers who have been able to span two or more specialties, and to simplify knowledge by coordination."[24] To the extent that professionalism meant specialization, it was of secondary value. On his Colorado expeditions Powell had permitted his men to make their observations but reserved to himself responsibility for drawing the major conclusions.[25] Similarly, in the Bureau he established the general directions, entrusting the details to "selected persons skilled in their pursuits."[26] But the teamwork of the Bureau was not the cooperation of professional equals; while enjoying wide latitude in pace and choice of work, some men still worked for others. They did not entirely control their science.

Not that the ethnologists were discouraged from drawing their own conclusions. For the official record, at least, McGee noted that they "were always encouraged to seek relations and educe principles, and to publish under their own names such results of their work *as were not inconsistent* with those of other investigators; for it was recognized that research is best promoted by encouraging the investigator."[27] And Powell observed in 1890 that

> the ethnologists who, as authors, prepare the publications of the Bureau, personally gather the material for them in the field, supplementing this material by a study of all the connected literature and by a subsequent comparison of all ascertained facts. The continuance of the work for a number of years by the same zealous observers and students, who freely interchange their information and opinions, has resulted in their training with the acuteness of specialists . . .

But this was an unanticipated development for the director, and the results went "far beyond the expectations entertained when the Bureau was originally organized."[28] When the progress of research permitted the comparison and grouping of phenomena, Powell did the synthesizing, gradually using the materials of his staff as "building blocks in his synthetic history of mankind."[29] In part the practice reflected Powell's sense that the science of the Bureau must present a united front to Congress, as McGee intimated; he thus guarded against misreading of the monograph studies by politicians and the public. At the same time, though, he once explained to Samuel Langley that his staff members were "learners" whose papers "contribute[d] to the data and simpler principles" of anthropology but required elaboration to yield significant generalizations.[30]

The nature of individual scientific roles and team effort in the early Bureau is best illustrated by first reviewing the collaborative projects that formed the central focus of the 1880s, then examining the individual careers of some of Powell's colleagues. In 1879 Powell launched three group projects "of a generally practical or economic character":[31] a linguistic classification; a synonymy of tribal and stock names; and a history of treaty relations between the federal government and the Indian tribes. The treaty study, referred to as a "Historical Atlas of Indian Affairs," anticipated future questions over land titles in the western territories. It became the personal project of Charles C. Royce, a part-time staff member. Although Royce finished it (and left the Bureau) in 1885 and Powell promised its appearance "as rapidly as possible," the work lay untouched until 1895, when Cyrus Thomas brought it up to date. The authoritative *Indian Land Cessions in the United States* finally appeared in 1899.[32]

While the treaty study developed as an individual project, the synonymy and language classification were the products of many minds and hands. The synonymy arose from Powell's conviction that the first task in any science is to achieve consensus on terminology. His experience in the Great Basin had demonstrated the need to order all the names used historically for each tribe or language group, in order to clear the way for further study and reveal historical affinities. As he noted in the first BAE annual report, "to follow any tribe of Indians through post-Columbian times is a task of no little difficulty. Yet this portion of history is of importance, and the scholars of America have a great work before them."[33] In theory this step should precede new research, but as it turned out the synonymy work proceeded concurrently with other Bureau interests, in a decidedly subordinate position. Fresh field work always seemed more urgent.

Otis Mason had begun a synonymy around 1873 as a card catalog. "I could not take one step without it," he remembered. With the founding of the Bureau he offered it to Powell, who suggested that Mason continue it under his direction.[34] Mason refused; Powell then asked Garrick Mallery to keep the synonymy up to date and expand it, but Mallery was less than enthusiastic and soon returned to his studies of sign-language and pictography. Eventually, though, Powell got the entire staff involved in the work, which became enmeshed with individual projects and with Powell's main goal, the linguistic classification. At first, it seems, Powell thought that the confusion over tribal names had to be clarified for progress in any field: anthropology simply had to have a "code of nomenclature rules similar in scope to those prevailing among zoologists."[35] During the first years, however, Powell and Henry W. Henshaw gradually came to the opinion that a synonymy was itself impossible without prior division of North American tribes into linguistic stocks.[36] Until 1885, when they completed the preliminary classification, the synonymy was placed on a back burner.

Powell's problem was a classic dilemma in the history of science: categories are necessary simply to deal with data; but the categories themselves easily become sources of distortion because shaping and selecting shade so easily into warping. For a man as sensitive as Powell to the charge of violating the inductive process, the problem was acute, and his shifting search for a firm ground in ethnology was readily apparent in these years. In addition, his staff was somewhat recalcitrant to work on the synonymy. The first half dozen years of the new Bureau were a period of excitement and productivity for the staff, who were busily extending and deepening studies begun during the seventies.

The synonymy received a flurry of attention around 1886, due mainly to the arrival of James Mooney at the Bureau, and the completion of the preliminary classification. Since boyhood, Mooney had been running his personal BAE in Indiana, and he arrived in Washington with an advanced synonymy (as well as a treaty study and linguistic work). According to a recent biography of Mooney, "Henshaw and Mooney spent several weeks [in 1885] on Mooney's synonymy and regrouped the almost 2,500 tribal names into linguistic categories."[37] The result was their landmark "List of Linguistic Families of the Indian Tribes North of Mexico, with Provisional List of the Principal Tribal

Names and Synonyms," a fifty-five-page booklet that Powell printed and that remained the guide to BAE linguistic and synonymy work until 1891.

On the strength of the Mooney-Henshaw guide, Powell returned to the synonymy, instructing the staff to suspend individual work. He placed Henshaw in charge of what was already becoming a "vast and complicated undertaking."[38] Henshaw was to take the immensely complex tribes of the Northwest Coast and California; Albert S. Gatschet's attention was divided between the southeastern region and the Pueblo and Yuman peoples; James Owen Dorsey handled the Athapaskan stock, in addition to his specialties, Caddoan and Siouan; Garrick Mallery and James Mooney undertook the most complicated (in terms of historical literature and nomenclature), the Algonquian and Iroquoian; Walter J. Hoffman aided Powell with the Shoshonean; and Jeremiah Curtin worked mainly in California but helped all around.[39]

At the end of fiscal 1886 Powell estimated that work on half of the linguistic families was finished; but a year later he again dropped the synonymy and each man returned to private endeavors. Henshaw continued to help Powell with the linguistic map and classification that, the director now reminded his readers, "properly precedes and forms the basis of the volume on synonymy."[40] The brief flurry of the preceding year had apparently been a false start. Still, in 1888 J. Howard Gore, member of the Anthropological Society of Washington and friend of Powell, announced that the synonymy was "far advanced toward completion" and would reach a thousand pages.[41] In 1890 the director announced that Henshaw was engaged in a "final revision" of the synonymy, but developments further delayed its appearance.[42] At this point Henshaw's health failed. He was transferred to field work in California; in 1893 he obtained an indefinite leave of absence and moved to Hawaii.

Henshaw's departure left the synonymy dangling. But more than this, the project itself continued to change character, as reflected in the variety of names attached to it: Dictionary of Indian Tribes, Dictionary of Tribal Synonymy, Tribal Synonymy of the American Indians, and finally, in 1895, Cyclopedia of the American Indians. Powell confessed in 1894 that "the work is of such character as not soon to be completed, since each new investigation yields additional information."[43] That was precisely the chief dilemma of the Bureau's first twenty years: how to undertake exciting, fresh research and also achieve the final synthesis of definite knowledge that was the goal of Powell's science. Reviewing the history of the synonymy project in 1895, he recognized that the constant influx of new information from the field had permanently altered the nature of the project, so that "the synonymy proper diminished relatively, while the body of general information became greatly expanded." The work had become a "great cyclopedia."[44]

After 1893, Frederick Webb Hodge gradually assumed more control of the project, and between 1896 and 1901 he and Cyrus Thomas devoted their attention to it, aided occasionally by others. Thomas, fresh from work on Royce's *Land Cessions*, pursued the assignment vigorously, finishing the Algonquian and Siouan stocks. But in 1901 Langley transferred Hodge to the Smithsonian, Thomas returned to his Mayan calendar studies, and James Mooney reluctantly inherited the synonymy.[45] It still lay in his file drawers when Powell died.

In the last years Langley repeatedly urged Powell and McGee to make haste with the Cyclopedia in order to mollify congressional critics. After Powell's death, Langley took tight control of the Bureau through Holmes, and he pushed the project, now finally renamed *The Handbook of American Indians North of Mexico*, at the expense of Bureau field research. Hodge became general editor of the greatly expanded work that included, in addition to synonymies, essays on every aspect of anthropological science and Indian life. He moved back to the Bureau, marshaled the entire staff, and hired outsiders to contribute essays. The work was largely finished by 1905 and began to appear in 1907, one year after Langley's death.

"What happened to it was what happened to the Bureau in other respects: men died, that was the chief difficulty," McGee said of the synonymy in 1903. Henshaw left; Dorsey, Pilling, Mallery, and Hoffman died; Mooney's Kiowa work was too important to suspend; and Langley distracted Hodge with other duties.[46] But the fate of the synonymy owed more to deep-running dichotomies of purpose and less to individual careers than McGee indicated. Virtually every annual report of the BAE between 1880 and 1900 began by explaining that individual researches were constantly interrupted by the higher demands of the collaborative projects, and year after year Powell promised the Synonymy or Cyclopedia to Congress and the public. But with the exception of the 1886–87 period, the project never received concentrated effort. Increasingly it came to be seen as a hindrance to individual research.

The linguistic map and classification of 1891, which fulfilled a vision shared by Jefferson, Gallatin, and Gibbs, proved to be the single most lasting and influential contribution of the early Bureau to American anthropology. From the beginning, linguistics was the heart of Powell's "New Ethnology," his clearest window into the mind of primitive man. And yet his emphasis on language is initially puzzling, given his background in geology and natural history and his own mediocre linguistic abilities. It was Joseph Henry who first suggested Indian studies to Powell as a proper field of inquiry, but the inspiration behind his work probably came from Gibbs and William Dwight Whitney. Gibbs, as we have seen, envisioned a continental map and took important steps in that direction by collecting hundreds of vocabularies.[47] Whitney's influence on Powell was subtler but perhaps stronger.

"Of the different attempts between the years 1860 and 1870, which *for the first time* began to extract from the mass of results accumulated by comparative grammar some generalizations about language, all were frustrated or without general value, except that of Whitney. . . ."[48] In these words Ferdinande de Saussure in 1909 recalled the powerful impact of Whitney on the transatlantic linguistic community of the latter nineteenth century. The power derived from Whitney's insistence, in his works on general linguistics *Language and the Study of Language* (1867) and *Life and Growth of Language* (1875), that language must be studied as a natural phenomenon obeying traceable laws, not as a semi-divine gift, and that it is deeply embedded in human institutions. He treated linguistics as a "cultural fact."[49] But the scientific analog that Whitney most frequently employed to describe linguistic change and growth was the same one that so deeply affected Powell's ethnology: uniformitarian geology.

> There is no way of investigating the first hidden steps of any continuous historical process, except by carefully studying the later recorded steps, and cautiously applying the analogies thence deduced. So the geologist studies the forces which are now altering by slow degrees the form and aspect of the earth's crust, wearing down the rocks here, depositing beds of sand and pebbles there, pouring out floods of lava over certain regions, raising or lowering the line of coast along certain seas; and he applies the results of his observations with confidence to the explanation of phenomena dating from a time to which men's imaginations, even, can hardly reach. The legitimacy of the analogical reasoning is not less undeniable in the one case than in the other.[50]

Whitney demonstrated the possibility of a humanistic study that was at once a moral and historical science. Indeed, his great appeal as a scientist, for Powell as for others, lay in his pervasive developmental historicism. For Whitney, Michael Silverstein has written, "explanation must be in terms of how the particular items get there, that is, in terms of how they arise, spread, and become productive, and run their course to obsolescence and atavism. Furthermore, this historical explanation deals with change that is gradual and regular; it is free from catastrophes, such as the floods and crumbling towers invoked by defenders of Mosaic chronology."[51] From this perspective, Whitney's and Powell's visions of scientific purpose—to abolish mystery from the science of man—were identical.

The fact that Whitney's European contemporaries explicitly acknowledged his influence has led to the judgment that he found less appreciative reception in the United States.[52] It seems likely, however, that in a number of particulars and, more importantly, in a general confidence in linguistics as a reliable basis for anthropology, Powell was a clear disciple of Whitney. In his conviction that grammar illustrates a unilinear evolution to highly inflective forms, and in his initial assumption (later rejected) that the American Indian languages could be traced back to a common ancestor, Powell could find authority in Whitney. Powell relied on lexical rather than grammatical data for his classification because grammar, Whitney taught, was partly adventitious, partly a phenomenon and index of stages of growth. Powell introduced the map and classification in words that showed his debt to Whitney:

> Grammatic stucture is but a phase or accident of growth, and not a primordial element of language. The roots of a language are its most permanent characteristics, and while the words which are formed from them may change so as to obscure their elements or in some cases even to lose them, it seems that they are never lost from all, but can be recovered in large part. The grammatic structure or plan of a language is forever changing, and in this respect the language may become entirely transformed.[53]

During the seventies both Henry and Powell looked to the Yale professor for aid and approval of their linguistic program. In early 1873, Henry spoke with Whitney and Trumbull "as to the charge of our ethnology now that George Gibbs has departed this life."[54] Powell was the apparent successor, but three more years passed before the Smithsonian Secretary, responding to Powell's initiative, turned over to him the Institution's collection of 668 North American language vocabularies.

Powell's first move was to revise Gibbs's "Instructions" of 1865, which had proved such a useful stimulus. With help from Whitney he enlarged the alphabet and vocabulary list by adding phrases and simple sentences to demonstrate grammatical structure, as Gibbs had intended.[55] During the summer of 1877 Powell and Whitney corresponded about a general alphabet for Indian languages. Their relationship exposed both Powell's respect for academic linguistics and his sensitivity to the lessons of field experience. Like Gibbs, he was a man straddling two worlds. While bowing to Whitney's "superior judgment" in linguistic questions, Powell wrote that he was anxious to test the alphabet "by practical use this summer in my own hands" and to make changes "as experience suggests." He urged a simple alphabet for cheap printing and wide circulation among the "general literature of the country"; Whitney's proposals offered, he objected, "no general plan which can be easily learned and remembered" by field workers.[56] For his part, Whitney simply reminded Powell that "you have no good reason for regarding and treating me as an authority in these matters . . . questions of alphabetizing are questions of expediency and compromise."[57]

Powell's ambivalence toward Old World linguistics came through in his correspondence with Whitney. Following Schoolcraft and Gibbs, he saw that mythology and belief systems remained hidden without knowledge of the languages in which they are expressed.[58] But the study of language in America must differ somewhat in purpose and method from the work of Greek and Sanskrit scholars, Powell reasoned. While they might look admiringly at the symmetry and complexity of Old World tongues, the American linguist could never adopt such a posture. The modern anthropologist, Powell exclaimed in 1884, "no longer looks into antiquity for human perfection, but he looks into the future of the world's history for the establishment of universal justice . . ."—and, he might have added, for models of language. "So we may laud the ingenious grammatic devices of ancient languages, but who would make Greek the vernacular of civilization?"[59] Powell studied languages not for themselves but for what they revealed about man's mental growth, past and future.

Always the surveyor and mapper, Powell set out to organize the linguistic diversity of North America. For this purpose he required simple instructions and a corps of workers, not the complex instruments of academics. After Powell received the Smithsonian vocabularies in 1876, the Rocky Mountain Survey veered noticeably toward ethnology. The materials in Powell's charge were hopelessly unsystematic. Because "those engaged in the work needed constant direction and were frequently calling for explanations," the following year he issued the *Introduction to the Study of Indian Languages*, a manual for the field.[60] But he soon grew dissatisfied with the first edition because the alphabet, prepared by Whitney, was too complicated, the word lists were too short, and the instructions were unclear. In 1880 he issued a much bulkier edition, including his own alphabet, fifty pages of "hints and explanations," 150 pages of vocabulary lists organized in thirty schedules, and four Morgan kinship charts in the cover pocket. Powell had created a portable course in ethnology for the untutored but zealous traveler.

It is worth noting that in the second edition Powell arranged the vocabulary schedules according to his newly established categories of human "activities," in order to connect the language study with other aspects of culture. He hoped thereby to involve the collector more deeply with specific peoples so as to extract maximum meaning from the data. The ideal was not simply a smattering of significant words to establish affinities with other tribes, but greater depth:

> It has been the effort of the author to connect the study of language with the study of the other branches of anthropology, for a language is best understood when the habits, customs, institutions, philosophy—the subject-matter of thought embodied in the language are best known. The student of language should be a student of the people who speak the language; and to this end the book has been prepared . . .[61]

The 1880 *Introduction* thus struck two themes: extensive coverage and intensive knowledge. In phrases that echoed the mythology of the beckoning American frontier, Powell's scientific virgin land called to potential students: "The field of research is vast: the materials are abundant and easily collected; reward for scientific labor is prompt and generous."[62] The vast open spaces of anthropological science invited personal investment.

Between 1880 and 1885, on the basis of vocabulary materials gathered by predecessors, collaborators, and the BAE (mainly Dorsey and Gatschet), Powell and Henshaw gradually filled in the linguistic map of North America. Henshaw appeared as the author of the 1885 classification—substantially the same as the better-known 1891 publication, for which Powell assumed major credit and responsibility.[63] Because the classification was a long-term, co-operative effort, and because Powell did not publish evidence for linguistic connections, assigning specific responsibility for the map and stock groupings has been difficult.[64] Still, the general outline of operations is clear, and it suggests the nature of the inner dynamics of the early Bureau.

If there was a Bureau inner circle around Powell—perhaps equivalent to the "Great Basin Lunch Mess" over at the Geological Survey offices of the time[65]—it consisted of James Pilling, James Stevenson (until his death in 1888), Garrick Mallery, and Henry Henshaw. By contrast, James Owen Dorsey and Albert S. Gatschet never enjoyed the director's full esteem, though he valued their talents and integrity.[66] Gatschet in particular became the "laboring work-horse and philologist clerk for Powell and Henshaw," with little of his own to show for it.[67]

Henshaw was the central staff figure in both the classification and synonymy work. A veteran of the Wheeler (Army) Survey, on which he had worked with Harry C. Yarrow and others, Henshaw was an avid naturalist and ornithologist. Chronically weak health, which had prevented him from matriculating at Harvard as a young man, plagued him all his life—a life lived alone for eighty years. Henshaw recalled that "it was Major Powell's opinion that a biologic training was a prerequisite to a successful career in anthropology, and this opinion he held to the last."[68] Powell looked to him to establish a respectable scientific nomenclature for anthropology, and it was probably Henshaw who determined on borrowing from biology the law of priority as the organizing principle for Amerindian linguistics (beginning with Gallatin's 1836 *Synopsis of the Indian Tribes*).[69] (William H. Dall, a naturalist whose work appeared in the first volume of Powell's *Contributions to North American Ethnology*, may also have influenced Powell's model.) Powell ambiguously credited Henshaw with the "final form" of the classification, and his reliance may have been more general than appears. C. Hart Merriam, a close friend for much of Henshaw's life, claimed that Powell intended him to be the next director of the Bureau.[70] Whatever Powell's intentions, Henshaw's health declined precipitously in the early nineties, and W J McGee replaced him as Powell's administrative officer, amanuensis, and presumptive heir.

Dorsey and Gatschet did the field work, aided to some extent by Jeremiah Curtin in California. Contrary to his own advice in the 1880 *Introduction*, Powell often assigned his men to groups with whom they had no familiarity. To some extent this was inevitable, given the massive undertaking. But in

Henry Weatherbee Henshaw, who served as Powell's linguistic
coordinator until 1892.

one instance, at least, he rejected Gatschet's separation of two Oregon languages—the conclusion from a prolonged study in the region—on the basis of a short reconnaissance by Dorsey.[71] Despite his European linguistic training, Gatschet was considered an astute observer and collector, but little more. While he and Dorsey collected, Powell and Henshaw compared. In his reports the director credited the vocabulary gathering expeditions in detail but remained silent about his own methods and criteria. Both scientific roles were necessary, but the higher functions involved less accountability to the public or Congress.

The linguistic work exemplified the unusual combination of openness and exclusiveness, even secrecy, that marked BAE work. It also illustrated the extent to which Dorsey and Gatschet, and in various ways all the BAE ethnologists, were incomplete scientists. The development of a "professional" consciousness, in Washington and elsewhere, required the transformation of this pattern into the modern concept of the field anthropologist, competent through training to collect and analyze his own observations. This development could not occur within the institutional structures of government anthropology. In Washington in the 1880s, functions were parceled out among different men.

To the early Bureau Powell brought men whom he knew and trusted. The major figures in this core of BAE founders were James C. Pilling, James Owen Dorsey, Albert S. Gatschet, and Garrick Mallery. For each of them the Bureau presented opportunity to expand researches already in progress. These individual projects, along with Powell's attempts at larger joint efforts, shaped the original BAE.

Perhaps closest to Powell as friend and amanuensis was James Pilling. A patient, painstaking, thoroughly upright man, Pilling was by all accounts admirable but not lovable, pleasant but cold—an unexciting personality. Those who failed to appreciate the value of his services could easily detest his plodding, filing-system mentality. The brilliant Clarence King was one such: "Do you want to do Powell a favor?" he advised a colleague. "Poison Pilling."[72]

Pilling's personality and methods produced a prodigious amount of work, however. A native of Washington state, Pilling attended Gonzaga College and taught himself the commercially valuable art of stenography. At age twenty he was a stenographer for congressional committees and commissions, and in this way came eventually to join Powell's Rocky Mountain Survey in 1875. For nearly four years he was "almost continuously" among Indians, faithfully recording Powell's vocabularies and stories. The two men formed a bond, as Powell fondly recalled:

Through many of the years of active life James and I were associated, in the office and in the field. Field work led us into the wilderness of

James Pilling, faithful clerk to Powell, in his library.

mountain and canyon, of forest and desert, away from the comforts and conveniences of civilization, where life itself was preserved by a constant struggle. In all this experience my boon companion never failed nor faltered, always doing more than his share in the struggle for existence and in the effort necessary to fill life with joy. He never rested from his labor when labor could be of value; he never lost courage, and courage was always in demand.[73]

Powell took care of his own, and he brought Pilling to the Bureau in 1879 as clerk and friend. When he succeeded Clarence King as director of the Geological Survey two years later, he eased the burden on BAE appropriations by moving Pilling, along with photographer Jack Hillers, executive officer James Stevenson, and himself, to the Survey payroll. Pilling became chief clerk of the Survey as well as clerk of the Bureau, retaining and expanding his bibliographical duties. These soon became all-consuming. His career project, begun in 1877, was nothing less than complete bibliographies of the literature on all the Indian languages of North America. If he did not know it in the beginning, Pilling soon realized that he could never complete such a massive task; in 1881 he wrote that "if I ever print my Bibliography I should like to insert a note telling why the work was never finished."[74]

Pilling persisted. Through the first decade of the Bureau, in tandem with the linguistic classification and the synonymy, Pilling's bibliographies grew steadily to thousands of titles. The meticulous file man received help from the entire Bureau staff and from interested individuals outside Washington who recognized the value of reference works.[75] The bibliographies remained Pilling's individual devotion, and he gave the last fifteen years of his life to them. He scoured the private and public libraries of the United States and Canada; when he went to Europe on personal matters, he spent most of his time in libraries and bookstores. In the process he established for the Bureau one of the finest ethnological libraries in the world.[76]

In 1885 Pilling sent out 100 copies of the 1,200-page *Proof-Sheets*, his preliminary bibliography, to collaborators for criticism and use.[77] But as new titles and information arrived almost daily, Pilling's work grew from a single volume to a series of large BAE *Bulletins*. The first linguistic stock completed was the Eskimo, which appeared as the Bureau's initial *Bulletin* in 1887. Eight more stock bibliographies had followed by Pilling's death in 1895.

After the death of his friend, Powell wrote somewhat ambiguously to Pilling's widow that the bibliographic work constituted a "monument to wisely directed labor."[78] Pilling's bibliographic labors indeed derived directly from Powell's larger purposes. The developing linguistic classification defined the categories of the bibliography, which progressed accordingly. More important, the history of Pilling's work typified the experience of the early Bureau. As Wallace Stegner has noted, despite the constant search and acquisition of new materials, "the aim was utter definitiveness, completion."[79]

The daily activities of the Bureau's office and field staff constantly frustrated the larger synthetic goals of Powell's anthropology. Originally envisioned as a definitive "pre-chore," a cornerstone of future research, Pilling's bibliographies emerged as a partial product. Pilling published only nine of fifty-eight language stocks, but they were the stocks with the largest, most scattered literature. A preparatory task grew into a major library research project and an unfinished but monumental personal accomplishment.

Pilling's drive to completeness also characterized the labors of another original member of Powell's staff, Colonel Garrick Mallery. A Pennsylvanian who traced his lineage back to the first decade of Puritan settlement, Mallery graduated from Yale in 1850, received a law degree from the University of Pennsylvania three years later, and at the onset of the Civil War had established a legal career in Philadelphia. In 1861, however, he abandoned the law to volunteer in the Union army. A year later he was severely wounded, captured, and exchanged; he returned to active duty in 1863. At the end of the war, Mallery accepted a commission in the regular army. After serving as secretary of state and adjutant general during the military occupation of Virginia, he worked for six years in the office of the chief signal officer, where he undertook meteorological researches. In 1876 he received command of Fort Rice (Dakota Territory), but his war wounds finally forced his retirement from the army in 1879.[80]

"Old habits of the Civil War left their mark of military drill on everyone who lived through it," Henry Adams perceived.[81] Major Powell's Bureau bore a few such marks. Among Washington circles of scientists and politicians who celebrated Civil War heroism and literate gentility, Mallery's "rugged manliness," educational and legal background, and conversational ease assured immediate and hearty acceptance. He seemed, in fact, the epitome of American Anglo-Saxon manhood: gallant soldier, broad scholar, man of science, genial companion, affectionate husband, staunch friend, and "high-bred gentleman," in the words of a lifelong friend.[82] As witty contributor to the Literary Society of Washington, president of the Philosophical Society of Washington, and BAE ethnologist, Mallery enjoyed great esteem in the capital until his death in 1894.

Mallery's interest in the North American Indians stemmed from his time in the Dakotas, where he found a "rude and interesting native picture record" that he analyzed as a primitive calendar. The following year he published "A Calendar of the Dakota Nation" as part of Ferdinand Hayden's survey of the territories.[83] It immediately attracted attention, and within two months Powell had obtained Mallery's transfer to the Rocky Mountain Survey. Mallery stayed with Powell for the rest of his life. When the founding of the Bureau coincided with his forced resignation from the military, the Colonel joined up with the Major.[84]

Colonel Garrick Mallery, lawyer, soldier, and stalwart scientist
of the BAE.

Over the next fifteen years, the Colonel, like Pilling, committed himself with rare devotion to a project that became an obsession: North American sign languages and picture-writing. And like the bibliographies and the synonymy, Mallery's pursuit became an uncompleted lifetime project because the data always outran the synthesis. But in the process Mallery, working through correspondents and his field researcher, Walter J. Hoffman, collected vast amounts of data on sign language, pictographs, and other forms of early Indian writing that would otherwise have disappeared unrecorded. His Bureau publications, lavishly illustrated with hundreds of color drawings, still remain a mine of information on phenomena that have since vanished.[85]

Between 1879 and 1894 Mallery worked steadily at his task. A preliminary goal was reached early with the publication of his *Introduction to the Study of Sign-Language* (1880), the third of Powell's proposed series of manuals for students and collaborators.[86] The same year, in accord with Powell's mode of operation, Mallery privately circulated to some correspondents a "Collection of Gesture Signs and Signals of the North American Indians, with some comparisons." These private and public stimuli produced a flood of data from across the country and overseas. Mallery immediately began synthesizing it into his *Sign-Language among the North American Indians for the first annual report.*[87] Although intended as tentative, *Sign-Language* was soon hailed as definitive. He then turned his attention to his original interest, pictographs; the results were another "preliminary paper" on pictographs (1886), and ultimately the 800-page *Picture-writing* opus of 1893.

Mallery carried forward the pattern of science-by-correspondence that Henry had found appropriate to the early Smithsonian, and Powell judged his methods and results as the best example of the fundamental plan behind the Bureau.[88] With the exceptions of two field trips in the late 1880s, Mallery remained an office worker, an editor of raw data. As Powell remarked of his work on pictography, the "primary authors" were unknown aborigines, for whom Mallery served as "discoverer, compiler, and editor."[89]

Within the Bureau framework, Mallery's purpose was clear: to discover the laws regulating early stages of linguistic evolution.[90] Gesturing and pictography, Powell believed, represented the typically "vague and indefinite, or chaotic" but unceasing efforts of primitive men to communicate through "thought symbols." The Indians of North America, "still groping blindly and widely for definite methods" at the time of White contact, illustrated among themselves the modes of picture-writing.[91] Mallery's efforts were expected to shed light on this early mental development.

The educated, stalwart Army colonel provided Powell with an unimpeachable investigator, a man of credentials in an area that invited speculation. Some investigators, Powell reminded his readers, had imagined "in the nebulous light of hieroglyphic symbols" connections between the Indians and other races of men, or had seen mysterious religious meanings in the aboriginal pictographs. Mallery had introduced a refreshingly objective and practical view:

> There was in him no bias toward a mystic interpretation, or any pre-determination to discover an occult significance in pictographs. . . . The probability appeared, from his actual experience, that the interpretation was a simple and direct, not a mysterious and involved process . . .[92]

While fully appreciating the poetic and imaginative features of primitive pictography, Mallery avoided "mystic symbolism" as a canon of interpretation; he presented facts "simply as facts."[93] Thus Powell celebrated with Mallery the new empirical age of post-Civil War America. Mallery turned to poetry himself to describe the new order:

> But now the cosmologic drama's o'er,
> Mithra's a myth, Great Pan pans out no more.
> Our world gives little scope to doctrine mystic—
> 'Tis wary, doubting, stern, and realistic;
> Takes every axiom on strict probation,
> And calls for propter hoc and demonstration.[94]

Mallery drew from his empirical rigor (if not from his poetry) an optimistic vision of human history. Herbert Spencer had argued that human militancy had paralyzed men with fear; gestures of greeting were signals of defense-lessness and terror. Reviewing collaborators' reports, Mallery answered that such salutations are in fact exchanged with greater frequency as civilization advances, "thus denoting a mutual sentiment or sympathy." "The history of salutations," he concluded, "illustrates the transition from egoism to altruism."[95]

In his vice-presidential address to the American Association for the Advancement of Science in 1889, the ethnologist turned to the implications of his work for the future of the American Indian. "Israelite and Indian: A Parallel in Planes of Culture" was an extended argument for psychic unity and against transoceanic contact. He went on to argue, as Powell had been reiterating for a decade, that study of the Indian was fruitless as long as anthropologists viewed the aborigines as a racial division of man rather than a stage of development. The Indians were not a people uniquely resistant to civilization, nor were they more naturalistic or spiritualistic than any people in their culture status. With "reasonable opportunities" the Indian would progress to civilization and Christianity.[96] The ineluctable trend to human unity would embrace all people, and "both Israelite and Indian will be lost in the homogeneous ocean which mankind seems destined to swell."[97]

In the obituary of his staunch friend, Powell especially noted his "scholarly taste" and "strong power of philosophic comparison."[98] The joining of the aesthetic and the intellectual reveals much about the wide respect that Mallery enjoyed. His scientific credentials lay in his Army virility, good taste and manners, elegant writing style, dedication to work, and adherence to a general evolutionary persuasion. A genial and witty raconteur, Mallery was a favorite at the gentlemanly literary and scientific societies of the capital. Because he embodied the ideal combination of soldier-scientist-litterateur, he lent important prestige to Powell's young anthropological research center at a time when the credibility of the science still lay in such general attributes. At Mallery's death in 1894 (within a few months of Pilling's and Dorsey's), Major Powell felt a deep personal and institutional loss.

Powell's feeling of loss is understandable, for the philosophical affinity between the two men was abundantly clear. Mallery, though, possessed a sensitive intelligence that was confined by his manners, moralisms, and philosophical categories. Powell shared the evolutionary worldview, and until his final years at least, it empowered him to great institutional and intellectual feats. But the structures that invigorate some men stifle others, and with Mallery there is a distinct sense of lost possibility. For example, in 1877 he delivered a paper before the Philosophical Society of Washington in which he convincingly refuted wishful assertions that North American Indians had worshipped a single God or Great Spirit. Mallery explained:

Doubtless in councils and other intercourse with Christians, Indian speakers employed the words *Manito, Taku Wakan,* and the like, in a sense acceptable to the known prejudices of their interlocuters, but that was through courtesy and policy, much as the strictest Protestant would once have found it convenient if not necessary, when at Rome, to speak respectfully to the Pope. The adoption of expressions as well as of ideas which were understood to be agreeable to or expected by the whites, is well illustrated in the use by western Indians of the terms "squaw" and "papoose," which are not in their languages, but are mere corruptions from the Algonkin. As all travelers insisted upon those words to signify woman and child, the tribes, as successively met, complied . . .[99]

Mallery's observations are commonsensical and yet astute, for he displays insight into patterns of accommodation and acculturation that was rare in his generation. But such insight came, could only come, in flashes, without elaboration and further pursuit. Similarly, the overriding conviction of human progress hid from him, perhaps mercifully, the tragic complexity behind his observations. But in those moments of insight lay the Colonel's true scientific, humanistic credentials.

William Turner advised Henry in 1851 that the only men suitably motivated to study the "mental idiosyncracies" of American Indians were the dedicated missionaries who spent long, arduous years at their posts.[100] The career of

James Owen Dorsey, a member of the Bureau from its founding until his death in 1895, demonstrated that the missionary spirit lived on, although attenuated and secularized, to the end of the century. If Pilling contributed the punctiliousness of the librarian, and Mallery the robust vigor of the Army man, the early Bureau found in Dorsey a sympathetic patience and a desire to understand in order eventually to save the Indian. Through all his immersion in the details of Indian linguistics and mythology, Dorsey always retained "in some measure his evangelical functions."[101] It was not an easy position to hold in the Bureau.

Born in Baltimore in 1848, Dorsey displayed a talent for languages even as a boy. He joined the Theological Seminary of Virginia in 1867 and became a deacon in the Episcopal church in 1871. Immediately Dorsey began missionary work among the Ponca Indians, a Siouan tribe of present-day Nebraska. After twenty-seven months he interrupted this work due to serious illness.[102]

When he left the Poncas in 1873, Dorsey was already speaking to the Indians without an interpreter and working on grammars and dictionaries of the Ponca language. Joseph Henry, an old family friend, aided and censored his work. Using a copy of Riggs's Dakota dictionary on loan from the Smithsonian, Dorsey examined the Indian tongues according to the categories of classical languages, carefully noting supposed similarities between Hebrew and Siouan tongues.[103] Since he was anxious to obtain Smithsonian support for publishing, he offered to send periodic accounts of his investigations and hoped for helpful suggestions from Henry's "philological collaborator." Others in the same line of work had only single informants, while he had 730 natives, Dorsey reminded one correspondent. Besides, other investigators operated from "improper motives."[104] However noble his motivations, Dorsey's early work, particularly the Hebrew connections, did not impress Smithsonian officials:

> But I would at the same time strongly advise to admit nothing but the bare materials without any kind of "comparisons" or would-be philological remarks. The work ought to be simple, clear, plain, and written in sober style. . . . Thus Mr. Dorsey will have to avoid in his work all sorts of digressions and everything else that savors of eccentricity and enthusiasm, especially those very crude and immature comparisons with Hebrew![105]

Dorsey returned eastward to a Maryland parish for five years in the midseventies, but neither his linguistic proficiency nor his mission was forgotten. When Powell began assembling his corps of ethnologists for the Rocky Mountain Survey in 1877, Henry recommended Dorsey. That year Powell engaged Dorsey to develop a grammar and dictionary of Ponca; in July 1878, Powell dispatched him to the Omaha reservation in eastern Nebraska for further field

Reverend James Owen Dorsey, linguist and ethnologist of the
Siouan peoples.

study. Dorsey stayed there nearly two years and returned as a member of the new Bureau.

Dorsey was hired as an expert on the Siouan languages and tribes, particularly the Omahas, Poncas, Quapaws, and Kansas. At the founding of the BAE, the Siouan family was known in greater detail than any other North American stock. The Bureau recognized eight Siouan languages, subdivided into twelve dialects. Of these, Dorsey devoted most of his attention to the four dialects he recognized in the language he called Cegiha: Ponca, Kansas, Osage, and Quapaw.

Dorsey's field experience among the Omahas and Poncas in 1871–73 and in 1878–80 provided the foundation for all his subsequent Siouan work; with only three exceptions he thereafter confined his work to Washington. In 1883 he traveled to Canada to investigate Tutelo, which Horatio Hale had recognized as a Siouan tongue; and to the Indian Territory to work with Quapaw speakers. Two years later, at Henshaw's insistence and very reluctantly, he undertook a four-month investigation of the linguistic groups of Oregon; and in 1892 he spent two months in Louisiana living with the last surviving speakers of Biloxi, which Gatschet had discovered as Siouan in 1887.[106]

Dorsey repeated the pattern of Powell and Mallery: intense early field work succeeded by an office career of collating and synthesizing, with only sporadic returns to the field. At times he struck a compromise of sorts by working with individual informants in Washington. This practice produced particularly fruitful results in 1887, when the Bureau hired George Bushotter, a Dakota who spoke Teton dialect, to record myths and legends. Over a six-month period Bushotter provided Dorsey with 258 manuscripts, as well as illustrative sketches, to which Dorsey added editorial notes and translations. The following year, John Bruyier, from the Cheyenne River Agency, worked on some of the Bushotter texts, demonstrating for Dorsey the differences between Teton among his people and the dialect of Bushotter's folk at the Pine Ridge and Lower Brulé reservations. In subsequent years Dorsey undertook similar informant work at his Washington office.[107]

Franz Boas once wrote that Dorsey's record of Ponca and Omaha literature, while severely limited, gave "deep insight into the mode of thought of the Indian," and he recommended Dorsey as a model, albeit an imperfect one, for linguistically based ethnography. In Boas's opinion, Dorsey largely ignored material culture and major aspects of ritual and social organization, but his work was still the best in 1906.[108] In actuality Dorsey did address many of these subjects. His publications included studies of dwellings, furniture, implements; migrations and war and mourning customs; kinship and marriage and social arrangements; as well as various collections of myths, stories, letters, dictionaries, and grammars. In his early work he even took notes on ethnobotany.

Dorsey always remained a student and active supporter of the interests of the peoples of the northern Plains. More than any other member of the original BAE, he resisted the strong surveying tendency by returning again and again to the languages, myths, rituals, and social arrangements of the Siouan peoples. He helped the Poncas write letters requesting improvements in reservation conditions, attended their councils, and personally wrote to the Commissioner of Indian Affairs on their behalf, all the while avidly attending to their language and social life. He observed sensitively and gathered his knowledge "without any force or artifice at all."[109]

This intimacy made possible a high standard in field method for the Bureau, and at least one novice, James Mooney, found a model in Dorsey's modest, sympathetic temperament.[110] Dorsey remarked acutely on the inconsistency of speakers of any language, noting that individuals change linguistic habits with age and that dialects are constantly in flux through contact. Thus, any grammar was an ideal, not a description of reality. In both his vocabulary work and grammar analysis, Dorsey resisted the imposition of Indo-European categories, insisting on the integrity of native systems.[111]

While he obediently adopted Morgan-Powell structures and terminology, Dorsey refused to theorize from his data, which as often as not contradicted Powell's expectations. Thus, Powell anticipated a process of differentiation in government functions among the Omaha; Dorsey's *Omaha Sociology* announced steady consolidation. As one historian has aptly concluded, "Dorsey's reports are an excellent example of how Powell's insistence on extensive field work by good observers did not function to prove Powell's theories, but instead provided information damaging to what the Director believed should be found."[112] Nonetheless, Powell managed to mold Dorsey's findings into appropriate shapes. At first Dorsey's investigations displeased the director, who ordered him to undertake a "special study" of anthropology—which meant reading Morgan's *Ancient Society*.[113] Although the "crude Hebraic comparisons" of his linguistics had long since disappeared, the former missionary was still inclined to see civilized notions of monotheism in primitive religions.[114] Once accommodated to the Morgan/Powell framework, though, Dorsey's empirical work yielded far-reaching conclusions for the director. When Dorsey's *Study of Siouan Cults* appeared in the 1890 report, Powell found "many important conclusions" standing "in the background" awaiting elucidation. Chief among them was confirmation of Powell's vision of primitive belief, in which supernatural powers are attributed to organic and inorganic objects. Dorsey had found that "it is safer to divide phenomena as they appear to the Indian mind into the human and superhuman, as many, if not most natural phenomena are mysterious to the Indian."[115] To Powell the iconoclastic lesson was clear. For three centuries, hasty observers had written of Indian belief in a single "Great Spirit." Taking this as a sign of

Albert Samuel Gatschet, Swiss-born linguist and student of
American Indian languages.

preparation for Christianity, generations of missionaries had sought to impose their God on it. Now the work of missionary Dorsey had finally exploded the myth: the savage mind knew no such concept.

While never a member of Powell's inner group, Dorsey was popular in the Bureau and was valued as an ethnologist and as a model of scientific method. From Powell's viewpoint he embodied the conflict between science and religion—an integral part of Powell's vision of mental evolution—in which empirical experience ultimately would override prejudice and superstition. His own career demonstrated the importance of prolonged, repeated, first-hand observations; perhaps the director viewed Dorsey's fieldwork as a kind of mental health cure on the Plains. Independent of untrustworthy interpreters, cautious, competent, Dorsey could present Indian beliefs with "unsurpassed fidelity."[116] He was a clear advance over deluded, pioneer missionary-ethnologists. As with Mallery, though, it is difficult to accept the contemporary Powellian evaluation of Dorsey. He did not embody conflict; rather, he combined deep human concern with stubborn attention to experienced truth. In sum, Dorsey brought forward the best of the American missionary tradition to the very edge of modern field ethnography. Perhaps Turner was correct after all: a truly human anthropology must retain within it something of the purged, sober mission.

In 1972 the following note was found among Albert S. Gatschet's notes for the synonymy: Every day from nine to ten, A. M.:

> Black the shoes.
> Fill bottles with coal oil.
> Clean & fill the lamp.
> Empty the waste-basket.[117]

That note might have served as the linguist's epitaph.

Gatschet personified the contradictory impulses of Washington anthropology. While he dispersed his energies at Powell's request over more than a hundred languages, he kept trying to return to his favorites, the Klamath Indians of Oregon. His linguistic ethnography of the Klamath, Boas judged in 1903, included "at the present time by far the best grammar of an American language in existence. If he had done nothing else but that he would have justified his work."[118]

Gatschet did much else. Between March 1877, when he joined Powell's Rocky Mountain Survey, and his forced retirement from the Bureau because of ill health in March 1905, he was an accomplished linguist and an indefatigable worker. A native of Switzerland, Gatschet attended the universities of Bern and Berlin, studying philology and theology. He emigrated in 1868 to New York, where he taught languages and contributed articles to scientific journals in both Europe and America. In 1872 Oscar Loew, a German botanist and linguist, returned to New York from the Wheeler Survey of the Southwest with sixteen Indian vocabularies, which he asked Gatschet to examine. To the countryman of Gallatin and Agassiz the experience opened a new world. His analyses appeared in the 1875 and 1876 reports of the Wheeler Survey, where Powell first saw Gatschet's name and work.[119] In March 1877, he accepted the Major's offer of a position on the Rocky Mountain team, with the understanding that he could publish any linguistic materials that he discovered in the manuscripts of the Smithsonian or in Powell's Survey.[120]

Gatschet's first assignment sent him to the Pacific coast to gather statistics on the tribes of Oregon and Washington Territory for the Bureau of Indian Affairs. Although the project was of a census nature, it marked the beginning of his Klamath studies.[121] His "Linguistic and General Researches among the Klamath Indians" appeared in the first report (1880). Like most of the first Bureau publications, it was a progress report. Using the language and texts as a basis, Gatschet ranged widely into the culture, embracing "mythic, ethnic, historic tales, grammar, and dictionary."[122]

Powell praised the Swiss immigrant for his unique ability to combine field experience with "high linguistic attainments of a general character." Here again Powell derived generalizations from Gatschet's painstaking Northwest work.[123] But the director had other priorities as well, and they soon began to impinge on Gatschet. In 1881 his detailed study of the Klamath language was already "in press," but it did not appear for nine more years, as Powell placed heavier burdens of the synonymy and the linguistic map on his linguist.

Between 1882 and 1890, Gatschet's career was marked by short, often fruitless foraging expeditions through the Southeast in search of remnant linguistic groups. There were a few startling discoveries, such as Biloxi; but the annual reports record some meager harvests. During the winter of 1881–82, for example, Gatschet traveled to South Carolina, where he located twenty surviving speakers of Catawba; then to New Orleans to record words and sentences from Choctaw speakers. He next spent two weeks with a small group of Chitimacha Indians, recording some 2,000 terms; and concluded his season with a vain search for three other groups. On his return Gatschet spent the rest of the year and the following two on Klamath.[124] In 1885, when Powell again superimposed the synonymy on his staff, Gatschet returned to the field: six weeks among Apaches in Texas, where without an interpreter he could not get trustworthy results; two months among reservation Kiowa and Comanches, where "the circumstances necessitated careful and numerous revisions of everything obtained"; and another month with the long-sought Atakapa of Louisiana, where he found the "sonorous, but strongly nasal" language spoken by "a few women living at the town." Other tribes visited on this sweep included Creek, Yuchi, Modoc, and Shawnee. Two he failed to locate.[125]

By 1888 Gatschet had rewritten the morphology of Klamath three times but was still digesting material for his region of the synonymy (eastern Florida to the Rio Grande). In 1890 he finally completed the Klamath grammar and wrote the last section, an "Ethnographic Sketch." It took another year to prepare the entire monograph for printing.[126]

As the Klamath work was emerging, Gatschet returned to ten years of unfinished notes on other tribes. But Powell had other plans. Gatschet, now approaching sixty, received the unenviable assignment of phonetically comparing the eastern and western dialects of the Algonquian family, a total of some forty to fifty dialects. It was an entirely new field for the aging linguist, and he spent the rest of his career, until 1905, diligently at work on it. He never produced another major study.

Judgments of Gatschet's work have varied widely. John R. Swanton, who joined the Bureau in 1901 (as successor to Dorsey) and knew Gatschet in his years of decline, suggested that while Dorsey became involved in the "mentality" of his subjects, Gatschet was purely a linguist.[127] Swanton was wrong. Gatschet was primarily a linguist in the sense that he, like Powell, viewed language as the key to ethnological study, and he devoted the larger proportion of his time to lexical and morphological analysis. But his Klamath work—as well as *Migration Legend,* which includes ethnographic materials from Creek, and which Swanton used heavily—demonstrates that his interests ranged well beyond language. The most qualified contemporary judge, Boas, was ambivalent. As we have seen, he highly praised Gatschet's work, but he also doubted that Gatschet could write the kind of analytical grammar that Boas envisioned for his *Handbook of North American Languages.* He avoided confronting his old friend while planning the project.[128]

Clearly Gatschet did not produce the major works that might have been expected from nearly three decades of labor. Regna Darnell has pointed out perceptively that standards changed in the Bureau between 1879 and 1895: the scattered bits and pieces of languages that filled out the linguistic map in 1891 had little value subsequently. But, as Boas knew quite well, Gatschet more than any other Bureau member was used for the director's ends and distracted from his own preferred work. Defending the old man's failure to publish, Boas reminded an investigating committee that Gatschet had been a tool to satisfy Powell's salvaging and surveying impulses:

By 1893 [Boas testified], Gatschet had accumulated such a vast amount of material that the only right thing for him to do would have been to sit down and write it out for publication. And he himself would have been only too glad to have had an opportunity to do so. His lack of publication is only a result of the policy of Major Powell, who wanted him to gather material for his general volume on the languages of the American Race.

Gatschet, concluded Boas, "has been by far the most eminent American philologist, away ahead of all of us."[129]

Gatschet was retired by the Bureau in 1905 and lived his last two years in poverty. Boas and others attempted unsuccessfully to ease the end with a pension from the new Carnegie Institution. Speaking of his former colleague, Otis Mason summarized his feelings: "For thirty years I have intimately known this scholar with an eye single to his researches concerning American Aboriginal languages. No other thought entered his mind. His permanent results are enormous."[130] Six months later Gatschet was dead.

Gatschet's dilemma was that of the early Bureau. He could not simultaneously produce the integrated studies of specific cultures that only years of concentrated exposure would have made possible, and also fill out Powell's map and synonymy. He bent to Powell's purposes partly because they suited his style, if not his scientific interests. A contributor but never fully an insider in Powell's organization, Gatschet preferred to work alone, methodically, thoroughly, honestly, and he was largely left alone. James Mooney warmly saluted the Bureau linguist, who "secure in his own honor . . . made no attempt to build up a reputation at the expense of other men, but gave to each his due credit.[131]

"When brought into close contact with the Indian, and into intimate acquaintance with his language, customs, and religious ideas," Powell lamented in 1891, "there is a curious tendency observable in students to overlook aboriginal vices and to exaggerate aboriginal virtues. It seems to be forgotten that after all the Indian is a savage . . ."[132] In this remarkably revealing statement Powell confessed to an unanticipated paradox. The tendency to subjective attachment, which resulted from prolonged exposure to specific peoples and which (Powell claimed) was particularly strong among students of language, warped scientific judgment as surely as did earlier negative estimates of the Indian based on prejudice. After more than a decade of Bureau activity, its director feared a loss of philosophical detachment.

Powell had always taken upon himself to keep before the Congress and the public the "great truths" of anthropological science; his entire scientific structure reflected this purpose and vision of his own role. Primary among these truths was the assertion that "the mind of man is everywhere practically the same, and that the innumerable differences of its products are indices merely of different stages of growth or are the results of different conditions of environment."[133] But why did Powell feel compelled at this time to restate his tenets of psychic unity and unilinear evolutionism and to remind his readers that "after all the Indian is a savage"?

The underlying moral and political question of BAE anthropology was the justice of the Indian's fate. This is not to suggest that the Bureau ethnologists operated under a cloud of guilt and penitence; on the contrary, with the possible exception of Charles Royce among the early staff, no man would have denied that the North American aborigines in one sense or another deserved their doom.[134] Powell and his associates worked not to question the outcome of history but to demonstrate why it had to be so, and possibly to ameliorate the process through science. By 1890 the general outline of human history and the major factors in determining the disparate fates of man seemed to be clear: Man had begun as one, but through a long period of prehistoric time had dispersed over the globe. From the point of dispersion, environmental influences had acted to determine differential rates of invention and growth and had gradually instilled permanent differences among races of men. Thus racial differences, while originally environmental, were nonetheless persistent and determinative of further growth or stagnation. However, since the beginning of European expansion and communication, the process of human differentiation had been reversed; the twentieth century would see the physical and cultural integration of all peoples in a global community.

This was essentially Morgan's optimistic prediction, which Powell, McGee, Mason, and Holmes elaborated in their own ways. Architectonically it also owed much to Spencer's suggestion of universal, alternating phases of integration and differentiation in all phenomena. But the emphasis on return to an egalitarian world fellowship demonstrates a spirit that was peculiarly American—and wishfully romantic.

Ill-equipped or unwilling to face the realities of growth, power, and destruction in their own society, Powell and his followers sought to rise above immediate experience by appeal to the categories of scientific understanding. In short, the insistence on the large vision, the "great truths," over immediacy and sentimental attachment was an appeal and escape from history to scientific abstraction. However tragic Indian-White relations may seem to the untutored, Powell wrote more than once, the scientific ethnologist, seeing the larger picture of past and future, knows better:

> Despite the pitiably frequent cases of personal and temporary injustice to the weaker race, the general policy has been guided by a deep-grounded recognition of the principles of justice and right on the part of both peoples . . . that the recognition of the rights of the aboriginal landowners has grown stronger and firmer with the passing of generations from the first settlement to the present, that the sympathy for the weaker race has increased with mutual understanding, and that the justice shown the red man is more richly tempered with mercy than during any earlier decade.[135]

In the light of such personal and social needs, the two-tiered structure of divided functions in the Bureau becomes intelligible. Like Henry before him and like his contemporaries Goode and Mason, Powell believed deeply in the moral education of the public. Despite appearances to the contrary, the story of man must be one of progress, and civilized man must stand at the apex. If not, then all was folly and absurdity and a cruel delusion. Powell depended on his staff to lay the empirical foundations of the New Ethnology, but the conclusions were predetermined by prior commitments. For this reason the Bureau men only controlled their data and observations to the degree that they concluded rightly. There was indeed, as John Swanton noticed, a "party line" in the Bureau.[136] But he and subsequent critics failed to appreciate the serious purposes beneath the Procrustean bed of Morgan/Powell evolutionism; belonging to a later generation, they could never understand the assurance and the hope it gave to men whose world was kaleidoscopically turning.

Notes

1. On the development of the social sciences after the Civil War, see Mary O. Furner, *Advocacy and Objectivity: A Crisis in the Professionalization of American Social Science, 1865–1905* (Lexington, 1975); Thomas J. Haskell, *The Emergence of Professional Social Science: The American Social Science Association and the Nineteenth-Century Crisis of Authority* (Urbana, 1977); and Hugh Hawkins, "The Ideal of Objectivity among American Social Scientists in the Era of Professionalization, 1876–1916," in Charles Frankel, ed., *Controversies and Decisions: The Social Sciences and Public Policy* (New York, 1976); also, Burton J. Bledstein, *The Culture of Professionalism: The Middle Class and the Development of Higher Education in America* (New York, 1976). Chapter 8 is especially suggestive.
2. Furner and Haskell specifically exclude anthropology from their studies.
3. Quoted in Haskell, *Emergence of Professional Social Science,* p. 97.
4. *Congressional Globe,* 40th Cong., 1st Session, 1867, p. 672; as quoted in Robert Winston Mardock, *The Reformers and the American Indian* (Columbia, 1971), p. 28.
5. Quoted in Don D. Fowler and Catherine S. Fowler, "Anthropology of the Numa: John Wesley Powell's Manuscripts on the Numic Peoples of Western North America, 1868–1880," Smithsonian Contributions to Anthropology 14 (Washington, D.C., 1971): 119.
6. Cf., Mardock, *Reformers and the American Indian,* Chapter 6: "Civilization or Extermination?" Mardock sees 1867 as the year of emergence of a humane peace policy, while 1876–79 were the "critical years" for removal and reservation policy (pp. 150–67).
7. Henry Adams, *The Education of Henry Adams: An Autobiography* (Boston, 1961), p. 309. The most complete account of the post-Civil War survey tradition is William H. Goetzmann, *Exploration and Empire: The Explorer and the Scientist in the Winning of the American West* (New York, 1966).
8. The original name was Bureau of Ethnology; "American" was added in 1894. The bill passed March 3, 1879 (U.S. Statutes 20:397). For background on the

consolidation movement and Powell's role in it and in the establishment of the Bureau, see William Culp Darrah, *Powell of the Colorado* (Princeton, 1951), pp. 237–54.

9.   The major sources are Darrah, *Powell of the Colorado*; Wallace Stegner, *Beyond the Hundredth Meridian: John Wesley Powell and the Second Opening of the West* (Boston, 1954); Thomas G. Manning, *Government in Science* (Lexington, 1967), a history of the first twenty years of the Geological Survey; and A. Hunter Dupree, *Science in the Federal Government: A History of Policies and Activities to 1940* (Cambridge, 1957), pp. 195–255.

10. *CNAE* 1 (Washington, D.C., 1877): ix.

11. Fowler and Fowler, "Anthropology of the Numa," pp. 12–13. See this discussion for a detailed account of Powell's itinerary and fieldwork between 1868 and 1880. The ethnological work had to be squeezed into spare moments. The work with Komas went slowly, as Powell complained to James Hammond Trumbull in 1876 (ibid., p. 119).

12. Ibid., p. 11. Powell's report is reproduced in this volume, pp. 97–119. Powell elaborated his statements before a congressional committee the following year.

13. Ibid., pp. 97–99.

14. Ibid., p. 116.

15. Ibid., pp. 117–18.

16. Ibid., pp. 99, 101.

17. Quoted in Darrah, *Powell of the Colorado*, p. 256.

18. BAE, *AR for 1895*, p. lxxxvi; Darrah, *Powell of the Colorado*, pp. 255–56.

19. *Report of the Secretary of the Interior for 1877*, vol. 1 (Washington, D.C., 1877), pp. 797–98.

20. I have dealt at length with the issue of utility in "Anthropology as Science and Politics: The Dilemmas of the Bureau of American Ethnology, 1879 to 1904," in Walter Goldschmidt, ed., *The Uses of Anthropology* (Washington, D.C., 1979), pp. 15–32. Passages from that article are reproduced here.

21. *Report of the Secretary of the Interior for 1877*, vol. 1 (Washington, D.C., 1877), p. ix.

22. See, esp., Regna D. Darnell, "The Professionalization of American Anthropology: A Case Study in the Sociology of Knowledge," *Social Science Information* 10, no. 2 (1972), pp. 83–103; C. M. Hinsley, "Amateurs and Professionals in Washington Anthropology, 1879 to 1903," in John V. Murra, ed., *American Anthropology: The Early Years* (St. Paul, 1976), pp. 36–68; and Timothy H. H. Thoreson, "Art, History, and Evolution," *Journal of the History of the Behavioral Sciences* 13 (1977): 107–25.

23. McGee to Hilgard, 17 July 1888, MP.

24. W J McGee, "Fifty Years of American Science," *Atlantic Monthly* 82 (1898): 320.

25. Stegner, *Beyond the Hundredth Meridian*, p. 146.

26. BAE, *AR for 1890*, p. xxi.

27. W J McGee, "The Bureau of American Ethnology," in George Brown Goode, ed., *The Smithsonian Institution, 1846–1896* (Washington, D.C., 1897), pp. 371–72. Emphasis added.

28. BAE, *AR for 1890*, pp. xxi–xxii.

29. Stegner, *Beyond the Hundredth Meridian*, p. 269.

30. Powell to Langley, 7 April 1900; as quoted in Virginia Noelke, "The Origin and Early History of the Bureau of American Ethnology, 1879–1910," Ph.D. diss. (University of Texas at Austin, 1974), p. 69.

31. BAE, *AR for 1885*, pp. 1–1i.

32. Charles C. Royce, "Indian Land Cessions in the United States," BAE, *AR for 1897* (Washington, D.C., 1899), pp. 521–964 (with introduction by Cyrus Thomas). Powell had hired Royce, who had been working independently, in 1879, without any authorization for entering the field of historical relations. Royce stayed two years, left the Bureau in 1881, returned again in 1883, and resigned permanently in 1885.

   The delay in publication has never been satisfactorily explained, but it was probably due to the political sensitivity of the issue. See my remarks in "Anthropology as Science and Politics," pp. 22–23.

33. BAE, *AR for 1880*, p. 76.

34. Mason to John G. Henderson, 8 June 1907, Otis T. Mason Papers, NAA; Mason to F. W. Hodge, 31 January 1907, Hodge-Cushing Papers.

35. BAE, *AR for 1866*, p. xxxv; BAE, *AR for 1885*, p. xliv.

36. BAE, *AR for 1886*, p. xxxv.

37. BAE, *AR for 1885*, p. xliii; BAE, *AR for 1886*, pp. xxxiii, xxxv. Powell and Henshaw were both impressed by Mooney's classification and synonymy work. See William L. Colby, "Routes to Rainy Mountain: A Biography of James Mooney, Ethnologist," Ph.D. diss. (University of Wisconsin, Madison, 1977), pp. 42–44.

38. BAE, *AR for 1885*, p. xlv.

39. BAE, *AR for 1886*, p. xxxv.

40. BAE, *AR for 1887*, p. xxix.

41. J. Howard Gore, "Anthropology at Washington," *Popular Science Monthly* 35 (1889): 790.

42. BAE, *AR for 1890*, p. xxxi.

43. BAE, AR for 1891, pp. xxxii, xxxv; BAE, *AR for 1894*, p. lxxxix; BAE, *AR for 1895*, p. lxxi; BAE, *AR for 1894*, p. lxxix.

44. BAE, *AR for 1895*, p. lxxi.

45. Hodge moved to the Smithsonian as acting curator of exchanges and assistant in charge of the office of the Secretary (Langley to Hodge, 31 January 1901, Hodge Papers, SW).

46. BAE-IN, pp. 248–51.

47. The idea of a linguistic map was not new with Gibbs. See Regna D. Darnell, "The Powell Classification of American Indian Languages," *Papers in Linguistics* 4, no. 1 (July 1971), pp. 73–76; and Mary Haas, "Grammar or Lexicon? The American Indian Side of the Question from Duponceau to Powell," *International Journal of Anthropological Linguistics* 35 (1969): 239–55. Gibbs's contribution has generally been ignored. Responding to Lewis Henry Morgan's "Suggestions Relative to an Ethnological Map of North America" (SI, *AR for 1861*, pp. 397–98), Gibbs outlined his concept of an "ethnological atlas" in letters of November and December 1862, to Joseph Henry, printed in SI, *AR for 1862*, pp. 87–93.

48. As quoted by Roman Jakobson, "World Response to Whitney," in Michael Silverstein, ed., *Whitney on Language: Selected Writings of William Dwight Whitney* (Cambridge, 1971), p. xxix.

49. Ibid., p. viii.

50. As quoted in ibid., p. xi.

51. Ibid., p. x.

52. Jakobson, "World Response," pp. xliii–xliv.

53. Powell, "Indian Linguistic Families," p. 12.

54. Henry Desk Diary, 15 April 1873, SIA.

55. SI, *AR for 1876*, pp. 35–36.

56. Powell to Whitney, 17 July and 27 August 1877, WDW Papers.

57. Whitney to Powell, 25 July 1877, NAA; as quoted in Regna D. Darnell, "The Development of American Anthropology, 1879–1920: From the Bureau of American Ethnology to Franz Boas," Ph.D. diss. (University of Pennsylvania, 1969), p. 65.

58. See, for instance, Powell's remarks in BAE, *AR for 1880*, p. xv.

59. "Address by Hon. John W. Powell," at inauguration of Corcoran School of Science and Arts (Washington, D.C., 1884), pp. 10,11.

60. *Introduction to the Study of Indian Languages*. 2d ed. (Washington, D.C., 1880), pp. v-vi.

61. Ibid., p. vi.

62. Ibid., p. viii.

63. J. W. Powell, "Indian Linguistic Families of America North of Mexico," BAE, *AR for 1885* (Washington, D.C., 1891), p. 142; Henry W. Henshaw and James Mooney, *Linguistic Families of the Indian Tribes North of Mexico, With a Provisional List of the Principal Tribal Names and Synonyms* (Washington, D.C., 1885); Regna D. Darnell, "The Powell Classification of American Indian Languages," *Papers in Linguistics* 4, no. 1 (July 1970), p. 79. See Darnell's Table I (pp. 100–08) for a list of changes between 1885 and 1891.

64. Darnell, "Powell Classification," pp. 82–85. For fuller discussion of the recent debate over authorship and additional references, see Darnell, "Development of American Anthropology," pp. 83–95.

65. Darrah, *Powell of the Colorado*, pp. 323–24; Thomas G. Manning, *Government in Science: The U.S. Geological Survey, 1867–1894* (Lexington, 1967), pp. 113–14.

66. See discussion of these men, below.

67. Colby, "Routes to Rainy Mountain," p. 49.

68. Henry W. Henshaw, "Autobiographical Notes," *The Condor* 22 (1920): 10.

69. Powell, "Indian Linguistic Families," pp. 8–10. Gatschet proposed a binomial, taxonomic linguistic classification that Powell found appealing. Powell noted ("Indian Linguistic Families," p. 23) of Gatschet's 1877 article on "Indian Languages of the Pacific States and Territories" (*Magazine of American History* 1) that Gatschet "advocates the plan of using a system of nomenclature similar in nature to that employed in zoology in the case of generic and specific names, adding after the name of the tribe the family to which it belongs; thus, Warm Springs, Sahaptin." Both the rule of priority and such taxonomic schemes no longer find application in linguistics, since languages do not conform to bi-

ological models. In no field of anthropology was the model of zoology clearer than in BAE linguistics.

70. Letter, 29 August 1930, printed in *American Anthropologist*, n.s. 33 (1931): 104.

71. Darnell, "Powell Classification," p. 83.

72. Quoted in Stegner, *Beyond the Hundredth Meridian*, p. 364.

73. Powell to Mrs. Pilling, 12 August 1895, reproduced in "James Constantine Pilling, 1846–1895" (privately printed memorial, 1895).

74. Pilling to Daniel Shea, 11 April 1881, NAA, quoted in Darnell, "Development," p. 63.

75. Ibid., 63–64.

76. Stegner, *Beyond the Hundredth Meridian*, pp. 263–64. In a personal communication to the author, William Sturtevant offered the following estimate of Pilling: "He was a very meticulous, accurate, and critical bibliographer. He included as much ms. material as he could locate, and all sorts of printed material—texts such as biblical translations, and letters and newspapers written in Indian languages, as well as brief vocabularies, grammars, etc. etc. He also included extremely useful brief biographies of many of the important authors. The results have been constantly and continuously referred to by generations of North Americanists. Bibliographic tools rarely get cited in publications, but they are used and save future scholars endless work and prevent ignorant errors."

77. J. C. Pilling, *Proof-Sheets of a Bibliography of the Languages of the North American Indians* (Washington, D.C., 1895).

78. Powell to Mrs. Pilling, 12 August 1895, in "James Constantine Pilling."

79. Stegner, *Beyond the Hundredth Meridian*, p. 264.

80. Robert Fletcher, "Brief Memoir of Colonel Garrick Mallery, U.S.A." (Washington, D.C., 1895, privately printed [copy in Smithsonian Institution Libraries]); John Wesley Powell, "Garrick Mallery," SI, *AR for 1895*, pp. 52–53.

81. Adams, *Education*, p. 366.

82. Fletcher, "Brief Memoir," p. 11.

83. Frederick Starr, "Anthropological Work in America," *Popular Science Monthly* 41 (1892): 301; Garrick Mallery, "A Calendar of the Dakota Nation," *Bulletin of the U.S. Geological and Geographical Survey of the Territories* 3:1 (Washington, D.C., 1877).

84. BAE, *AR for 1883*, pp. lii–liii; BAE, *AR for 1889*, pp. xxvi–xxvii.

85. Mallery's major publications were: *Sign-language among North American Indians, compared with that among other People and Deaf-mutes*, BAE, *AR for 1880*, pp. 263–552; *Picture-Writing of the American Indians*, BAE, *AR for 1889*, pp. 1–807.

86. Garrick Mallery, *Introduction to the Study of Sign-Language among the North American Indians as Illustrating the Gesture-speech of Mankind* (Washington, D.C., 1880).

87. The dates are confusing because of publication delays. *Sign-language* appeared in the 1880 report, but the report was not issued until 1881, which gave Mallery additional months to prepare his paper. Delays subsequently became more severe. Thus, for instance, Mallery's *Picture-writing* was part of the 1889 report, but did not appear until 1893. Bureau reports for the intervening years,

moreover, show that Mallery was still working on his report throughout this time. In addition to the normal delays of publication and government bureaucracy, Powell's desire to mollify Congress probably led him to promise reports before they were finished. Constant acquisition of new materials also led to unending revisions.

88. BAE, *AR for 1880*, p. xxv.
89. BAE, *AR for 1893*, p. xxxi.
90. BAE, *AR for 1889*, p. xxx; Darnell, "Development," p. 132.
91. BAE, *AR for 1893*, pp. xxxi–xxxii.
92. BAE, *AR for 1883*, p. lv.
93. Ibid, p. lvi.
94. Garrick Mallery, "A Philosophic Phantasy," read before the Philosophical Society of Washington, 18 February 1893 (privately printed, n.d.).
95. Garrick Mallery, "Greeting by Gesture," *Popular Science Monthly* 38 (1891): 644.
96. Garrick Mallery, "Israelite and Indian: A Parallel in Planes of Culture,"*Popular Science Monthly* 36 (1889–90): 52–76, 193–213 (quotations pp. 207, 210). In Mallery's (and Powell's) view, civilization had to precede Christianity: "Christianity, belonging to the plane of civilization and to that only, sits on a savage or barbarian as a bishop's mitre would on a naked Hottentot." (p. 208)
97. Ibid., p. 209. Mallery had expressed the same views in 1877, before his Bureau career began. See Mallery, "Some Common Errors Respecting the North American Indians," *Bulletins of PSW* II (Washington, D.C., 1875–1880), pp. 175–81.
98. SI, *AR for 1895*, p. 53.
99. Mallery, "Some Common Errors," p. 177.
100. "Professor Turner's Letter on Indian Philology: (12/16/51)," SI, *AR for 1851*. pp. 97–98.
101. BAE, *AR for 1890*, p. xliii; cf. Darnell, "Development," pp. 122–23, on Dorsey's double role as missionary and scientist.
102. "James Owen Dorsey," SI, *AR for 1895*, p. 53.
103. Dorsey to Henry, 18 March 1873; Dorsey to Rev. Joseph Packard, 24 March 1873, Rhees Papers, SIA.
104. Dorsey to Henry, 8 April 1873; Dorsey to Packard, 24 March 1873, Rhees Papers, SIA.
105. F.L.O. Roehrig to Henry, 18 March 1873, SIA; quoted in Darnell, "Development," p. 11.
106. Darnell, "Development," pp. 86–87; BAE, *AR for 1883*, pp. xli–xlii; BAE, *AR for 1885*, p. xxxvi; BAE, *AR for 1893*, p. xl.
107. BAE, *AR for 1887*, p. xxix; BAE, *AR for 1888*, p. xxxvii. Although the Bushotter interviews were the most extensive, subsequent informant work in Washington also lasted long periods. In 1889 Samuel Fremont (Omaha) stayed five months; Little Standing Buffalo (Ponca), two months; during 1890 George Miller (Omaha), three months; in 1891, an anonymous Quapaw visited for four months; and in 1894 Dorsey recorded Winnebago texts for an unspecified period from one Philip Longtail. On Dorsey's collaboration with

Bushotter, see Raymond J. DeMallie, "George Bushotter: The First Lakota Ethnographer," in Margot Liberty, ed., *American Indian Intellectuals: 1976 Proceedings of the American Ethnological Society* (St. Paul, 1978) pp. 91–102.

108. Franz Boas, "Some Philological Aspects of Anthropological Research," *Science* 23 (1906): 641–45. Reprinted in George W. Stocking, Jr., *The Shaping of American Anthropology, 1883–1911: A Franz Boas Reader* (New York, 1974), p. 185.

109. Noelke, "Origin and Early History," pp. 145–46.

110. Colby, "Routes to Rainy Mountain," pp. 49–51.

111. Darnell, "Development," p. 112.

112. Noelke, "Origin and Early History," p. 148.

113. BAE, *AR for 1882,* p. xxxv.

114. BAE, *AR for 1890,* p. xlvi.

115. Ibid., p. xlv.

116. Ibid., pp. xlv–xlvi.

117. From a note in BAE photograph files, NAA.

118. Boas testimony, BAE-IN, p. 943; A. S. Gatschet, "The Klamath Tribe and Language of Oregon," *Contributions to North American Ethnology* 2 [parts 1 and 2] (Washington, D.C., 1890).

119. A. S. Gatschet, "Report on the Pueblo Languages of New Mexico, and of the Moquis in Arizona: their affinity to each other and to the languages of the other Indian tribes," in *Annual Report of the U.S. Geological Survey West of the 100th Meridian for 1875* [Appendix LL of annual report of Chief of Engineers for 1875] (Washington, D.C., 1875); A. S. Gatschet, "Analytical Report upon Indian dialects spoken in southern California, Nevada, and on the lower Colorado River, etc.," in *Annual Report of the U.S. Geological Survey West of the 100th Meridian for 1876* [Appendix JJ of annual report of the Chief of Engineers for 1876] (Washington, D.C. 1876).

120. James Mooney, "Albert Samuel Gatschet, 1832–1907," *American Anthropologist,* n.s. 9 (1907): 561–62; Gatschet testimony, BAE-IN, p. 553; BAE, *AR for 1880,* p. xiii. Although both Dorsey and Gatschet joined Powell as "ethnologists," this description was intended mainly to distinguish them from the geologists, botanists, etc., on the Survey. The focus of their work was understood to be linguistic; in particular they were to compare the several hundred Powell and Smithsonian vocabulary lists (see Darnell, "Development" p. 318; Mooney, "Gatschet'" p. 562).

121. BAE, *AR for 1880,* p. xiii; Mooney, "Gatschet," p. 562.

122. BAE, *AR for 1880,* pp. xx–xxii.

123. BAE, *AR for 1881,* p. xxi; see, e.g., Powell's discussion of the development of separate modifiers through the "law of phonic change" and "economy," in BAE, *AR for 1880,* pp. xxi–xxii.

124. BAE, *AR for 1882,* pp. xxxi–xxxiii; BAE, *AR for 1883,* p. xlvii; BAE, *AR for 1884,* p. xxxiii.

125. BAE, *AR for 1885,* pp. xxxiv–xxxvi.

126. BAE, *AR for 1886,* p. xxxvi; BAE, *AR for 1889,* p. xvii; BAE, *AR for 1890,* pp. xxxii–xxxiii; BAE, *AR for 1891,* p. xxiv.

127. Swanton testimony, BAE-IN, p. 540; Darnell, "Development," pp. 112–13 (footnote).

128. Darnell, "Development," p. 287; Boas testimony, BAE-IN, p. 925.

129. Boas testimony, BAE-IN, p. 944. Boas considered Gatschet's assignment to Algonquian "the greatest mistake that Powell made" in administering the Bureau. (Boas testimony, original, unrevised copy, BAE-IN, p. 943.)

130. Mason to H. S. Pritchett, 26 September 1906, NAA.

131. Mooney, "Gatschet," p. 566.

132. Powell, "Indian Linguistic Families," pp. 35–36.

133. Ibid.

134. See remarks on Royce in Hinsley, "Anthropology as Science and Politics," pp. 22–23.

135. BAE, AR for 1897 (Washington, D.C., 1899), pp. lvi–lvii.

136. John R. Swanton, "Notes Regarding My Adventures in Anthropology and with Anthropologists," ms., pp. 33–34, NAA.

VII

Heroes and Homelessness:
Reflections on
Frank Hamilton Cushing,
James Mooney, and BAE Anthropology

"The fate of our times," Max Weber wrote toward the end of his life, "is characterized by rationalization and intellectualization and, above all, by the 'disenchantment of the world.'"[1] Weber was not the only observer and critic who perceived that by 1900 western civilization could boast of great achievements but little mystery. Henry Adams thought that the American people "were wandering in a wilderness much more sandy than the Hebrews had ever trodden about Sinai; they had neither serpents nor golden calves to worship. They had lost the sense of worship. . . ."[2] Fairy tales were for children, myths were for savages. But if enlightened civilization yielded power over both nature and man, it left many dissatisfied souls.

At the emotional center of American culture stood the home. The stable, comfortable Victorian household protected stoutly against unpredictable social and economic forces outside, but it was an unexciting haven. As middle-class Americans slowly discovered, the age of science and industry left little room for imagination, mystery, and romance. If one can measure by tastes in magazine fiction, by the end of the century a large reading public was turning outward to far-flung scenes for vicarious excitements. A flaccid, neurasthenic society seemed to require exotic tonics, because there was little heroism at home. For people feeling acutely the confines of closing frontiers, the North American Indian emerged once again as a source of national reinvigoration.

As Richard Slotkin has brilliantly demonstrated, American literature and national mythology have been populated from the beginning by a series of intermediaries between savagery and civilization: captives, hunters, frontiersmen, Indian fighters, mountain men. In each case the mediating figure, through immersion in the wilderness and savage ways, returns to civilization with a gift, or boon, to his troubled people. From the forest and savagery he learns the secret of regeneration and prosperity.[3] By 1880, as the days of the frontiersman were rapidly fading, the heroic stature of boon-bringer passed for a time to the scientific explorer—the naturalist and ethnologist. The salvage

Frank Hamilton Cushing, young genius of the Bureau of
American Ethnology, c. 1879.

ethnology of these years was, therefore, potentially more than curiosity collecting, for the ethnologist offered a gift of romantic aboriginal cosmology to a callow, disenchanted people. Those who succeeded most fully in this quest were individuals who, like their predecessors on the fictional and actual frontiers of American history, were themselves homeless and partially estranged. A degree of alienation was both precondition and product of the quest.

It may be true that, as Susan Sontag observed, anthropologists have institutionalized homelessness as an integral part of professional training and identity. Conformist abroad and critic at home, the anthropologist struggles constantly with ambivalence toward his own society and those he studies.[4] Whatever the current situation in the profession, cultural distance was decidedly undesirable in the world of Powell's Bureau. Committed to the mores and values of contemporary American life, Powell hardly intended to institutionalize any degree of alienation in Washington. Yet the BAE, like the early Smithsonian, became a haven for some individuals to whom restlessness or idiosyncracy permitted no comfortable home in society. In their searches for alternative modes of understanding, these individuals contributed, not to the professionalization of American anthropology, but to the richness of its heritage.

In 1880 the Southwest presented the most alluring ethnographic fields in North America. An invigorating climate; sedentary populations of artisans in weaving, pottery, and silver; mysterious, bird-like cliff-dwellers of the remote past; possible links between the high civilizations of Central America and the North American aborigines: these were some of the appealing aspects that fed a popular romance with the Southwest that blossomed into commercial exploitation with the new century. The lower canyon country of New Mexico and Arizona became the primary regional focus of Bureau work, and Powell displayed a particular proprietary interest in the pueblo peoples. Among those who worked in the region were Frank Hamilton Cushing, James and Matilda Stevenson, Washington Matthews, and Jesse W. Fewkes. Interests overlapped and ambitions often clashed, with Matthews, Cushing, and Army lieutenant John G. Bourke forming a cordon against what they considered the incursions of the Stevensons, Fewkes, and others. The Indian cultures of the region apparently fostered unusual attachment and possessiveness, and under the exposure of public popularity anthropology in the Southwest became heavily infused with personal style.

Frank Hamilton Cushing (1857-1899) certainly had style. Cushing was the precocious young genius of Bureau ethnology, and Powell doted paternally on this chronically ill, eccentric, and uncontrollable spirit. Cushing remains enigmatic.[5] Matilda Stevenson considered him a fool and a charlatan.[6] Powell and McGee called him a genius for his ability to enter fully into savage thought, while Boas stated that Cushing's genius "was his greatest enemy" and suggested that all his work would have to be done over.[7] Alfred Kroeber valued Mrs. Stevenson's sobriety above Cushing's flamboyance and judged their work accordingly. On the other hand, Claude Lévi-Strauss has seen in Cushing a brilliant, intuitive precursor of structuralism.[8] Cushing remains a live issue even today.

According to Cushing's own account of his childhood, at the family homestead in western New York the sickly, premature child spent years in social isolation and self-education into the ways of the woodland Indians. Avoiding formal schooling and "relieved of the constant waste of mentality through the friction of social relation," his mind followed its own channels.[9] The account may well be, like many such biographical statements of the period, a retrospective search for scientific roots. Its importance lies not in historical accuracy but in the fact that Cushing chose to portray his early life in a certain manner. Immediately in his reconstructed biography one faces the single consistent thread of Cushing's life: his insight that reality, whether the individual life or the group experience, is a psychological construct.[10] Each person structures his own world, and each group its collective experience, according to categories and patterns that must be understood and respected.

Cushing possessed a gift that was rare in his (or any) time: a tentativeness toward truth, values, and mores. Perhaps it was the excessive freedom of an unstructured or self-structured youth that encouraged levity and distance from his culture and branded him a wayfarer. His insistence on creating as well as discovering—that is, his free insertion of imagination in his work—placed Cushing on the fringes of any scientific community. He spurned institutional bonds, though he readily used individuals and organizations for his own purposes. He never valued institutional loyalty. In similar fashion he found little use for the language, channels, and forms of dialogue within established scientific circles. Not that he denied the importance of method in ethnology. In an early letter to Otis Mason he lamented that "America has no *Science* of Ethnology or Archaeology, and (I may add) that every Boer who has correctly or incorrectly described an arrowhead or a simple mound, is at once considered an archaeologist and styles himself, 'Professor.'"[11] Previous literature on the Zuñi pueblo, he told Baird soon after arrival in the Southwest, was "nothing," and he felt confident that "my *method must* succeed."[12] And at one low point in his career, when he thought he was dying in 1889, Cushing begged Bourke to "let the world know of my hard work and say that my method was the correct one in ethnological investigation. . ."[13] But Cushing was far too idiosyncratic to recognize the primacy of a scientific peer audience or to contribute in a major way to its creation. He knew personal friendships and bitter feuds, but he never developed a strong sense of professional community.

In 1874, when he was seventeen, Cushing sent a brief report of his New

York arrowhead collections to Baird, who printed it in the Smithsonian report. The following year Cushing entered Cornell University to study with naturalist Charles Hartt, but soon left for Washington. At Baird's invitation he lived in the Smithsonian towers and assisted Charles Rau with the Philadelphia Centennial collections.[14] Cushing found Rau irascible, and the old German's method of classifying implements did not satisfy Cushing's growing conviction that the anthropologist must understand motive through ethnographic data, and method through personal experiment.[15] The only way to grasp the subtle influences in aboriginal art, he wrote some years later, is "through experiments with original materials with one's own hands, limited in action to the appliances of the original local stone age conditions in each given case, and in almost blind submission to their influences and promptings."[16] "Blind submission" to nature's promptings was as alien to Charles Rau's neat, controlled cabinets as it was illicit in American society generally.

After the Centennial, Cushing remained in touch with Baird, but the Smithsonian could not take him on and he had to wait three years for a field opportunity.[17] The first BAE expedition, under Powell's compatriot of the seventies, James Stevenson, left for the Southwest in August 1879, to make "as careful a study as circumstances will permit of the Pueblo Ruins and caves of that district of country. . ."[18] The expedition was impelled by persistent concern, expressed through Congress to Baird, that foreign emissaries were ransacking the Southwest of its archaeological and ethnological treasures. In 1876 Ephraim G. Squier had advised the Peabody Museum (somewhat prematurely, as it has turned out) that foreigners had already turned Mexico into an ethnological wasteland, and now the southwestern United States seemed similarly threatened.[19] The BAE/Smithsonian venture became a perennial "Ethnological campaign" against such intruders.[20] Accordingly, the emphasis lay on material collections, after which the expedition might turn its attention to "language, customs, and habits, mythology, government, architecture, etc., etc.—"[21]

Spencer Baird's central role in Cushing's Zuñi experience has been obscured by time and by the romanticization of Cushing. Cushing joined the Stevenson expedition as the representative of Baird and the National Museum, and he reported directly to Baird even after his transfer to the Bureau in 1882.[22] Baird had insisted on including a special investigator of a single pueblo on the Stevenson reconnaissance group, and he recommended Cushing. He also requested regular reports from his man. For his part, Cushing viewed himself somewhat as a bird thrown out of the nest: he was determined to fly or die in the attempt. He would, Cushing assured Baird, "obey orders like a private"; after nearly a year at Zuñi, he confessed that "On the whole, then, I am *far* from sorry you have decided to keep me down here 'till I've done something."[23] Initially at least, the Zuñi experience was as much exile as involvement. In either case, Cushing's infatuation with the Zuñis was neither immediate nor reciprocal. At an early date he reported to Baird that "it is solely with the wish to make my visit to this Pueblo of a little scientific use, that I would *consent* even to remain here." Inability to communicate, constant physical discomfort, "disgusting" food made his first weeks utter misery.[24]

Still, it was Cushing's decision to stay at Zuñi when the rest of the Stevenson party moved on, and both Baird and Powell acceded to his wishes with apprehension. At first neither Cushing nor his superiors had a clear notion of the length of time that would be involved in his Zuñi work. "I think very well of leaving Cushing in pueblo country to complete his investigations," Baird informed Stevenson. "It will be difficult for him to get so completely on the inside track of this people again, as he appears to be now." To Putnam, who was watching with reserved approval from the Peabody Museum in Cambridge, Baird wrote that "It gives us great pleasure to have the endorsement of such eminent critics as yourself for our action in keeping Mr. Cushing in the Zuñi country for so long a time and of our intention of maintaining him in that service as long as may be necessary."[25] The Cushing experiment was being observed from the East with great interest.

As his stay lengthened into years and stories filtered back to eastern newspapers about the "White Indian," rumors arose questioning Cushing's moral state. The Smithsonian and the Bureau stoutly defended him, and Cushing fought back effectively through a series of popular articles in *Century Magazine* on "My Adventures at Zuñi," as well as by bringing back to the pueblo, in 1882, a White bride. The ambivalent nature of his undertaking—both the appeal and the revulsion—as seen from the bounds of his own culture was significant in determining the nature of Cushing's work and the timing of decisions. He had to balance carefully between two cultures.

He gradually came to sense the deep complexity of Zuñi life. It was like a veil lifting slowly before his eyes, as he told Baird:

> As gradually their language dawns upon my inquiring mind not the significance of these ceremonials alone but many other dark things are lighted up by its meanings. They are the people who built the ruins of Cañon Bonito. In their language is told the strange history of these heretofore mysterious remains each one of which has its definite name and story. The handworks on the rock face and the pictograph of a 'Primitive civilization' in the light of this language and tradition reveal their mysteries at once with their proof . . . Perhaps not a more conventional people may be found than these pueblos.

The secret of his success, Cushing continued, was his method: he observed Zuñi ceremonies and customs with "unfeigned reverence," never laughing. As a result, he claimed, "they love me, and I learn."[26]

Cushing exaggerated his acceptance. He was hardly an object of veneration at Zuñi, despite his efforts to portray as much. There is in fact evidence that he forced his will and presence on frequently unreceptive people (though perhaps not as vigorously as Matilda Stevenson, who ultimately had to guard her living quarters).[27] Still, Cushing's inquiries steadily widened into questions of history and origins. In an important statement of early 1880, he outlined fifteen broad areas of research to Baird and Powell, and he reported his most important discovery to date: that the arts, industries, and ceremonies of the pueblo peoples were governed by rigid rules, measures, and patterns, "formulas" as he called them, transmitted through generations by means of "ancient talks." These were the keys to understanding past history and current practices, he thought. Now deeply absorbed in Zuñi life, Cushing estimated another year and a half would be required for thorough knowledge of the language, prayers, and ancient instructions.[28]

Powell and Baird were excited with Cushing's progress. Powell's annual reports devoted considerable space to detailing the Zuñi experiences. Clearly here was an exceptional ethnologist, whose "devotion, energy, and tact" had gained him admission to the Order of the Bow and the position of "Assistant Chief" of the pueblo, the director reported. While biding his time to gain entrance to the "ancient epic rituals," Cushing explored the cemeteries, ruins, caves, shrines, and grottoes of the valleys with great material and theoretical profit. By the time of his return in March 1884, Cushing was convinced that he had located the seven lost cities of Cibola of the Spanish chroniclers— demonstration, he argued, of the reliability of Indian stories and traditions when properly interpreted.[29]

However sincere his enthusiasm, Cushing overestimated his advance in understanding the Zuñis, and his very presence was a disrupting factor in the pueblo. As a Bow Priest the ethnologist gained access to the sacred as well as the secular organization of the tribe, and he considered his admission "the greatest of all the achievements of my life perhaps; for it breaks down the last shadow of objection to my gaining knowledge of the sacred rites. . ."[30] By virtue of his office, though, Cushing aligned himself with the traditional tribal leadership in battles against other Zuñi families and "progressive" White influences, such as missionaries, traders, politicians, and Army personnel. The roles of ethnologist and tribal spokesman were incompatible for him. Cushing's life at Zuñi was consequently marked by disputes over horse stealing, lost Army mules, missionary influence, and land claims of Whites.

One such dispute caused the Bureau anguish and probably led to Cushing's recall to Washington in 1884. The son-in-law of John H. Logan, senator from Illinois and candidate for vice-president, had filed a claim for some 800 acres of the Nutria Valley, which had mistakenly been omitted from the 1877 Zuñi Reservation boundaries. When Cushing led the tribe's successful fight to reclaim the land, an infuriated Logan visited Zuñi in 1882, declared Cushing a fraud, and launched an attack against the ethnologist and the Bureau.[32] Significantly, the main focus of attack was his supposed moral degradation through prolonged exposure to Indians. Responding to criticism of his lifestyle, Cushing reassured Baird that his methods were "the results of my deliberate and best judgment," and that his relation with the Zuñis had always preserved his honor.[33] In an unpublished "interview" with himself in June 1883, Cushing again addressed this sensitive issue. He found himself "sincere in his motives, honest in his assertions, and in spite of his undeniable but voluntary and acknowledged 'degradation' to have retained fully his moral character and self-respect. . ."[34] The Logan dispute revealed not only the political pressures that could be brought to bear on Powell's organization but also the vulnerability of Cushing's style of field work in the 1880s, not least due to the self-doubts that critics could instill in an introspective ethnologist.

Politicians were not Cushing's only source of friction. He and the Stevensons competed more than they cooperated, and Cushing's growing fame added to the animosity. Washington Matthews, who was an Army man, the first careful student of Navaho life, and a staunch friend of Cushing's, cordially disliked both James and Matilda Stevenson, and he wrote to Cushing in caustic phrases of their attitudes and methods:

> "Colonel"! Stephenson [sic] came down on us a week ago with half a dozen tenderfeet, including professor Gore Harry Biddle, the son of a Virginia senator, a young Mr. McElhone, brother of a potent newspaperman, Mr. Mindelieff [sic], an artist, and several other "judicious" appointments. Stephenson staid with us, and we blew your trumpet all the time he was here & he kept rather "mum." A portion of the party are gone to Zuni to get materials to make an immense model of the Pueblo, the biggest model they have yet made. . . . Stephenson has gone to Santa Fe for some inscrutable purpose and expects to bring Powell back with him in a few days. Mrs. Stephenson came to Crane's Ranch and stopped there, so we have not seen her fair face nor listened to her gentle voice. Perhaps she wanted an invitation to [Fort] Wingate but she didn't get one.[35]

The ill-feeling toward the Stevensons, which Cushing certainly shared, centered on their high-handed manner with the Indians, their supposed failure to give proper credit to informants, their essential lack of respect for the pueblo peoples, and their political connections. Matthews particularly resented the financial support that they enjoyed through the Bureau and their presumptuous claims of knowledge based on short visits. "I suppose that you have heard that the Stevensons poached on my preserve last fall," he confided to Cushing in 1886. "They went there to duplicate my work, with a stenographer and far more means and materials than had ever been placed at my disposal. . ."[36] After Cushing's recall, the Zuñi field was open to his competitors: "There will, I think, be no necessity for your bringing in your

Victorian America meets the Southwest: Matilda Stevenson in Taos country; interior of Stevenson's Washington home.

Indians from Zuñi or for your coming out here again," Matthews informed him with sarcasm. "I saw Col. Stevenson at Wingate. He assured me that Mrs. Stevenson had learned to talk both Zuñi and Spanish fluently and was obtaining no end of valuable information from the Indians. From the way she is working I think she will get all that is worth getting before long. The Indians are just unbosoming themselves to her. Col. S. too has explored a number of caves around Zuñi and made wonderful discoveries. . ." In 1891 Matilda was still "working her sponge for all it was worth."[37]

Bourke, Matthews, and Cushing believed that they had come to the Southwest not merely to take but to exchange with mutuality and sympathy. To be sure, there is no question that Cushing bullied the Zuñis for information, especially at first; and both Bourke and Matthews felt acutely the constrictions of Army duties on their scientific ambitions—jealousy played a role in their judgments of the Stevensons and, later, of Jesse Fewkes. But more importantly, they reacted against invasion and exploitation by mere passersby, observers who could not, they felt, understand complex secrets that were revealed only with time and patience. "Got into the medicine-lodge and saw things I never dreamt of. Would you imagine that the rascals, who have neither ornamented robes, skins, or pottery, or carven idols, have nevertheless a complete system of pictographic myth symbolism?" Thus Matthews announced his discovery of Navaho sand-painting to Cushing in 1884. Eight years later he reported another personal breakthrough:

> I have made great strides in my knowledge of Navajo rites &c within the past years (But this is *private* to *you*), particularly during the past winter, & I have gained a position among the shamans that I had never hoped to get. Now they *urge* information and opportunities on me— nothing is witheld; I have been baptized and confirmed & have partaken of the Lord's supper (or its undoubted analogue) with them, and they urge on me a final ceremony of consecration which I doubt if my constitution will stand. But I keep all this quiet.[38]

Intimacy always carries a heavy burden of responsibility, and for some individuals it is difficult to glimpse the sacred and secret without also sharing veneration for it. It seems that for Cushing and Matthews, at least, profound ethnological experiences brought awareness of possible violation and betrayal of the Zuñis and Navahos. This was an especially painful dilemma for men who sensed the barrenness and irreverence of their own civilization. In order to bring regenerating knowledge to their own people, they necessarily violated trusts to others. The dilemma was insoluble, and it may have contributed to Cushing's reticence in publishing.[39]

On the 1879 expedition Cushing complained to Baird that while Stevenson was a good business manager (he served as executive officer of the Bureau and the Geological Survey), he treated Cushing like a boy. Subsequent experiences confirmed Cushing's misgivings about the Bureau, which he shared with Matthews and Bourke. At one point in 1881 he decided to seek an Army commission in order to "cultivate arms as a profession, & science as a recreation I love." Despite Bourke's support and the endorsement of General Philip Sheridan, the appointment never materialized.[40] Bourke, who at the time was considering retirement from the Army in order to devote himself to Apache studies, suspected that the Bureau had blocked Cushing's appointment. The problem, Bourke advised his friend, was that Cushing's excellence had alienated the BAE corps. He consequently could expect little help, because his reputation "will destroy or dim that of many an old plug who has grown fat and greasy. . ."[41] "You haven't a friend too many," he warned Cushing; without them he could be destroyed by the BAE:

> A congregation of penny-dips will not be disposed to let an electric light enter among them. You know well that I have always distrusted those people and that in our conversations long ago we both concluded not to lean upon them too much.

Bourke advised him to locate a good cattle ranch near Zuñi, "near enough so that you can have their protection and they your counsels," possibly financed by "N.Y. and Boston capitalists."[42] At the same time Cushing should cultivate a "European reputation" with Edward B. Tylor, Spencer, and others:

> America offers no suitable field for you. Very few of our people care for the Indians and nearly all of them manifest a suspicion of a man who presumes to consider their manners, customs, and ideas worthy of note and preservation.[43]

Integrity intact but harboring doubts about the Bureau, Cushing was ordered to Washington in January 1884, to write up four and half years of field work. He spent more than two years in the capital but never began the expected work. Powell pushed him to complete his Zuñi linguistics in preparation for a full study of mythology and social arrangements. The only immediate result for the BAE was a brief study of pueblo pottery.[44]

Cushing's frail health gave way under office rigor in late 1886, when he took an indefinite leave of absence from the Bureau and returned to the Southwest. But he did not return alone. Perhaps remembering Bourke's advice, Cushing had located a rich Boston capitalist, and he went back to the arid country as director of the Hemenway South-Western Archaeological Expedition, endowed by Boston blueblood Mary Hemenway. Cushing's interests had been moving for some time from ethnology to history and archaeology, and the Hemenway project offered him the opportunity to follow his imagination wherever it led. For two years he combed the Arizona ruins that had increasingly fascinated him and that held, he was convinced, keys to the past civilizations of the region, and perhaps of North and Central

America generally. Cushing produced glowing reports of significant finds, but it was all fragmentary. In 1889, just as the expedition might have been expected to reach significant results, Cushing collapsed again and was forced to return to the East, and Mrs. Hemenway replaced him with a Harvard-trained naturalist, Jesse Walter Fewkes.

Fewkes's appointment infuriated Cushing and initiated a decade-long feud. Confined to his New York homestead, unable or unwilling to produce the final report on the expedition, Cushing fumed against his successor. Fewkes had taken his manuscript data; had accused him of mismanagement, intemperance, and insanity; and had published without giving proper credit, Cushing railed.[45] Matthews comforted Cushing, reminding his friend that "the Codfish" (Fewkes) was completely unqualified for the Hemenway:

> Our Boston friend, while in Zuñi never spoke a word of Zuñi and didn't know a word of Spanish. He never employed either Graham or 'Nick' the only English-speaking men in Zuñi, yet he learned everything about them in two months. What a pity it is we have not a few more such brilliant lights in Ethnography![46]

William T. Harris, mediator between Cushing and Mrs. Hemenway, patiently reminded Cushing of the real issue: he had produced only fragments from an investment of $100,000. As of June 1891, there were no hard accusations against him, only "hard suspicions." All Mrs. Hemenway wanted was the final report. In response to Cushing's threat to abandon the work altogether, Harris explained his moral obligation and exposed his shortcomings as a scientist in painfully clear language:

> If you give up that work it seems to me that you will make the greatest mistake of your life. Because you see all your special articles on various themes hinge upon the validity of your work of simple observation and inventory. You have nothing to show on that side that is published and secondly you cannot defend yourself from the almost universal charge that is made and will be made against your work, that it is visionary, rather than scientific. You have left the results of the South-West Expedition in such a form that a scientific report upon it made by specialists would undoubtedly prove that you had abused the trust placed in you by Mrs. Hemenway, and had taken no care to save the results of your investigations, step by step, just as such results are saved by scientific expeditions.
>
> You know what the astronomers call the personal equation. In dealing with the religious and philosophical ideas of a lower people we must be very careful not to read into their poems ideas which have come to consciousness only with modern nations. There will be the suspicion that you have consciously or unconsciously modified the data given you by

the natives and this will seriously diminish the credit which your articles should have. But if you prove your right to be trusted as to data, you must prove it by writing minute and clear histories or records of your discoveries.[47]

The early years of the Hemenway Expedition under Cushing (it continued until the patroness's death in 1894) were a turning point in his career and in Southwestern archaeology. Highs and lows were inseparable with Cushing. At the moment of his greatest promise and in a position of critical leadership, he suffered dreadfully from heat and his various bodily ills, which had worsened. The expedition was bedevilled by relic-hunters who destroyed bones and artifacts, and Cushing had difficulty keeping order and momentum. He was completely unfit as a leader. Frederick Webb Hodge, who accompanied the expedition and later became both a brother-in-law and harsh critic of Cushing,[48] recalled that the director, perhaps because he was so ill, took few field notes but "depended largely on long accounts written in letter form to Mrs. Hemenway and to Sylvester Baxter." Baxter was a Boston journalist who served as home secretary and popularizer of the expedition back East. These reports "contained a great deal of bunk"—hypotheses and ambitious plans.[49] According to Hodge, Cushing simply failed to function well:

> The location of artifacts on the maps was done at Cushing's insistence, as he made no notes himself and he thought that by locating the 'finds' on the maps his memory would be aided when the time came to write the final report. Illness prevented Cushing, at times, from visiting the diggings from Camp Hemenway nearby; at other times he fiddled away his time in making flags for the tents and other useless trifles. Sometimes weeks passed without the laborers having any supervision excepting that given by the intelligent Mexican laborer Ramon Castro. Cushing was jealous of note-taking by anybody but himself.[50]

The digging was not thorough, and Cushing's interpretations of the finds were often based on his imagination. Thus, for instance, he explained "ultra mural" houses (structures beyond the pueblo walls) in terms of a supposed caste system, whereas it was, Hodge argued, "more reasonable to suppose that they were merely shelters occupied when the farming work was in progress, as in the case of Zuñi today."[51] Partly as a result of Cushing's slipshod methods, the Hemenway Collection, now in the Peabody Museum of Harvard, still awaits thorough study. He never wrote a final report.

The famous incident of the jewelled frog perhaps indicates Cushing's state of mind at Camp Hemenway. Having seen a shell frog from the ruins of southern Arizona in the possession of a Phoenix businessman, Cushing secretly "improved" a plain, frog-shaped shell found at Los Muertos to look like an aboriginal product. Some years later Hodge told the story of Cushing's deception:

> Some days later he appeared [from his tent] holding in his clenched hand a beautiful mosaic frog. That he had intended to palm it off as a specimen found in the ruins, I have no doubt. When he opened his hand and showed the object to me, I did not exclaim, but spoke of it casually as his own handiwork, as if he was aware that I knew he had made it, whereupon he said, "But it looks too new." This, coupled with the secrecy with which the frog was manufactured, confirmed my belief that he had intended to represent it as of Indian manufacture, but on account of its newness had abandoned the idea and thought of preserving it only as a model.
>
> Some time later, Prof. Edward S. Morse visited Los Muertos. . . . It was, I believe, in the evening of the day of his arrival that Cushing brought out the frog, and showed it to Morse, first holding it in his closed hand as before. As soon as Morse put eyes on it, he exclaimed. 'Great Lord, Cushing, where did you find that?' Cushing responded, nonchalantly, 'In a jar in Ruin III.'
>
> In his own belief, Cushing had won, for if the frog could deceive Morse, it would deceive anyone. The result was that Morse took the frog to Boston and showed or gave it to Mrs. Hemenway, never suspecting that the object was anything but genuine. It was thus that the frog found its way into the Hemenway collections.[52]

Cushing's own account naturally presented a different perspective on the matter. Responding in 1898 to Putnam's request for a statement as to the genuineness of the frog, Cushing struggled to explain how he worked on the specimen step by step with primitive materials and methods. He wrote in part:

> When I had completed these preliminary operations I mistakenly endeavored to solidify the more fragile parts by gently heating the entire surface,—by which the work coalesced in such manner that the portions restored were almost indistinguishable from the others. Then hoping to bring out the difference again, I cautiously rubbed the surface on a piece of suspended buckskin, using as the safest buff I could find the fine loam of the ruins. This did not accomplish what I intended & I frankly acknowledge it was a mistake, but a conscientious mistake. . .
>
> Since this was the first recognizable specimen of its kind that had to my knowledge been found; since I used such care in its restoration, and since subsequently another specimen identical with it in general and in several specific characteristics has been found . . . , you may without hesitation

exhibit this example not only as the first type specimen, but also, as
accurate and authentic.[53]

The entire performance, from the specimen reconstruction (told with some
pride, one senses) to the final confession of conscientious error and claim of
authenticity, was pure Cushing.

The Hemenway expedition was at once the greatest opportunity, trial, and
failure of Cushing's life, and he never entirely recovered from its impact. The
heightened self-pity and martyrdom of his later years found expression in
another confession to Putnam:

> In the vain efforts of a sick man, to meet the demands or desires of
> friends and fellow workers, my efforts too often become scattered, my
> sense of proportion or relative importance distorted, and my power to
> do any special & practical work, any one thing as it should be done,
> deferred or hazarded.
>
> It is this, my dear sir, [that has] led men . . . to pronounce me a false
> claimer, a vain speculator, a fraud, a drunkard, a pretender to the illness
> that is my mortal scourge and slow living death. And these men have
> no pity in judgement and they are such as would undo you and me alike
> if they could.[54]

Ignoring Harris's advice, Cushing abandoned the Hemenway work and
returned to the BAE and his pending Zuñi materials. Between 1892 and
1894 he produced the beautiful *Outlines of Zuñi Creation Myths* and a series
of shorter pieces, along Powellian lines, on the development of mental concepts
and manual agility. From a scholarly viewpoint these were the most disciplined
and productive years of Cushing's life.[55]

The prolonged office work again proved burdensome and depressing to
Cushing. In 1894 Powell secretly arranged with William Pepper, Cushing's
personal physician and provost of the University of Pennsylvania, to send
Cushing to Florida for a rest and archaeological reconnaissance.[56] The health
trip produced scientific bonanzas. As before at Zuñi and Camp Hemenway,
the first reports glowed with the enthusiasm of fresh discovery. Cushing's
early observations in the coastal shell mounds occupied two pages in the
Bureau's 1895 report, and the data led to far-reaching hypotheses:

> Some of these pile-dwellings appeared to Mr. Cushing to stand in definite
> relation to certain of the shell mounds, particularly those of definite
> form, and through this relation he is able to gain some insight into the
> origin and development of mound building among the American abo-
> rigines, this insight being in part due to his intimate acqaintance with
> Indian modes of thought.[57]

The above statement, which seemed to promise a major insight into North

American aboriginal mound building, was based on a preliminary survey of the site that lasted less than one day in May 1895.[58]

The full expedition, partly financed by Phoebe Hearst and consisting of Cushing, his wife, and seven workers, arrived in late February 1896, and excavated for two months. Cushing returned to Washington in May; the fifty-nine boxes and eleven barrels of relics arrived somewhat later in Philadelphia for his reconstruction and analysis. Cushing never returned to Florida.

He also never finished classifying and arranging the collections, which remain unique in Florida archaeology.[59] Instead, Cushing became embroiled in a nasty dispute with Bureau photographer William Dinwiddie, who in the summer of 1896 accused the ethnologist of falsifying another shell specimen. Cushing's aides on the expedition all vouched for the authenticity of the find and for his honesty; Powell and the Bureau rallied around him; and Dinwiddie was fired for insubordination.[60] Cushing and his friends saw the episode as another attack on his character. "So after all the hub-bub," Matthews reflected, "the only one to suffer as a result of 'the Cushing slander' is poor little Dinwiddie, with his wife and children, he was only a catspaw for more designing men. . ."[61]

The Dinwiddie affair dragged on for months, disturbing the clear Key Marco waters and sapping Cushing of his limited energy; or so he claimed to Pepper. He hoped to complete the Key Marco report by early 1898, but chronic illness and the inconvenience of traveling to Philadelphia to examine the collection delayed the work. In October 1898, the collection moved to Washington, but Cushing died five months later.[62]

In each of the major phases of his career—Zuñi, Hemenway, the Pepper Expedition—Cushing left promising insights or discoveries unfinished. In each case, too, he experienced incapacitating illness and acrimonious personal relationships. At the time of his sudden death he was busily planning, with Powell's doting approval, yet another undertaking, this time with Powell, in the shell-heaps of Maine. So, had he lived, the pattern would have continued. Cushing could not be tied to institutions or individuals, but used them even as he depended on them—Baird's Smithsonian, Powell's Bureau, Hemenway's Expedition, Pepper and Stewart Culin's University Museum—to pursue his own erratic course. He lived for the great moments of discovery; they were a necessity for him. Cushing had no time for the deadening chores of scientific polish and proof. The flash of brilliance, promising insight, far-reaching theory—then Cushing was moving on, leaving the litter of his research strewn across the Southwest and elsewhere for others to pick up, if they could. Here was genius of a sort, but its credentials came increasingly under question, as William Harris informed Cushing. When Harvard-trained Fewkes succeeded self-taught Cushing on the Hemenway project, the change symbolized a generation's experience. Brilliant intuition alone went only so far.

Two years before his death, Cushing explained to the Board of Indian Commissioners "the need of studying the Indian in order to teach him." His address summarized the Bureau's reform philosophy: that Indian policy must be based on accurate knowledge rather than sentiment, fervor, prejudice, or ignorance. The BAE, Cushing explained, was not devoted to anthropology as a science alone, but aimed to understand the Indian's

> very nature, his mood of mind, his usages, his attitude, all in order that we may be better able to treat him as a subject or ward, and to aid him to overcome in his sadly unequal struggle with an advancing and alien civilization, so that he may be fitted to survive among us and not be further degraded or utterly destroyed.[63]

In order to understand the Indian, Cushing instructed, we must go to him as brothers, fully comprehend his inmost nature, study his past, "learn how he came to be what he is, and thus learn how to make him other than what he is." Rather than bludgeon the aborigine with Christianity and civilization, Whites must not immediately require the Indian to abandon his traditions, but wean him away through understanding and example:

> Of all the people on this continent, not excluding ourselves, the most profoundly religious—if by religion is meant fidelity to teachings and observances that are regarded as sacred—are the American Indians. . . For with them, sociologic organization and government and the philosophy and daily usages of life are still so closely united with religion, that all their customs, which we consider as absurd and useless, grow from it as naturally and directly as plants grow from the soil. . . . It is, then, most dangerous to tell the Indians of the baselessness of their beliefs, the uselessness of the customs and ceremonies founded upon them. Why strike at the very root of the life whereby they maintain their communities, by striking at these things before the appointed time?

Only through "searching knowledge," Cushing advised, could the government representatives teach "these latter-day barbarians, as we style them."[64] Sudden transitions tragically destroyed the revered traditions of Indian life, traditions that are loved "in a way that passes our comprehension, for we are weaned from love of our traditions":

> We do not want to go to them, then, and weaken their sense of morality founded on the traditions they believe, and so venerate, by saying that these are wrong, for we never in a lifetime, with the utmost effort and labor, can blot out of their minds what their fathers and mothers have taught them when young, of reverence for these traditions, and replace it with equally influential reverence of our own.[65]

It was reverence and mystery that Frank Cushing sought, at Zuñi pueblo, in the buried secrets of Los Muertos, among his imagined Key-dwellers of western Florida. Today Cushing is remembered and valued chiefly as a precursor in need of refinement and discipline. But Cushing's message to his own age speaks even more directly to ours. His message was this: A truly rich culture must not deny or eradicate the deep mythological and imaginative wellsprings of the soul. Beneath the vast cultural diversity of mankind lies a spiritual commonality, a level of intuitive communication.[66] The poetic and artistic powers of man exist independently of positive rational knowledge, and they constitute an equally valid, necessary, and deeply satisfying mode of dealing with the cosmos. The scientific world of observation and deduction that was in the making with such fanfare by anthropologists and others during Cushing's lifetime was tragically limiting and impoverished, despite its unprecedented yield of power. He realized as much. The institutional and personal storms that marked his life attested to his unfitness for the new century he never saw. The heartfelt eulogies by fellow anthropologists at his early death revealed that they too felt an irreplaceable loss, as if a part of themselves had been suddenly snatched away.

James Mooney (1861-1921) was an Irish Catholic and a journalist. His ethnic heritage and early newspaper career determined the deepest patterns of his anthropology. Even as a child of Irish immigrants in Richmond, Indiana, Mooney was conscious of separation from the mainstream of American culture. His estrangement grew with time. From the age of eight until he joined the Bureau of Ethnology, at twenty-four, in 1885, Mooney worked for a newspaper in his home town. Like his Irish sensibility, Mooney's journalistic bent never left him. Throughout his career in anthropology he was associated and concerned with politically and culturally oppressed peoples—Irish or Native American—and he was fascinated by modes of communication. From these roots came the central questions of his anthropology: How do oppressed people transmit the binding elements of their culture from one generation to the next? How do those who are defeated and dispersed nonetheless preserve identity and tradition?

Political consciousness came to Mooney as a birthright. While most of his colleagues explained the demise of the American Indian in racial or developmental terms, human fate for Mooney was the product of history and relative power. Although in early writings he occasionally adopted the rhetoric of evolutionism, Mooney did not take decline and subordination as signs of mental or cultural inferiority. Misfortune brought forth no judgment from him because as a Catholic Irishman he knew that "failure" said nothing about inherent worth. Social and political disintegration was a historical fact, not a moral state.[67]

Mooney realized no less than Powell that Indian cultures in their pristine, precontact forms were fast disappearing; consequently, there was a strong element of urgency and salvage in his work. However, perhaps because of his historical perspective and Irish nationalist sympathies, Mooney came to see Indian cultures as living and changing, struggling to survive under extremely demoralizing conditions. As he poignantly demonstrated in his monograph on the ghost-dance (1896), the aboriginal cultures of North America were human responses to hopelessness, misery, and social chaos.[68] Mooney was one of the first to recognize in Indian degradation the trauma of acculturation and adjustment to loss of power.

To a degree that was exceptional in his generation, Mooney's ethnology was grounded in painstaking historical reconstruction. His library and bibliographic research elicit admiration and gratitude from students even today; his major monographs on the Cherokee, the Ghost Dance, and the Kiowa are indispensable classics. But the Cherokees still consider Mooney their outstanding historian not merely because he told the story of their trials drawing on both Indian and White materials and memories, but also because he saw that history exists in the mind of the present as much as in documents. The persistent strength of oral tradition and unwritten knowledge comes from the deep roots they take in the personality and daily habits of the individual. Mooney discovered first among the eastern Cherokees what Cushing found in Zuñi pueblo: that the past lived vibrantly in the present and still controlled central aspects of aboriginal cultures. Mooney, like Cushing, sought to isolate the most secret keys that defined the past and determined present behavior. He would later locate such keys in the heraldry of the southern Plains peoples; among the Cherokees of the North Carolina mountains, he found them in sacred "formulas" of healing, love, and hunting. In these formulas, Cherokee history lived on. Perhaps Mooney's greatest contribution was to expand and redefine history so as to embrace Indian experience, and to incorporate this into his ethnology.

As a boy Mooney loved lists. When he was ten he wrote down names of sewing machine manufacturers and kept statistics on European languages. A short time later he began to direct his energies toward American Indians, gathering information on tribal names, languages, migration histories, boundaries, and treaty relations. In a fashion remarkably similar to Powell's program, by age sixteen Mooney had developed, on his own in Indiana, a large map of the tribes of North America.[69] In 1882 Mooney first applied to the Bureau, but Powell rejected him because of his lack of linguistic experience and the shortage of funds at the Bureau. He was turned down again the following year, and again in 1884. Finally in 1885 he traveled to Washington for a personal interview. This resulted in an unsalaried opportunity to prove himself.[70]

Mooney made immediate, significant contributions to the Bureau synonymy; his arrival in fact stimulated a flurry of activity for a year or so.[71] But the tentativeness of his hiring seems to have persisted; he never shared

James Mooney, newspaperman, student of Cherokee and Plains ethnography.

Powell's favor or joined the inner circle at the Bureau. He worked with Mallery on the synonymy but became friends with Gatschet and Matthews. It was Matthews who did the most to shape Mooney. Despite his Army affiliations and friendship with the favored Cushing, Matthews was no confidante of Powell's; as we have seen, he felt slighted and unappreciated at the Bureau. After Matthews's death in 1905, his wife, Caroline, wrote to Charles Lummis that the failure of the Bureau to provide an obituary of her husband was perfectly consistent: "The Bureau of Ethnology has ignored him as it always has done in the past. . ."[72] But Mooney was fortunate that in 1885 Matthews was stationed for a period in Washington and working in the Bureau. As sons of Irish immigrants to the Midwest (Matthews grew up in Iowa), the two men shared an important ethnic and religious bond. Mooney, who eventually did write Matthews's obituary in the *American Anthropologist*, attributed his success as an ethnologist to his Irish heritage:

> By a faculty of mingled sympathy and command he won the confidence of the Indian and the knowledge of his secrets, while by virtue of that spiritual vision which was his Keltic inheritance, he was able to look into the soul of primitive things and interpret their meaning as few others have done.[73]

Matthews offered Mooney four points of guidance for field work: learn the language; be authoritative but sympathetic; record everything precisely; and avoid preconceptions.[74] Mooney apparently listened carefully. His first field trip, to the eastern Cherokees in the North Carolina hills, was originally commissioned to examine remnant dialects for the linguistic map. But Mooney immediately envisioned much wider purposes. In his first seasons (1886 and 1887) he established the field methods that always characterized his work. Like Cushing and Matthews, he emphasized patience, indirection in questioning, and mutuality of exchange.

Mooney's field success was attributable in part to the fact that he astutely but sympathetically took advantage of the social disintegration and economic poverty of the Cherokees. He began with material culture, inquiring about purchase of artifacts, expressing interest in manufacturing techniques, gently probing into sources of daily habits and customs. Severe economic hardship may have facilitated purchase of articles (including written formulae for the BAE) among these people, as among most other Native American groups by the second half of the century. Mooney further demonstrated serious purpose by working assiduously on the complicated Cherokee language. He soon discovered that the combination of sincere interest and calculated flattery usually, but not always, opened the way to establishing the individual informant relationships that he enjoyed and utilized to such profit.[75]

Mooney found the Cherokee men of knowledge secretive, proud, and competitive; furthermore, "at present each priest or shaman is isolated and independent":

> It frequently happens, however, that priests form personal friendships and thus are led to divulge their secrets to each other for their mutual advantage. Thus when one shaman meets another who he thinks can probably give him some valuable information, he says to him, "Let us sit down together." This is understood by the other to mean, "Let us tell each other our secrets." Should it seem probable that the seeker after knowledge can give as much as he receives, an agreement is generally arrived at, the two retire to some convenient spot secure from observation, and the first party begins by reciting one of his formulas with the explanations. The other then reciprocates with one of his own, unless it appears that the bargain is apt to prove a losing one, in which case the conference comes to an abrupt ending.[76]

The key to Mooney's Cherokee work was his ability to penetrate and participate in this system of knowledge exchange. Gaining trust to enter this exclusive circle of knowledge required time and sensitivity; and, of course, Mooney had to have something to give as well. Matthews's success among the Navaho shamans in the same period was due largely to his standing as a physician, which permitted a cross-cultural exchange of privileged information: his anthropology was in part professional dialogue. Mooney did not formally possess similar expertise, but he had amassed a large store of Irish lore, stories, and medical remedies. With these he was able to claim a place of respect within the dwindling circle of Cherokee medicine men.

If cooperation and exchange faltered, however, Mooney had other methods at his disposal. The independence that derived from social disintegration also led to jealousy and vanity among the Cherokee men of knowledge. Mooney played on these feelings. He acquired his first book of written Cherokee formulas, the Swimmer manuscript, by appealing to his informant's pride:

> Mooney reminded Swimmer that there were only a few men of knowledge left and that the only purpose of recording myths was to let the world know how rich the Cherokee culture had been. If Swimmer could not give him complete information, perhaps someone else within the tribe could. Mooney also told him that shamans from other tribes sent songs and myths of a similar nature to Washington. . . . Swimmer said he knew as much or more than any medicine man in his tribe, and he would tell all he knew to prove it.[77]

Mooney succeeded handsomely as an ethnologist, and his success complicated relations in the Bureau. His early years in Washington, until about 1890, were, like Cushing's years at Zuñi, a period of struggling self-assertion.

One suspects that his preference for the field, like Cushing's long absences from Washington, reflected desire for physical and intellectual autonomy as much as commitment to preserving Indian cultures. Powell was a formidable, powerful figure in the eighties, a man of heroic proportions. It was no simple matter for a young man to declare independence or to differ openly, even with a director committed to individual fulfillment. As a result, the Bureau annual reports sometimes contained muted arguments between Powell and his ethnologists, as he sought to correct rather than censor wayward notions.

Mooney soon began to test his tether. Powell was certainly impressed with the Cherokee results, particularly the unique written formulas Mooney had acquired for the Bureau. But signs of potential and profound rift emerged early. Powell's brief remarks introducing Mooney's *Sacred Formulas of the Cherokees,* in the seventh annual report, damned the work with faint praise. Attempting to place aboriginal zootheism in its proper developmental niche, the director reminded the reading public that "zoic mythology degenerates into folk tales of beasts, to be recited by crones to children or told by garrulous old men as amusing stories inherited from past generations. . ." By so displaying his commitment to civilized rationality, Powell implied that Mooney's discoveries had little value other than as "vestiges" of earlier systems.[78]

Mooney understandably estimated his own work more favorably (as do most others today); but his evaluation was grounded in a different perspective and purpose. Mooney's vitality and sympathy at this early point are best conveyed in his own words:

> The formulas contained in these manuscripts are not disjointed fragments of a system long since extinct, but are the revelation of a living faith which still has its priests and devoted adherents, and it is only necessary to witness a ceremonial ball play, with its fasting, its going to water, and its mystic bead manipulation, to understand how strong is the hold which the old faith yet has upon the minds even of the younger generation.

> It is impossible to overestimate the ethnologic importance of the materials thus obtained. They are invaluable as the genuine production of the Indian mind, setting forth in the clearest light the state of the aboriginal religion before its contamination by contact with the whites. . . .

> These formulas furnish a complete refutation of the assertion so frequently made by ignorant and prejudiced writers that the Indian had no religion excepting what they are pleased to call the meaningless mummeries of the medicine man. This is the very reverse of the truth. The Indian is essentially religious and contemplative, and it might almost be said that every act of his life is regulated and determined by his religious belief. It matters not that some may call this superstition. The difference is

only relative. The religion to-day has developed from the cruder super-
stitions of yesterday, and Christianity itself is but an outgrowth and
enlargement of the beliefs and ceremonies which have been preserved
by the Indian in their more ancient form.[79]

The reference to Christianity was an early sign of Mooney's movement
toward a cross-cultural perspective based on the suspicion that cultural phenomena are functions of social, economic, and political conditions rather than
indices of mental growth. It is important to note, however, that Mooney's
position emerged within the intellectual atmosphere of the BAE. Powell's
system of mental evolutionism was always flawed and open to radical
challenge. While Powell chose to emphasize the gulfs and distances separating
savage and civilized men, other observers, including some members of his
own staff, formally embraced the stage-sequence framework but were nonetheless struck, not by the disparities, but by the similarities in belief and
behavior among all men. Why were they impressed in such a manner? As
in Mooney's case, personal temperament and prior experience deeply influence
basic perspective in anthropology, shaping the personal politics of the
science. As he grew older Powell increasingly accented the great psychic and
social leaps at critical points in his conjectured human development, while
Mooney, with equal legitimacy and oftentimes similar language, pointed to
continuity and behavioral kinship among men. He was exploring the possibility that Indian cultures represented not simpler, undeveloped human experiences, but full, complex models that were in no meaningful sense distinct
from civilization.

This awareness, which dawned in the Cherokee work, became possible only
when Mooney viewed the Cherokees as more than a dying cultural remnant.
Nineteenth-century ethnology was built on the assumption of Indian decay,
and the BAE had been founded within that tradition. As long as he pursued
the professed institutional purposes of the Bureau—salvaging linguistic and
material pieces—the intellectual perimeter of Mooney's work would be confined. But Mooney bent the institution to his personality and desires, and
he was inclined to see vigor, not decay. However gradual the personal process,
the result was a perceptual switch that set Mooney on a path diverging widely
from Powell's.[80] By 1900, when he published *Myths of the Cherokee*,[81] Mooney
had long since abandoned Powell's developmental approach to mythology in
favor of ethnohistorical questions. His biographer has stated that it "made
more sense to him to study myth exchange within the context of tribal trading
and raiding patterns."[82] In the face of Powell's strong predilection for viewing
Indian mythology as a system of thought rather than a historical product,
and considering Mooney's subordinate status in the Bureau, his historicism
required courage and conviction. Why did this approach seem more reasonable
to him; what factors determined Mooney's preference?

In pursuing Mooney's anthropology to its sources, it is instructive to consider briefly the contrasting career of Jeremiah Curtin, the myth-collector who worked for the Bureau at intervals during the eighties and nineties. Curtin (1835-1906), born in Wisconsin territory and educated at Harvard during the Civil War, omnivorously studied languages and recorded folktales and myths around the world, from the Modocs and Wintus of California to the Irish and the Slavs. Despite a common Irish heritage, midwestern roots, mutual interest in both Celtic and American Indian mythology, and overlapping sojourns at the Bureau, Curtin and Mooney curiously never developed any professional or personal relationship. Age may have been a factor, since Curtin was a considerably older man, but then, so was Washington Matthews. The breach between Curtin and Mooney was deeper than age.

Curtin saw globally: "Not greatness dwarfs men, but littleness, petty surroundings, petty associates, petty interests dwarf."[83] Externally at least, Curtin was certainly not petty. He could never be tied to focused study or a single spot; he never owned a home and, except for brief periods of BAE office work, rarely stayed in one place more than a few months. For decades his faithful wife accompanied him everywhere as companion and secretary. Unquestionably a talented polyglot—he knew dozens of languages with various degrees of proficiency—Curtin skimmed a score of cultures, enduring terrible privations and enjoying cosmopolitan luxuries. So did his wife.

When he was in Washington, Curtin was a favorite of Powell's; he dedicated *Creation Myths of Primitive America* (1898) to the one-armed explorer through whom, he said, "the world has learned more of the great primitive race of our country than it learned from the discovery of the continent till the day when the Bureau was founded."[84] It is evident from his published statements that Curtin accepted Powell's theories and purposes. He had little interest in aboriginal histories. The myths of the American Indians, he believed, together formed a coherent system that was characteristic of a primitive plateau of mentality.[85] They had "philosophies of life and systems of religion which resembled one another, but were greatly varied in detail; the underlying ideas were mainly the same, but the working out varied from tribe to tribe." Curtin saw the Western Hemisphere as an extensive "museum of the human mind in its earlier conditions." He valued Indian mythology as a "treasure saved to science by the primitive race of America," not as a living presence or means of further inquiry.[86]

Curtin's field practice fitted his purposes. He claimed, like a successful ethnologist, to have been "adopted" by the Seneca, but the honor was a meaningless gesture that occurred on his first day at the reservation near Versailles, New York. In Curtin's words, "Then I ate an ear of corn and I was an Indian. . . . After receiving the congratulations of the crowd, I went back to Versailles, leaving the Indians to partake of their feast."[87] Curtin did subsequently return to the Seneca and in time developed relatively stable informant relations with people who were already highly acculturated into local White society. Among the Modocs, Klamaths, and Wintus of the west coast, however, Curtin was more a detached consumer than a committed investigator: "Whenever one Indian failed me, I sent for another and, while waiting, I kept my nerves steady by reading Persian," he wrote of one visit.[88] In sum, Curtin was never really more than a sojourner anywhere, even in Washington: "In the Bureau (in 1885-86) I was occupied with the Alaskan work but I found time to read Hebrew and Persian, and with the assistance of Smith, a Cherokee Indian, I learned the Cherokee language. Evening hours were given to study."[89]

The contrasts between Mooney and Curtin—in personality, method, experience, and basic concerns—point to the complexity in the shaping of an ethnologist. Curtin was restless and homeless, but he was not alienated from or critical of his civilization. While at Harvard he had easily adopted the style and values of mid-century Boston as it entered its "New England Indian Summer": he wrote with polish but no passion; he traveled widely, but his nerves were numbed to the pain and sorrow of Indian fate. His goal was to contribute to the library of humanist knowledge, not to participate in history or pass judgment on it.

Mooney came to the BAE with a critical edge that was soon sharpened by work among a defeated but persistent people. The remarkable fact is that Mooney, perhaps because he lacked a thorough grounding in Powellian philosophy or a variant evolutionism, saw the persistence in Cherokee defeat. Mooney's own persistence and struggle may have been determinative. For him, nothing came easily. A shy and reticent man, he did not possess the flair or ease of Curtin. To him the human world was enigmatic, an accidental series of affairs, anything but a progressive rise to civilized reason. The measure of Mooney's growth was an increasing tentativeness toward knowledge. "I am not infallible or omniscient," he reminded Matthews in 1897, "& every field trip serves only to convince me more than before that at the best a white man can only hope to gather scraps around the edge of his Indian subject."[90]

In 1890 Mooney turned to the Plains region and shelved his Cherokee notes for nearly a decade. The switch was occasioned by an outbreak of the ghost-dance among the Arapaho, Cheyenne, and other tribes from the Mississippi to California, but Mooney's work in the Southeast had already led him to the Indian Territory to study the western Cherokee. On the basis of linguistic and historical evidence, Mooney had argued, following Horatio Hale's suggestion, that the Tutelo and related groups of the Southeast were survivors of the parent stock of western Siouan tribes, who at some point had been driven out of the Southeast by Algonquian and Iroquoian interlopers. Mooney's case was largely circumstantial and hotly debated, but it indicated his growing historicism and drew his attention westward.[91]

His famous memoir on *The Ghost Dance Religion and the Sioux Outbreak of*

1890, which appeared in the Bureau's 1893 annual report (published in 1896), marked his maturity as reporter, historian, and ethnologist; it has remained the major source of his enduring reputation. The ghost-dance had been misrepresented by agents of the Bureau of Indian Affairs and by eastern newspapers as preparation for war. Mooney soon discovered that the fears were unfounded and that the dance pointed to deep historical and ethnological puzzles:

> In the fall of 1890 the author was preparing to go to Indian Territory, under the auspices of the Bureau of Ethnology, to continue researches among the Cherokee, when the Ghost dance began to attract attention, and permission was asked and received to investigate the subject also among the wilder tribes in the western part of the territory. Proceeding directly to the Cheyenne and Arapaho, it soon became evident that there was more in the Ghost dance than had been suspected, with the result that the investigation, to which it had been intended to devote only a few weeks, has extended over a period of more than three years, and might be continued indefinitely, as the dance still exists (in 1896) and is developing new features at every performance.[92]

Mooney observed and participated in the ghost-dance during three field seasons (1891–93), chiefly among the Arapaho, Sioux, Kiowa, and Cheyenne. He carefully wrote down a multitude of songs, and in 1893 became one of the first ethnologists to use a gramophone in the field. Because the songs contained the structure of the religion, he argued, analysis of their symbolism would yield insights into the mythology and customs of each tribe. At the ceremonies Mooney carefully watched face and body movements, the gestures of the medicine-men, and the symptoms and timing of trances. His research into the history of the spread of the ghost-dance, and his pilgrimage, at the end of 1891, to Wovoka, the Paiute prophet who lived on Walker Lake reservation in Nevada, convinced Mooney that the dance was a ceremony of peace and brotherhood, a movement of cultural revitalization among desperately poor, nearly hopeless peoples. Wovoka's written statement of religious principles, as Mooney analyzed it, contained the basic elements of every religion: ethical precepts, a spiritual mythology, and exhortation to ritual observance. The ghost-dance religion was a "revolution" that came "but once in the life of a race."[93] While each of the tribes interpreted Wovoka's message according to its own myths, they all shared the messianic faith as "the only viable alternative in a world of insufferable oppression."[94]

The massacre at Wounded Knee, which occurred as Mooney was preparing for the field in the last days of 1890, and the stunning ignorance and corruption of BIA agents, moved Mooney to anger that he transformed into poignant descriptive passages. After reviewing the evidence and official reports of Wounded Knee, he concluded in a balanced tone "that the first shot was fired by an Indian, and that the Indians were responsible for the engagement; that the answering volley and attack by the troops was right and justifiable, but that the wholesale slaughter of women and children was unnecessary and inexcusable."[95] Even less forgivable was the failure to send a medical or burial team to the site for three days. Mooney described the scene:

> The bodies of the slaughtered men, women, and children were found lying about under the snow, frozen stiff and covered with blood. . . . Almost all the dead warriors were found lying near where the fight began, about Big Foot's tipi, but the bodies of the women and children were found scattered along for 2 miles from the scene of the encounter, showing that they had been killed while trying to escape. . . . A number of women and children were found still alive, but all badly wounded or frozen, or both, and most of them died after being brought in. Four babies were found alive under the snow, wrapped in shawls and lying beside their dead mothers, whose last thought had been of them. They were all badly frozen and only one lived. The tenacity of life so characteristic of wild people as well as of wild beasts was strikingly illustrated in the case of these wounded and helpless Indian women and children who thus lived three days through a Dakota blizzard, without food, shelter, or attention to their wounds. It is a commentary on our boasted Christian civilization that although there were two or three salaried missionaries at the agency not one went out to say a prayer over the poor mangled bodies of these victims of war.

> A long trench was dug and into it were thrown all the bodies, piled one upon another like so much cordwood, until the pit was full, when the earth was heaped over them and the funeral was complete. . . . Many of the bodies were stripped by the whites, who went out in order to get the "ghost shirts," and the frozen bodies were thrown into the trench stiff and naked. They were only dead Indians. As one of the burial party said, "It was a thing to melt the heart of a man, if it was of stone, to see those little children, with their bodies shot to pieces, thrown naked into the pit."[96]

Powell valued Mooney's ethnological labors, but he was undoubtedly pleased that it did not appear in print until 1896. While Mooney was in the field in early 1891, *Illustrated American* and several eastern newspapers began a campaign for an official investigation into the roles of the army and Bureau of Indian Affairs in recent events, especially Wounded Knee. The editors of *Illustrated American,* circulating a petition in Washington, called on both Powell and Mason. Both refused to sign. Mason, according to the magazine, replied that "we never express ourselves vehemently upon political matters. It isn't healthy to do so." *Illustrated American* also reported its meeting with Powell:

I next visited Major Powell, the head of the Geological Survey, and one of the best posted men on Indian affairs in this country. He refused to sign the petition on the ground that it would embroil him in a controversy with the Secretary of the Interior. (And, by the way, all these department heads seem to be in mortal dread of Secretary Noble.) Major Powell further said that he had no doubt that the Sioux had suffered to an extreme degree. He heartily wished that the appeal to Congress should be successful.[97]

Powell had good reason to be circumspect, since he was under heavy attack from critics of the Geological Survey, who would force him to resign from the Survey two years later. But more disturbing than Mooney's accusation of Army "butchery" at Wounded Knee and his transparent Indian sympathies were his speculative cross-cultural comparisons between the ghost-dance and other religious movements of revitalization among the oppressed, including early Christianity. This aspect of Moooney's work, which presaged theoretical and comparative work in cultural deprivation in the twentieth century, was unwelcome heterodoxy in Langley's Smithsonian and Powell's Bureau. Mooney's suggestion that Christian doctrine might be founded on dreams and visions appalled Langley, who admonished Powell that "such words . . . had better have been left unwritten. They give the ill-wishers of the Bureau a powerful means of attack, if attention is called to them, which I trust it will not be."[98] Powell agreed and regretted that Mooney's statements in an official government publication might "provoke hostile criticism."[99] Characteristically, in his introduction to the annual report the director repaired the damage as best he could:

It may be observed that caution should be exercised in comparing or contrasting religious movements among civilized peoples with such fantasies as that described in the memoir; for while interesting and suggestive analogies may be found, the essential features of the movements are not homologous. Most of the primitive peoples of the earth, including the greater part of the American Indians, represent the prescriptorial stage of culture. . . . while white men represent the scriptorial stage. Now, the passage from the earlier of these stages to the later, albeit partially accomplished among different peoples, probably marks the most important transition in the development of human culture or the history of the race; so that in mode of thought and in coordination between thought and action, red men and white men are separated by a chasm so broad and deep that few representatives of either race are ever able clearly to see its further sides. . . . Thus, many of the movements described in this chapter were among people separated from the ghost dance enthusiasts by the widest known cultural break as well as by the widest known break in fiducial development; and whatever the superficial resemblance in the movements, there is a strong presumption against their essential homology.[100]

The experiences of the early nineties drove Mooney further away from the "party line" of the Bureau. His meticulous research, mainly in official government documents, protected him from reprisal from those outside the Bureau who objected to his account of Wounded Knee, but within the BAE Mooney seems to have become increasingly isolated. At the World's Fair in Chicago in 1893 he clashed with Cushing over display techniques, and in the field he began to find the Bureau's procedures irksome and constricting. At one point he exploded to Henshaw:

> I have spent the last two weeks in a dirty tepee, sleeping on the ground and living on crackers and coffee, because I wouldn't eat a sick colt. I come back to find my vouchers returned and no money and [have] to dodge the traders and stand off a mob of wild Indians. . . . When I return I must have money . . . from some source and after that I can sit down and make vouchers to suit all the red tape requirements of the treasury.[101]

The trajectory of Mooney's career pointed to intensive history and ethnography of specific cultures at the very time that Powell, with the aid of W J McGee, was beginning his final, rigid evolutionary synthesis. Mooney, intellectually (and often physically) isolated and possessed by a sense of urgency to record the disappearing way of life of the southern plains, spent two-thirds of his time in the field, usually among the Kiowa, over the next decade. Finding in the Kiowa the most conservative tribe of the region, in 1893 he started the most intensive, prolonged field study of his life. He focused on two points: discovery and analysis of Kiowa calendar counts, and reproduction and study of the symbolism of Kiowa heraldry (tipi and warrior shield designs). The dual emphasis had a logic. The calendar studies offered insight into the Kiowas' view of their own recent history; in 1898 Mooney published *Calendar History of the Kiowa Indians,* now recognized as a meticulously researched classic. The heraldry studies that Mooney extended to the Cheyenne and others but never completed, were a promising window into social organization and the world of dreams and visions.[102]

McGee, who acted as ethnologist in charge of the Bureau after 1893, had little understanding or patience with Mooney's ethnohistorical interests, and he grew progressively annoyed with Mooney's political and personal activities on behalf of his Indian friends. McGee wanted published work; he saw no reason why an ethnologist could not go to the field and make his observations one year and write them up the next, as he did with the Seri Indians in 1894 and 1895.[103] When Mooney complained of illness in a difficult 1895 season, McGee advised him that if his health did not "permit effective operations," he should stop wasting Bureau money. Hurt and angry, Mooney retorted that

"During all these months that I have been almost fighting for my life to carry through to completion a piece of work that might bring credit to the bureau . . . an occasional expression of official concern might have served to brace up failing energies, but this goes far to kill what strength is left."[104] He returned to Washington early, as McGee ordered.

Mooney came to despise McGee for his arrogance and ignorance. But quite aside from personalities, well before the turn of the century Mooney realized that the framework of social and mental development into which Powell and McGee insisted on placing his studies was sterile. He saw, furthermore, that Powell's program for anthropology no longer served a useful purpose and must give way to fresh ideas. In 1903 Mooney received an opportunity to state views orally that he would certainly have hesitated to commit to writing. Testifying before the Smithsonian committee looking into practices in Powell's Bureau, Mooney was initially reticent, but when requested to state his personal views on organizing research he summarized nearly two decades of experience.

The era of the survey was over in anthropology, Mooney observed. Linguistic stock classification, he contended, bore little relation to environmental/cultural types, which was a far more meaningful classification for study and museum display.[105] Given the small corps of ethnologists available, Mooney judged, to undertake to study every tribe would only result in "a lot of bad work."[106] His plan was to map out the major type areas and concentrate on typical "study tribes" for each group, as he had done with the Cherokee for the southeastern woodland type, and the Kiowa for the southern plains. He estimated that about thirty such "broadly defined types" could be established north of Mexico. Mooney's description of the plains type revealed the importance he placed on environment and his broad scope of interrelationships:

> For instance, we will take the plains, stretching, say, from the Saskatchewan down to the Rio Grande, generally a timberless region, occupied originally by the buffalo as the principal game animal; and the Indians consequently were nomadic in their habits. They could not manufacture anything that was easily breakable, and for that reason did not have pottery . . . and they did not have the wood carving of the Pueblo tribes, and they did not do much basket work, for lack of material. They depended on the buffalo, and had to follow him, so they had to have portable houses, and could not build stone or adobe houses. They had the tipi, and it was made of skin. They developed certain arts all along that line; and along with the tipi as the center of the house life they had certain other things that belonged to the same kind of hunting and nomadic life. They did not have agriculture, and as they did not have that, they did not have certain of the arts and objects that sedentary tribes had. They did not have the Green Corn Dance that belonged especially to agriculture, but they did have certain things that the tribes to the east and the west of them did not have.[107]

The work must be done quickly, Mooney told the committee. Defending his practice of spending so much time in the field, Mooney confessed that his notes would be of limited use to another student, since they were "shorthand notes, to be interpreted from my own knowledge and experience, for final writing."[108] But the field work could not wait: "I do not think much of the desk ethnologist, on general principles, and I know from being out there—well, being with any tribe—how rapidly this thing is passing away."

Now, for instance, I have just come from one great ceremonial, and I have seen it four times. I saw it ten years ago for the first time, and I have seen it twice since, and then this last time. It would be impossible to make anybody in the east realize the difference between that ceremonial the first time I saw it and this last time. And I can judge from that that in five years it will be wiped [out]; it will not be there at all; it will have vanished.

Now I am most of my time with the Kiowas. I hope to work them up as a complete tribal study. I picked them out about twelve years ago, after having seen a great many tribes, as being the best study tribe upon the plains, and the most conservative—as being the most Indian. I have been with them on this last trip, for a year and a half, and in all that time I have not seen one man in Indian dress in that tribe. When I went to them there were not half a dozen families in the tribe living in houses. They were all in tipis and in tipi camps. . . . There were not a dozen men who ever wore a hat. They had feathers in their hair, and they painted their faces whenever they went any place. The man with whom I made my home—I lived in tipis then for several years during the time I was with them—had eight rings in one ear and five in the other. He lived in a tipi and under an arbor in summer, always had his full buckskin on when it was time for buckskin; and he never went to a military post, or to a dance, or to anything else, without spending a couple of hours at least to dress and paint up. Now he is in a house, and has chickens and a corn field, and stoves and clocks and beds; and he has taken out his rings and cut his hair, and he looks like a dilapidated tramp.

Now, that sort of thing is going on everywhere, and I do not think an ethnologist can afford to spend much time in the office under such circumstances. When a man gets broken down he can afford to sit at a desk; but I believe it is better to take the chances of having some of this note material lost, and to spend this present time in investigation.[109]

When Mooney described to the committee the indirect, cumulative nature of field note-taking, his terms exposed clearly the chasm that separated his anthropology from the natural-science tradition of Powell and the early Bureau. People, Mooney had found, simply could not be observed and described in the same manner as birds or geological deposits:

A man investigating another kind of a subject perhaps, some natural science, is making his own investigations, in his laboratory; he is alone, and as he discovers a fact he can note it there. But I am talking to an Indian—well, say I am talking to an Indian about his shield, and he tells me that this shield was dreamed by a certain man. Then I get a dream origin for my myth note-book; I get a name with a translation for my—well, for my dictionary, if you please, or glossary, and I get a statement on name giving for some other investigation, and before I am done with it, he may mention a plant, and some use for that plant, and there may be some origin for that, and after an hour's talk with him, I have probably struck a dozen threads for investigation; and that would all be on two or three pages. And the rest of those same lines or threads would be on other pages in other notebooks. Now, when it comes to writing those out for the final publication, it must be all overhauled, and all the material from the different places put together. In that way, as you can see, each one of these things will be scattered all through the note material. [110]

Mooney was not alone with the insights of his field experiences. He had learned from Dorsey and Matthews; Cushing, too, had sensed the depth of Zuñi life. Matilda Stevenson, whom Powell detested but tolerated in the Bureau because of her political connections, steadily deepened her knowledge of Zuñi and Zia pueblos over several decades. By all accounts an insensitive field worker, [111] Stevenson nonetheless came to see the importance of prolonged exposure. She had written her BAE monograph *The Zuñi Indians*, [112] she explained in 1903, because

I felt the need of some definite publication, a sort of foundation of some tribe, and my aim in the Zuñi work was to probe to the very core of their philosophy, their religion, and sociology and to make such a book as would be of positive value to the student of ethnology . . . I hoped to get something that the student could take hold of and read and then start on any line of study he might desire. It takes a good part of a life to get a work like that. . . . No one can pursue a profound study in any special line in ethnological work without having a foundation to go upon, because their religion, their sociology, their whole life, is so entangled, so gnarled together, that you cannot study one line without the other unless you are familiar with their life. [113]

At the founding of the BAE, vocabulary lists and circulars of inquiry had still been basic methodology. They had introduced system and consistency but had discouraged flexibility in the field—the flexibility that Mooney had in mind when he stated that "The Indian is an uncertain quantity. You get him in one place and in another place. He is not a man whom you can talk with right straight along."[114] Years in the field, made possible by the institutional freedom of the Bureau, had taught Mooney a patient willingness to let specific conditions determine the immediate direction of inquiry. But flexibility was not capitulation. As we have seen, Cushing suffered accusations of having become a savage, and Mooney's sympathy with Indian political concerns created considerable friction. Yet neither man "went native," and in most respects, such as Mooney's aversion to sexual or scatological references in print, both adhered to contemporary American mores. What set them apart was their gradual realization that just as grammatical categories must be altered in learning Indian languages, the anthropologist must suspend, not abandon, inherited notions of social organization, scientific knowledge, artistic beauty, even moral categories, if he is to come to understand another people. This was a difficult and troublesome stance, for it involved willingness to doubt and surrender, albeit temporarily, the hard-won certainties of industrial civilization. As Henry Adams remarked of the 1890s, "one could not stop to chase doubts as though they were rabbits."[115]

By the new century the BAE had inadvertently spawned, in certain individuals, a critical perspective and an ethnographic emphasis that had been largely unknown only twenty years before. There is an understandable temptation to see in Mooney or Cushing forebears of modern professional anthropology, particularly when they appear against a background of nineteenth-century evolutionary enthusiasts. In a recent study of Cushing, Joan Mark credits him with developing "an American science of anthropology" and argues for his priority in conceiving and developing, in his Hemenway years, the culture concept usually attributed to Boas.[116] Cushing did use the term "cultures" in his writings of the 1890s, in contexts which leave little doubt that he meant integrated, holistic, historically determined phenomena. But for Cushing (and Mooney), intellectual discoveries had no direct bearing on the structures of scientific institutions. They did not perceive that certain avenues of inquiry, especially in the social sciences, must be guaranteed freedom from external interference in order to proceed. Similarly, Cushing never followed his concept of culture to its clear institutional implication: that anthropologists must be trained to recognize and allow for the cultural and personal bias of their observing. The element lacking (from current perspective) in Mooney and Cushing, the blind spot that places them in their own time, was their inability to see the intimate linkage between intellectual life and the institutional structures in which it necessarily takes place.

The structures of nineteenth-century anthropology no less than those of today permitted favorable conditions of growth for some inquiries, while others withered for lack of nourishment. Boas realized as much, and between 1896 and 1905 he stated clearly the limitations and possibilities, as he saw them, of the government bureau and the museum as institutional forms for anthropological science.[117] Over the following decade he brought about the major alterations in both the intellectual and institutional contours of American anthropology that would establish his dominance in the profession by 1920. But the driving force in the Boasian revolution, and the reason that one could speak of a "profession" by 1920, came precisely from that combination of institutional and intellectual structure: through the university department Boas consciously institutionalized a new constellation of ideas capable of being tested and elaborated by a subsequent generation of trained students.

Intimacy between institutions and ideas is a fundamental condition of modern intellectual life.[118] Beyond the annual meetings and journals of communication, the professional condition means that the survival and development of ideas depend heavily on the barrenness or fertility of institutional soil. And, as Boas quickly learned, institutions by their very natures offer widely varying conditions for growth. Because they possessed little institutional perspective, Mooney and Cushing, for better or worse, were not "professional" anthropologists. To the limited extent that they concerned themselves with perpetuating theory or method through testing and refinement, they relied, like Powell, on example rather than on training others to follow them. As Mooney confessed, he was willing to take the risk of leaving behind piles of undigested, possibly unusable field notes. Of equal importance, their audience was the American nation, not a well-defined academic peer group. As Joan Mark has perceptively observed, Cushing "glorified in the cleverness of the Zuñi people, and implicitly in his own cleverness, in being able to follow along and trace the interconnections in their culture. He was an insider telling the rest of the world something it did not know. For later anthropologists the approach was more often that of scientists telling one another things about a group of people which the people did not know about themselves."[119]

The cases of Mooney and Cushing demonstrate that professionalism, in Washington anthropology or elsewhere, did not come naturally or without a cost. The national moral service that Joseph Henry had foreseen for American anthropology remained a possibility for Cushing, Mooney, and their colleagues. They could not make the adjustment to a more rigorous, constructed professional audience and its horizons. If they were not anthropologists of the sort that we would recognize today, it was only because they held to grander goals. Professionals, no, but they were exceptional, committed men.

Notes

1. Max Weber, "Science as Vocation," in H. H. Gerth and C. Wright Mills, eds., *From Max Weber: Essays in Sociology* (London, 1948), p. 155.

2. Henry Adams, *The Education of Henry Adams: An Autobiography* (Boston, 1961), p. 328.

3. Richard L. Slotkin, *Regeneration Through Violence: The Mythology of the American Frontier, 1600–1860* (Middletown, Conn., 1974).

4. Susan Sontag, "The Anthropologist as Hero," in E. N. Hayes and T. Hayes, eds., *Claude Lévi-Strauss: The Anthropologist as Hero* (Cambridge, 1970), pp. 188–89.

5. I have borrowed this point from Joan Mark, "Frank Hamilton Cushing and an American Science of Anthropology," *Perspectives in American History* 10 (1976): 482.

6. Notation on reverse of a photograph of Cushing presented to the Southwest Museum by F.W. Hodge in 1950. I am indebted to William Sturtevant for this reference.

7. Boas quoted in Neil Judd, *The Bureau of American Ethnology: A Partial History* (Norman, Okla., 1967), pp. 62–63; F. W. Hodge to E. DeGolyer, 3 April 1946, Hodge-Cushing Papers.

8. Alfred Kroeber, "Frank Hamilton Cushing," *Encyclopedia of the Social Sciences* II (New York, 1930–35): 657; Mark, "Frank Hamilton Cushing," p. 485.

9. "Necrology: Frank Hamilton Cushing," BAE, *AR for 1900*, p. xxxv. The author was almost certainly McGee, but materials in Cushing's papers indicate that the oft-repeated stories of Cushing's childhood originated with him.

10. See Mark, "Frank Hamilton Cushing," pp. 484–86.

11. Cushing to Mason, 30 September 1876, Hodge-Cushing Papers.

12. Cushing to Baird, 29 October 1879, NAA.

13. Bourke Diary, 30 May 1889; as quoted in Robert Poor, "Washington Matthews: An Intellectual Biography," M.A. thesis (University of Nevada-Reno, 1975), p. 45.

14. F.H. Cushing, "Antiquities of Orleans County, New York," SI, *AR for 1874*, pp. 375–77; Baird to Cushing, 3 December 1875, SIA.

15. Cushing to Lucien Turner, 15 May 1879, Hodge-Cushing Papers.

16. F.H. Cushing, "The Germ of Shore-Land Pottery," *Memoirs of the International Congress of Anthropology* (Chicago, 1893), p. 234.

17. See, e.g., Baird to Cushing, 12 July 1878, NAA, for an example of their continued close contact.

18. Powell to James Stevenson, 4 August 1879, M. C. Stevenson Papers, NAA.

19. Squier to Robert Winthrop, 15 February 1875, Peabody Museum Papers, HUA.

20. The phrase was Baird's. Baird to "Dear James," 10 July 1883, M. C. Stevenson Papers, NAA.

21. Powell to Stevenson, 8 September 1880, M. C. Stevenson Papers, NAA.

22. Despite Powell's claim that he "first sent Mr. Cushing to Zuñi" (BAE, *AR for 1898,* p. xlvii), it was Baird who guided Cushing's course in the early years.

23. Cushing to Baird, 18 July 1880, NAA.

24. Cushing's severe gastrointestinal problems plagued him for years. In 1883, E. N. Horsford, a Boston admirer, offered to pay Cushing's fare back to Washington and begged Powell to let him return: "Cushing has repeatedly written me of his terrible suffering from dyspepsia. . . . I see a little of the martyr spirit which alarms me. We cannot afford to indulge in such sacrifice." (Horsford to Powell, 19 November 1883, NAA).

25. Baird to Stevenson, 8 September 1880, M. C. Stevenson Papers, NAA; Baird to Putnam, 8 April 1882, Peabody Museum Papers, HUA.

26. Cushing to Baird, 9 October 1879, NAA.

27. Triloki Nath Pandey, "Anthropologists at Zuñi," *Proceedings of the American Philosophical Society* 116, no. 4 (1972), pp. 322–28.

28. Cushing to Baird and Powell, 18 February 1880 (draft), NAA. This important letter included Cushing's list of fields for study at Zuñi: language (prerequisite); industrial and art "formulas"; religious instructions, prayers, and songs; religious materials (masks, etc.); plume sticks; astronomic monuments; "Zuñi culture compared to other indigenous American Civilizations"; gesture language survivals; kinship patterns; ancient ruins; primitive condition of the Shiwe; origin of current mythological usages; "effects of natural phenomena and physical environment on nature belief"; philosophy of games; recording oratory, folklore, and mythology.

29. BAE, *AR for 1884,* pp. xxv–xxix, xxxii–xxxv.

30. Cushing to Baird, 4 December 1881, as quoted in Pandey, "Anthropologists at Zuñi," p. 323.

31. Ibid., p. 326. The most complete recital of these events occurs in Raymond Stewart Brandes, "Frank Hamilton Cushing: Pioneer Americanist," Ph.D. diss. (University of Arizona, 1965). Brandes's work, the only full-length study of Cushing, is valuable for basic facts and anecdotal material. See also Bernard L. Fontana, "Pioneers in Ideas: Three Early Southwestern Ethnologists," *Journal of Arizona Academy of Science* 2 (1960): 124–29.

32. Pandey, "Anthropologists at Zuñi," pp. 325–26.

33. Cushing to Baird (draft, n.d.), NAA.

34. Ms. "Interview," 9 June 1883, Hodge-Cushing Papers; as quoted in Pandey, "Anthropologists at Zuñi," p. 326, and in Brandes, "Frank Hamilton Cushing," p. 107.

35. Washington Matthews to Cushing, 8 August 1881, Hodge-Cushing Papers. Reference courtesy of Robert Poor.

36. Matthews to Cushing, 17 August 1886, Hodge-Cushing Papers. Reference courtesy of Robert Poor.

37. Matthews to Cushing, 4 November 1884, Hodge-Cushing Papers; and Matthews to Cushing, 18 November 1891, Hodge-Cushing Papers.

38. Matthews to Cushing, 4 November 1884, Hodge-Cushing Papers; Matthews to Cushing, 5 April 1892, Hodge-Cushing Papers. Reference courtesy of Robert Poor.

39. As suggested by Philip Phillips in his introduction to Cushing, *Exploration of Ancient Key Dwellers' Remains on the Gulf Coast of Florida* (New York, 1973). However, Cushing failed to produce consistently, in instances where this consideration played no part.

40. Cushing to Bourke, 13 August 1881; Sheridan to Bourke, 8 June 1882, Hodge-Cushing Papers.

41. Bourke to Cushing, 7 June 1882, Hodge-Cushing Papers.

42. Bourke to Cushing, 25 November 1882 and 30 June 1884, Hodge-Cushing Papers.

43. Bourke to Cushing, 30 September 1884, Hodge-Cushing Papers.

44. BAE, *AR for* 1885, p. xlvii; F.H. Cushing, "A Study of Pueblo Pottery, as Illustrative of Zuñi Culture Growth," BAE, *AR for 1883*, pp. 467–521.

45. Cushing to "My Dear Friend," 27 August 1891 (draft), Hodge-Cushing Papers.

46. Matthews to Cushing, 7 January 1891 and 23 July 1889, Hodge-Cushing Papers.

47. Harris to Cushing, 9 November 1891, Hodge-Cushing Papers.

48. On Hodge's hostility, see Mark, "Frank Hamilton Cushing," p. 481, fn.

49. Hodge to Emil W. Haury, 5 October 1931, and handwritten notes, PMA.

50. Ibid.

51. Ibid.

52. Ibid.

53. Cushing to Putnam, 4 January 1898 (copy of letter of June 1897), PMA.

54. Cushing to Putnam, 4 January 1898, PMA.

55. Brandes, "Frank Hamilton Cushing," pp. 161–67, discusses this period.

56. The Florida excursion is treated in F. H. Cushing, *Exploration of Ancient Key Dwellers' Remains on the Gulf Coast of Florida*, ed. with intro. by Philip Phillips (New York, 1973); in Brandes, "Frank Hamilton Cushing," pp. 167–205; and in Marion Spjut Gilliland, *The Material Culture of Key Marco Florida* (Gainesville, 1975). Gilliland presents a judicious account of the Cushing expedition, including the Dinwiddie accusation against Cushing, discussed below. She concludes that Cushing was innocent and the painted shell was genuine (p. 183).

57. BAE, *AR for 1895*, p. lvii.

58. Gilliland, *Material Culture*, p. 4.

59. Cushing, *Key Dwellers' Remains*, p. xvii.

60. Gilliland, *Material Culture*, presents the case and reproduces relevant documents. Dinwiddie had made slanderous statements about other Bureau staff members as well (McGee to Powell, 27 October 1896, copy in BAE-IN, NAA).

61. Matthews to Cushing, 21 January 1897, Hodge-Cushing Papers. Reference courtesy of Robert Poor.

62. Gilliland, *Material Culture*, p. 5.

63. F. H. Cushing, "The Need of Studying the Indian in Order to Teach Him," *28th Annual Report of the Board of Indian Commissioners* (Washington, D.C., 1897 [reprinted by A. M. Eddy, Albion, New York, 1897]), pp. 3–4.

64. Ibid., pp. 9–10.

65. Ibid., p. 12.
66. Mark, "Frank Hamilton Cushing," p. 482.
67. The major source for this discussion of James Mooney is the recent, thorough biography of Mooney by William Colby: "Routes to Rainy Mountain: A Biography of James Mooney, Ethnologist", Ph.D. diss. (University of Wisconsin-Madison, 1977). I am deeply indebted to Mr. Colby for permitting me to use his unpublished study and other materials.

"The nineteenth-century Irish saw themselves as the victims of history," Arthur M. Schlesinger, Jr., writes in *Robert Kennedy and His Times* (New York, 1978). "Memories of dispossession and defeat filled their souls. They had lost their national independence, their personal dignity, their land, even their language, to intruders from across the sea" (p. 3).
68. James Mooney, *The Ghost-Dance Religion and the Sioux Outbreak of 1890,* BAE, *AR for 1893,* Part 2 (Washington, D.C., 1896).
69. John R. Swanton, "James Mooney," *American Anthropologist* 24 (1922): 209.
70. Colby, "Routes to Rainy Mountain," p. 42.
71. See the discussion in Chapter VI.
72. Caroline Matthews to Charles F. Lummis, 22 May 1905, CFL Papers. Reference courtesy of Robert Poor.
73. James Mooney, "In Memoriam: Washington Matthews," *American Anthropologist* 7 (1905):520.
74. Colby, "Routes to Rainy Mountain," p. 52.
75. Ibid., p. 76.
76. James Mooney, "Sacred Formulas of the Cherokees," BAE, *AR for 1886* (Washington, D.C., 1891), p. 309.
77. Colby, "Routes to Rainy Mountain," pp. 81–82, 84.
78. BAE, *AR for 1886* (Washington, D.C., 1891), pp. xxxix–xl.
79. Mooney, "Sacred Formulas," pp. 309, 318–19.
80. On the "gestalt" switch as analog to the process of scientific discovery, see Thomas Kuhn, *The Structure of Scientific Revolutions* (Chicago, 1962).
81. James Mooney, *Myths of the Cherokee,* BAE, *AR for 1898,* Part 1 (Washington, D.C., 1900), pp. 3–548.
82. Colby, "Routes to Rainy Mountain," p. 172.
83. Jeremiah Curtin, *The Memoirs of Jeremiah Curtin* (Madison, 1940), p. 383.
84. Jeremiah Curtin, *Creation Myths of Primitive America in Relation to the Religious History and Mental Development of Mankind* (Boston, 1898).
85. Ibid., pp. xi–xxxix, presents Curtin's synthesis of American creation myths. It is of interest that Curtin, a prolific writer, noted in his *Memoirs* (p. 687) that he struggled to compose this introduction.
86. Curtin, *Memoirs,* pp. 637–38, 502.
87. Ibid., p. 319.
88. Ibid., p. 367.
89. Ibid., p. 382.
90. Mooney to Matthews, 4 July 1897, Matthews Papers, MNCA.
91. James Mooney, "Siouan Tribes of the East," *BAE Bulletin* 22 (Washington, D.C., 1894). For an assessment see Colby, "Routes to Rainy Mountain," pp. 133–35.

92. Mooney, *The Ghost-Dance,* p. 653.
93. Colby, "Routes to Rainy Moutain," p. 232.
94. Ibid., p. 200.
95. Mooney, *The Ghost-Dance,* p. 870.
96. Ibid., pp. 876-79. Robert Underhill, historian of the Puritan slaughter of the Pequot Indians in May 1637, recalled that the Pequots "brake forth into a most doleful cry; so as if God had not filled the hearts of men for the service, it would have bred in them a commiseration towards them." (Larzer Ziff, *Puritanism in America: New Culture in a New World* [New York, 1974], p. 91.) The cant of conquest has a haunting echo.
97. I am indebted to William Colby for providing this information.
98. Langley to Powell, 25 May 1897, NAA.
99. Powell to Langley, 26 May 1897, SIA.
100. BAE, *AR for 1893* (Washington, D.C., 1896), pp. LX–LXI.
101. Mooney to Henshaw, 8 June 1891, NAA; as quoted in Colby, "Routes to Rainy Mountain."
102. James Mooney, *Calendar History of the Kiowa Indians,* BAE, *AR for 1896* (Washington, D.C., 1898), pp. 129–445; Colby, "Routes to Rainy Mountain," pp. 321–22. John C. Ewers has recently evaluated Mooney's Kiowa field work, especially his oral history, in his introduction to the Smithsonian Institution Press reprint of the *Calendar History* (Washington, D.C., 1979). John C. Ewers's *Murals in the Round: Painted Tipis of the Kiowa and Kiowa-Apache Indians; An exhibition of tipi models made for James Mooney of the Smithsonian Institution during his field studies of Indian history and art in southwestern Oklahoma, 1891–1904* (Washington, D.C., 1978), an exhibition catalog for the Renwick Gallery of the National Museum of American Art, presents the first sizable publication of Mooney's tipi data.
103. McGee's career is the subject of Chapter VIII.
104. As quoted in Colby, "Routes to Rainy Mountain," p. 320.
105. Mooney Testimony, BAE-IN, p. 968.
106. Ibid., p. 969.
107. Ibid., p. 970.
108. Ibid., p. 973.
109. Ibid., pp. 974–75.
110. Ibid., pp. 983–84.
111. See, e.g., the account of Stevenson in Pandey, "Anthropologists at Zuñi." It should be noted, however, that Stevenson bore burdens, as the pioneer woman field anthropologist in the Southwest, that none of her male contemporaries shared or recognized. Merely being taken seriously as a scientist was a major accomplishment for a woman in the Bureau. Stevenson's "pushiness" undoubtedly grew in part from intense pressures. For sympathetic portraits, see Nancy O. Lurie, "Matilda Coxe Stevenson," in *Notable American Women, 1607–1950* 3 (Cambridge, 1971): 373–74; and Lurie, "Women in Early American Anthropology," in June Helm, ed., *Pioneers of American Anthropology: The Uses of Biography,* American Ethnological Society monographs, No. 43 (Seattle and London, 1966), pp. 29–81.
112. Matilda Coxe Stevenson, *The Zuñi Indians: Their Mythology, Esoteric Fraternities,*

and Ceremonies, BAE, *AR for 1902* (Washington, D.C., 1904), pp. 1–608.

113. Testimony of M. C. Stevenson, BAE-IN, p. 353.

114. Mooney Testimony, BAE-IN, p. 982.

115. Adams, *Education,* p. 232.

116. Mark, "Frank Hamilton Cushing," passim. For a balanced, closely researched essay on Cushing, see Jeese Green's introduction to his edited *Zuñi: Selected Writings of Frank Hamilton Cushing* (Lincoln, Neb., 1979). Green's full notes display painstaking research and address many of the events discussed earlier in this chapter. By contrast, John Sherwood's recent article on "Frank Cushing, Boy Wonder of the Smithsonian's Old Bureau of Ethnology" (*Smithsonian* 10, no. 5 [1979], pp. 96–113), merely rethreshes old straw.

117. See Chapters VIII and IX.

118. George W. Stocking has begun to investigate and elaborate this point for twentieth-century American anthropology in "Ideas and Institutions in American Anthropology: Toward a History of the Interwar Period," intro. to Stocking, ed., *Selected Papers from the American Anthropologist, 1921-45* (Washington, D.C., 1976), pp. 1–50.

119. Mark, "Frank Hamilton Cushing," p. 484.

VIII

Fin-de-Siècle: The Rise and Fall of William John McGee, 1893–1903

As the nation neared the end of the nineteenth century, severe dislocations and sharp contrasts marked American public and private life. At Chicago in 1893 the White City rose in splendor on the shore of Lake Michigan to celebrate (a year late) 400 years of conquest, expansion, and progress, while a few blocks away the nation's worst depression already gnawed away at the masses of urban poor. The World's Fair lasted less than a year; its anthropology collections would form the nucleus of Marshall Field's ambitious Columbian Museum. The depression lasted until 1897, leaving a different legacy: sober realities of suffering and inequality that even the jingoistic distractions of the Spanish-American War could not conceal. If Chicago was America, the state of civilization was brutally clear: personal exertion and private charity had failed to sustain a free, mobile society. People, millions of them, were caught. Henceforth new commitments and new social forms would be required to preserve stability—never mind equality. "For a hundred years, between 1793 and 1893," Henry Adams reflected, "the American people had hesitated, vacillated, swayed forward and back, between two forces, one simply industrial, the other capitalistic, centralizing, and mechanical." Now they "slipped across the chasm."[1]

For his own part, Adams learned to ride a bicycle.[2] The release of the outdoors in the nineties—bicycling, sports, naturalist clubs, wilderness fiction—came as an antidote to cluttered parlors and closed frontiers.[3] But it was also, perhaps, a sign of altered possibilities. If effective economic and political freedoms were diminished, personal freedoms would fill the void; if few individuals owned their productive lives, many could buy into the life of consumption. Thus, beneath the apparent incongruities and paradoxes of the decade lay the coherence of modern life, a complementarity between immense power and impotent individuals—individuals, like Adams, "landed, lost, and forgotten, in the centre of this vast plain of self-content."[4]

W J McGee has been largely forgotten in American anthropology today. Yet in his ten-year career as anthropologist, from 1893 to 1903, he rose to the height of the profession in this country. At the time of his abrupt departure from Washington in 1903, Alice Fletcher spoke of him as "a man of growing power" in anthropology, and Franz Boas saw in him "the main stay" of sound government anthropology.[5] Fletcher and Boas valued McGee because he played a central role in establishing anthropology as a respectable scientific pursuit at the turn of the century. He vigorously promoted the science, wielding influence less by original contributions than by position—his close relationship to Powell, marriage to Anita Newcomb, and incessant activity in local and national scientific societies. Throughout his career McGee boosted government science: in the eighties, Survey geology; in the nineties, BAE anthropology; from 1907 to his death, Interior Department conservation.

McGee was a master of synthesis. One contemporary wrote that his great strength was "the skillful use of the results of others." John Swanton made the same point less charitably, recalling that McGee "did not impress me as a profound thinker but as intensely desirous to win scientific consideration, and while aping originality . . . desperately feared to depart from the 'party line' of his day . . ."[6] Swanton was accurate but not entirely to the point. McGee served an idea of science, not a specific field; he valued generalization based on broad experience over specialization. As one colleague lamented in 1916, he belonged to a dying breed, "whom there seems to be a tendency to crowd out now . . ."[7]

McGee arrived in Washington in 1883 from a rural Iowa upbringing that included less than eight years of schooling, many seasons of farming, and brief experiments in blacksmithing, inventing, and surveying.[8] Born prematurely and seemingly subject to every possible disease, McGee grew up as "a very sickly, delicate child" on his parents' small farm outside Farley, in eastern Iowa. Triumph over childhood infirmities that led to adult robustness later became a part of the McGee legend. So did self-education. During later years of fame McGee elaborated a "self-made" image, claiming to have taught himself German, Latin, higher mathematics, and law. This was fabrication. The simple fact is that throughout his boyhood and adolescence his work was the farm, and he had little access to even a small library.[9]

In many ways, McGee never left Iowa. Until late in life he retained his state residency, cultivated the powerful Iowa politicians in Washington, who provided him with an important power base, and capitalized on the image of self-made country boy. But he always held in tension contradictory sentiments about his poor roots, making virtue of an undeniable biography, building grand systems of scientific philosophy while telling his daughter nostalgic tales of elementary school foot-races and of taking the hay wagons to town in the hot midwestern summers. Like his friend and fellow Iowan, novelist Hamlin Garland, McGee straddled two worlds: that of the "old red schoolhouse on the hill" and that of Washington science.[10] It was his personal tragedy that McGee never found peace or acceptance in either. By 1912 he was exiled from both. Having cut communication with his Iowa relatives and his wife and children, he passed away alone in a room at the Cosmos Club in Washington.

McGee's early work was on glacial geology. It was audacious, characterized by a slim foundation of careful, even brilliant observation and a large super-structure of theory. He moved easily from present formations to imaginative reconstruction of earlier processes and structures. His geology always contained a distinctly romantic streak; his visionary faculty seemed irrepressible. Powell recognized a kinship, brought him to Washington in 1883, and entrusted major projects to him: a thesaurus of American geological formations and a preliminary geological map of the United States. Their relationship was solidly built on tacit understanding: "McGee, I know what I want; you know what I want. Figure a way to do it before next March."[11]

McGee always figured a way. Learning rapidly and working furiously at his administrative tasks and his own research in the U. S. Geological Survey, within a short period he was exuding self-confidence, influence, and success from Washington. It seemed to one friend that "your fly-wheel is running more smoothly now even than when you used to . . . study panoramic geology at the rate of 40 miles per day; or face highwaymen on dark roads, unarmed, on principle; or make [map] sections for [Israel] Russell in Salt Lake and sub voce swear yourself into a seriously hyperaemic condition."[12] McGee's driving ambition and political malleability fitted him well to government organiza-tion. He fully realized that adjustment was the key to power in organizational science.

He adjusted in various ways. In 1888 he married Anita Newcomb, second daughter of Simon Newcomb, America's foremost astronomer and a powerful influence in the capital. Anita's mother opposed the marriage and her father simply ignored his son-in-law.[13] If McGee needed further motivation, this rejection surely provided it. Anita became a driving force behind his career for the next fifteen years.

In the early years, "Beauty" and "Don," as they affectionately called one another, made the requisite efforts, molding their life together around in-dividual needs and capacities. Anita devotedly accompanied him to the fields of Iowa in 1888, where she examined his genealogy while he displayed his new wife and prepared his old Iowa survey for publication. Subsequently she represented him at professional meetings and joined expeditions in the Po-tomac region. For his part, McGee realized that his wife, as one historian has observed, had "more intellectual than domestic capacity."[14] He encouraged her to pursue medicine and anthropology. She entered Columbian University's School of Medicine and emerged as an M.D. in 1892—a singular achievement for a woman at the time. In the same year she joined the Anthropological Society of Washington and remained a member until 1905.[15]

Participation in scientific societies further enhanced McGee's social status in the capital. He considered such gatherings indispensable to American science. Much of the "substantial scientific progress" of the country came from local societies, contended McGee, for they occupied a critical position between the general populace and organized science; they formed an "intermediate link" between the increasingly isolated specialist and the layman.[16] Specialization bothered McGee deeply, but he responded ambivalently. He defended his own practice of coining new terms because, he argued, new ideas required them. This might be a mistake, he confessed, because science was after all the servant of man; but he was often too busy to reach back to the "cradle terms" of English for the sake of the public.[17] In McGee's view, "specialists grow up through the indifference of the masses and their inability to keep pace with the investigator." At the same time, the knowledge of the specialist was "soon blasted by the poison of its own egoism, unless the richer part of its substance is guided toward the general mass of society."[18]

Ideally the scientific society, embracing educated and intelligent laymen as well as experts, should counteract specialization by diffusing knowledge in reasonably sophisticated form. It might also serve as a badge of membership for men lacking family background.[19] Upon arrival in Washington, McGee lost no time in applying to the array of organizations in the capital. He immediately joined the Anthropological Society, and over the next two decades he delivered twenty-two papers and served as an officer for fifteen consecutive years.[20] But the ASW was only the beginning. Sensing new needs and opportunities, McGee became a driving force in the National Geographic Society, the Geological Society of America, the Columbian Historical Society, and the American Anthropological Association. When the ASW fell on hard times in 1898, McGee and Boas personally took over joint ownership of the *American Anthropologist* and kept it afloat until the founding of the national association four years later.[21] At the founding of the Washington Academy of Sciences in 1898, McGee was the only person belonging to all twelve constituent societies.

Despite the multiple memberships, McGee never felt accepted in Washington. His daughter remembered that "for years my environment had no more use for my father than if he had been a coal-heaver."[22] Marriage into the Newcombs was a major step, to be sure, and in Anita he gained a source of encouragement and further status. But he also brought upon himself expectations that his salary, always anomalously high for a government employee and sufficient for a comfortable life, could never fully satisfy. Not that Anita whipped her husband along in his career. The challenges were always self-imposed with McGee. He loved Anita as he loved science; his doctor wife became a symbol of the social and scientific attainment he never completely knew. He was always impelled to continue proving his worth to his wife and her family, to Washington, and perhaps to himself.

Success and time hardened McGee. By the early nineties he was a powerful force in Washington society. Yet in these years of promise a strident tone

An outing to the soapstone quarry in west Washington, D.C.:
W J and Anita McGee to the left; Otis Mason, center, with stick;
geologist Rollin D. Salisbury to far right, with umbrella.

had already entered his work. Having served his apprenticeship in science, he was now prepared to judge others. His Iowa survey, published in 1890, along with his work on the Potomac region, served as accreditation. The publications, the marriage, the societies—all announced his arrival. But along with them came intemperance and haughtiness, signs of the officious government scientist.

Under intense fire from congressional critics and western mining, timber, and land entrepreneurs, Powell resigned as director of the U. S. Geological Survey in 1893. He retired to the Bureau, bringing along McGee as protégé and heir apparent. The following year Powell underwent a second operation on his painful right arm; he had begun the slow decline to his death in 1902. During these years McGee, operating as "ethnologist in charge," directed the Bureau of American Ethnology. Powell's demise marked McGee's ascendancy in Washington science.

Institutional relations had always been highly personal on the Mall. Powell's friendships with Spencer Baird, Smithsonian Secretary from 1878 to 1887, and with Baird's successor (1887–1906), Langley, were critical in determining Bureau autonomy. Powell had accepted Henry's advice, encouragement, and support as a protégé. With Baird positions were more equal. Powell respected Baird as a brilliant scientific organizer, a fine zoologist and, most importantly, a man who "knew how to marshal significant facts into systems, and to weld them into principles."[23] But Powell also considered the BAE a personal enterprise, placed within the Smithsonian only to insure its independence. He stoutly resisted external control over personnel, appropriations, or research priorities.

The battle for autonomy centered perennially on the "Secretary's reserve." Powell's original plans for the BAE did not involve expeditions for the U.S. National Museum, but Baird maintained that the Bureau must also serve as a collecting arm of the Museum. In November 1879, he announced that he was setting aside one fourth of the BAE's $20,000 appropriation for purchasing or discovering material for the Museum.[24] Baird's motives were scientific and political, as Langley later explained:

It is a recognized fact among all the natural sciences that objects and specimens are as necessary to researches as explorations and notes in the field. This fact was pointed out by Secretary Baird to Major Powell, but, as he was largely interested in linguistics, and was disposed to sacrifice other things to his favorite studies, the collecting of material was largely disregarded, until Secretary Baird insisted, as he told me, upon his view of the wishes of Congress to have some objects well worthy to show as part of the results of the explorations.[25]

The Secretary's reserve remained an informal arrangement, and thus a bone of contention, year after year. As BAE appropriations increased and stabilized at $40,000 from 1883 to 1892, the $5,000 reserve represented a smaller bite of the total. But Powell's research ambitions grew even faster than the funding, so that the reserve became more rather than less irritating. It was an encroachment, a reminder of dependence. In July 1883, for instance, Baird instructed Powell regarding funds for the coming year. He told the director that Congress was "extremely impatient" for material collections, since foreign governments were rapidly "sweeping the localities" of North America for treasures. While Baird complained of the large BAE salaries, he informed Powell of his decision to hire James G. Swan for Northwest Coast work, taking $3,600 of Bureau money—a generous year's salary at the time. His own expenditures, "without the formalities of reference to the director of the Bureau of Ethnology," the Secretary needled Powell, had been "very productive, and will compare favorably with the result of outlays of a similar amount by the Bureau."[26] For the remainder of Baird's tenure, Powell grudgingly tolerated the reserve, working around it but never accepting its validity.

Astronomer Samuel P. Langley came to the Smithsonian from Allegheny Observatory in Pittsburgh less than a year before Baird's death. When he became the Smithsonian's third Secretary in 1887, Washingtonians hardly knew him. They knew little more of him at his death nineteen years later. Fifty-three years old, unmarried and without family ties, Langley arrived alone and lived a lonely life in the capital. Reserved, shy, socially inept, belonging to an older generation, Langley was generally perceived as cold and aloof. He had few friends; according to one of them, "his hunger for real friendship and affection was pathetic."[27]

Powell was one of those few, cherished friends. In the last decade of his life he and Langley vacationed together and exchanged papers on their philosophies of science.[28] When Powell and Holmes traveled to Cuba in 1900, Langley asked them repeatedly to join him in Jamaica, where he was studying the flight of turkey buzzards.[29]

The intimacy with Powell interfered with Langley's control of the Bureau. In 1891 he proposed to assume direct supervision of Bureau personnel and appropriations. Powell lashed out to defend his prerogatives:

> To take from the director the planning of the work, the appointment of employees, and the disbursement of moneys, and to have these duties assumed by the secretary of the Smithsonian, would place the secretary in the position of performing the duties of a Bureau officer, and the director of the Bureau of Ethnology would be but a chief of division, or clerk, to carry out his plans. I regret that you should consider it necessary to pursue this course. So far as I know, up to the present time the work has been carried on without criticism, the accounts have all

been settled in the treasury promptly, the publications of the Bureau have been well received by the scholars of America and of the world, and the service has inspired the confidence of the Congress.[30]

One month after joining the BAE, McGee challenged Langley's authority to set aside the reserve, thereby reopening an old wound.[31] Over the next decade Langley grew to despise and distrust the new ethnologist. While Powell lived, the tense and suspicious relations between the Smithsonian staff and the BAE did not erupt into open conflict, despite accusations of shoddy business methods in the Bureau. Langley fostered an exterior of amiable scientific neutrality. But it was an uneasy, unstable condition.

McGee came to the Bureau simply as an ethnologist, but the title did not match his self-image, salary, or ambition. Accordingly, in September 1893, he began signing correspondence as "ethnologist in charge." The new title went unchallenged but not unnoticed; it became a small but significant irritant in Bureau/Smithsonian relations in coming years.

As an ethnologist, McGee once again had to apply himself assiduously. For six months he studied Powell's principles of sociology and mental evolution. His first article, "The Siouan Indians: A Preliminary Sketch," which appeared in the 1894 annual report as an introduction to Dorsey's posthumous *Siouan Sociology*, demonstrated that he was a good disciple.[32] "Siouan Indians" was a model of Powellian anthropology in approach and conclusions. Drawing heavily on Dorsey's notes, McGee first demonstrated mastery of the literature on the Siouan stock. He then reviewed the Sioux according to the standard categories: language, arts and industries, social institutions, beliefs, physical traits. His summary elaborated Powell's theories and placed the Siouan stock in its "proper" place among North American tribes and human development generally. He offered little that was new, but forcefully restated Powellian orthodoxy.

After 1893 Powell indulged his interest in the origins of human institutions to an obsessive degree, and McGee suited his fieldwork to those concerns. Having completed his office and library apprenticeship in anthropology in his first year, McGee prepared in the fall of 1894 to gain his spurs in the field. Taking $2,000 from the Secretary's reserve, he organized an expedition to the Southwest to collect artifacts from the Papago and neighboring tribes, and from the cliff ruins of Arizona and New Mexico.[33] He left Washington in mid-October, outfitted in Tucson, and dropped south across the border into Sonora. McGee stopped briefly at numerous Papago villages, but spent a good deal of his time noting weed growth and local soil and water conditions.[34] The party lost a week in delays with Mexican officials. Since Mexican law prohibited collecting antiquities—the main purpose of the trip—McGee made small collections of modern Papago materials. The first half of the trip was an aimless trek through northern Mexico in search of primitive, unacculturated Indians.

The party arrived in Hermosillo at the end of the month, where they tarried several days. Here McGee heard for the first time of the wild, bloodthirsty Seri Indians, only a few miles away, along the coast of the California Gulf and on Tiburon Island.[35] At last he confronted a significant challenge: native inhabitants of the forbidding Sonora desert, never studied by White Americans and reportedly the most hostile people of North America. McGee expected to find here men and women living in near-bestial conditions, American examples of the heretofore-only-theorized primal savagery. His expectations, not surprisingly, were met.

With Mexican government permission to enter "Seriland," as McGee's men dubbed the desert region, the party proceeded westward to the coast adjacent to Tiburon Island, guided by an aging Mexican, Pascual Encinas, who as a young man had pushed the Seri off their lands. The McGee party finally located a temporary Seri settlement of about sixty individuals. They stayed for several days, but the interviewing occurred in one thirty-six-hour period.[36] McGee recorded a 400-word vocabulary, took numerous group and individual photographs, collected artifacts for the Museum, and observed Indian habits. McGee was back in Washington by the end of November, after forty days' absence, only a handful of which were actually spent in contact with Indians.[37]

The following year McGee returned to study the warlike Seri in depth. The expedition was ill-fated from the start, largely due to the leader's bravado and incompetence. The party left Tucson on November 9, 1895, by a slightly different route than the previous year and spent several days examining, drawing, and photographing ruins and collecting artifacts. McGee then headed directly for Costa Rica, where he had found the Seri rancheria the preceding year. The Seri had abandoned the site and reportedly moved out to Tiburon.

McGee decided to pursue. While Señor Encinas constructed a crude boat at his ranch, McGee explored and mapped parts of the nearby mountains in his vain search for the elusive Indians. McGee, Encinas, and company then "with much difficulty" hauled "la lancha Anita" across the narrow desert to Kino Bay on the Gulf of California. With ten days' food rations and five days' water supply, McGee organized his eleven-man party and headed up the coast to a point opposite Tiburon Island.

After five days of delay due to severe gales, part of the expedition crossed the strait "El Infiernillo." On returning for the rest of the party, however, two men encountered a gale and were blown twenty-five miles down the coast, where, as McGee reported, the Anita was "practically wrecked on a desert island." Four days later the men had worked their way back up the coast, met the returning ranchhands (from whom they obtained fresh water) at Kino Bay, and reunited with the three members of the party ("who had suffered much thirst") still waiting upcoast to cross to the island.

In the meanwhile McGee and his party on Tiburon were trying to stay alive by traveling inland for water and building a driftwood raft. When the boat finally reappeared, McGee set out across the island with renewed vigor in pursuit of the Indians. Most of the energy of the party was spent hauling water, with armed guards to protect against the "considerable and constant" threat of Seri ambush. McGee found some artifacts, including a balsa canoe-raft, and some deserted encampments, but he never contacted a single Seri.

When the men's shoes and moccasins were worn out, McGee called off the chase. But his problems were far from over. The party, "now practically barefoot," crossed to the mainland but found themselves without food or water, miles from Encinas's ranch, and "still constantly under the eyes of Seri warriors watching from a distance," presumably waiting to attack. At this point McGee set off alone for Kino Bay, twenty-five miles away, for help. But on reaching the rendezvous point he found it abandoned, and in eighteen hours trekked miles across the desert to the ranch. He returned with supplies to his waiting party and on the last day of 1895 they were all safely back at the ranch.

On January 3, 1896, his last day in Mexico, McGee made one final attempt at Seri ethnology: an interview with Fernando Kolusio, an outcast Seri who had lived for decades with Encinas. McGee closed five-and-a-half pages of notes with the following observation:

Culusio [sic] was very small when he left the tribe; he is now old, somewhat deaf, and has nearly forgotten the language. It is my judgment that his information is practically worthless except when corroborated. So the inquiry is not continued.[38]

Thus ended the 1895 Seri expedition.

These expeditions constituted McGee's fieldwork in ethnology, and he relied on them for his anthropological credentials. It is, therefore, not unfair to ask what the Seri and Papago trips actually accomplished. The ethnological value of the second expedition was virtually nil. Despite McGee's attempts to picture a dangerous, heroic adventure among bloodthirsty savages, the hunt for the Seri emerges as a series of blundering, foolish decisions by an ignorant and glory-hungry greenhorn. Somehow the entire party survived in spite of McGee. Furthermore, his notebooks of the trip, replete with self-conscious comments on dwindling food supplies and romantic appellations (Camp Thirsty, Camp Disappointment, Camp Despair), clearly imitated Powell's first Colorado expedition. Down to naming the boats—"la lancha *Anita*" for Powell's *Emma Dean*—his performance was pathetically derivative.[39]

The first trip provided McGee's Seri information, gathered in a very brief period at an encampment of some sixty starving, miserably poor souls. From this he constructed a 300-page monograph, "The Seri Indians," which appeared after long delay in the 1896 BAE report.[40] "Rarely in the annals of

W J McGee in dangerous "Seriland," 1895.

anthropology has so much been written based on so little field work," Bernard
Fontana wrote of it.[41]

What did McGee find? He found the savages he sought. On Powell's ladder
of culture, McGee discovered, the Seri occupied a bottom rung, and he
stretched his rich vocabulary to define their near-bestial state. Every facet of
Seri life exhibited a preoccupation with animal life; they were "zoosematic
in esthetic, zoomimic in technic, zootheistic in faith, and putatively zoocratic
in government." Even their language seemed "largely mimetic or onomato-
poetic."[42] Although he gathered extremely sparse data on language and mythology, the "coincident testimony" of all other aspects of their lives consigned
the Seri to "the lowest recognized plane of savagery."[43]

The most conspicuous fact of Seri life was isolation, in habitat and more
importantly in thought. The fear and animosity that neighboring Papago
Indians displayed toward them, the sullen dislike for Encinas (known locally
as "conqueror of the Seri" and viewed by the Seri as a "hated trainer") made
them resemble "a menagerie of caged carnivores" to McGee. Even in the face
of Caucasian gifts and goodwill, the Indians showed only "curiosity, avidity
for food, studied indifference, and shrouded or snarling disgust," although,
he noted, they were cheerfully affectionate among themselves. McGee saw
an "intuitive and involuntary" loathing for outsiders, a highly developed,
inbred "race-sense" to match their beautiful bodies.[44]

For the Seri, McGee found, were a singularly attractive people; men and
women of all ages appeared "notably deep-chested and clean-limbed quick
steppers," not unlike "human thoroughbreds." As the published photographs
and drawings of bare-chested women attest, McGee was struck by Seri beauty
and grace. The animal-like physiques and movements resulted, he concluded,
from the rugged environment and isolation from other tribes, which had
permitted mutually reinforcing mind and body developments. Consequently
the Seri were even farther away from their neighbors "in feeling than in
features, in function than in structure, in mind than in body."[45]

The animal likeness emerged everywhere. Unable to photograph a Seri
hunter in shooting position, McGee concluded that Seri archery was a fluid
movement, not a static position, another sign of bestial behavior. The Seri
habit of hunting pregnant animals revolted McGee and reminded him that
"the very sight of pregnancy or travail or newborn helplessness awakens [in
the savage mind] slumbering blood-thirst and impels to ferocious slaughter."
Here one could see the roots of the shocking barbarities of Seri history, "tragedies too terrible for repetition save in bated breath of survivors..."[46] McGee had probably heard many such stories through the
"bated breath" of Pascual Encinas and his Mexican ranch hands, who had
fought a war of near-annihilation against the Seri for years. The second-hand,
hearsay influence of McGee's hosts runs throughout his demeaning account.

The Seri, in sum, confirmed Powellian evolution. First, they demonstrated that human evolution was to be traced in the mind, not in physical features (although these provided useful supplementary evidence). While they possessed some animal affinities physically, this low group of savages demonstrated that "the nearest and clearest indications of bestial relationship are to be found in the psychical features"; the Seri possessed a "burgeoning yet still bestial mind."[47] Secondly, the Seri illustrated the impact of immediate physical environment on all institutions at such a low level of development. Powell could not have asked for a more complete validation of his philosophy.

In his anthropology as in his geology, McGee combined perceptive field observations with a fertile imagination. Some of his field data have stood the tests of subsequent students; his imaginative interpretations have not. Reviewing his work in 1931, Alfred Kroeber found his observations "excellent but slender in range," permeated with conjectures and doubtful assumptions.[48] Kroeber's judgment has been echoed more recently by Bernard Fontana, who finds McGee "an incredibly astute observer, a kind of human Kodak."[49] Speculations and value judgments aside, Fontana contends, McGee produced a valuable and on many points essentially accurate baseline ethnography of a little-studied people. Be that as it may, the point is that for McGee the speculations constituted the valuable part of the study. Furthermore, the pure data of the field diary and the ethnographer's preconceptions cannot be so easily separated. As Kroeber's Seri work clearly showed, McGee's assumptions about his subjects and his anxiety to place them clearly in a developmental sequence warped his observations.

Kroeber corrected McGee on three major points: the pedestrian habit and footspeed of the Seri, their absence of a tool sense, and hostility to aliens, particularly to racial mixture. Kroeber found that Seri tools, like all their material culture, lacked order and polish, but in contrast to McGee he credited the people with "excellent practical mechanical sense."[50] Most importantly, McGee had erred grievously in stressing Seri cultural isolation.[51] "They are strictly, indeed fiercely, endogamous, alien connection being the blackest crime in their calendar and invariably punished by death," McGee had claimed.[52] But McGee wrote in total ignorance of neighboring Pima and Yuma cultures. He never saw that the Seri must be understood as a problem in local ethnohistory, not as a people with "congenital deficiencies or abnormalities" resulting from isolation, or instinctive animal impulses hindering social development. In sum, Kroeber concluded, the Seri

> relate culturally to other peoples much as might be anticipated from their geographical position and subsistence opportunities. The Seri problem consequently has to be removed from the category of those which hold out a hope or illusion of being particularly significant for the solution of basic questions or broad hypotheses. . . . The thorough study of this culture will involve much grinding physical hardship and possibly

some danger. It is to be hoped that when the work is undertaken, it will not be in a spirit of personal adventure, with emphasis on the external difficulties to be overcome, but with a serious desire and competence to secure facts and understanding.[53]

McGee, never even a mediocre linguist, could not begin to understand Seri tales and mythology. He was thus restricted to the visual. While sufficient for geology, this was crippling in ethnology. As Kroeber noted, it was in the social and religious aspects of Seri life, "where verbal communications are as important as observation," that McGee's work was most questionable.[54]

The Seri Indians served to establish McGee's credentials in his adopted science, at least as far as Washington anthropologists were concerned. But the Seri study was less important for McGee's personal growth than the fascination with desert life that he found in the Southwest. Two brief studies of desert ecology, "The Beginning of Agriculture" and "The Beginning of Zooculture," certify that his jaunts were not a total scientific loss. McGee's desert studies were highly perceptive. In the words of Clark Wissler, he "presented concisely the interrelations of plant and animal life as constituting a kind of community and then observed man in this setting."[55] He found that desert plants adjusted in various delicate ways to aridity, among them leaflessness, waxiness, and greenness. While plants made such adjustments, McGee observed, desert animals exhibited traits of cooperation with other animals as well as plants in order to withstand the rugged environment. Sometimes the cooperation involved only minor modifications in behavior and no "loss of individuality," as McGee put it. This arrangement he termed communality. Other adjustments involved intimate interdependence with other creatures, which he called commensality. In phrases reminiscent of Darwin's "tangled bank," McGee described the community of life centering on the saguaro cactus:

The flowers are fertilized by insects . . . and the seeds are distributed by birds; for it is manifest that the finding of the plants by flying things is facilitated by their great stature. Moreover the flowers are brilliantly white in color and attractive in perfume, while the fruit is gorgeously red and sweetly sapid. Still further it is manifest that the typical placing of branches is the most economical possible at once for the pumping of water from below and for bringing the flowers and fruits at the extremities within easy sight of the cooperating insects and birds. So it would appear that the saguaro is a monstrosity in fact as well as in appearance—a product of miscegenation between plant and animal, probably depending for its form and life-history, if not for its very existence, on its commensals.

The lesson was clear: subhuman organisms in the desert displayed incipient social organization against the common environment. Moreover, this "subhuman communality" frequently resulted not only in solidarity but stronger "individuality" among plants and animals.[56]

Man represented the final step in a direction determined before him. By consuming seeds and fruits and redistributing the seeds of useful plants, the Papago "entered into the vital solidarity of the desert," partially conquering the soil and increasing the sum total of desert life. Although the modern Papago made no attempt to control water supply, McGee saw in the archaeological ruins of northern Mexico indications of a higher antecedent culture that had practiced irrigation. The beginning of environmental control thus began among the subhuman desert species, whereas with man, "strength lies in union; and progress in combination leads to solidarity." Agriculture was the final stage of this process. "So, whatever its last estate," McGee concluded, "in its beginning agriculture is the art of the desert."[57]

McGee's theories on the domestication of animals followed a similar logic and drew likewise on the Papago notes. Observing Papago toleration and use of vultures, quails, doves, coyotes, and cows, McGee analyzed various degrees of intimacy in the human-animal relations of the desert. In all cases, however, the arrangements were essentially collective, that is, between groups of people and groups of animals. Individual ownership was rare. McGee inferred that associations arose in mutual toleration and were mainly a collective phenomenon. Plant, animal, and human formed a continuum of intellectual development: the plant responded imperfectly, almost passively, to environmental pressures, displaying only the "germ of instinct"; instinctual animals showed the "germ of reason" in gathering together and cooperating more effectively; only man consciously bred and exterminated species for his benefit, multiplying "both vitality and mentality." Taken as a whole, southwestern desert life traced out a "comforting and promising course of development."[58]

The southwestern trips of 1894 and 1895 convinced McGee that social organization began in the arid regions of the world, where the forbidding environment forced all forms of life to cooperate in order to survive. Typically, this vision was both speculative and structured, at once founded upon yet divorced from observation. Once again the quest for origins led the ethnologist away from the immediate, sensible world to a misty past of imagined races of primeval animal-men. Just as for Powell the trips down the deepening canyons of the Colorado River had been journeys into the past, McGee traveled back in time in Sonora, hoping to find the roots of human society.

"Practically we bought the Seris out," McGee wrote to Holmes after his first trip.[59] It was a small collection from Indians who had almost nothing to give or sell. But if the collection was meager and the second trip a disaster, McGee returned with a heightened reputation as explorer and scientist. Between

1895 and 1900 he reached his zenith. As Powell withdrew, his protégé took control of the Bureau, dictating Powell's correspondence and composing the annual reports. "I knew it all," he testified. "I drafted every plan of operations, and wrote every report, and drafted every important letter, letters from Major Powell as well as from myself." Powell devoted his office time after 1895, McGee's stenographer remembered, almost entirely to *Truth and Error;* he did not dictate "more than the smallest percent" of the letters he signed. During the summers, when Powell was in Maine, "every particle of control" remained in McGee's hands.[60] To Powell's widow, McGee was poignantly explicit about the last years:

> In his office life I knew the condition better than anyone else, and sought in every way to have his best side kept outward. The fact remains that since the final operation on his arm in Baltimore [in 1894] the Major never wrote a report or any other important official paper; for while sometimes he was undoubtedly able to do so, he was oftener unable, and even in his best hours the strain of the work and the need for gathering half-forgotten details would have been injurious . . . during the later years of the Bureau he seldom saw the reports until they were shown to him in printer's proofs.[61]

Press clipping services solicited McGee—a sure sign of notoriety. He engaged in ceaseless activity in the social and scientific circles of the capital. Above all, McGee emerged as the dominant spokesman for Powellian evolutionism and his own vigorous championing of American science, technology, and mature nationhood. As vice president of section H of the AAAS (1897) and as three-time president of the Anthropological Society of Washington (1898–1900), McGee made good use of professional forums. He took these opportunities between 1897 and 1902 to bring together his thoughts on anthropology, science, evolution, and American life in a culminating *fin-de-siècle* performance.

The passing of the old century called forth nostalgia and celebration for the stunning accomplishments of recent decades, while the coming of the new century inspired anxiety and optimism. The Iowa farmboy knew nostalgia and anxiety well, but he subordinated them to an aggressive, positive vision of the future. With the sum of human experience laid before them, what had Washington anthropologists learned? What laws had emerged? History and science, especially anthropology, showed that the trend of human development was toward unity of all races and cultures, a single world community on the highest cultural plane. On the individual level, McGee discerned a trend toward greater strength: "Perfected man is overspreading the world."[62] At the same time, the races of the world were rapidly mixing. White and Red had produced some fine specimens of humanity; White and Black mixtures included such men as Frederick Douglass and Booker T. Washington. The difficulty in interracial mixing was its frequently illicit nature among the lowest representatives of either race, rather than among the "eminent Othellos and dignified Desdemonas" of the country. Mixture was fundamentally a class, not a race problem. To McGee it was apparent that "the predominant peoples of the world are of mixed blood," and that mixing would continue. The law of humanity was "convergence in brain and blood."[63]

The laws of the animal and plant realms so brilliantly elucidated by Darwin had no human application. Having uniquely overshadowed and controlled nature's forces, man no longer diverged into varieties in response to environmental stimuli. Darwin and Spencer notwithstanding, "when the entire field of man's experience . . . is surveyed, it becomes clear that the human genus is not dividing into species . . . but is steadily drifting toward unity of blood and equality of culture."[64]

Other fields confirmed the physical trends. Discriminating five stages of human mental development, McGee found that the sum of mental powers increased considerably with each successive stage. Psychology corroborated racial observations: "Thought is extending from man to man and from group to group and gaining force with each extension, and . . . all lines converge toward a plane higher than any yet attained."[65] The course of pre-Columbian history in North America showed a "series of convergent and interblending lines, coming up from a large but unknown number of original sources scattered along the various coasts of the continent." Evidence from all aspects of cultural life led to the same conclusion: Man had reversed the patterns of lower life to take control. The twentieth century would see human unity in blood and culture.

America stood at the head of advancing humanity, and the lessons of the national history indicated the future. The mingling of peoples had gone so far that the American had become "the world's most complex ethnic strain," and American culture embraced all others. The United States was a nation of strength; "The selection of the strong by pioneering has been repeated over and over again, and the prepotent progeny have gone back to vitalize the weaker vessels with little loss of their own vigor . . . ."[66] What was the role of the anthropologist in this "prepotent" culture? Simply to put men in touch with the laws of their own nature so that they would aid the progress of humanity. As McGee pointed out in an 1897 address on "The Science of Humanity," man had always been a favorite theme of artists and scholars, but until recent years he had remained a "vast chaos of action and thought . . . that last citadel of the unknown."[67] But now the human body and brain, like all other material things, "will be controlled and reconstructed for the good and glory of intelligent Man."[68] The anthropologist would show the way to a fully human future.

But would the people follow? Science, as Joseph Henry believed, had no meaning without application to human need, and utility was also integral to McGee's concept of science. Fortunately, a generation after Henry's death McGee could rejoice that America had become, in its institutions and daily habits, a nation of science. It was a sign of the times that

> most men of civilized and enlightened lands are coming to appreciate the coin of experience above the dust of tradition, and are gradually entering, whether intentionally or not, into the ways of Science. Only a generation ago the very name of Science was the symbol of a cult to one class of thinkers and a juggler's gaud to another class; today Science is an actual part of everyday life of all enlightened folk.[69]

For McGee, the fate of a disenchanted world rested in the hands of the scientist, who combined virtue and altruism. With an appreciative, scientific citizenry behind him, how could the scientist fail?

Yet if the new century looked bright for enlightened humanity, clouds were gathering on the horizon of McGee's own career. Samuel Langley had never wanted McGee in the Bureau to begin with. When Powell first proposed moving him from the Survey in 1893, Langley resisted, arguing that while McGee was a man of "uncommon force and ability," he was not qualified by temperament or training to administer a scientific bureau. Langley acquiesced only with the understanding that McGee would never succeed to the directorship.[70] "I did this at a time when Mr. McGee was nearly a stranger to me, on the testimony of his unfitness for that place," Langley confided in 1902. "Now that I have known him for ten years, I see no reason to change my opinion."[71]

Langley distrusted McGee's brand of science. While he wanted a socially relevant Bureau, the Secretary felt that McGee's pronouncements on current racial and social issues, which appeared more frequently every year, were hardly impartial. To Langley, the role of the scientist amounted to presenting data and results without interpretation, particularly without the musings in which McGee indulged at government expense. Where problems of philosophy were concerned, Henry Adams wrote, Langley "liked to wander past them in a courteous temper, even bowing to them distantly as though recognizing their existence, while doubting their respectability."[72] Unfortunately McGee crossed over and shook hands with them. In 1902 Langley informed Daniel Coit Gilman that after Powell's death he intended to purge the Bureau so that "in accordance with the well-established policy of the Smithsonian Institution, its scientific work shall be limited to the observation and recording of phenomena . . . and that its sanction shall not be given to theoretical or speculative work."[73]

Politics partially determined Langley's position. By the turn of the new century he was under heavy pressure to reform the BAE. In the eyes of most congressmen the original purpose and chief goal of the Bureau had been eminently practical: to furnish the national legislature with reliable scientific information for dealing with the American aborigines. Langley could point at least to Royce's *History of Land Cessions of the Indian Tribes,* finally published in 1899, as a utilitarian product. But practical work was more often promised than produced. The BAE had wandered far from such enterprises, congressmen complained, citing such papers as McGee's work on the Seri and James Mooney's "Myths of the Cherokees" as examples of wasting public funds.[74]

In early 1902, when Powell's death seemed imminent, Langley decided to take action. The time had come for the BAE "to begin a new career, and to show that in this new life it can be useful to Congress in the way that Congress wants." He blamed McGee for the declension in Bureau fortunes. "The possible death of Major Powell is so near a contingency, and the unfortunate affairs of the Bureau have aroused such opposition in Congress to its continuance," he wrote to his aide, Richard Rathbun, "that I am more disposed than heretofore, if possible, to say that Mr. McGee must not hope to occupy that position [the directorship] while I am responsible for his official acts."[75]

In February, Langley asked Holmes to take over the Bureau on Powell's death. Holmes balked, protesting that he could not do such a thing to his friend. McGee, he said, was Powell's chosen successor, a politically powerful midwesterner, and "the strongest man in Anthropology today in America, if not in the world . . ."[76] Shortly after this conversation, Joseph Cannon, chairman of the House Appropriations Committee and near-dictator of the House of Representatives, notified Langley that he would approve the upcoming BAE appropriations only if Langley would personally direct Bureau affairs and produce something to justify its existence. Further discomfited, Langley told Holmes that after Powell, the new relationship between the Smithsonian and the Bureau would "materially differ" from the old; he would place the BAE on the same footing as other divisions of the Smithsonian, something he had "foreborne to do." If the Bureau was to last, "its work must be popularized and shown to be practical," and it would have to be guided directly from the Smithsonian. Through the next months he vainly urged on McGee and Powell the importance of pursuing vigorously the long-delayed *Cyclopedia of Indian Tribes.*[77]

In early September, McGee traveled to Baddeck, Nova Scotia, on the pretext of a "general reconnaissance of the survivors of the Micmac, Molisit, and related Algonquin tribes" of upper New England, but in reality to lay future plans with Smithsonian Regent Alexander Graham Bell.[78] On September 15, Mrs. Powell summoned McGee to be with the old Major in his final hours; he passed away on September 23. Whatever private assurances the dying Powell may have given his protégé in Maine, McGee returned to Washington without an official blessing. The day after the funeral McGee requested his own promotion, and during the next two weeks McGee's numerous friends in politics and science flooded Langley's office with supporting letters.[79]

Langley appointed Holmes, and McGee declared war on them both. American anthropologists almost without exception sided with McGee, and in the weeks of late October and November they expressed their views clearly. On October 14, Alice Fletcher described the situation to Boas, who responded with a telegram and the first of many letters on McGee's behalf. Frederick Ward Putnam had already advised Langley that ethnologists were expecting McGee's appointment: "It would be a serious mistake if he is rot appointed." George A. Dorsey at the Field Museum, Frank Russell at Harvard, and Stewart Culin at the University Museum in Philadelphia, expressed similar sentiments.[80]

McGee organized a lobbying effort aimed at the Smithsonian Regents to discredit Langley. During October, Regent Richard Olney, for instance, received protests from Boas, Russell, *Science* editor James McKeen Cattell, and professors of geology Albert Perry Brigham at Colgate, H. LeRoy Fairchild at Rochester, and Ralph S. Tarr at Cornell.[81] The campaign soon developed into a general attack on Langley's administration. To his friends outside Washington, McGee pictured Langley's decision as merely the latest move in a long-term scheme aimed at "the undermining and reduction, if not complete abolition" of the Bureau. "Matters are now in such shape," he wrote Russell, "that the Bureau can be retained and rehabilitated only by joint and determined efforts on the part of the anthropologists of the country . . ." The issue, according to McGee, boiled down to a single question: "Shall Major Powell's monument as the greatest scientific man in America be perfected, or shall envy and jealousy be permitted to scatter the stones?"[82]

In the course of the debate over the Powell succession, Franz Boas emerged as a spokesman for the still-inchoate but growing professional consciousness among American anthropologists. While most anthropologists probably shared Boas's reservations about Langley, Boas's vigorous support of McGee at this time requires its own explanation, for it was very personal and highly significant. Boas had arrived in the United States in the mid-eighties, but it was a full decade before he gained institutional stability at Columbia University. He served briefly as geographical editor for *Science*, undertook fieldwork on the Northwest Coast sponsored by the British Association for the Advancement of Science, and between 1889 and 1892 taught anthropology at Clark University. In 1893 he came to Chicago as chief assistant to Frederick Putnam at the Columbian Exposition. Having nowhere to go at the close of the Fair, he agreed to stay on to organize the inherited anthropology exhibits for the new Field Columbian Museum. He hoped to stay on in Chicago permanently, but he was displaced by William H. Holmes and resigned in the spring of 1894. It was a year and a half before the New York appointments, at Columbia and the American Museum, materialized.[83]

The Chicago experience was extremely bitter for Boas, but it taught him important lessons of politics and science, one of which was the limitations of the museum as an institution of scientific anthropology. Thus, when he began to develop his own plans for the future science, the Bureau was a major part of them. The BAE was the only institution in the country willing to underwrite and publish the work in linguistics and mythology that Boas considered integral to a complete science of anthropology. Museums, by contrast, seemed interested only in material collections. Since the early nineties, Boas had been talking with McGee and Powell about preserving full texts as the basis for future linguistic and ethnological work, and the Washington men had responded.[84] Between 1893 and 1903 the BAE supported a great deal of Boas's work by purchasing linguistic manuscripts and notebooks from him at a total cost of about $4,000. This support was critical not only for his livelihood but for Boas's personal scientific growth.

As Boas saw the issue, the Bureau had maintained a balance and fullness in American anthropology that aided harmonious and healthy progress. "The interests of anthropological science," he instructed Langley, "requires [sic] . . . that those lines of human activities that do *not* find expression in material objects—namely language, thought, customs, and I may add, anthropometric measurements—be investigated thoroughly and carefully." The Bureau was the only American institution dealing with the "general problems" of anthropology. Furthermore, other anthropologists working in museums, such as George A. Dorsey at Field, had similarly discovered that museum funds were simply not available for "purely theoretical work."[85]

Thus Boas approached McGee's dispute with clear preferences: he valued support for his linguistic and mythology work, and hoped for its continuance; he was fully prepared to befriend McGee against the man who had taken his place in Chicago; and he deplored the possible domination by the museum. While he avoided disparaging Holmes, Boas distinguished between the talents of a museum man and those of other anthropologists. Holmes's natural gifts led him to a thorough appreciation of visual objects, Boas admitted, but his interest in "that part of anthropology that deals with ideas alone" was slight. And it was precisely such matters that formed the BAE's principal work. Placing Holmes in charge would inevitably mean subordinating the Bureau to "museum interest."[86] Finally, with Holmes as head curator of anthropology at the National Museum and director of the Bureau, no good could possibly come to an already overworked man and understaffed museum.[87]

But the real issue lay beyond "museum influence" or the vitality of either institution. Langley, through his presumptuous interference with the Bureau succession and his disregard of the opinions of American anthropologists, struck at the integrity and independence of anthropology. In 1902 the status of the fledgling science remained so precarious that anthropologists felt such a blow keenly. By exercising his "personal inclination" without regard to the opinions of concerned scientists, Langley had introduced a dangerous element of uncertainty that threatened the very existence of the Bureau; and he had instilled, said Boas, "a feeling of general instability in the scientific service of the government which we hoped had been entirely overcome by this time."[88]

Furthermore, by appointing Holmes "chief" rather than "director," Langley had demonstrated his intention to control the Bureau. But in its stage of development at the turn of the century, American anthropology above all required individuals with generous conceptions of its needs and possibilities. Langley did not have them; whatever his other faults, Boas argued, McGee did possess such understanding: "It is easy to criticize McGee . . . because his mannerism, and his tendency to bring out the ultimate bearings of single observations, make easy points of attack. But all this has nothing to do with McGee's intelligent understanding of the work of the Bureau, nor with his administrative ability."[89]

Although Langley never abolished or intended to abolish the Bureau, Boas subsequently found his doubts justified. Langley insisted on gathering up the dangling threads of investigations that had been dragging along since the early days. It was time to clean house: to close off investigations and begin summing up the results of two decades of work on the American Indian. Boas was astonished at Langley's insistence on final results. Anthropologists could not simply decide that the final results were in, he answered, any more than Langley could submit the final report on his astrophysical work. The work of the Bureau, just like investigation in any other field of science, he explained to Charles D. Walcott, "should of course be such that with the advance of studies each line of research should be deepened and made more useful," not abruptly terminated. Anthropology was a continuing, ongoing experience; Langley's failure to comprehend that fact amounted to a "fundamental error of judgment."[90]

McGee's case was lost from the start, because Langley was determined not to promote him. Far from destroying the BAE, Langley believed, with some justification, that he was saving it from almost certain demise at the hands of politicians who were no longer awed by Powell and were now demanding useful results. Langley wanted, in short, to return the Bureau to its original role of 1879, as an informational arm of the Congress and the people. As he explained it to himself in a memorandum, "On [Powell's] death a new day begins for the Bureau—partly a reversion to the policy of his own vigorous years."[91] Until his own death four years later, Langley concentrated all BAE resources on the long-awaited *Handbook of American Indians* (formerly the *Cyclopedia*), which he intended as a practical manual for congressmen and constituents.

McGee made his final eight months in the Bureau utter misery for everyone. In Mexico he contracted typhoid, from which he never completely recovered. Nor did he ever recover from the decisions of Langley—that "frog nestled in the shelter of the Smithsonian," the "Senegambian in the woodpile," in McGee's rich phrases—or his deceitful friend Holmes.[92] For months he sniped at Holmes and contributed no work of his own. (He took fifty-seven days of sick leave in the first three months of 1903.)[93] He turned bitterly on his former friend, accusing him of adopting Langley's policy of "fair words and foul acts," and reminding Boas that "you saw Holmes' cloven foot in Chicago, but I see both of them and the forked tail as well."[94] For a time Holmes tried to placate McGee and serve Langley at the same time, but he soon became disgusted with McGee's attacks.[95]

The crisis came in the summer of 1903. In April, officials of the Bureau discovered evidence of forgery and embezzlement by Frank M. Barnett, a minor employee. Barnett was apprehended and tried, but his misdeeds led in July to a general inquiry by Smithsonian officials into the operations of the Bureau during the Powell/McGee tenure.[96] Throughout the sweltering Washington midsummer, Langley's investigating committee took more than 1,000 pages of testimony from Bureau anthropologists (including Boas, who held an unsalaried position as honorary philologist) and staff members.

The investigation ranged widely but returned again and again to McGee's shortcomings as administrator and scientist. Boas returned to New York after his testimony, convinced that the investigation was a witchhunt. The records tend to confirm his impression.[97] The committee combed McGee's correspondence since 1893. They were appalled to find letters relating to private affairs, stock transactions, real estate settlements, political affairs, and other matters unrelated to official business.[99] As if the letters were not sufficiently damaging, his own stenographer confirmed McGee's working habits in a vengeful letter to Matilda Stevenson, who happily turned it over to the Smithsonian committee. Her boss, Caroline Dinwiddie reported, spent a great amount of time on personal business at the cost of the BAE. "Over and over again I spent weeks of office time on articles which were published in *Harper's*, the *Atlantic Monthly*, *The Forum*, etc., for which he was paid magazine rates." She spared nothing: "In my judgment, such a man is absolutely unfit for an administrative office. His whole policy is autocratic in the extreme, and no man dares do independent work under his tutelage."[99] Clearly the Bureau under McGee had not possessed the spirit of "Barnum's happy family," as later claimed by a friendly Washington newspaper.[100]

A series of "mistaken enterprises and dangerously faulty methods" was laid at McGee's door. His fruitless trip to Nova Scotia at the time of Powell's death did not go unnoticed; nor his Mexico jaunt at government expense the following November.[101] His performance after October 1902, probably sealed his fate. Rathbun noted that his attitude toward the Smithsonian Secretary had been offensive, "disloyally outspoken and malicious," and had begun to spread to others. [102] Particularly irksome was his effort during the recent period to organize a Bureau of Archaeology and Ethnology under the International Archaeological Commission. McGee seemed to be preparing a place for himself elsewhere while still on the BAE payroll.

McGee defended himself, but without effect. In the Bureau, private and public often mixed, and individuals often made sacrifices for science, even to the extent of personally making up deficits, he explained. [103] As far as the "unofficial" work was concerned, McGee saw no conflict because he honestly saw no distinction between activities within and without the Bureau, between the so-called personal and public. A man's science was of a piece. It was essential, he believed, that every collaborator of the Bureau, "according to .his powers and his lights," should be connected with "general scientific progress" in order to confirm "the character and standing of these men who are engaged in the researches relating to American Indians." McGee's profession of faith on this point is so enlightening that it bears repetition in full:

> I have thought it important that every scientific collaborator of the Bureau should be a member of the Anthropological Society of Washington, and I think that it is important that every collaborator of the Bureau should be a member of the newly established [American] Anthropological Association. I have thought that the reputation of the Bureau would depend to a considerable extent on the scientific standing of the several officers and collaborators and I have thought . . . that the scientific standing of the collaborators, determining that of the office, would depend upon the amount of work they did in connection with these voluntary scientific associations. It may be a fad on my part, but . . . one of which I am not at all ashamed, to hold that the scientific activity of this country of ours finds its best expression in the voluntary scientific associations . . . [which] have placed this country where it is in the scientific world today. . . . The fact that salaries are paid out of appropriations made by the government or paid in other ways is largely an incident in connection with the scientific development of the individuals who constitute the scientific element in this country, and it is for that reason that my policy has always been an extremely liberal one with respect to my own activity and the activity of other collaborators of the Bureau in general scientific work, in the maintenance of scientific societies, in making contributions very largely of a gratuitous character. . . . That has been my policy throughout. [104]

McGee set forth a conception of government science that stressed the development of the individual, not of an organization or a delimited body of knowledge. Because the organization derived from individual enterprise, the government's proper role was strictly supportive, not directive. To McGee, furthermore, everything he did outside his home was in the public interest; and yet his personal scientific growth was always involved, which ultimately benefited the public.[105] The 1903 investigation revealed, among other things, that this vision of government science was already under heavy attack from a new breed of functionaries who emphasized loyalty to the institution over either personal development or loyalty to science in general.

The committee's verdict was predictable. Although McGee was not fired, his position was abolished, and he resigned at the end of July, as expected. The blistering indictment found him guilty of unsystematic financial methods; carelessness and possible corruption in purchasing manuscripts, chiefly from Boas and Fletcher; gross negligence of the manuscript collections; and hostility toward Langley.[106] McGee left Washington under a heavy cloud.

Over the next four years McGee's personal life crumbled, as he and Anita permanently separated. He returned to government work in 1907, however, as a member of the Department of Agriculture. That summer, while camping in the California Sierras, he and Gifford Pinchot laid the plans for what became the conservation movement of the early twentieth century.[107] McGee fulfilled his scientific life in these years. Whitney Cross observed that "it was McGee, and neither Powell, Ward, nor any other of their fellows, who directly and specifically transmitted the common beliefs of the trio into the twentieth century conservation movement."[108] Powell's Irrigation Survey had been an early and abortive attempt to apply the lessons of science to an unruly political and social world. In the conservation movement McGee combined the lessons learned from Powell and his own experiences with desert and water into a final attempt to guide American society scientifically. "All the compensatory drives from a disease-ridden body, a ruined career, and a broken marriage," Cross concluded, "heightened his lifelong devotion to the general welfare for a final decisive stroke of public service."[109]

In the spirit of Morgan and Powell, McGee ended his life condemning wasteful American capitalism and turning to the model of aboriginal America for alternative modes of organizing society and resources. Pinchot recalled that McGee made him see that "monopoly of natural resources was only less dangerous to the public welfare than their actual destruction." Adopting the iconoclastic view of American history coming into vogue among progressive reformers, McGee preached that the dreams of the Founding Fathers had been subverted as "the People became in large measure industrial dependents rather than free citizens." This had occurred because the national habit of giving away land and resource rights to individuals had developed into an unprecedented "saturnalia of squandering the sources of permanent prosperity." In his dying years McGee called for a nobler patriotism, honesty of purpose, a warmer charity, a stronger sense of family, and "a livelier humanity, in which each will feel that he lives not for himself alone but as a part of a common life for a common world and for the common good . . ."[110] McGee never lost faith—the Iowa fields were there to the end. A champion of American individualism in science, technology, and commerce throughout his life, in the end he foresaw and demanded its demise in order to return to what the desert had shown him: that man, like all life, must band together for the common welfare. This was the lesson and promise of anthropology for the new century.[111]

Science meant order and system to Powell and McGee. It was synonymous with philosophy—they used the terms interchangeably—because scientific understanding transcended the flux and confusion of daily experience to provide perspective on events. Still, any theoretical framework must have some foundation in empiricism, and McGee extended Powell's system almost to the point of caricature. He became an easy target.

In McGee's demise were indications of a major cultural change. By the turn of the new century, the federal government no longer provided the environment for personal fulfillment as defined by Powell. At the same time, the insistence of Schoolcraft, Morgan, Gibbs, and Powell on an open science and on the general "scientific development of individuals" argued against the critical, exclusive university training that Boas would bring. Powell's institution, like its predecessors, sought to perpetuate and preserve an accepted, cherished style and set of American values, not evaluate them in order to consider alternatives.

Powell's Bureau of American Ethnology, like McGee, reached the political and historical limits of a tradition. American anthropologists of the nineteenth century had appealed to and placed faith in the same constituency that Joseph Henry strove to create and encourage in science: the intelligent, stalwart, presumably large middle section of Americans with moderate leisure and freedom from pecuniary pursuit. Their science amounted to a form of moral uplift; their middle-class helpers would serve as the leavening for a nation. Perhaps it was a myth, but men build institutions on myths. By the end of the century that democratic homogeneity was clearly crumbling, in Chicago and across the nation, under racial and social strife, taking with it the foundations of an institutional order. Not coincidentally, new criteria and groupings arose to provide identity, order, and purpose for anthropology.

Notes

1. Henry Adams, *The Education of Henry Adams: An Autobiography* (Boston, 1961), pp. 344–45.
2. Ibid., p. 330.
3. See John Higham, "The Reorientation of American Culture in the 1890s," in

John Weiss, ed., *The Origins of Modern Consciousness* (Detroit, 1965), pp. 25–48.

4. Adams, *Education*, p. 330.

5. Fletcher to Boas, 14 October 1902, BP; Boas to McGee, 3 August 1903, MP.

6. Charles Keyes, "W J McGee, Anthropologist, Geologist, Hydrologist," *Annals of Iowa*, series 3, vol. 2 (1913), p. 187; John R. Swanton, "Notes regarding my adventures in anthropology and with anthropologists," ms. (ca. 1944), pp. 33–34, NAA.

7. Remarks of Alfred C. Lane, quoted in *The McGee Memorial Meeting of the Washington Academy of Sciences* (Baltimore, 1916), p. 90.

8. On McGee's early years, see Emma R. McGee, *Life of W J McGee* (privately printed, Farley, Iowa, 1915); F. H. Knowlton, "Memoir of W J McGee," *Bulletin of the Geological Society of America* 24 (1912): 18–29; N. H. Darton, "Memoir of W J McGee," *Annals of the Association of American Geographers* 3: 103–10; Whitney R. Cross, "W J McGee and the Idea of Conservation," *Historian* 15 (1953): 148–62; *The McGee Memorial Meeting;* F. W. Hodge, "W J McGee," *American Anthropologist* 14 (1912): 683–86; and Anita Newcomb McGee to Gifford Pinchot, 5 June 1916, GP.

9. Remarks of Emma McGee, quoted in *McGee Memorial Meeting*, p. 90; *Life-History Album* belonging to Klotho McGee Lattin, p. 9, in which Anita McGee recorded the full list of McGee's illnesses; Anita McGee to Pinchot, 15 June 1916, GP.

10. "Stories told to Klotho McGee," typescript in author's possession. The schoolhouse reference occurs in McGee's biographical entry in the membership lists of the Explorers Club of New York, which he joined at its founding in 1905.

11. Quoted in William C. Darrah, *Powell of the Colorado* (Princeton, 1951), p. 316.

12. Willard Johnson to McGee, 10 June 1885, MP.

13. Personal interview with Klotho McGee Lattin, 31 December 1973.

14. Cross, "W J McGee," p. 152.

15. Ms. membership list, Anthropological Society of Washington Papers, NAA.

16. McGee to F. P. Venable, 25 March 1887, MP.

17. McGee to J. P. Lesley, 7 October 1892, MP.

18. W J McGee, "The Science of Humanity," *American Anthropologist,* o.s. 10 (1897): 246.

19. James Kirkpatrick Flack, *Desideratum in Washington: The Intellectual Community in the Capital City, 1870–1900* (Cambridge, 1975).

20. Membership and officer records, ASW Papers, NAA.

21. On McGee's role in founding the American Anthropological Association, see George W. Stocking, Jr., "Franz Boas and the Founding of the American Anthropological Association," *American Anthropologist* 62 (1960): 1–17.

22. Personal interview, 31 December 1973.

23. J. W. Powell, "The Personal Characteristics of Professor Baird," *Bulletin of the PSW* 10 (Washington, D.C., 1887): 71.

24. Don D. Fowler and Catherine S. Fowler, "John Wesley Powell, Ethnologist," *Utah Historical Quarterly* 37 (1969): 170; notes on "Reserve Fund," 13 January 1903, BAE-IN.

25. Langley memorandum, "The Bureau of Ethnology," n.d., BAE-IN.

26. Baird to Powell, 7 July 1883, copy in MP.

27. Cyrus Adler, "Samuel Pierpont Langley," SI, *AR for 1906*, pp. 531–32.

28. See, e.g., Powell to Langley, 20 December 1901, NAA.

29. W. H. Holmes, WHH 8, sections 1 and 2.

30. Powell to Langley, 11 June 1891, copy in BAE-IN.

31. Langley, "Memorandum," 2 August 1893, copy in BAE-IN. McGee presented four reasons against the reserve. Langley refused to discuss it.

32. W J McGee, *The Siouan Indians: a Preliminary Sketch*, BAE, *AR for 1894*, pp. 157–204; James Owen Dorsey, *Siouan Sociology*, ibid., pp. 205–44.

33. Powell to Langley, 9 August 1894, NAA.

34. Seri notebooks, 24 October and 25 October 1894, MP.

35. Bernard L. Fontana, "The Seri Indians in Perspective," in W J McGee, *The Seri Indians of Bahia Kino and Sonora, Mexico* (Glorieta, New Mexico, 1971 [reprint of the BAE, *AR for 1896*]), no pagination.

36. Ibid.

37. The 1894 trip is summarized from McGee's viewpoint in BAE, *AR for 1895*, pp. lxii–lxv. For a closer summary see Fontana, "The Seri Indians."

38. Seri notebooks, MP.

39. Ibid.

40. "The Seri Indians," BAE, *AR for 1896*, pp. 1–298 (with a comparative lexicology of Seri-Yuman by J.N.B. Hewitt, pp. 299–344). Government publication dates generally ran about two years behind the reporting fiscal year. McGee delayed the report at least one extra year for his Seri article—so long, in fact, that the report was prepared first and the bulk of his "Seri Indians" was later inserted with separate pagination.

41. Fontana, "The Seri Indians."

42. BAE, *AR for 1896*, p. 294.

43. Ibid., p. 295.

44. Ibid., pp. 130–33.

45. Ibid., p. 161.

46. Ibid., p. 203.

47. Ibid., p. 295.

48. Alfred Kroeber, "The Seri," *Southwest Museum Papers* 6 (Los Angeles, 1931): 18, 52.

49. Fontana, "The Seri Indians."

50. Kroeber, "The Seri," p. 25.

51. Ibid., pp. 24–28.

52. W J McGee, "Expedition to Papagueria and Seriland: A preliminary note," *American Anthropologist*, o.s. 9 (1896): 97–98.

53. Kroeber, "The Seri," p. 53.

54. Ibid., p. 48.

55. Clark Wissler, "W J McGee," in *Encyclopedia of the Social Sciences* 5: 652–53.

56. W J McGee, "Beginning of Agriculture," *American Anthropologist*, o.s. 8 (1895): 368–69.

57. Ibid., pp. 374–75.

58. W J McGee, "Beginning of Zooculture," *American Anthropologist*, o.s. 10 (1897): 228–29.

59. McGee to Holmes, 6 December 1894, MP.

60. McGee testimony, BAE-IN, pp. 125, 127; Caroline Brooke Dinwiddie to Matilda Coxe Stevenson, 21 February 1902, BAE-IN.

61. McGee to Emma Dean Powell, 19 November 1902, BAE-IN.

62. W J McGee, "The Trend of Human Progress," *American Anthropologist*, n.s. 1 (1899): 414.

63. Ibid., pp. 419, 421.

64. Ibid., p. 424. McGee elaborated these thoughts fully in "Man's Place in Nature," *American Anthropologist*, n.s. 3 (1901): 1–13.

65. Ibid., p. 435.

66. Ibid., pp. 445–47. For another statement of the same theme, applied to the Spanish-American War and its evolutionary significance, see McGee's "The Course of Human Development," *Forum* (1898): 56–65.

67. W J McGee, "The Science of Humanity," *American Anthropologist*, o.s. 10 (1897): 271.

68. Ibid., p. 272.

69. W J McGee, "Cardinal Principles of Science," *Proceedings of the Washington Academy of Sciences* 2 (1900): 7–8.

70. Handwritten note, addressed to R. R. Hitt, n.d., SIA.

71. Langley to Richard Rathbun, confidential note, 15 February 1902, BAE-IN.

72. Adams, *Education*, p. 377.

73. Langley to Gilman (draft), 24 November 1902, SIA.

74. Langley to Holmes, 19 November 1902; "Papers on the work of the Bureau by Secretary and others" and "Memorandum of conversation between Senator O. H. Platt and the Secretary," 11 November 1902, both in BAE-IN. Langley was fully aware of congressional opinion and shared much of the concern over the tendency to provide work of "purely scientific & abstract interest." Langley, "Memorandum of what I am saying to Mr. Cannon," n.d., BAE-IN.

75. Langley to Rathbun, 15 February 1902, BAE-IN.

76. Holmes, WHH 9, section 1: "Chiefship period, BAE, 1902–1910," in Library of the National Museum of American Art and the National Portrait Gallery, SI. The meetings took place on 13 and 14 February 1902.

77. Fragment of letter from Langley, 12 April 1902, SIA.

78. McGee to himself, 9 September 1902, commissioning his trip; unsigned memorandum noting that McGee went to Baddeck "ostensibly to study Indians. There is no record of any Indians having been visited"; McGee to Bell, August 1902; handwritten note of Anita N. McGee, 15 September 1902; all in BAE-IN.

79. McGee to Langley, 27 September 1902, SIA; Memorandum of S. P. Langley, 9 October 1902, BAE-IN. The complex maneuverings of October and November 1902, are well documented but not recounted here.

80. Fletcher to Boas, 14 October 1902, BP; Putnam to Langley, n.d., SIA. The Dorsey, Culin, and Russell correspondence is also in the Secretary's incoming correspondence for these years, SIA.

81. The letters to Olney are in the Secretary's incoming correspondence, SIA.

McGee also conferred with Boas and other anthropologists at the meeting of the Congress of the Americanists in New York during the week of October 21. McGee later denied any involvement in organized efforts on his behalf.

82. McGee to Russell, 29 October 1902; McGee to Henderson, 30 October 1902, BAE-IN. These letters later served as evidence of McGee's disloyalty to Langley. McGee's appeal to the memory of Powell was serious, for his veneration and love for his mentor were clearly sincere. (Although for his own purposes McGee could be ugly. To Stephen Peet, whom he had always treated rather shabbily, he complained in November 1902: "I have been carrying an invalid for ten years and working for two . . . [McGee to Peet, 17 November 1902, Peet Papers, Beloit College Archives].) McGee's hatred for the Smithsonian officials ran so deeply that he defiantly refused to hand over Powell's brain, in his possession, to the National Museum until June 1906—surely a powerful symbolic gesture! Richard Rathbun, for his part, so despised McGee that he advised against accepting it. Daniel S. Lamb received the Major's brain in the Army Medical Museum on June 15, 1906. (Rathbun to Adler, 29 May 1906, SIA.)

83. On Boas's trials in this period, see Curtis M. Hinsley and Bill Holm, "A Cannibal in the National Museum: The Early Career of Franz Boas in America," *American Anthropologist* 78 (1976): 306–16.

84. Boas to Powell, 18 January and 19 March 1893, NAA.

85. Boas to Langley, 15 October 1902, SIA; Boas to Bell, 18 June 1903, BP.

86. Boas to Alexander Graham Bell, 7 August 1903, BP.

87. Boas to Langley, 3 December 1903, SIA. Indicative of Boas's reputation with the Langley staff was the comment of Richard Rathbun to Cyrus Adler on this letter: "Our friend takes himself very seriously." See also Boas to Bell, 9 November 1902, BP.

88. *Science* (21 November 1902), p. 831.

89. Boas to Bell, 7 August 1903, BP.

90. Boas to Charles P. Bowditch, 17 December 1903; Boas to Charles D. Walcott, 7 December 1903, BP.

91. Langley, "Strictly private memorandum of what I am saying to Mr. Cannon," BAE-IN.

92. McGee to W. A. Croffut, 10 February 1904, MP.

93. "Memorandum of annual and sick leave had by W J McGee . . . up to 6/30/03," BAE-IN.

94. McGee to Boas, 21 December 1902 and 16 June 1903, BP.

95. Holmes, WHH 9, section 1.

96. The records of the 1903 investigation (BAE-IN) are in the NAA of the SI. The significance of the investigation for Washington anthropology generally is the subject of the following chapter. The discussion here treats only the impact on McGee.

97. Boas to McGee, 3 August 1903, and to Carl Schurz, 12 August 1903, BP.

98. Adler *et al.* to Langley, 24 September 1903, p. 39, BAE-IN. Hereafter referred to as Adler Committee report.

99. Caroline Brooke Dinwiddie to Matilda Stevenson, 21 February 1902, BAE-IN. This letter, written when Powell lay near death in February 1902, may have been solicited by Stevenson—who loathed McGee—as evidence against him.

100. *Washington Evening Times,* 16 October 1902.

101. McGee testimony, p. 621, BAE-IN.

102. Handwritten notes by Rathbun, n.d., and McGee testimony, pp. 787–88, BAE-IN.

103. McGee testimony, p. 660, BAE-IN.

104. McGee testimony, pp. 821–22.

105. It should be noted that the public/private distinction and the question of the proprietary rights of the individual in the scientific organization plagued Langley, too, as shown in an 1894 letter to George Brown Goode:

> It is equally recognized that a subordinate may, in the course of his official work, make original observations which, in a scientific sense are his, rather than the Institution's; and it probably never will be practicable to formulate a rule or system of rules which will discriminate satisfactorily in every case as to the moral right of publication of such facts, especially as it is, in the nature of the case, indeterminable what part of his work is really official, what is purely personal and independent, and what is due to the thought, method, or experience of his scientific mind.

But, he added, there must be an ultimate authority for "the necessities of administration." (Langley to Goode, April 1894, assistant secretary's incoming correspondence, 1881–1896, SIA.)

106. Adler Committee report, pp. 40–42. The committee placed entire responsibility for the shortcomings of the Bureau on McGee. As Boas pointed out, this was not completely just, since McGee had worked within limits set by Powell (Boas testimony, pp. 946–51). Boas concluded that "whatever was good went to the credit of Powell and whatever was bad went to the discredit of McGee" (p. 951).

107. Remarks of Joseph A. Holmes, quoted in *McGee Memorial Meeting,* p. 20.

108. Cross, "W J McGee," p. 156; Gifford Pinchot, *Breaking New Ground* (New York, 1947). For McGee's central role in the conservation movement, see also Samuel P. Hays, *Conservation and the Gospel of Efficiency: The Progressive Conservation Movement, 1890-1920* (Cambridge, 1959), pp. 102-07.

109. Cross, "W J McGee," p. 160. For a recent, thorough assessment of McGee's contributions to the conservation movement, see Michael J. Lacey, "The Mysteries of Earth-Making Dissolve: A Study of Washington's Intellectual Community and the Origins of American Environmentalism in the Late Nineteenth Century," Ph.D. diss. (George Washington University, 1979), pp. 284–342.

110. W J McGee, "The Conservation of Natural Resources," *Proceedings of Mississippi Valley Historical Association* 3 (1909–10); quoted in Roderick Nash, ed., *The American Environment: Readings in the History of Conservation* (Reading, Mass., 1968), pp. 41–45.

111. See, for instance, McGee's address, "Principles underlying water rights," closing the 19th National Irrigation Congress, 7 December 1911, in *Official Proceedings of the Congress* (Chicago, 1912), pp. 309–20. McGee insisted on the "essential principle of natural equity" that "All the water belongs to all the People" (p. 318).

IX

Crisis and Aftermath: Smithsonian Anthropology under William Henry Holmes, 1902–1910

Washington, D.C., in 1900 was the capital of American politics and, in some fields, science as well. No longer an isolated outpost in an unproven republic, in the years since the Civil War the capital city had blossomed into a consequential intellectual center; it had become a locus of ideas in action. Government science stood at its apex in substantive contributions and in reputation, not yet visibly overtaken by graduate schools, private research foundations, and industrial research laboratories. The magnet of scientific power would never again draw men so strongly to Washington, nor would the preeminence outlast the First World War; but the early years of the new century were a heady, inspiring moment for national scientific service.

President Theodore Roosevelt carried into his administrations (1901–08) a reassertion of national vigor and expansion of the executive branch that relied heavily on a community of scientists and on a belief in impartial government service. The community and the belief were both offspring of the post-Civil War decades of tumultuous demographic and economic growth. Roosevelt's chief institutional innovation, the federal regulatory agency, presupposed a corps of objective investigators; in most of the major domestic political disputes of the Roosevelt and Taft years—pure food and drug, conservation of natural resources, railroad and social welfare legislation—government scientists played central informational and catalytic roles.

Scientific men and women constituted the heart of Washington intellectual and social life as the century turned. For thirty-five years a fertile and flourishing intellectual community had gradually created a set of forums for discussion and enlightenment: the Philosophical, Literary, Anthropological, and Biological Societies of Washington formed the nucleus of this constellation of social groupings. In 1898, when thirteen societies joined to establish the "interlocking directorship" of the Washington Academy of Sciences, the capital seemed to arrive at intellectual maturity.[1]

Washington's intellectual community was built upon a substratum of common concerns and purposes. Powell, McGee, and sociologist/paleobotanist Lester Frank Ward were prominent in ignoring disciplinary boundaries to address what they saw as the fundamental issues of their day. "What was going forward in the intellectual lives of these men in the last decades of the century," one historian has recently observed, "was the interpretation of the social meaning of the doctrine of evolution. The whole experience had powerful moral and religious dimensions, and the basic question they dealt with was this: are cosmogenesis, biological evolution, and human social evolution driven by processes cognate to us all as moral beings, or are they indifferent and alien to us?"[2] The questions bequeathed by Darwin had evolved by the 1890s into a set of highly charged issues with direct political import: With what costs and benefits does man presume to alter the courses of nature and of human society? On what ground may man claim a hand in shaping his own fate? Washington was the appropriate scene of debate, for on the resolution of these questions hinged the very legitimacy of government science.

By the time of America's entry into the First World War, the question of the propriety of an activist government had been settled by economic and social developments, not by the arguments of Ward, William Graham Sumner, or Herbert Croly. Management efficiency and scientific expertise soon became the watchwords of a generation busily erecting an "organizational society" in which those who could claim status as scientists assumed important advisory roles in policy-making.[3] Not surprisingly, with the new century "every year brought more scientists into federal service." Scientific bureaus began to proliferate after 1900: the National Bureau of Standards, Bureau of Mines, Bureau of the Census, and the Forestry Service all appeared between 1901 and 1905. Under the powerful influence of figures like Charles D. Walcott and Gifford Pinchot, emphasis moved noticeably toward applied research for public utility, leaving basic work to the growing university departments or foundations like the Carnegie Institution of Washington (1902) and the National Geographic Society (1888).[4]

Washington cultural life was consequently weak in the arts and weighted toward the scientific. Still, Henry James considered the capital a "City of Conversation," somehow not entirely absorbed by politics.[5] The growing bureaucracies and international cares that came with the world war would undermine the social ease of nineteenth-century Washington, erasing the vestiges of southern small-town sleepiness that Henry Adams recalled. But in 1900 the city had reached a cultural apex. "More and more," an English visitor remarked, "Washington becomes the Mecca of the United States."[6]

The Smithsonian Institution, situated expansively on the Mall, shifted with political and scientific winds. Smithson's original bequest of $515,000, augmented over the years by private gifts, had risen in fifty years to more than $900,000, yielding in 1900 an annual private operating fund of some $60,000. This sum represented a mere fraction of the Institution's expenditures, however. Now embracing the ever-growing National Museum, the Astrophysical Observatory, the National Zoological Park, and the BAE, the

Smithsonian absorbed half-a-million dollars a year. The Museum, as Henry had anticipated, depended entirely on Congress for its annual sustenance of $250,000.[7]

The Smithsonian had never enjoyed true political neutrality under Henry or Baird, and the scope of its activity in an age enamored of science and aware of public service assured that the Institution would be exposed to national politics as never before. Between the Spanish-American War and the First World War, Smithsonian science generally and BAE anthropology in particular were caught in the throes of major social adjustments. Professing scientific impartiality for his Institution, Secretary Samuel Langley found it prudent to stress public service, even as the Smithsonian moved away from the central dynamics of American science. But Langley's notion of service bore little resemblance to Henry's nineteenth-century sense of moral uplift. Langley sought to apply science immediately to current concerns, and he desired to educate the museum public to a limited degree through entertaining, eye-catching exhibits. The change from Henry to Langley had occurred incrementally, but it involved abdication of a vital ethical element. Powell was a pivotal and fascinating example of the transformation. As we have seen, he originally promised useful functions for ethnology, then withdrew into esoteric interests, never again to emerge as a policy advisor in Indian affairs (although the course of his career was radically different in geology). Like Henry, he believed deeply in ultimate public enlightenment through doing as well as dispensing science. This dream was dead by the time of Powell's death. The hardening class lines of American science and society had already determined that the mass of Americans would merely consume, not experience their science.

The enormous growth of the Smithsonian; its consequent vulnerability to political pressures; the turn to applied research in government science in the Roosevelt years; and the use of the museum as public entertainment: these were some of the related historical trends that combined to push BAE anthropology for a time into Henry Adams's fin-de-siècle dead-water, "where not a breath stirred the idle air."[8] The timing was most unfortunate for the place of government anthropology in the emerging national profession. At the very period when Boas at Columbia and Putnam at Harvard were training a new generation of American ethnologists, linguists, and archaeologists, Langley and Holmes faced the apparent bankruptcy of Powell's scientific vision with little vigor of their own. While self-trained amateurs were rapidly passing out of acceptance, the Bureau had neither facilities nor philosophy for training men and women. Dependent on others for its staff, the Bureau became dependent on the outside for new ideas as well.

Broadly sketched, then, the fate of the Bureau after Powell had less to do with individual personalities than with deeply running social and scientific currents. The BAE was the victim of historical movements both within and beyond anthropology. On the one hand, a public sinking ever further into ignorance and impotence demanded titillation more than edification from tax-supported bureaus and museums of science. Politicians responded predictably, and among Washington anthropologists, the "museum interest," as Boas aptly phrased it, gained dominance over research in nonmaterial culture. On the other hand, the cadre of new university professionals in anthropology, abandoning a public voice, soon moved off into debates among themselves. The Bureau of American Ethnology, child of a past world, was left without respectable program or purpose.

Powell's scientific world crumbled in the summer of 1903. The torrent that washed away W J McGee's career in anthropology had been building for years, held back only by Powell's massive presence. During the eighties his structure had been useful in focusing work and framing questions. But beginning in the early nineties his health steadily deteriorated and he progressively withdrew from active participation in the Bureau. The last decade was a long, sad decline. Between 1890 and 1895, old and trusted collaborators departed and were replaced by McGee, who cared for Powell as he prepared to succeed him. By 1900, stagnation had overtaken the Bureau. No new projects appeared, and the valuable work that did continue grew from seeds sown much earlier (such as Mooney's work) or from Boas's efforts to revise BAE linguistics.[9]

The Smithsonian investigation in the summer of 1903 brought these political, professional, and personal matters to a head. The testimony of Boas, McGee, Fewkes, Stevenson, Mooney, and others revealed in detail the underpinnings and daily operations of Powell's organization. As they freely discussed their concerns about the Bureau's methods, they revealed that it had reached an untenable position in anthropology. By the end of July it was clear that in the new century Powellian science no longer satisfied either public or nascent professional needs. Four related issues emerged: lack of scientific planning; institutional loyalty; the appropriate role of the individual in science; and withholding of materials from publication. All of them touched on Powell's cherished assumptions.

The primary question, as committee chairman Cyrus Adler posed it, was "whether the work of the members of the scientific staff of the Bureau was being pursued in accordance with some general system so that it might . . . show definite results in a reasonable time; or whether it was being done upon individual opinion, according to individual tastes . . ."[10] In the early years, Frederick Webb Hodge answered, Powell had outlined the collaborative projects. Of these, two were long since finished and the third, the synonymy, was still limping along, hampered by the constant accumulation of new data and shuffled from one reluctant staff member to the next, an unwanted stepchild of Powell's fertile mind. [11] Outside of these general projects, pursued sporadically over the years, BAE anthropology amounted to private pursuits. Jesse Fewkes, who had joined the staff in 1897, complained that in his experience things has just "drifted along" without guidance. Investigations had always been determined more by personality than by problem: "If they could get a good man to do work in any field," he stated, "they got him, and he brought in his results, and they catalogued them under the different sciences." Correlation of effort was totally absent: "Anyone that wants to go out [in the field] makes a strong appeal and he goes out," Fewkes added. He contrasted the Washington work with the American Museum of Natural History's current program, the Jesup Expedition organized by Boas:

> Take the New York people. They start with a question of the trail of migration of the Indian from the Old to the New World via Behring Strait, the so-called Jesup expedition. Men are sent to different points to study. There is a correlated plan of effort to which the endeavors of these men are directed.

What the Bureau needed, he suggested, was "a certain definite plan," in which "we could work in harmony, and it would be much better." [12]

John N. B. Hewitt, a member of the Bureau since the mid-eighties, confirmed Adler's impression that the Bureau was not a "close corporation." "You could work in the same office with an ethnologist, ten of you in all, for ten years, and although you were speaking acquaintances, you do not seem to have collaborated very closely," Adler surmised. Hewitt agreed that "each man had his own work and stuck to it." [13] As a result, Matilda Stevenson summarized, Powell and McGee's organization had become not "a Mecca for scientific men to come to and to believe in," but "a place at which scientific men all over the country shrug their shoulders." [14]

Powell's tendency to accumulate materials without publishing them bothered the committee deeply. The hoarding was a result of his desire to release only final results—Powell's "determinate knowledge"—and it had infuriated contemporaries for years. A decade earlier, in fact, Otis Mason had described to Langley the resistance to Powell's Bureau from elsewhere in the country. Opponents at that time, as Mason saw it, included Putnam, Alice Fletcher, and Daniel Brinton, and their reasons for dissatisfaction included "the alleged exclusive spirit of the Bureau in reference to material in its possession and withheld both from publication and from the privilege of investigation." [15] At about the same time another critic had reminded the Washington men that the public and the scientific community had more interest in the scientific process than in the grand generalizations that arrogant government men chose to reveal. [16] This proprietary attitude had prevented respected anthropologists, such as Putnam and Brinton, from enjoying access to Bureau data. It had even kept the researches of some BAE personnel, such as Gatschet, from reaching the public. [17] Joseph H. McCormick, who worked with the Bureau on a part-time basis in the nineties, added that "the criticism that I find in travelling over the country by outside anthropologists is that by the time the material is published it is old and practically valueless, because it has been anticipated by other colleges and museums or something of that sort." [18] Boas deplored Powell's retention of material, which had resulted, he said, in large amounts of unfinished, possibly useless material. Boas's criticism was part of his general stance on the importance of publishing data. While government science should not be limited to publication of facts without "ultimately trying to draw the widest, and consequently most useful inferences," he suggested, at the same time no scientist had the right "to present the conclusions he has drawn without giving to the world the facts on which his conclusions are based." [19]

Boas's remarks to the committee exposed additional dilemmas in the young profession of anthropology. By the turn of the century, Boas, as previously discussed, was formulating his own plans for anthropology in the United States. The Bureau was pivotal for the future of linguistic work; indeed, during Holmes's tenure as BAE chief, Boas took complete charge of Bureau linguistics. But the previous arrangements between Boas and the Bureau for his linguistic work and that of his students encountered deep suspicion from Smithsonian officers. To the committee Boas defended his joint expeditions of the previous decade for the Bureau and the American Museum. The joint efforts, he argued, had provided linguistic material for the Bureau and ethnographic data for the Museum at minimum cost. For John Swanton's early Haida work, for example, the BAE paid only his salary of $700, while the New York museum took care of all field expenses. In return the BAE received a Haida grammar and a large collection of texts. The equivalent results by the BAE alone would have cost an additional $1,200, Boas estimated. Furthermore, the cooperation was a natural division of interests:

> I wanted to have full information on the social organization of the Haida, and to get this it was necessary to collect, in the original language, the whole history of the families. We cannot handle all these texts in New York; we have not the means of working out grammars; we cannot engage men to do philological work. Therefore, we could afford to turn over the philological work to the Bureau of Ethnology . . . [20]

The integrated nature of anthropology was uppermost in Boas's mind, and it required multiple approaches to cultural phenomena. This dissolved questions of institutional loyalty. The investigator cared only about the intricacies of the problem at hand, with no thought of the ultimate disbursement of his findings. In the cases of his own students Boas instructed them to collect certain things and to collect with everything they get information in the native language and to obtain grammatical information that is necessary to explain their texts. Consequently the results of their journeys are the following: they get specimens; they get explanations of the specimens; they get connected texts that partly refer to the specimens and partly refer simply to abstract things concerning the people; and they get grammatical information. The line of division is clear; the grammatical material and the texts go to the Bureau, and the specimens with their explanations go to the New York Museum. There is no conflict of any sort.[21]

Under close questioning Boas detailed his methods of working up linguistic materials. He proceeded by stages, during which the notecards moved back and forth between Washington and New York. At each point he "endeavored to put it in such shape that anyone familiar with linguistic methods might take it up, if for some reason or other I could not complete it."[22] Boas's sense of incompleteness and tentativeness in his science marked his testimony throughout.

Smithsonian officers found Boas's methods unorthodox. While he stressed an open-ended, unfinished science, with loyalty transcending local institutions, the committee asked for final products and exhibited a proprietary attitude. They were impatient with tentativeness and distrustful of divided allegiances. The constant recall of materials to New York for further work was particularly irksome. If these linguistic manuscripts were the property of the Bureau, they asked, why were most of them still with Boas? What had the Bureau paid for? The demand for complete materials to justify congressional appropriations indicated growing pressures and frustration with an apparently endless enterprise. It was a lack of understanding that undermined Boas's work with Washington, thus contributing to the isolation of Bureau anthropology over the coming years.

Amidst the swirling institutional change of this period, Boas was unquestionably the central figure, as even Cyrus Adler and his committee grudgingly recognized in 1903. In promoting his view of a broad-based science, Boas had first to reorient the attachments of anthropologists. This was to be, in fact, as important as any specific theoretical or methodological point inculcated by university training. Having suffered personally from the vagaries of local cliques and institutional myopia, Boas was convinced that the parochial pride and gentlemanly enthusiasms that had inspired much nineteenth-century American science must give way to wider horizons and higher intellectual standards. Local academies of science, he lectured Charles D. Walcott in 1902, had outlived their usefulness. Arguing for national publication series framed around disciplinary interests rather than local activities, Boas admitted that "The objection might be raised that by combining forces in this manner each academy would lose its individuality. Personally I should consider this

Franz Boas posing as a Kwakiutl hamatsa dancer for a National
Museum diorama, 1895.

a most desirable effect, but it is very probable that the emotional interest in the welfare of the local bodies may outweigh among many individuals the more general interest in the advancement of science."[23]

In this instance, as in his fight with McGee for exclusive membership in the new American Anthropological Association (which he temporarily lost to McGee's preference for an open organization),[24] Boas stood athwart deep historical patterns of his adopted country. Nor were these the only fronts on which he fought. Anthropology as he foresaw it required full cooperation between museums and those institutions, such as the BAE or university departments, with main interests in nonmaterial culture. But the hoped-for collaboration repeatedly failed—in Chicago, Philadelphia, Washington, New York. In each case personalities and unique conditions played roles, but with the exception of Harvard's Peabody Museum, where the university department grew from an established museum, the consequences were always the same.[25] On this issue Boas was stymied for years, and his frustration was a measure of the strength of the interests that he confronted. But he never abandoned the ideal of a university-museum complex. Writing to Berthold Laufer in 1918 regarding the establishment of an East Asiatic Institute, Boas described the situation he had known through much of his career:

> It is, of course, perfectly clear that as long as we have a single professorship without any prospect for occupation for young people, we shall never make any headway, no matter how good a professor may be; neither will your museum work be effective, unless it is placed on a wider basis. My idea would be to take up the plan as we had it in mind about fifteen years ago or more, namely: outline an institution in which both university and museum work should be represented, and in which provision should be made that the young people to be trained will find useful occupation for a number of years until the country is well enough advanced in interest to take up the work in different centers.[26]

Laufer pursued his career at the Field Museum in Chicago, which provides an instructive illustration of the institutional flux and the prominence of Boas after the turn of the century. In Chicago the failure to meld university and museum anthropology was almost total.[27] The officers and trustees of the Field Museum were ambitious and hopeful that their museum in the midwestern capital would soon overtake other museums of natural history and anthropology, and they set out in 1894 to obtain the best collections that money could buy. Frederick Putnam had hoped that the Field would become "an everlasting memorial of the [1893] Exposition," particularly of his own department of anthropology at the fair, but by 1894 it was clear to him that the "grand opportunity for science [had been] made such a football" that local politics rather than science would dominate.[28] Putnam warned Edward H. Thompson, his archaeological agent in Yucatan, to avoid Chicago: "You need a quiet, conservative, scientific life in order to do your best work. In Chicago all would be drive and rush and largely sensational effects. That is what they are now after, and it is natural in a place which has started out with great hopes and plenty of money and a feeling that money will do anything. By and by they will realize that while money is an important factor in the work, it alone will not make a scientific institution."[29]

During the formative months of the Field Museum in early 1894, Boas outlined a plan of development for the department of anthropology. The Boas plan featured two points: increased collections from different continents to illustrate the main theme of the department, namely, human development under different environments; and completion of the American collections, which already constituted eighty percent of the total acquisitions and which Boas considered among the most valuable in the country. Boas was attempting, in short, to balance the educational and scientific functions of the Museum.[30] Over the next decade, first under Holmes (1894–97) and then under George A. Dorsey, the Boas plan guided the department's growth, but not in Boas's spirit. In 1897, for instance, Holmes instructed Dorsey to undertake an absurdly ambitious collecting trip for the Museum. Dorsey's itinerary took him to Montana, Washington, British Columbia, California, and the Southwest, all in the course of a few weeks. His purposes were diverse: "You are to endeavor in the first place to secure collections illustrating the physical characteristics of the principal Ethnic groups visited, and in the second to collect materials and data for the construction of certain culture groups illustrative of the great culture provinces into which your work may carry you." Holmes's further instructions made clear that the goal of Dorsey's reconnaissance bore little resemblance to Boas's call for in-depth, holistic study. Holmes, always as much artist as anthropologist, aimed at eye-catching synopses of peoples:

> The goal is the erection of Museum group exhibits representing at least four of the principal ethnic groups, viz: the hunter peoples of the great plains, the cedar-carving peoples of the Northwest Coast, the basket-making tribes of California, and the stone house builders of Arizona and New Mexico. The general idea of these Museum exhibit groups is that they should include life size models of the men, women, and children of the typical community selected to represent the group, and that these figures should be represented as engaged in some characteristic occupation and surrounded by such of their belongings as may be conveniently brought together and displayed.[31]

Dorsey, who succeeded Holmes as curator of anthropology and remained in that position until 1915, continued to dream of amassing the premier collections of North American aboriginal cultures.[32] Due to his Chicago appointment, which came at an early age, his training under Putnam (and later briefly under Boas), and his clear independence of Washington, Dorsey enjoyed a potentially powerful position in American anthropology. But like Holmes in Washington, Dorsey seems never to have asserted himself against the desires of the museum director and patrons; nor did he make overtures of cooperation toward Frederick Starr and the fledgling anthropology department at the University of Chicago.

Boas sensed Dorsey's tendency to drift. Dorsey deeply respected Boas and wished above all to be included among his inner circle. Boas's influence was "the greatest factor in our science today," he wrote on the occasion of the Boas *Festschrift* in 1907. "I for one believe that I fully realize what this means, but I can only come to a full realization of it all when I try to conceive what we were before you came among us and what we would have been had you not come. Every worker in anthropology is indebted to you, and the amount of his success may be measured by the extent of his indebtedness. It seems to me that I can wish for nothing higher than that your students may be worthy of their master."[33] If Dorsey expected to be recognized as one of those worthy students, he was disappointed. Berthold Laufer, who worked with Dorsey at Field Museum and whom Boas valued most highly among American workers in 1903,[34] once referred to Dorsey's "terrifying superficialness"; it was an estimation that Boas shared.[35]

The upstart nature of Chicago science annoyed Boas no less than it had Putnam. Moreover, there was his own humiliation in Chicago in 1894 to chill Boas's interest in Dorsey's museum. Introducing Fay-Cooper Cole to Boas in 1906, Dorsey explained that he was especially "desirous that he should receive the benefit of your instruction in linguistic methods, and in the second place, I am desirous that he should obtain the ability to define and investigate ethnological problems from your point of view." Cole dutifully arrived at Columbia at mid-semester and reported progress to Dorsey, but Boas was not impressed: "Of course, I shall do what I can for Mr. Cole, but he seems to be too much in a hurry, and expects to be able to do too much inside of the two months and a half of this term that remain."[36] The following year Dorsey arranged to spend two months studying linguistics with Boas, in connection with his Pawnee studies, as "sufficient proof, if any were needed, of my serious desire to have the benefit of some work with you." Although he came to New York, Boas was unreceptive. "I think that if you want to get familiar with linguistic methods," he advised the Chicagoan, "you have to allow more time for it than you seem to think necessary. It seems to me that Mr. Cole was altogether too hasty in his work and tried to cover too much in a very short time. Of course, the whole matter was new to him, and he may have the impression that he learned a great deal, but it is only a most elementary foundation that he got. If you simply want to know how we go about linguistic work, of course you can get that idea within a reasonable time, and I shall be very glad to do all I can to help you. I have, of course, my own researches on hand, and I shall not be able to give more than a certain limited time to you, unless I should want to take up the study of Pawnee myself."[37]

The relations with Dorsey and the Field Museum demonstrate that Boas was a tough taskmaster for his science, tolerating little frivolity where his students were concerned—and he chose those students himself. The outstanding quality of J. Alden Mason, he judged, was that "he appreciates how much he has to learn." Of William Mechling, who was a student at Harvard in 1916, Boas was uncertain "on account of the ease with which he was distracted from his work by amusements of various sorts." (Although Boas hastened to add that "I do not hold this particularly against him, because a good many young men who turn out very good later on have that characteristic.")[38] The frequent remarks about personality linked Boas with the world of Powell and McGee, indicating that there was still strong paternalism within Boasian professionalism. In Leslie Spier, Boas recognized and sympathized with a kindred spirit, and his comments are worth recording:

> He is very careful and painstaking, and knows something about biological, archaeological, and ethnological character. He has ideals and is true to them, even if his loyalty brings about discomforts. Connected with this is a certain unyielding position which is easily taken for conceit, but I feel that, as he grows older, he outgrows the difficulties which result from this peculiarity.

> He is without doubt the most independent and intelligent thinker that I have had for a long time. He still lacks the broad foundation that a man like [H.K.] Haeberlin had, but he is a serious student and absolutely truthful in his search for truth. He used to be rather difficult in his personal relations with other people, but his angles and corners are wearing off very rapidly and he is quite a different man now from what he used to be a few years ago. Some people think that he is conceited, but that is a very unfair judgment. It is rather shyness and intolerance of dogmatism that gives the impression.[39]

It is doubtful that Boas ever wrote more lucid descriptions of himself than these reflective passages on Spier.

Thus between 1900 and 1920, Boas's influence grew steadily through his own driving energies and those of his students, and new centers of activity, such as Chicago and Berkeley, claimed increasing attention and funds. Powell's Bureau, however, emerged from the 1903 investigation tarnished and demoralized. In the late summer, John Swanton described to Boas the uncomfortable conditions under Langley's "dictatorship":

> I think this atmosphere of suspicion, meanness, and political pulling and hauling about the worst for any young man of energy and high scientific ideals. I see a splendid field open to the Bureau, but until it

is headed by a real able sympathetic ethnologist I do not believe it can properly make use of its opportunities. Where editors and private secretaries flourish while scientific workers are backlisted [sic], where compilation is made to count for more than original research, and where talk runs on saving a hundred dollars [rather than] on solving ethnological problems, what scientific future can we look forward to and what inducements are there for scientists?[40]

The Powell-McGee Bureau appeared an inefficient, highly exclusive agency, molded by Powell's theories despite claims of inductive science. While jealously guarding materials from outsiders, the BAE had suffered from lack of a research program beyond the whims of individuals. Finally, it was irrelevant to public needs.

There was truth in the picture, for the Bureau had indeed been founded on the individual. Matilda Stevenson recalled that "my instructions were usually these from Major Powell: 'Go and do the best you can, you know best how to pursue your work and I know that you will accomplish all that is possible.'"[41] If this meant lack of planning, it was because Powell's early scientific career had confirmed his faith that the path to general truth lay in ever-greater accumulation of facts and that the scientist must follow his genius. He assumed that if one ethnologist died, any competent successor could work up the notes—thus his willingness to withhold materials for years. Again and again, early personal experiences seemed to determine the institutional forms and behavior of later years. McGee caught this important truth for his and perhaps every generation when, late in life, he wrote to Walcott: "You may recall that both Powell and I began scientific work at our own cost and not for salary; and we never got over the habit."[42]

In the wake of the investigation a number of blueprints for future Bureau anthropology appeared, all of them designed to return the agency to public purpose. By 1900 many influential Americans were deeply concerned about the quality of the "American stock" and the effects of mixing with Indians, Blacks, Orientals, and others, and they demanded that the government discover the scientific facts about race mixture. In early 1904, attempting to mollify congressional critics and avoid appropriation cuts, Langley and Alexander Graham Bell, a Regent of the Smithsonian, drew up an outline of future BAE work for Congress. Langley did not welcome active Smithsonian involvement in social questions, but encouraged by Bell, he proposed to expand agency activities to include studies of the peoples of Samoa and Hawaii, and he included an ambitious "Biological Study of the People of the United States." Langley voiced both a concern for the country's racial state and a faith in applied anthropology:

The ethnic elements of all nations and races are assembling in America, and are rapidly coalescing. It is the first occurrence of its kind known in history, and is the beginning of an era fraught with the deepest possible interest, historic, scientific, and national. It affords a great, and probably a last, opportunity to witness and record the intermingling of the racial elements of the world and the resultant physical, mental, moral, and pathologic interactions in all stages and in every phase. Shall the opportunity be neglected by the American Government? It is a self-evident fact that a knowledge of the elements with which a nation has to deal is the first essential to intelligent administration of these elements . . . Science can have no greater purpose than to lay the foundation for the future molding of the racial destinies of the United States—to so determine the results of the mingling of white, black, red, and yellow races on the longevity, fecundity, vigor, liability to disease, moral and intellectual qualities, and to so fully understand the operations of heredity and the effects of changing social and climatic conditions, as to frame and administer wise laws regarding these subjects, and to direct the policy of the thousands of institutions that deal with the racial welfare of the nation.[43]

Bell approved Langley's plan, but in revising the proposal he stressed the importance to the nation of the biological or, as he preferred, ethnological survey. Bell saw a "new people" gradually evolving in the United States, and he hoped that "the final result should be the evolution of a higher and nobler type of man—and not deterioration of the nation."[44]

In his last report as acting director of the BAE (1902), McGee had outlined his own "Applied Ethnology," which included a prominent place for laboratory and field work in physical anthropology. Noting that "the time is at hand for applying the principles of the New Ethnology to American aborigines as ethnic constituents of a growing citizenship," McGee observed that "many of the practical problems connected with immigration, Chinese exclusion, the occupation of Porto Rico, Hawaii, and the Philippines, and the education of the colored race can finally be solved only in the light of ethnologic principles. . . . These and other weighty considerations have led to the inauguration of researches in physical anthropology." He explained to Boas that he intended to develop beside the "purely scientific branch" of the Bureau a "practical branch" to determine "the citizenship value of both pure and mixed Indians." It was time "to utilize the principles developed during the formative period [of Bureau anthropology] and to apply them to the welfare of the nation." McGee prepared another outline, which Boas presented to the Smithsonian Regents on McGee's behalf in December, in which he pictured himself as the proponent of a socially relevant agency and reminded the Regents that "it was my purpose gradually to transform the Bureau from a special and purely scientific office to one of more general and practical character."[45] This had never come about, he contended, because Powell had argued that "We must leave something for McGee, and besides, I am an old man now, and I do not want to do it."[46]

Predictably, Boas presented the most ambitious program. He had a great stake in Bureau operations, and he tended to blame Powell rather than McGee for the Bureau's loss of direction and contraction in scope. Powell's antipathy to physical anthropology had kept the Bureau from developing into the "Ethnological Survey" of the American population (including Blacks, mestizos, and mulattos) that Boas also foresaw. In addition to work in physical anthropology, Boas emphasized investigations with "practical bearings," such as the effects of White education and missionary teaching on Indian amalgamation with White society.

In late 1903 he prepared a prospectus on the "Organization of the Bureau of American Ethnology," presented to the Smithsonian Regents late in that year. His program deserves attention. Boas defined two broad areas of activity for the Bureau: further study of the early, unwritten history of the American Indians, as Powell had pursued; and study of the "Effects of Social and Climatic Adaptation and of Race Mixture in America." Under Powell the purely scientific had received emphasis, while application had been largely ignored. Boas proposed to correct this imbalance with a reinvigorated Bureau.[47]

Physical anthropology was the heart of Boas's plan. For years he had promoted and directed anthropometric studies as an integral part of anthropology. In *Science* magazine Boas argued that "the physical and mental characteristics of Indian half-bloods, of negroes and mulattoes, and the effects of adaptation and amalgamation of the many European nationalities that settle in our country" were proper fields of work for the Bureau. And he told Bell that anthropologists had wished for years that the Bureau would be extended to include race mixture, so that reliable information would be available to guide legislation on race problems.[48]

To the Regents, Boas outlined a five-year, $800,000 program for the Bureau. (The annual BAE budget at the time varied between $30,000 and $40,000.) Comparing the Bureau to the American Museum of Natural History, he found that the BAE spent $6,000 working up every $1,000 of field work, while the corresponding office expense in New York was only $1,600. Since the large permanent staff at the Bureau meant high administrative expenditures, Boas advised that the Bureau start with a small core of young scientists and cooperate extensively with anthropologists employed by other institutions, just as he had worked with Powell. Bureau money should be confined to research and, unlike past practice, never be used to pay for specimens for the National Museum. By cutting the staff to a minimum, Boas estimated, general administration could be limited to about $21,000 a year.

But this was only the administrative budget. He divided Bureau activities into the "historical" work of the ethnologists and the "amalgamation of races" work of the physical anthropologists. Typically, Boas fitted his vision to his audience, matching urgency with large demands. Boas predicted that within twenty years the North American tribes would have disappeared altogether, so that the ethnological work was necessarily limited in time. He estimated that about 450 separate field trips (of unspecified length) would be necessary to record the ethnology of the vanishing tribes of North America. This work would be done by "special agents," not regular Bureau employees. Although fewer than ten trained men were available in 1903, Boas thought that a sufficient number could be trained within five years to cover everything. He proposed a similar program of special agents for archaeological work, noting that here, too, at least ten competent archaeologists could be trained in five years. The entire ethnological budget, including permanent BAE ethnologists, special agents, archaeologists, and administration, rose from $76,000 in the first year to $170,000 in the fifth.

This large allotment still did not include the work in physical anthropology, which was the "general anthropological survey" that Boas envisioned. While the historical work would eventually die out with its subject matter, Boas predicted that the work of the physical anthropologists "will prove to be beneficial in so many different lines, that its continuance and expansion will become necessary."[49] Here again trained men were not immediately available, so that in the first year only $12,000 would be required for this work. Boas anticipated that as the purely ethnological work decreased and eventually ceased altogether, the importance of the applied anthropology would grow and ultimately dominate the Bureau. In this way the Bureau would develop by 1920 into a complete, ongoing "Anthropological Survey" of the racial elements of the nation.

The Bureau of Ethnology never became an anthropological survey of the American people. Holmes proved to be a weak administrator who permitted the Bureau to slide under the supervision of Langley and, after Langley's death in 1906, of Charles D. Walcott, an old friend from Geological Survey and Chicago days. Bureau correspondence passed through the Institution's offices, and the BAE offices moved from the Adams building on F Street down to the Mall. Thus was the Bureau subordinated and disciplined to the larger institution, so that "airplane builders and geologists were now making final decisions in the field of anthropology." In her study of the Holmes years, Virginia Noelke has further concluded that while Powell "left the BAE without a clear definition or purpose," eight years later "Holmes left a scientific agency which had no important role in either the field of anthropology or in the [government] bureaucracy."[50] Unable to compete with foundations and universities for funds and trained personnel, the Bureau also had difficulty living up to political demands for applied science.

The dilemmas of the Bureau extended well beyond the shortcomings of Holmes. Even with more assertive leadership, the Bureau after Powell would

William Henry Holmes with a friend on the Washington Mall,
summer of 1871; and in his office at the BAE, winter of 1904.

have been buffeted about by currents of professional change. While new people were in training with Boas and Putnam and soon with Kroeber, the BAE staff was aging. Mooney and Stevenson continued field work whenever possible, but John Swanton's unceasing linguistic and ethnological work represented the only infusion of fresh enthusiasm. Significantly, Swanton was a student of both Putnam and Boas. Holmes was not unaware of the problem, but he was powerless. He wisely freed Swanton for field work while most of the staff was manacled to the *Handbook,* and he bemoaned the lost opportunities caused by government restrictions:

It is a constant regret to me that the Bureau is not able to add to its forces at least a few of the promising young students trained by . . . teachers in the field of anthropology, but the conditions under which our work is directed make this next to impossible.

To another correspondent Holmes specified one of those conditions when he noted simply that "few die and none resign in the Government service."[51]

Holmes was a tired man of fifty-six when he reluctantly assumed the reins of the Bureau. For this shy but proud man, the nasty dispute with McGee was a shattering climax to more than two decades of government science. His own archaeological field work was largely over by 1902, and he spent the rest of his long life (until 1933) defending opinions formed early on, notably his skepticism toward all claims for Paleolithic man in the New World. As Boas had anticipated, museum matters occupied most of Holmes's attention, and he traveled frequently on museum and exposition business. Part of 1904 was devoted to the International Congress of Americanists in Stuttgart and a subsequent tour of European museums reminiscent of Mason's tour of 1889. In 1908–09, Holmes traveled to Santiago, Chile, for the first Pan-American Scientific Congress. In the intervening years domestic fairs, such as the James-town Tercentennial of 1906 and the Alaska-Yukon-Pacific Exposition (Seattle, 1908), drained him further.

Honors came to Holmes now, and after years in the shadows of Powell and McGee he savored them. William H. Dall thought the recognition long overdue: "There is more or less human nature mixed up with all the affairs of man, and pure justice is strictly supernatural and not to be counted on here below," Dall wrote in congratulating Holmes on his election to the National Academy of Science in 1905. Holmes may have been, as his daughter-in-law claimed, "an avowed materialist," but he selected Dall's letter for inclusion in his scrapbook memoirs.[52] In Chile, too, he basked in honor at the Pan-American meetings: "I dined with the [Pedro] Moutts in Santiago Chile 1909; sat at his left and he pared a peach for me and ordered a special bottle of wine," Holmes inscribed on a photograph of the Chilean president.[53]

Holmes wished at long last to place archaeology in a central position within American anthropology.[54] New World archaeology, ethnology, and historical research had traveled separate paths through the nineteenth century, but a hope for synthesis had grown, especially with southwestern and Central American students, from the 1870s. Putnam had rejoiced to Morgan in 1876 that "the data exists for a better understanding than we have had before & that such men as Morgan & [Adolphe] Bandelier are living & ready for the work. My own work," he continued, "has been so entirely from objects & not from books that I find much in all you & he write that is confirmatory of what I do from specimens as to prove that careful work from both these sources will in time clear up much which is now dark and mysterious."[55] Bandelier, too, saw the necessity of multiple approaches, but he leaned to library and ethnological research, and he disdained archaeologists for their ignorance of the Spanish chroniclers and of living peoples: "It is my firm belief," he had advised Morgan, "that much more can be realized out of the aboriginal clusters in Mexico, Guatemala, and in Yucatan as they are found at this present day, than from any survey of Palenqué, Uxmal, and Chichen-Itza."[56]

Thus recognition of the desirability of collaboration had dawned, even as personal and institutional limitations prevented implementation. Discounting or choosing to postpone archaeological work, Powell had pursued the North American mounds survey partly as a result of congressional and Smithsonian pressures. By contrast, Holmes felt that as archaeology entered the twentieth century, it stood prepared to make essential, unique contributions to the science of man. To the assemblage in Stuttgart he announced that "when the results achieved [by archaeologists] are supplemented by the rich materials furnished by a study of the living peoples, they must go far toward illuminating the pages of the story of humanity which the Old World has been gradually but surely revealing."[57]

Holmes promoted Bureau archaeology in two ways: by continuing his crusade against claims for Paleolithic man in America, and by supporting Jesse W. Fewkes's work in the Southwest and the Caribbean. While he no longer took to the field himself, the Chief worked through others, notably Gerard Fowke, in explaining away signs of glacial or preglacial man in America. Holmes's determined efforts derived in part from his conviction, established years before, that Old World categories must not be imported and imposed on American prehistory. "So far as the use of the terms 'paleolithic' and 'neolithic' are concerned they may both be omitted from the literature of American archeology without loss if not to possible advantage," he stated in 1904. At the same time, he confessed, American scholars had failed to establish a convincing cultural chronology:

Hundreds of ancient caves have been searched with only negative results; glacial gravels have been examined with great care but the returns are exceedingly meager; river terraces, and kitchen midden deposits, yield nothing of particular value, and the results, when viewed as a whole, instead of enlightening the mind, fill it rather with confusion. It is within the bounds of possibility that this confusion may in a measure be due to the presence in America of an autochthonous race element.[58]

Holmes's blindness resulted from the focus of his vision: seeking major statements about New World race history, insisting on seeing widespread, disparate observations as a whole, he discouraged study of local microchange. While he was aware of new trends, he served old purposes.

Much the same can be said of Fewkes's archaeology in the Southwest and the Caribbean. Fewkes seems to have been widely disliked and distrusted; Cushing was only the first of his detractors. The antipathy may have been due in part to his loyalty to Langley, the Smithsonian, and the needs of the National Museum. While he was certainly never a mere pot-hunter, institutional bonds and his own inclinations did delimit his archaeology.[59] Because he followed Cushing and Bandelier in the Southwest and was familiar with developments at the Peabody Museum, Fewkes was sensitive to the possibilities of an approach to the prehistory of the Southwest such as both Putnam and Holmes had hoped to establish. Fewkes's article, "The Prehistoric Culture of Tusayan," published in 1896, in fact suggested such a program.[60]

But Fewkes was unable to follow through. After his discovery of the striking Sikyatki pottery in the mid-nineties, he continued southwestern research into Hopi ethnology and history with funds drawn by Langley from the Secretary's Bureau reserve. Then, following the Spanish-American War, he switched to the Caribbean for collecting and theorizing about the roots and spread of Antillean culture. Like the BAE flirtation with Hawaiian ethnology in these years (which produced minimal results), Fewkes's Caribbean foray followed the course of empire more than the logic of science. His work, while pioneering, was less than notable, and at times he elected to purchase collections rather than excavate deeply. After the establishment of Mesa Verde National Park in 1906, Fewkes assumed responsibility for preparing various sites for public visit, exclusively excavating major cliff dwellings and mesa cities.[61]

Despite indefatigable labors, Fewkes lacked focus or depth. In the nineteenth-century tradition of the Cyrus Thomas mounds survey, he undertook reconnaissance of large areas, addressing broad questions and amassing material collections. In contrast to Alfred V. Kidder's decades of work at Four Corners and Pecos, Fewkes did not excavate fully or consider local developments sufficiently. While the nature of his archaeology could produce occasional new discoveries, they were theoretically sterile.

Holmes pushed government anthropology in another important new direction, but here too the locus of innovation was the National Museum. Reversing Powell's priorities, he brought serious work in physical anthrplogy to Washington for the first time by hiring Aleš Hrdlička and setting up a division for him in the Museum. Over the following decades Hrdlička became a fixture in Smithsonian anthropology and a dominant force in his profession. The story of Holmes and Hrdlička lies beyond the scope of this discussion, but it should be noted that the two men built a firm rapport based on several commonalities: skepticism toward Paleolithic man, dislike of Boas and Germans generally, loyalty to the Smithsonian Institution, and stubborn scrappiness. In his dying days Holmes wrote to his old friend that "[I] miss you, miss you very much. . . . And those lunch hours were a tonic which there is nothing to replace." For his part Hrdlička recalled (to Frederick Hodge) stirring scientific battles and lamented that "one after another of the 'old guard' is passing away. . . . Ten years hence there will be hardly a soul left of our generation, but this is quite all right if only one could be more hopeful of some of the youngsters."[62]

The Holmes years, in sum, were a prolonged struggle to define new purpose and interest for the Bureau. The constant awareness of public scrutiny warped and inhibited its anthropology. Holmes extended the BAE reach to the Caribbean and the Pacific; he became a strong proponent of government preservation of antiquities and sought a major role for the Bureau in their management; he encouraged Swanton's field work and Fewkes's archaeology, while abdicating Bureau linguistics almost entirely to the man most capable of advancing it, Boas. Finally, he sought out and supported Hrdlička for the Museum. The Bureau was hardly moribund as a scientific agency, but it continued to drift.

The professional difficulties of Holmes's organization were distilled in the major publication and preoccupation of the Bureau: *The Handbook of American Indians North of Mexico.* The *Handbook* appeared in two large volumes (1907, 1910) under Langley's insistent direction and Hodge's dutiful, competent editing. As it finally emerged, the *Handbook* was not so much the culmination of Powellian anthropology as a testimony to changed times, both in Washington and in American anthropology. While referring to public utility Powell had intended his "cyclopedia" as a scientific tool for intelligent laymen. Langley appealed to the memory of the Major but ordered a handbook for politicians and their favored constituents in order to bolster appropriations and his sagging reputation. The volumes were immensely popular but—final irony for a bureau founded by Powell—so few were placed at the Bureau's disposal that requests had to be turned down.

The *Handbook* was a model of nineteenth-century popular science—a generation late. Drawing on virtually the entire anthropological community, Holmes and Hodge mixed invaluable synonymy, bibliography, history, census statistics, and respectable ethnography with occasional judgmental generalization. Of the Eskimo, for example, Henshaw and Swanton wrote: "In disposition the Eskimo may be described as peaceful, cheerful, truthful, and honest, but exceptionally loose in sexual morality." Elsewhere in the article the authors distinguished the several branches of the Eskimauan stock, as determined by Boas and others' meticulous work, and provided a full bibliography.[63]

Holmes described the *Handbook* as a "comprehensive treatise" that would give rise to a supplementary series of specialized handbooks, including Boas's *Handbook of American Indian Languages* (1911) and Holmes's *Handbook of Aboriginal American Antiquities* (1919).[64] The *Handbook of American Indians* did occasion some new research and summary of past years' work, especially among the Bureau staff, but the enterprise was fundamentally at odds with the developing profession of anthropology. It was not simply that the project kept the BAE staff at their desks for at least five years. More importantly, the *Handbook*, a reflection of Langley's attitude toward anthropology, assumed a contracting rather than an expanding, deepening field. The compilation, Hodge predicted, "will eventually represent a complete summary of existing knowledge respecting the aborigines of northern America."[65] Hodge was restating Powell's old dream of comprehensiveness and ultimate knowledge, but by 1906 this was an expectation that had been belied and undermined by the history of the Bureau itself. The image of anthropology as a terminal enterprise, dying out with its subject matter, directly contradicted the notions of continuity and an inquiring community being nurtured, at great personal expense and exertion, in Cambridge, New York, and elsewhere. Quite aside from its clear merits as a resource book in anthropology, the *Handbook* was a fascinating historical product of clashing suppositions and grinding institutional change.

Boas's estrangement from Washington anthropology grew after 1903, despite his position as Honorary Philologist in the Bureau; but it did not in itself condemn Smithsonian anthropology to backwardness or irrelevance. The alienation was, rather, indicative of deep differences of critical perspective within the American anthropological community. Those differences never surfaced for direct confrontation. In retrospect it is possible to watch Boas building his case piece by piece, in linguistics, racial studies, and ethnology, against the linked formal categories of nineteenth-century evolutionism.[66] If his critique was largely complete in its basic elements by 1896, its implications were not apparent to many at the time; nor was he in a position to present it forcefully. The Spanish-American War of 1898, Boas later claimed, was his "rude awakening," for it revealed the American nation to him as "a young giant, eager to grow at the expense of others, and dominated by the same desire of aggrandizement that sways the narrowly confined European states."[67] As the myth of American exceptionalism burst for Boas, his sense of urgency to combat American intolerance and ignorance increased. He became more strident and aggressive.

The consequences of American war and imperialism were thus radically different for Boas and for the Washington men. Finally established at Co-

lumbia University and the American Museum, Boas began two decades of
academic entrepreneurship, deeply enmeshing himself in teaching, administrative machinations, and untiring promotion of anthropology. As his
appeals to Morris K. Jesup, Phoebe Hearst, Archer Huntington, and others
demonstrate, he was entirely pragmatic, perfectly willing to take advantage
of the whims of America's capitalist elite to promote his science.[68] Just as
Powell had worked twenty years earlier to carve out scientific autonomy within
the only institution then capable of funding anthropology, the federal government, Boas now labored singlemindedly toward independent bases for a
critical social science.

Boas's institutional drive followed directly from the deepest lessons of his
anthropology and from his American experience. In the United States, he
came to see, the strength of unreasoning tradition and emotional attachments
still blinded men to the truths of humane intelligence: that "others may abhor
where we worship," and that consequently self-restraint rather than self-
assertion is the highest duty of the nation.[69] Under such discouraging conditions, Boas's moral science required an institutional base from which to
promote rational inquiry free of economic indebtedness, political dependence,
or cultural myopia. In short, the basic tenets of Boasian anthropology, the
structures he worked to create, and his long crusade against racial, ethnic,
and cultural intolerance formed a single fabric of activist, humane social
science. In 1916 he stated once again the basic point of his dispute with
Mason and Powell in 1887, but it was now confirmed by thirty years of
personal and professional history:

> As a matter of fact, the number of people in our country who are willing
> and able to enter into the modes of thought of other nations is altogether
> too small. The American, on the whole, is inclined to consider American
> standards of thought and action as absolute standards, and the more
> idealistic his nature, the more strongly he wants to "raise" everyone to
> his own standards. For this reason the American who is cognizant only
> of his own standpoint sets himself up as arbiter of the world.[70]

For Smithsonian/BAE anthropologists, the expansionism and domestic issues of the Roosevelt years taught differently. As discussed above, Holmes
no less than Boas encouraged an expanded scope for anthropology, first to
Central and South America, then to the U.S. insular possessions. For Boas
it was a question of combating American narcissism and provincialism with
exposure to other cultures; his intentions had changed little since the 1893
Exposition. It is difficult to find any such critique in the scientific expansionism of Holmes or Langley. Their science in the public service, it must
be said, came to mean loyalty to American ways.

As he reached the height of his career in the science of man, Holmes, it
turned out, was no less prone than McGee had been to making grand pro-

nouncements on human affairs of the past, present, and future. In his version of human evolution the role of physical environment was somewhat greater than it had been for Powell, thus removing some of the stigma of cultural backwardness. But his evaluation of aboriginal New World cultures was low, and his environmentalism lay as a thin veil over a racial hierarchy. The evolutionism that Holmes had adopted at an early point did not promote greater tolerance; rather it became another tool for legitimizing conquest and the submission of other peoples. The less fortunate peoples of the earth, he believed, owed their status not to inherent racial inadequacies but to traits acquired from specific environmental conditions. They were doomed in either case, of course, but they had been equal at the creation. This was a comforting thought for men who, like Holmes, still believed in the American ideals of freedom and individual opportunity. If men had begun biologically unequal to the struggle, thereby scientifically predestined to extinction or prosperity, human evolution lost all moral meaning. If, on the other hand, all men had begun with equal possibilities but in a cosmos of differing environments, some of which encouraged thrift and inventiveness while others retarded such progress, success and prosperity could be earned and justified. Holmes's anthropology was always a curious blend of biology, religion, and politics, and perhaps it offered reassurance to people in the midst of urbanization, social stratification, and ambivalent imperialism. Certainly it satisfied Holmes. He implied a stern but just creative force, and portrayed a world in which the hard-working, thrifty individual, like the hardy, tempered race, rightly succeeded. In Holmes the apology and explanation for Anglo-Saxon dominance at home and abroad, for the disappearance of "inferior" types everywhere, found a staunch scientific spokesman.

More than half a century separated Henry Schoolcraft's 1846 ethnological prospectus to the first meeting of Smithsonian Regents from the BAE blueprints of Boas, McGee, and Langley in 1903. In that interval immense changes took place in the intellectual and institutional scaffolding of American anthropology. Yet in retrospect the developments appear gradual, piecemeal; continuities more than discontinuities seem to characterize the overlapping generations of Schoolcraft and Henry, Morgan, Powell, even Boas.

Science in nineteenth-century America was a moral enterprise. The modern attitude of respect, even veneration, of scientific expertise in this country rests on its strictly secular, problem-solving function: the scientist possesses the treasured knowledge necessary for keeping social and technological machinery running more or less smoothly. Higher claims are accepted only at great risk. In the last century, by contrast, scientists of Joseph Henry's persuasion believed that they were entrusted with the moral conscience and future welfare of America. Surrounded by a grasping, impious culture, the scientist had a momentous task: to turn men back, as their clerical fathers and grandfathers had done, to nature and nature's God by exposing them to the brilliant order of the universe.[71] At the same time, appropriately, the public would presumably show respect and appreciation for the scientist as the modern shepherd. Not surprisingly, from this viewpoint the needs of society and scientist achieved a comfortable accord.

The role of the American scientific elite, then, embraced two tendencies that coexisted uneasily. The scientist must spread scientific experience among the people as a means of spiritual uplift and social harmony—salvation would have to be known directly, not through hearsay. Concurrently, though, the drive to exclusiveness which rested on the assumption that only the few were truly capable or inclined to devote their lives to science, demanded recognition of separate status. The latter need impelled both the drive against frauds and imposters and efforts to establish means of formal accreditation that characterized American science a hundred years ago. These proved to be difficult tasks. In anthropology, which straddled the classical curricula of moral and natural philosophy, character rather than expertise tended to count heavily. Current theories of perception taught that every man sees clearly and faithfully if not distorted by impure motives—the motives of the scrambling marketplace. Furthermore, desire for scientific coverage of a large continent before its destruction by heavy waves of population led to reliance on honesty rather than formal credentials. Under the circumstances, anthropological observation was necessarily a popular phenomenon.

And yet distinctions did gradually emerge. The scientific experience that the Smithsonian offered to the lay public was really limited to observation; the Institution heightened functional differences by emphasizing gatherers on one hand, theorizers on the other. It at once connected and distinguished among the elite and the democracy in science. Circular questionnaires from Henry King to Schoolcraft, Morgan, Gibbs, and Powell explicitly invited participation even while they directed and systematized, thereby channeling field work.

The Bureau of American Ethnology inherited these patterns and habits. The early BAE struggled to establish scientific criteria in the face of assumptions that resisted formal credentials. Employment in a government bureau had, by the 1890s, itself become a major index of scientific status. Indeed, one of the multiple purposes for which Powell astutely used his publications was the building of his staff. The emphasis varied with the individual. Cushing was the intuitive genius, Mallery the stalwart, honest investigator, J. O. Dorsey the conscientious, sympathetic Christian. There was room for all kinds, but that very flexibility meant that at root the Bureau's requirements remained simple and subjective: honesty and character.

Powell's categories guided the Bureau. His scientific philosophy was grounded in the conviction that most human thought was filled with delusion and error, usually caused by arrogant, unfounded speculation. The Major conceived of his Bureau as a tool for dissolving mystery, for reducing the puzzles of aboriginal America to understandable historical sequences. In theory this was to be accomplished through ever-greater accumulations of data. In the early years especially, the premium lay on new, exciting discoveries—for Cushing, Mallery, and McGee, in fact, the great discovery of profound significance became obligatory.

There was a palpable sense of excitement and promise in those years. The organization of science in Washington was informed by an evolutionary vision that anticipated a single world brotherhood of man, a unified, ecumenical cosmos. The image of American linguistic development—from many small groups speaking diverse, mutually unintelligible languages, to ever-greater concentrations of common culture—seemed to point the way. The multifarious inventions that Mason and Goode organized in the Museum, right up to the telephone and telegraph, seemed to bond men ever more tightly in a common fate. Perhaps most striking to the Washington men was the racial amalgamation already in the process of homogenizing all mankind into a single biological strain. As they looked into the future, they saw that the American Indian, like the Negro, was destined to be absorbed into a swelling stream of common mankind.

The visions of assimilation and of evolution to a world culture might have encouraged resignation and discouraged efforts to reform or aid the Indian. Indeed, the BAE was accused repeatedly by the Bureau of Indian Affairs and others of hampering efforts to educate and civilize the Indians. Powell did not seek, however, simply to preserve Indian customs for scientific study, but rather, as he had first argued in 1874, to provide scientific grounds for gradual, humane reform. But while wise public policy depended on scientific knowledge, he also aggressively insisted that man must take control and responsibility for his destiny, by discovering the laws of nature and employing them for man's welfare. The ambivalence between reform action and positive knowledge is clear in the following summary by McGee of BAE goals:

> Ethnologists, like other good citizens, are desirous of raising the Indian to the lofty plane of American citizenship; but they prefer to do this constructively rather than destructively, through knowledge rather than ignorance, through sympathy rather than intolerance—they prefer to pursue in dealing with our immature race the course found successful in dealing with the immature offspring of our own flesh and blood. *Incidentally*, they desire to record those steps in mental and moral progress visible among our aborigines, with the view of tracing the mental and moral progress of all mankind, and thereby more wisely guiding efforts toward future betterment.[72]

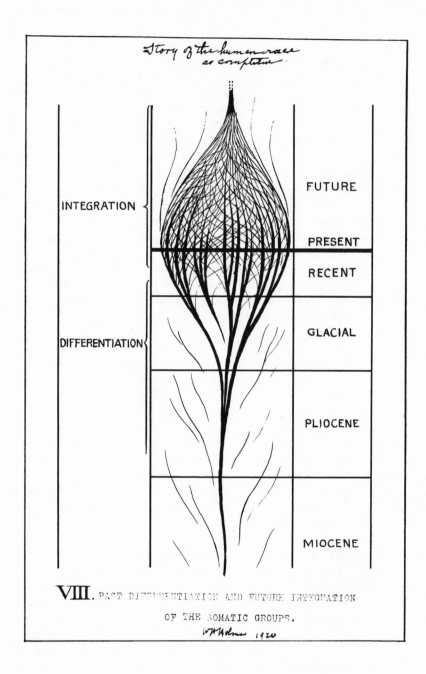

"Story of the Human Race as Completed," sketch by W. H. Holmes, 1920.

Acting on these beliefs, Powell and the Washington anthropologists helped to usher in a new era of government-supported, institutional science. But even as they "organized anthropologic research in America," they retained the contradictory expectations of an earlier period. Like their countrymen busily building the economic, social, political, and educational structures of twentieth-century America, they were ill-prepared for the implications of their acts. Their vigorous assertion of human control sprang from a profound fear that control had already been lost, or abdicated, not to a natural but to a technological, corporate environment that separated man from man.

Here lay the irony for Powell's generation: they molded the forms of modern society but were not modern men. Powell and McGee were interdisciplinary scientists in a sense that cannot be fully recaptured, since they looked for character and certain habits of thought before specific knowledge. Mason retained a piety and wonder toward his work, as well as a simplistic notion of taxonomic science—both revealed his antebellum roots. Powell provided an institutional environment in the Bureau that, in the end, began to alter anthropology in method and data by encouraging a sense of capacity and identity among some staff members. It was a major contribution, but largely unintended.

Unintended results: these more than anything else marked the course of Washington anthropology, as they characterize so much of our modern history. The contours of modern American anthropology formed beyond the borders of intention. They were never really mapped out ahead, even by Boas—though to be sure, he, like Putnam, Brinton, and Powell had his dreams and plans. On the contrary, while they celebrated man's powers of control, Powell and his Washington coworkers backed into the future, carrying into a new century the glorious experiences of one world even as they built another.

Notes

1. James K. Flack, *Desideratum in Washington: The Intellectual Community in the Capital City, 1870–1900* (Cambridge, 1975), p. 158.
2. Michael James Lacey, "The Mysteries of Earth-Making Dissolve: A Study of Washington's Intellectual Community and the Origins of American Environmentalism in the late Nineteenth Century," Ph.D. diss. (George Washington University, 1979), p. 3.
3. Jerry Israel, ed., *Building the Organizational Society: Essays on Associational Activities in Modern America* (New York, 1972).
4. Constance McLaughlin Green, *Washington: Capital City, 1879–1950* (Princeton, 1963):200-01. On the early years of the Carnegie Institution of Washington, see Nathan Reingold, "National Science Policy in a Private Foundation: The Carnegie Institution of Washington," in Alexandra Oleson and John Voss,

eds., *The Organization of Knowledge in Modern America, 1860–1920* (Baltimore, 1979), pp. 313–41.

5. Ibid., pp. 190, 195–96.

6. Ibid., p. 188.

7. Figures are taken from SI, *AR for 1900,* p. LVII.

8. Henry Adams, *The Education of Henry Adams: An Autobiography* (Boston, 1961), p. 331.

9. Boas judged that Powell lost control of the Bureau at an early date because the field of investigation was simply too vast and complex for the series of handbooks that Powell originally planned. Every worker went his own way, Boas thought; and this "chance development" intensified after about 1895. Boas to Robert S. Woodward, 13 January 1905, BP.

10. BAE-IN, p. 838, NAA. (Page numbers refer to the revised transcript of testimony.)

11. Ibid., pp. 288–89.

12. Ibid., pp. 279–83.

13. Ibid., p. 501.

14. Ibid., p. 386.

15. Mason to Langley, 23 June 1891, SIA.

16. E. W. Claypole, "Prof. G. F. Wright and his Critics," *Popular Science Monthly* 42 (1893): 776.

17. Regna D. Darnell, "The Development of American Anthropology, 1879–1920: From the Bureau of American Ethnology to Franz Boas," Ph.D. diss. (University of Pennsylvania, 1969), pp. 81–82.

18. BAE-IN, p. 881.

19. Ibid., pp. 927, 942.

20. Ibid., pp. 918–22.

21. Ibid., p. 922.

22. Ibid., pp. 915–17. For a fuller discussion, see C. M. Hinsley, Jr. and Bill Holm, "A Cannibal in the National Museum: The Early Career of Franz Boas in America," *American Anthropologist* 78 (1976): 306–16.

23. Boas to Walcott, 21 January 1902, BP.

24. George W. Stocking, Jr., "Franz Boas and the Founding of the American Anthropological Association," *American Anthropologist* 62 (1960): 1–17.

25. On museum-university conflicts, see Darnell, "Development," pp. 166–234; and Darnell, "The Emergence of Academic Anthropology at the University of Pennsylvania," *Journal of the History of the Behavioral Sciences* 6 (1970): 80–92.

26. Boas to Laufer, 11 February 1918, FMA.

27. On early Chicago anthropology, see George W. Stocking, Jr., *Anthropology at Chicago: Tradition, Discipline, Department* (Chicago, 1979).

28. Report to the Director [of the 1893 Exposition] for July 1893, FWP; Putnam to C. O. Whitman, 14 March 1894, FWP.

29. Putnam to Thompson, 19 May 1894, FWP.

30. Boas to F. J. V. Skiff, 2 March 1894, FMA.

31. Holmes to George A. Dorsey, 12 May 1897, FMA.

32. See, e.g., Dorsey to Skiff, 17 January and 18 January 1901, FMA.

33. Dorsey to Boas, 24 April 1907, FMA.
34. Boas to Walcott, 7 December 1903, BP. In this interesting letter Boas reviewed and individually evaluated virtually the entire anthropological community.
35. Laufer to Boas, 13 April 1908, BP; quoted in Darnell, "Development," p. 206. Alfred Kroeber has left the following commentary on this point: "George Dorsey once confided to me, in the Palace Hotel in San Francisco before the earthquake of 1906, that Boas was like a tree all over which there grew as fruits those whom he admitted to his friendship—to participation and identification, in modern terms. But those not so admitted would never be close to Boas, and Dorsey himself, for all his trying, remained wholly shut out. For those who remember Dorsey and his energy, self-reliance, competitiveness, and hard-boiled man-of-business manner, this will seem a strangely affecting confession. It shows Boas functioning as a powerful father figure, cherishing and supporting those with whom he identified in the degree that he felt they genuinely were identifying with him, but, as regards others, aloof and probably fundamentally indifferent, coldly hostile if the occasion demanded. A true patriarch, in short, with patriarchal strength and outlook." Kroeber, "The Place of Boas in Anthropology," *American Anthropologist* 58 (1956): 151–59.
36. Dorsey to Boas, 2 February 1906 and 2 March 1906; Boas to Dorsey, 7 March 1906, FMA. Relaying Boas's comment to Cole, Dorsey advised, "Don't let this worry you but do what you can to counteract this impression."
37. Dorsey to Boas, 24 September 1906; Boas to Dorsey, 1 October 1906, FMA.
38. Boas to Dorsey, 27 April 1903; Boas to Laufer, 28 November 1916, FMA.
39. Boas to Laufer, 26 February 1919 and 9 February 1920, FMA.
40. Swanton to Boas, 16 August 1903, BP.
41. BAE-IN, p. 352.
42. McGee to Walcott, 26 January 1910, GP.
43. Minutes of the annual meeting of the Board of Regents, 27 January 1904, SIA. The Langley proposal was actually drafted some months earlier by Holmes. See Holmes to Langley, in WHH 8, sec. 4.
44. Bell to Langley, 3 February 1904, SIA.
45. BAE, *AR for 1902*, pp. ix–xiv; McGee to Boas, 18 September 1903, SIA.
46. BAE-IN, pp. 253–57.
47. Franz Boas, "Organization of the Bureau of American Ethnology," n.d., BP. Boas outlined his ideas briefly before the investigating committee (pp. 933–36, 939–40), but this ms. is a fuller statement.
48. *Science* (21 November 1902), p. 828; Boas to Bell, 9 November 1902, BP; see also Boas to Charles P. Bowditch, 17 December 1903, BP.
49. Boas, "Organization," p. 9.
50. Virginia Noelke, "The Origin and Early History of the Bureau of American Ethnology," Ph.D. diss. (University of Texas at Austin, 1975), pp. 232, 322.
51. Holmes to Frederick Starr, 16 May 1905, NAA; Holmes to G. Stanley Hall, 25 April 1905, NAA. Both letters quoted in Noelke, "Origin and Early History," p. 313.
52. Mary Holmes to Aleš Hrdlička, 22 January 1933, Hrdlička Papers, NAA; W. H. Dall to Holmes, 20 April 1905, WHH 9: 136.

53. WHH 9: 108.

54. See, e.g., "The Place of Archeology in Human History," the introduction to Holmes's *Handbook of Aboriginal American Antiquities, BAE Bulletin* 60, Part I (Washington, D.C., 1919), pp. 1–8.

55. Putnam to Morgan, 18 December 1876, LHM.

56. Bandelier to Morgan, 13 March 1880, LHM.

57. W. H. Holmes, "Contributions of American Archeology to Human History" (21 August 1904), in WHH 9: 227–28.

58. Ibid., pp. 226–27.

59. Noelke, "Origin and Early History," pp. 271, 273. The following discussion of Fewkes draws on Noelke's treatment, pp. 271–77, though the interpretation is mine.

60. J. W. Fewkes, "The Prehistoric Culture of Tusayan," *American Anthropologist,* o.s. 9 (1896): 151–73.

61. Arthur H. Rohn, "The South and Intermontane West" in James E. Fitting, *The Development of North American Archaeology* (Garden City, 1973), p. 190.

62. Holmes to Hrdlička, 3 October 1932; Hrdlička to F. W. Hodge, 24 October 1932, Hrdlička Papers.

63. Frederick W. Hodge, ed., *Handbook of American Indians North of Mexico, BAE Bulletin* 30, Part I (Washington, D.C., 1907), pp. 433–37.

64. Holmes, *Handbook of Aboriginal American Antiquities,* p. xiii.

65. Hodge, *Handbook of Indians,* p. viii.

66. George W. Stocking, Jr., "The Basic Assumptions of Boasian Anthropology," in Stocking, ed., *The Shaping of American Anthropology, 1885–1911: A Franz Boas Reader* (New York, 1974), pp. 1–20.

67. Ibid., pp. 331–32.

68. Ibid., pp. 283–306, esp. 301–03.

69. Ibid., p. 332.

70. Ibid.

71. This nineteenth-century "culture of science" has been brilliantly elucidated by Edward Lurie in his *Nature and the American Mind: Louis Agassiz and the Culture of Science* (New York, 1974).

72. W J McGee, *The Red Man and Helper* (Carlisle, Penn., 1904), p. 2. Emphasis added.

Bibliography

BOOKS AND MONOGRAPHS

Abbott, Charles C. *Primitive Industry*. Salem, Mass.: George A. Bates, 1881.

Adams, Henry. *The Education of Henry Adams: An Autobiography*. Boston: Houghton Mifflin, 1961.

Atwater, Caleb. *Description of the Antiquities of Ohio and Other Historical States. Transactions and Collections of the American Antiquarian Society.* 1. Worcester: American Antiquarian Society, 1820.

Bancroft, George. *History of the United States*. 14th ed. Boston: Little, Brown, 1854.

Bartlett, John R. *The Progress of Ethnology, an Account of Recent Archaeological, Philological, and Geographical Researches in Various Parts of the Globe, tending to elucidate the Physical History of Man. Transactions of the American Ethnological Society* 2. New York: 1848.

Bell, Whitfield J., ed. *A Cabinet of Curiosities: Five Episodes in the Evolution of American Museums*. Charlottesville: University of Virginia Press, 1967.

Berkhofer, Robert F., Jr. *The White Man's Indian: Images of the Indian from Columbus to the Present*. New York: Random House, 1978.

Blackwood, Beatrice. *The Classification of Artifacts in the Pitt Rivers Museum, Oxford*. Oxford: Pitt Rivers Museum, 1970.

Bledstein, Burton J. *The Culture of Professionalism: The Middle Class and the Development of Higher Education in America*. New York: W. W. Norton, 1976.

Boas, Franz. *The Mind of Primitive Man*. New York: Macmillan Co., 1911.

Boller, Paul F., Jr. *American Thought in Transition: The Impact of Evolutionary Naturalism, 1865–1900*. Chicago: Rand McNally, 1969.

Brew, John O., ed. *One Hundred Years of Anthropology*. Cambridge: Harvard University Press, 1968.

Cappon, Lester, J., ed. *The Adams-Jefferson Letters*. Chapel Hill: University of North Carolina Press, 1959.

Carter, Paul A. *The Spiritual Crisis of the Gilded Age*. DeKalb: University of Northern Illinois Press, 1971.

Coulson, Thomas. *Joseph Henry: His Life and Work*. Princeton: Princeton University Press, 1950.

Croll, James. *Climate and Time in Their Geological Relations: A Theory of Secular Changes of the Earth's Climate*. New York: D. Appleton and Co., 1875.

Curtin, Jeremiah. *Creation Myths of Primitive America in Relation to the Religious History and Mental Development of Mankind*. Boston: Little, Brown and Co., 1898.

————. *The Memoirs of Jeremiah Curtin*. Madison: Wisconsin State Historical Society, 1940.

Cushing, Frank Hamilton. *My Life at Zuñi*. Santa Fe: Peripatetic Press, 1941.

————. *Outlines of Zuñi Creation Myths*. BAE, AR for 1892, pp. 321–447. Washington, D.C.: GPO, 1896.

————. *Zuñi Breadstuff*. New York: Museum of the American Indian, Heye Foundation, 1920.

————. *Zuñi Folk-Tales*. Introduction by J. W. Powell. New York: G. P. Putnam's Sons, 1901. Reissued with introduction by Mary Austin. New York: Knopf, 1931.

Dall, William H. *Spencer Fullerton Baird: A Biography*. Philadelphia: J. B. Lippincott Company, 1915.

Daniel, Glyn E. *A Hundred Years of Archaeology*. London: Duckworth, 1950.

Daniels, George H. *American Science in the Age of Jackson*. New York: Columbia University Press, 1968.

————. *Nineteenth-Century American Science: A Reappraisal*. Evanston: Northwestern University Press, 1972.

Darnell, Regna. *Readings in the History of Anthropology*. New York: Harper & Row, 1974.

Darrah, William Culp. *Powell of the Colorado*. Princeton: Princeton University Press, 1951.

Darwin, Charles. *The Descent of Man and Selection in Relation to Sex*. 2d ed. New York: D. Appleton and Co., 1922.

Deuel, Leo. *Conquistadores Without Swords: Archaeologists in the Americas*. New York: Schocken, 1967.

Dickens, Charles. *American Notes*. Philaldelphia: Nottingham Society, n.d.

Dupree, A. Hunter. *Science in the Federal Government: A History of Policies and Activities to 1940*. Cambridge: Harvard University Press, 1957.

Eiseley, Loren. *Darwin's Century: Evolution and the Men Who Discovered It*. Garden City: Doubleday & Co., 1958.

Ewers, John C. *Murals in the Round: Painted Tipis of the Kiowa and Kiowa-Apache Indians; An exhibition of tipi models made for James Mooney of the Smithsonian Institution during his field studies of Indian history and art in southwestern Oklahoma, 1891–1904*. Washington, D.C.: Smithsonian Institution Press, 1978.

Fitting, James E., ed. *The Development of North American Archaeology: Essays in the History of Regional Traditions*. Garden City: Doubleday, 1973.

Flack, James Kirkpatrick. *Desideratum in Washington: The Intellectual Community in the Capital City, 1870–1900*. Cambridge, Mass.: Albert Schenkman, 1975.

Fowler, Don D., and Fowler, Catherine S., eds. *Anthropology of the Numa: John Wesley Powell's Manuscripts on the Numic Peoples of Western North America,*

1868–1880. Smithsonian Contributions to Anthropology 14. Washington, D.C.: Smithsonian Institution Press, 1971.

Fowler, Don D., and Matley, John. *Material Culture of the Numa: The Powell Collection, 1868–1876.* Smithsonian Contributions to Anthropology. Washington, D.C.: Smithsonian Institution Press, 1975.

Frankel, Charles, ed. *Controversies and Decisions: The Social Sciences and Public Policy.* New York: Russell Sage Foundation, 1976.

Fredrickson, George M. *The Black Image in the White Mind: The Debate on Afro-American Character and Destiny, 1817–1914.* New York: Harper & Row, 1971.

Furner, Mary O. *Advocacy and Objectivity: A Crisis in the Professionalization of American Social Science, 1865–1905.* Lexington: University of Kentucky Press, 1975.

Gatschet, Albert Samuel. *The Klamath Tribe and Language of Oregon.* Contributions to North American Ethnology 2. Parts 1 and 2. Washington, D.C.: GPO, 1890.

Gerth, H. H., and Mills, C. Wright, eds. *From Max Weber: Essays in Sociology.* London: Routledge and Kegan Paul, 1948.

Gibbs, George. *The Memoirs of the Administration of Washington and Adams, edited from the Papers of Oliver Wolcott, Secretary of the Treasury.* New York: 1846.

Gilliland, Marion Spjut. *The Material Culture of Key Marco, Florida.* Gainesville: University of Florida Presses, 1975.

Goetzmann, William H. *Exploration and Empire: The Explorer and the Scientist in the Winning of the American West.* New York: Alfred A. Knopf, 1966.

Goldschmidt, Walter, ed. *The Uses of Anthropology.* Special Publication of the American Anthropological Association no. 11. Washington, D.C.: American Anthropological Association, 1979.

Goode, George Brown, ed. *The Smithsonian Institution, 1846–1896: The History of its First Half-Century.* Washington, D.C.: Devine Press, 1897.

Green, Constance McLaughlin. *Washington: Capital City, 1879–1950.* Princeton: Princeton University Press, 1963.

————. *Washington: Village and Capital, 1800–1878.* Princeton: Princeton University Press, 1962.

Green, Jesse, ed. *Zuñi: Selected Writings of Frank Hamilton Cushing.* Lincoln: University of Nebraska Press, 1979.

Guralnick, Stanley M. *Science and the Ante-Bellum American College.* Memoirs of the American Philosophical Society 109. Philadelphia: American Philosophical Society, 1975.

Harris, Marvin. *The Rise of Anthropological Theory: A History of Theories of Culture.* New York: Thomas Y. Crowell Co., 1968.

Haskell, Thomas L. *The Emergence of Professional Social Science: The American*

Social Science Association and the Nineteenth-Century Crisis of Authority. Urbana: University of Illinois Press, 1977.

Haven, Samuel F. *Archaeology in the United States.* Smithsonian Contributions to Knowledge 8. Washington, D.C.: GPO, 1856.

Hayes, E. N. and Hayes, T., eds. *Claude Lévi-Strauss: The Anthropologist as Hero.* Cambridge: MIT Press, 1970.

Hays, Samuel P. *Conservation and the Gospel of Efficiency: The Progressive Conservation Movement, 1890–1920.* Cambridge, Mass.: Harvard University Press, 1959.

Helm, June, ed. *Pioneers in American Anthropology: The Uses of Biography.* Seattle: University of Washington Press, 1966.

Henry, Joseph. *The Papers of Joseph Henry,* edited by Nathan Reingold. Vol. 1: December 1797–October 1832: The Albany Years. Washington, D.C.: Smithsonian Institution Press, 1972.

Hodge, Frederick W., ed. *Handbook of American Indians North of Mexico.* Part 1. *BAE Bulletin* 30. Washington, D.C.: GPO, 1907.

Holmes, William Henry. *Handbook of Aboriginal American Antiquities. BAE Bulletin* 60, Part 1. Washington, D.C.: GPO, 1919.

Hooker, Arthur, ed. *Official Proceedings of the Nineteenth National Irrigation Congress, held at Chicago, Illinois, U.S.A., December 5–9, 1911.* Chicago: R. R. Donnelly & Sons Co., 1912.

Huddleston, Lee Eldridge. *Origins of the American Indians: European Concepts, 1492–1729.* Austin: University of Texas, 1967.

Israel, Jerry, ed. *Building the Organizational Society: Essays on Associational Activities in Modern America.* New York: Free Press, 1972.

James, Edward T., ed. *Notable American Women, 1607–1950: A Biographical Dictionary.* Cambridge: Belknap Press of Harvard University Press, 1971.

Jefferson, Thomas. *Notes on the State of Virginia.* In Foner, Philip S., ed., *Basic Writings of Thomas Jefferson.* Garden City: Halcyon House, 1944.

John Wesley Powell: Proceedings of a Meeting Commemorative of his Distinguished Services, held in the Columbian University under the Auspices of the Washington Academy of Sciences, February 16, 1903. Proceedings of the Washington Academy of Sciences 5:99–187. Washington, D.C.: Judd and Detweiler, 1903.

Jones, Joseph. *Antiquities of Tennessee.* Smithsonian Contributions to Knowledge 22. Washington, D.C.: GPO, 1882.

Judd, Neil. *The Bureau of American Ethnology: A Partial History.* Norman: University of Oklahoma Press, 1968.

Kardiner, Abram, and Preble, Edward. *They Studied Man.* New York: Mentor Books, 1963.

Kolakowski, Leszek. *The Alienation of Reason: A History of Positivist Thought.* Translated by Norbert Guterman. Garden City: Doubleday & Co., 1969.

Kroeber, Alfred L., *et al. Anthropology Today: An Encyclopedic Inventory.* Chicago: University of Chicago Press, 1953.

Kuhn, Thomas. *The Structure of Scientific Revolutions.* Chicago: University of Chicago Press, 1962.

Laguna, Frederica de, ed. *Selected Papers from the American Anthropologist, 1888–1920.* Evanston, Ill.: Row, Peterson and Co., 1960.

Liberty, Margot, ed. *American Indian Intellectuals. 1976 Proceedings of the American Ethnological Society.* St. Paul: West Publishing Co., 1978.

Lowie, Robert H. *History of Ethnological Theory.* New York: Holt, Rinehart and Winston, 1937.

Ludewig, Hermann E. *The Literature of American Aboriginal Languages.* Edited by Nicolas Trübner, with additions and corrections by William W. Turner. London, 1858.

Lurie, Edward. *Nature and the American Mind: Louis Agassiz and the Culture of Science.* New York: N. Watson, 1974.

Lyell, Charles. *The Geological Evidences of the Antiquity of Man.* 4th ed., rev. London: John Murray, 1873.

McCulloh, James H. *Researches, Philosophical and Antiquarian Concerning the Aboriginal History of America.* Baltimore: F. Luces, Jr., 1817.

McGee, Emma R. *Life of W J McGee.* Farley, Iowa: privately printed, 1915.

McGee, W J, ed. *Proceedings of a Conference of Governors in the White House, Washington, D.C., May 13–15, 1908.* Washington, D.C.: GPO, 1909.

McGee, W J. *The Seri Indians of Bahia Kino and Sonora, Mexico.* BAE, *AR for 1896.* Washington, D.C.: GPO, 1898. Reprinted with introduction by Bernard L. Fontana. Florieta, N.M.: Rio Grande Press, 1971.

McGee Memorial Meeting of the Washington Academy of Sciences. Baltimore: Williams and Wilkinson Co., 1916.

McKusick, Marshall. *The Davenport Conspiracy.* Iowa City: The University of Iowa, 1970.

McVaugh, Rogers. *Edward Palmer: Plant Explorer of the American West.* Norman: University of Oklahoma Press, 1956.

Mallery, Garrick. *Picture-Writing of the American Indians.* BAE, *AR for 1889,* pp. 1–907. Washington, D.C.: GPO, 1893.

————. *Sign-language among the North American Indians, compared with that among other People and Deaf-Mutes.* BAE, *AR for 1880,* pp. 263–552. Washington, D.C.: GPO, 1881.

Manning, Thomas J. *Government in Science: The U.S. Geological Survey, 1867–1894.* Lexington: University Press of Kentucky, 1967.

Mardock, Robert W. *The Reformers and the American Indian.* Columbia: University of Missouri Press, 1971.

Mason, Otis T. *Aboriginal American Basketry: Studies in a Textile Art Without Machinery.* USNM, *AR for 1902,* pp. 171–548. Washington, D.C.: GPO, 1903.

Mayer, Brantz. *Mexican Archaeology and History.* Smithsonian Contributions to Knowledge 9. Washington, D.C.: GPO, 1857.

Mitra, Panchanan. *A History of American Anthropology.* Calcutta: University of Calcutta, 1933.

Mooney, James. *Calendar History of the Kiowa Indians.* BAE, AR for 1896. Washington, D.C.: GPO, 1898. Reprinted with an introduction by John C. Ewers. Washington, D.C.: Smithsonian Institution Press, 1979.

―――. *The Ghost-Dance Religion and the Sioux Outbreak of 1890.* BAE, AR for 1893, Part 2. Washington, D.C.: GPO, 1896.

―――. *Myths of the Cherokee.* BAE, AR for 1898, Part 1. Washington, D.C.: GPO, 1900.

―――. *Sacred Formulas of the Cherokees.* BAE, AR for 1886. Washington, D.C.: GPO, 1891.

―――. *Siouan Tribes of the East.* BAE Bulletin 22. Washington, D.C.: GPO, 1894.

Morgan, Lewis Henry. *Ancient Society: or, Researches in the Lines of Human Progress from Savagery through Barbarism to Civilization.* Edited by Eleanor Burke Leacock. Cleveland: World Publishing Co., 1963.

―――. *Systems of Consanguinity and Affinity in the Human Family.* Smithsonian Contributions to Knowledge 17. Washington, D.C.: GPO, 1871.

Morton, Samuel George. *An Inquiry Into the Distinctive Characteristics of the Aboriginal Race of America.* Boston, 1842; Philadelphia, 1844.

―――. *Crania Americana, or a Comparative View of the Skulls of the Various Aboriginal Nations of North and South America. To Which is Prefixed an Essay on the Varieties of the Human Species.* Philadelphia, 1839.

Murra, John V., ed. *American Anthropology: The Early Years. 1974 Proceedings of the American Ethnological Society.* St. Paul: West Publishing Co., 1976.

Nash, Roderick, ed. *The American Environment: Readings in the History of Conservation.* Reading, Mass.: Addison-Wesley, 1968.

Nott, J. C., and Gliddon, G. R. *Types of Mankind, or Ethnological Researches based upon the ancient monuments, paintings, sculptures, and crania of races, and upon their natural geographical, philological, and Biblical history.* Philadelphia: Lippincott, Grambo and Co., 1854.

Oehser, Paul H. *The Smithsonian Institution.* New York: Praeger Publishing, 1970.

―――. *Sons of Science: The Story of the Smithsonian Institution and its Leaders.* New York: Henry Schuman, 1949.

Oleson, A., and Brown, S. C., eds. *The Pursuit of Knowledge in the Early American Republic.* Baltimore: The Johns Hopkins University Press, 1976.

Oleson, A., and Voss, J., ed. *The Organization of Knowledge in Modern America, 1860–1920.* Baltimore and London: The Johns Hopkins University Press, 1979.

Pearce, Roy Harvey. *Savagism and Civilization: A Study of the Indian and the American Mind.* Baltimore: The Johns Hopkins University Press, 1965.

Pilling, James C. *Proof-Sheets of a Bibliography of the Languages of the North American Indians.* Washington, D.C.: GPO, 1895.

Pinchot, Gifford. *Breaking New Ground.* New York: Harcourt, Brace, 1947.

Pott, P. H. *Naar Wijder Horizon: Kaleidscoop op ons beeld van de Buitenwereld.* The Hague: Mouton & Co., 1962.

Powell, John Wesley. *Truth and Error.* Chicago: Open Court, 1898.

Prichard, James C. *Researches in the Physical History of Man.* Edited by George W. Stocking, Jr. Chicago: University of Chicago Press, 1973.

Rau, Charles. *The Archaeological Collection of the United States National Museum, in Charge of the Smithsonian Institution.* Smithsonian Contributions to Knowledge 22. Washington, D.C.: GPO, 1876.

_____. *Observations on Cup-shaped and other Lapidarian Sculptures in the Old World and in America.* Contributions to North American Ethnology 5. Washington, D.C.: GPO, 1882.

_____. *Prehistoric Fishing in Europe and North America.* Smithsonian Contributions to Knowledge 25. Washington, D.C.: GPO, 1884.

Reingold, Nathan, ed. *Science in Nineteenth-Century America: A Documentary History.* New York: Hill and Wang, 1964.

Resek, Carl. *Lewis Henry Morgan: American Scholar.* Chicago: University of Chicago, 1960.

Schlesinger, Arthur M., Jr. *Robert Kennedy and His Times.* New York: Ballantine Books, 1978.

Schoolcraft, Henry Rowe. *Information regarding the history, condition and prospects of the Indian tribes of the United States: collected and prepared under the direction of the Bureau of Indian Affairs.* 6 vols. Philadelphia: Lippincott, Grambo & Co., 1851–57.

_____. *Personal Memoirs of a Residence of Thirty Years with the Indian Tribes on the American Frontiers.* 1851. Reprint. New York: Arno Press, 1975.

Silverberg, Robert. *Mound Builders of Ancient America: The Archaeology of a Myth.* Greenwich: New York Graphic Society, 1968.

Silverstein, Michael, ed. *Whitney on Language: Selected Writings of William Dwight Whitney.* Cambridge: MIT Press, 1971.

Slotkin, Richard L. *Regeneration Through Violence: The Mythology of the American Frontier, 1600–1860.* Middletown, Conn.: Wesleyan University Press, 1974.

Smith, Henry Nash. *Virgin Land: The American West as Symbol and Myth.* New York: Random House, 1950.

Somkin, Fred. *Unquiet Eagle: Memory and Desire in the Idea of American Freedom, 1815–1860.* Ithaca: Cornell University Press, 1967.

Spencer, Herbert. *First Principles.* Reprinted from 5th London ed. New York: A. L. Burt, 1880.

_____. *The Study of Sociology.* Introduction by Talcott Parsons. Ann Arbor:

University of Michigan, 1961.

Squier, Ephraim G. *Aboriginal Monuments of New York.* Smithsonian Contributions to Knowledge 2. Washington, D.C.: GPO, 1851.

————. *The Serpent Symbol and the Worship of the Reciprocal Principles of Nature in America.* New York: G. P. Putnam, 1851.

————. , and Davis, Edwin H. *Ancient Monuments of the Mississippi Valley: Comprising the Results of Extensive Original Surveys and Explorations.* Smithsonian Contributions to Knowledge 1. Washington, D.C.: GPO, 1848.

Stanton, William. *The Great United States Exploring Expedition of 1838–1842.* Berkeley: University of California Press, 1975.

————. *The Leopard's Spots: Scientific Attitudes Toward Race in America, 1815–1859.* Chicago: University of Chicago Press, 1960.

Stegner, Wallace. *Beyond the Hundredth Meridian: John Wesley Powell and the Second Opening of the West.* Boston: Houghton Mifflin, 1954.

Stevenson, Matilda Coxe. *The Zuñi Indians: Their Mythology. Esoteric Fraternities, and Ceremonies.* BAE, AR *for 1902.* Washington, D.C.: GPO, 1904.

Stocking, George W., Jr. *Anthropology at Chicago: Tradition, Discipline, Department.* Chicago: The University of Chicago Library, 1979.

————. *Race, Culture and Evolution: Essays in the History of Anthropology.* New York: Free Press, 1968.

————., ed. *Selected Papers from the "American Anthropologist," 1921–1945.* Washington, D.C.: American Anthropological Association, 1976.

————. *The Shaping of American Anthropology, 1883–1911: A Franz Boas Reader.* New York: Basic Books, 1974.

Thomas, Cyrus. *Report on the Mound Explorations of the Bureau of Ethnology.* BAE, AR *for 1891,* pp. 3–730. Washington, D.C.: GPO, 1894.

Thoreson, Timothy H. H., ed. *Toward a Science of Man: Essays in the History of Anthropology.* The Hague: Mouton, 1976.

Trollope, Anthony. *North America.* New York: Harper & Brothers, 1862.

Van Tassel, David D., and Hall, Michael G., eds. *Science and Society in the United States.* Homewood, Ill.: Dorsey Press, 1966.

Weiss, John, ed. *The Origins of Modern Consciousness.* Detroit: Wayne State University Press, 1965.

Whitman, Walt. *Walt Whitman: Complete Poetry and Selected Prose and Letters.* Edited by Emory Holloway. London: Nonesuch Press, 1938.

Whitney, William Dwight. *Language and the Study of Language: Twelve Lectures on the Principles of Linguistic Science.* New York: Charles Scribner & Co., 1867.

Whittlesey, Charles. *Ancient Works in Ohio.* Smithsonian Contributions to Knowledge 3. Washington, D.C.: GPO, 1852.

Wiebe, Robert H. *The Search for Order, 1877–1920.* New York: Hill & Wang, 1967.

Willey, Gordon R., and Sabloff, Jeremy A. *A History of American Archaeology.* San Francisco: W. H. Freeman and Co., 1974. 2d ed., 1980.

Wissler, Clark. *The Relation of Nature to Man in Aboriginal America.* New York: 1926. Reprint. New York: AMS Press, 1971.

Wright, George Frederick. *The Ice Age in North America and its Bearings upon the Antiquity of Man.* Oberlin: Bibliotheca Sacra Co., 1889.

————. *Man and the Glacial Period.* New York: D. Appleton, 1892.

Ziff, Larzer. *Puritanism in America: New Culture in a New World.* New York: Viking Press, 1973.

PERIODICALS

Abbott, Charles C. "Occurrence of Implements in the River Drift at Trenton, New Jersey." *American Naturalist* 7 (1873):204–09.

————. "Second Report on the Paleolithic Implements from the Glacial Drift in the Valley of the Delaware River near Trenton, N.J." *Eleventh Annual Report of the Peabody Museum* (1878):225–57.

————. "The Stone Age in New Jersey." *American Naturalist* 6 (1872):144–60, 199–229.

Adler, Cyrus. "Samuel Pierpont Langley." SI, *AR for 1906,* pp. 515–533.

Boas, Franz. "Museums of Ethnology and their Classification." *Science* 9 (1887):587–89.

————. "The Occurrence of Similar Inventions in Areas Widely Separated." *Science* 9 (1887):485–86.

————. "The Study of Geography." *Science* 9 (1887): 137–41.

Buettner-Janusch, John. "Boas and Mason: Particularism versus Generalization." *American Anthropologist* 59 (1957):318–24.

Bushnell, David I., Jr. "Drawings by George Gibbs in the Far Northwest, 1849–1851." Smithsonian Miscellaneous Collections 97, no. 8 (1938).

Chamberlin, Thomas C. "The Method of Multiple Working Hypotheses." *Science,* o.s. 15 (1890):92–96; later expanded in *Journal of Geology* 5 (1897):837–48.

Cockerell, T. D. A. "Spencer Fullerton Baird." *Popular Science Monthly* 68 (1906):63–83.

Collier, Donald, and Tschopik, Harry, Jr. "The Role of Museums in American Anthropology." *American Anthropologist* 56 (1954):768–79.

Cox, William VanZandt. "George Brown Goode: A Memorial Sketch." *American Monthly Magazine,* January 1897, pp. 1–11.

Cross, Whitney R. "W J McGee and the Idea of Conservation." *Historian* 15 (1953):148–62.

Cushing, Frank Hamilton. "Antiquities of Orleans County, New York." SI, *AR for 1874*, pp. 375–77.

———. "Exploration of Ancient Key Dwellers' Remains on the Gulf Coast of Florida." *Proceedings of the American Philosophical Society* 35 (1896):329–448. Reprinted, with introduction by Philip Phillips. New York: AMS Press, 1977.

———. "The Germ of Shore-Land Pottery." *Memoirs of the International Congress of Anthropology*, pp. 217–34. Chicago, 1894.

———. "The Need of Studying the Indian in Order to Teach Him." Albion, N.Y.: A. M. Eddy, 1897. Reprint of original in *Twenty-Eighth Annual Report of the Board of Indian Commissioners*. Washington, D.C.: GPO, 1897.

———. "A Study of Pueblo Pottery, as Illustrative of Zuñi Culture Growth." BAE, *AR for 1883*, pp. 467–521. Washington, D.C.: GPO, 1886.

Darnell, Regna. "The Emergence of Academic Anthropology at the University of Pennsylvania." *Journal of the History of the Behavioral Sciences* 6 (1970):80–92.

———. "The Powell Classification of American Indian Languages." *Papers in Linguistics* 4 (1971):79–110.

———. "The Professionalization of American Anthropology: A Case Study in the Sociology of Knowledge." *Social Science Information* 10, no. 2 (1972), pp. 83–103.

———. "The Revision of the Powell Classification." *Papers in Linguistics* 4 (1971):233–57.

Darton, N. H. "Memoir of W J McGee." *Annals of the Association of American Geographers* 3 (1912):103–10.

Dexter, Ralph W. "Putnam's Problems Popularizing Anthropology." *American Scientist* 54 (1966):315–32.

Dorsey, James Owen. "Siouan Sociology." BAE, *AR for 1894*, pp. 205–44. Washington, D.C.: GPO, 1897.

Duponceau, Peter Stephen. "Report of the Historical and Literary Committee to the American Philosophical Society, January 9, 1818." *Transactions of the Historical and Literary Committee of the American Philosophical Society* 1. Philadelphia, 1819.

Fewkes, Jesse Walter. "The Prehistoric Culture of Tusayan." *American Anthropologist*, o.s. 9 (1896):151–73.

Fletcher, Robert. "Brief Memoir of Colonel Garrick Mallery." Washington, D.C.: privately printed, 1895.

Fontana, Bernard L. "Pioneers in Ideas: Three Early Southwestern Ethnologists." *Journal of the Arizona Academy of Science* 2 (1963):124–29.

Fowler, Don D., and Fowler, Catherine S. "John Wesley Powell, Anthropologist." *Utah Historical Quarterly* 37 (1969):152–72.

Freeman, John F. "Religion and Personality in the Anthropology of Henry Schoolcraft." *Journal of the History of the Behavioral Sciences* 1 (1965):301–13.

————. "University Anthropology: Early Departments in the United States." *Kroeber Anthropological Society Papers* 32 (1965):78–90.

Gatschet, Albert S. "Analytical Report upon Indian dialects spoken in southern California, Nevada, and on the lower Colorado River, etc." *Annual Report of the U.S. Geological Survey West of the 100th Meridian for 1876.* Washington, D.C.: GPO, 1876.

————. "Report on the Pueblo Languages of New Mexico, and of the Moquis in Arizona: their affinity to each other and to the languages of the other tribes." *Annual Report of the U.S. Geological Survey West of the 100th Meridian for 1875.* Washington, D.C.: GPO, 1875.

Gibbs, George. "The Intermixture of Races." SI, *AR for 1864,* pp. 375–76.

————. "On the Language of the Aboriginal Indians of America." SI, *AR for 1870,* pp. 364–67.

————. "A Physical Atlas of North America." SI, *AR for 1866,* pp. 368–69.

Gilbert, Grove Karl. "John Wesley Powell." SI, *AR for 1902,* pp. 633–40.

Goode, George Brown. "The Genesis of the U.S. National Museum." USNM, *AR for 1891,* pp. 273–380.

————. "Museum-History and Museums of History." *Papers of the American Historical Association* 3 (1889):495–519.

————. "The Principles of Museum Administration." *Annual Report of the Museums Association of Great Britain for 1895.* York: Coultas & Volans, 1895.

Gore, J. Howard. "Anthropology at Washington." *Popular Science Monthly* 35 (1888):786–95.

Gould, Stephen Jay. "Morton's Ranking of Races by Cranial Capacity: Unconscious Manipulation of Data May Be a Scientific Norm." *Science* 200 (5 May 1978):503–09.

Gruber, Jacob. "Ethnographic Salvage and the Shaping of Anthropology." *American Anthropologist* 72 (1970):1289–99.

Haas, Mary. "Grammar or Lexicon? The American Indian Side of the Question from Duponceau to Powell." *International Journal of Anthropological Linguistics* 35 (1969):239–55.

Hallowell, A. Irving. "The Beginnings of Anthropology in America." In *Selected Papers from the American Anthropologist, 1888–1920,* edited by Frederica de Laguna. Evanston, Ill.: Row, Peterson and Co., 1960, pp 1–90.

————. "The History of Anthropology as an Anthropological Problem." *Journal of the History of the Behavioral Sciences* 1 (1965):24–38.

Henshaw, Henry W. "Autobiographical Notes." *The Condor,* vol. 21, no. 3 (1919), pp. 102–107; no. 4, pp. 165–171; no. 5, pp. 177–181; no. 6, pp. 216–222; vol. 22, no. 1 (1920), pp. 3–10; no. 2, pp. 55–60; no. 3, pp. 95–101.

Hinsley, Curtis M., and Holm, Bill. "A Cannibal in the National Museum: The Early Career of Franz Boas in America." *American Anthropologist* 78

(1976):306–16.

Hodge, Frederick Webb. "W J McGee." *American Anthropologist* 14 (1912):683–86.

Hoffman, Walter J. "The Menomini Indians." BAE, *AR for 1893*, pp. 11–328. Washington, D.C.: GPO, 1896.

Holmes, William Henry. "Museum Presentation of Anthropology." *Proceedings of the American Association for the Advancement of Science* 47 (1898):485–88.

———. "Primitive Man in the Delaware Valley." *Science*, n.s. 6 (1897):824–29.

———. "Report on the Ancient Ruins of Southwestern Colorado, examined during the summers of 1875 and 1876." *10th Annual Report of the United States Geological and Geographical Survey of the Territories.* Washington, D.C.: GPO, 1878.

Hough, Walter. "Otis Tufton Mason." *American Anthropologist* 10 (1908):661–67.

Hrdlička, Aleš. "Physical Anthropology in America." *American Anthropologist* 16 (1914):508–54.

Hymes, Dell H. "Kroeber, Powell, and Henshaw." *International Journal of Anthropological Linguistics* 3, no. 6 (1961), pp. 15–16.

Kayser, Elmer Louis. "Columbian Academy, 1821–1897: The Preparatory Department of Columbian College in the District of Columbia." *Records of the Columbia Historical Society* (1971), pp. 150–63.

Keyes, Charles R. "W J McGee, Anthropologist, Geologist, Hydrologist." *Annals of Iowa* series 3, vol. 2 (1913), pp. 6–10.

Knowlton, F. J. "Memoir of W J McGee." *Bulletin of the Geological Society of America* 24 (1912):18–29.

Kohlstedt, Sally. "A Step Toward Scientific Self-Identity in the United States: The Failure of the National Institute, 1844." *Isis* 62 (1971):339–62.

Kroeber, Alfred L. "Frank Hamilton Cushing." *Encyclopedia of the Social Sciences* 2 (New York, 1930–35):657.

———. "The Place of Boas in Anthropology." *American Anthropologist* 58 (1956):151–59.

———. "Powell and Henshaw: An Episode in the History of Ethnolinguistics." *International Journal of Anthropological Linguistics* 2, no. 4 (1960), pp. 1–5.

———. "The Seri." *Southwest Museum Papers* 6 (1931).

Lamb, Daniel S. "The Story of the Anthropological Society of Washington." *American Anthropologist* 6 (1904):564–79.

Langley, Samuel P. "Memoir of George Brown Goode." Washington, D.C.: National Academy of Sciences, 1897.

LeConte, Joseph. "The Factors of Evolution." *The Monist* 1 (1890–91):321–35.

Lowie, Robert H. "Reminiscences of Anthropological Currents in America Half a Century Ago." *American Anthropologist* 58 (1956):995–1016.

McGee, W J. "The Beginning of Agriculture." *American Anthropologist*, o.s. 8 (1895):350–75.

_____. "The Beginning of Zooculture." *American Anthropologist*, o.s. 10 (1897):215–30.

_____. "Cardinal Principles of Science." *Proceedings of the Washington Academy of Sciences* 2 (1900):1–12.

_____. "The Course of Human Development." *Forum* 26 (1898):56–65.

_____. "The Earth the Home of Man." *Special Papers of the Anthropological Society of Washington* 1, no. 2. Washington, D.C.: Anthropological Society of Washington, 1894.

_____. "Expedition to Papagueria and Seriland: A Preliminary Note." *American Anthropologist*, o.s. 9 (1896):93–98.

_____. "Fifty Years of American Science." *Atlantic Monthly* 82 (1898):307–20.

_____. "Man and the Glacial Period." *American Anthropologist*, o.s.6 (1893):85–95.

_____. "Man's Place in Nature." *American Anthropologist* 3 (1901):1–13.

_____. "Necrology: Frank Hamilton Cushing." BAE, *AR for 1900*, pp. xxxv–xxxviii.

_____. "Paleolithic Man in America: His Antiquity and Environment." *Popular Science Monthly* 34 (1888):20–36.

_____. "The Science of Humanity." *American Anthropologist*, o.s. 10 (1897):241–72.

_____. "The Siouan Indians: A Preliminary Sketch." BAE, *AR for 1894*, pp. 157–204. Washington, D.C.: GPO, 1897.

_____. "The Trend of Human Progress." *American Anthropologist* 1 (1899):401–47.

Mallery, Garrick. "A Calendar of the Dakota Nation." *U.S. Geological and Geographical Survey of the Territories Bulletin* 3, no. 1. Washington, D.C.: GPO, 1877.

_____. "Greeting by Gesture." *Popular Science Monthly* 38 (1890–91):477–90.

_____. "Israelite and Indian: A Parallel in Planes of Culture." *Popular Science Monthly* 36 (1889–90):52–76, 193–213.

_____. "A Philosophic Phantasy." Read before the Philosophical Society of Washington, 18 February 1893. Privately printed, n.d.

_____. "Some Common Errors Respecting the North American Indians." *Bulletin of the Philosophical Society of Washington* 2 (1875–80):175–81.

Mark, Joan. "Frank Hamilton Cushing and an American Science of Anthropology." *Perspectives in American History* 10 (1976):449–86.

Mason, Otis T. "Aboriginal American Harpoons: A Study in Ethnic Distribution and Invention." USNM, *AR for 1900*, pp. 189–304.

_____. "Aboriginal American Zootechny." *American Anthropologist* 1 (1899):45–81.

_____. "Basket-Work of the North American Aborigines." USNM, *AR for 1884*, Part 2, pp. 291–316.

_____. "The Birth of Invention." SI, *AR for 1892*, pp. 603–11.

————. "Cradles of the American Aborigines." USNM, *AR for 1887*, pp. 161–212.

————. "The Educational Aspect of the United States National Museum." *Johns Hopkins University Studies in Historical and Political Science* 8 (1890):505–19.

————. "Ethnological Exhibit of the Smithsonian Institution at the World's Columbian Exposition." *Memoirs of the International Congress of Anthropology*, pp. 208–16. Chicago, 1894.

————. "Influence of Environment upon Human Industries or Arts." SI, *AR for 1895*, pp. 639–65.

————. "The Leipsic Museum of Ethnology." SI, *AR for 1873*, pp. 390–409.

————. "North American Bows, Arrows, and Quivers." SI, *AR for 1893*, pp. 631–79.

————. "The Occurrence of Similar Inventions in Areas Widely Apart." *Science* 9 (1887):534.

————. "Primitive Travel and Transportation." USNM, *AR for 1894*, pp. 237–593.

————. Review of *Korean Games* by Stewart Culin. *American Anthropologist*, o.s. 9 (1896):22–23.

————. "The Scope and Value of Anthropological Studies." *Proceedings of the American Association for the Advancement of Science for 1884:* 365–83.

————. "Technogeography, or the Relation of the Earth to the Industries of Mankind." *American Anthropologist*, o.s. 7 (1894):137–61.

————. "Throwing-Sticks in the National Museum." USNM, *AR for 1884*, Part 2, pp. 279–91.

————. "Traps of the Amerinds: A Study in Psychology and Invention." *American Anthropologist* 2 (1900):657–75.

————. "The Ulu, a Woman's Knife, of the Eskimo." USNM, *AR for 1890*, pp. 411–16.

————. "Vocabulary of Malaysian Basketwork: A Study in the W. L. Abbott Collections." *USNM Proceedings* 35 (1908):1–51.

————. "What is Anthropology?" Washington, D.C.: Smithsonian Saturday Lectures, 1883.

Molella, Arthur, and Reingold, Nathan. "Theorists and Ingenious Mechanics: Joseph Henry Defines Science." *Science Studies* 3 (1973):323–51.

Mooney, James. "Albert Samuel Gatschet, 1832–1907." *American Anthropologist* 9 (1907):561–65.

————. "In Memoriam: Washington Matthews." *American Anthropologist* 7 (1905):514–23.

Morton, Samuel George. "Account of a Craniological Collection." *Transactions of American Ethnological Society* 2. New York, 1848.

Osborn, Henry Fairchild. "Goode as a Naturalist." *Science*, n.s. 5 (1897):374–79.

Pandey, Triloki Nath. "Anthropologists at Zuñi." *Proceedings of the American Philosophical Society* 116 (1972):321–37.

Powell, John Wesley. "Competition as a Factor in Human Evolution." *American Anthropologist*, o.s. 1 (1898):297–321.

————. "Darwin's Contributions to Philosophy." *Proceedings of the Biological Society of Washington* 1 (1882):60–70.

————. "From Savagery to Barbarism." *Transactions of the Anthropological Society of Washington* 3 (1885):173–96.

————. "Human Evolution." *Transactions of the Anthropological Society of Washington* 2 (1883):176–208.

————. "Garrick Mallery." SI, *AR for 1895*, pp. 52–53.

————. "James Owen Dorsey." SI, *AR for 1895*, pp. 53–54.

————. "Museums of Ethnology and their Classification." *Science* 9 (1887):612–14.

————. "The Personal Characteristics of Professor Baird." *Philosophical Society of Washington Bulletin* 10 (1887):71–77.

————. "Sketch of Lewis H. Morgan." *Popular Science Monthly* 18 (1881):114–21.

————. "The Three Methods of Evolution." *Philosophical Society of Washington Bulletin* 6 (1884):27–51.

Rau, Charles. "Artificial Shell-Deposits in New Jersey." SI, *AR for 1864*, pp. 370–74.

————. "Indian Pottery." SI, *AR for 1866*, pp. 346–55.

————. "Memoir of C.F.P. von Martius." SI, *AR for 1869*, pp. 169–78.

————. "North American Stone Implements." SI, *AR for 1872*, pp. 395–409.

Reingold, Nathan. "The New York State Roots of Joseph Henry's National Career." *New York History* 54 (1973):132–44.

Royce, Charles C. "Cessions of Land by Indian Tribes to the United States: Illustrated by those in the State of Indiana." BAE, *AR for 1880*, pp. 247–62.

————. "The Cherokee Nation of Indians." BAE, *AR for 1884*, pp. 121–378.

————. "Indian Land Cessions in the United States." Introduction by Cyrus Thomas. BAE, *AR for 1897*, pp. 521–964.

Sherwood, John. "Frank Cushing, Boy Wonder of the Smithsonian's Old Bureau of Ethnology." *Smithsonian* 10, no. 5 (1979), pp. 96–113.

Starr, Frederick. "Anthropological Work in America." *Popular Science Monthly* 41 (1892):289–307.

Stevens, John Austin. "A Memorial of George Gibbs." SI, *AR for 1873*, pp. 219–25.

Stocking, George W., Jr. "Franz Boas and the Founding of the American Anthropological Association." *American Anthropologist* 62 (1960):1–17.

————. "The History of Anthropology: Where, Whence, Wither?" *Journal of the History of the Behavioral Sciences* 2 (1966):281–90.

————. "On the Limits of 'Presentism' and 'Historicism' in the Historiography of the Behavioral Sciences." *Journal of the History of the Behavioral Sciences* 1 (1965):211–17.

Sturtevant, William C. "The Authorship of the Powell Classification." *International Journal of Anthropological Linguistics* 25 (1959):196–99.

————. "Does Anthropology Need Museums?" *Proceedings of the Biological Society of Washington* 82 (1969):619–50.

Swanton, John R. "William Henry Holmes." *National Academy of Sciences Biographical Memoirs* 17:223–52. Washington, D.C.: National Academy of Sciences, 1937.

Thoreson, Timothy H. H. "Art, Evolution, and History: A Case Study of Paradigm Change in Anthropology." *Journal of the History of the Behavioral Sciences* 13 (1977):107–125.

Trumbull, James Hammond. "On the Best Method of Studying the North American Languages." *Transactions of the American Philological Association* 1 (1869–70):55–79.

Washburn, Wilcomb E. "The Museum and Joseph Henry." *Curator* 8 (1965):35–54.

Wilson, Daniel. "Lectures on Physical Ethnology." SI, *AR for 1862–63,* pp. 240–302.

Wilson, Thomas. "The Smithsonian Institution and its Anthropological Work." *Journal of the Royal Anthropological Institute of Great Britain and Ireland for 1890:* 509–15.

Wissler, Clark. "W J McGee." *Encyclopedia of the Social Sciences* 5 (1930):652–53.

ADDRESSES, CIRCULARS, PAMPHLETS

American Ethnological Society. *Indian Languages of North America. AES Circular* 1. New York, June 1852.

Baird, Spencer F. *General Directions for Collecting and Preserving Objects of Natural History.* Washington, D.C., 1848.

Gibbs, George. *Instructions for Archaeological Investigations in the U.S.* SI, *AR for 1861,* pp. 392–96.

————. *Instructions for Research Relative to the Ethnology and Philology of America.* Smithsonian Institution Miscellaneous Collections 7. Washington, D.C.: GPO, 1863.

————. *Instructions relative to the Ethnology and Philology of America. Appendix A: Physical Characters of the Indian Races; Appendix B: Numerical Systems.* Smithsonian Contributions to Knowledge 15. Washington, D.C.: GPO, 1865.

Goode, George Brown. *Classification of the Collection to Illustrate the Animal Resources of the United States: A List of Substances Derived from the Animal*

Kingdom, with Synopsis of the Useful and Injurious Animals and a Classification of the Methods of Capture and Utilization. Washington, D.C.: GPO, 1876.

————. *The Organization and Objects of the National Museum.* USNM Circular 15. Appendix 4. USNM Proceedings 14. Washington, D.C.: GPO, 1881.

Henry, Joseph. "Address of Prof. Joseph Henry." *Fifth and Sixth Annual Reports of the American Museum of Natural History*: 44–50. New York, 1874.

Henshaw, Henry W., and Mooney, James. *Linguistic Families of the Indian Tribes North of Mexico, with a provisional list of the Principal Tribal Names and Synonyms.* Washington, D.C.: GPO, 1885.

Hunter, Alfred. *A Popular Catalogue of the Extraordinary Curiosities in the National Institute arranged in the Building belonging to the Patent Office.* Washington, D.C., 1859.

King, Henry. *Directions for Making Collections in Natural History, prepared for the National Institution for the Promotion of Science.* Washington, D.C., 1840.

Mallery, Garrick. *Introduction to the Study of Sign-language among the North American Indians as Illustrating the Gesture-speech of Mankind.* Washington, D.C.: GPO, 1880.

Mason, Otis T. *Ethnological Directions Relative to the Indian Tribes of the United States.* Washington, D.C., 1875.

Pilling, James C. *Proof-Sheets of a Bibliography of the North American Indians.* Washington, D.C.: Smithsonian Institution, 1885.

Poinsett, Joel R. *Discourse on the Objects and Importance of the National Institution for the Promotion of Science, established at Washington, 1840. Delivered at the First Anniversary.* Washington, D.C., 1841.

Powell, John Wesley. *Address Delivered at the Inauguration of the Corcoran School of Science and Arts, in the Columbian University, Washington, D.C., October 1, 1884.* Washington, D.C.: Gibson Bros., 1884.

————. *Introduction to the Study of Indian Languages with Words, Phrases and Sentences to be Collected.* Washington, D.C.: GPO, 1877. 2d ed., 1880.

Rhees, William J. *Guide to the Smithsonian Institution and National Museum.* Washington, D.C., 1859.

————. *Visitor's Guide to the Smithsonian Institution and National Museum.* Washington, D.C., 1880.

Schoolcraft, Henry Rowe. *An Address, Delivered before the Was-Ah-Ho-De-No-Son-Ne, or New Confederacy of the Iroquois, at its Third Annual Council, August 14, 1846.* Rochester, 1846.

————. *Incentives to the study of the Ancient Period of American History. Address to the New York Historical Society, 17 November 1846.* New York, 1847.

————. *Plan for the Investigation of American Ethnology: to include the facts derived from other parts of the globe, and the eventual formation of a Museum of Antiquities and the peculiar Fabrics of Nations: and also the collection of a library of the Philology of the World, manuscript and printed.* New York, 1846.

Yarrow, Harry Crécy. *Introduction to the Study of Mortuary Customs among the North American Indians.* Washington, D.C.: GPO, 1880.

UNPUBLISHED WORKS

Beckham, Stephen Dow. "George Gibbs, 1815–1873: Historian and Ethnologist." Ph.D. dissertation, University of California at Los Angeles, 1969.

Bieder, Robert Eugene. "The American Indian and the Development of Anthropological Thought in the United States, 1780–1851." Ph.D. dissertation, University of Minnesota, 1972.

Brandes, Raymond Stewart. "Frank Hamilton Cushing: Pioneer Americanist." Ph.D. dissertation, University of Arizona, 1965.

Colby, William L "Routes to Rainy Mountain: A Biography of James Mooney, Ethnologist." Ph.D. dissertation, University of Wisconsin-Madison, 1977.

Darnell, Regna D. "The Development of American Anthropology, 1879–1920: From the Bureau of American Ethnology to Franz Boas." Ph.D. dissertation, University of Pennsylvania, 1969.

Erickson, Paul A. "The Origins of Physical Anthropology." Ph.D. dissertation, University of Connecticut, 1974.

Freeman, John F. "Henry Rowe Schoolcraft, 1793–1864." Ph.D. dissertation, Harvard University, 1960.

Jacknis, Ira. "The Field Columbian Museum Expedition to the Northwest Coast, 1897." Unpublished paper.

————. "Franz Boas and Museums of Anthropology in America, 1880–1920." Unpublished paper.

Lacey, Michael J. "The Mysteries of Earth-Making Dissolve: A Study of Washington's Intellectual Community and the Origins of American Environmentalism in the Late Nineteenth Century." Ph.D. dissertation, George Washington University, 1979.

Noelke, Virginia H. "The Origin and Early History of the Bureau of American Ethnology, 1879–1910." Ph.D. dissertation, University of Texas at Austin, 1974.

Poor, Robert. "Washington Matthews: An Intellectual Biography." Master's thesis, University of Nevada-Reno, 1975.

Tax, Thomas G. "The Development of American Archeology, 1800–1879." Ph.D. dissertation, University of Chicago, 1973.

ARCHIVAL MATERIAL

This study draws largely on unpublished archival material, some of it opened for the first time. In addition to the collections listed below, I enjoyed access to copies of the incoming and outgoing correspondence of Joseph Henry, gathered, from various collections, at the Joseph Henry Papers, Smithsonian

Institution, under the editorship of Nathan Reingold. These letters are cited in the notes by original collection.

Beloit.
Beloit College Archives.
Stephen D. Peet Papers.

Boston.
Harvard University Archives.
Peabody Museum Papers.
Frederick Ward Putnam Papers.
Peabody Museum Archives.
Papers of Frank Hamilton Cushing and the Hemenway South-Western Archaeological Expedition.

Chicago.
Field Museum Archives.
Franz Boas Files.
George A. Dorsey Files.

Los Angeles.
Southwest Museum.
Frederick Webb Hodge/Frank Hamilton Cushing Papers.
Charles F. Lummis Papers.

Madison.
Wisconsin State Historical Society.
George Gibbs Family Papers.
Increase Lapham Papers.

New Haven.
Yale University Library.
Elias Loomis Papers.
William Dwight Whitney Papers.

New Orleans.
Tulane University Medical Library.
Joseph Jones Papers.

Philadelphia.
American Philosophical Society.
Franz Boas Papers.
John Fries Frazer Papers.

Princeton.
Princeton University Library.
Joseph Henry Collection.

Providence.
John Carter Brown Library.
John Russell Bartlett Papers.

Rochester.
University of Rochester Library.
Lewis Henry Morgan Papers.

San Marino.
Henry E. Huntington Library and Art Gallery.
William J. Rhees Papers.

Santa Fe.
Museum of Navaho Ceremonial Art.
Washington Matthews Papers.

Washington, D.C.
George Washington University Archives.
Catalogues and Prospectuses of the Columbian College Preparatory
    School, 1861–84; GWU, Bulletins, 1871–84.
Library of Congress.
Anita Newcomb McGee Papers.
William John McGee Papers.
Gifford Pinchot Papers.
Ephraim George Squier Papers.
**Smithsonian Institution, Library of the National Museum of American
Art and the National Portrait Gallery.**
William Henry Holmes, "Random Records of a Lifetime Devoted to Science
    and Art, 1846–1931." 20 vols.
Smithsonian Institution, National Anthropological Archives.
William L. Abbott Papers.
Anthropological Society of Washington Papers.
Bureau of American Ethnology Letterbooks, 1879–1920.
Bureau of American Ethnology Letters Received, 1879–1910.
Aleš Hrdlička Papers.
Records of the 1903 Investigation of the BAE.
Matilda Coxe Stevenson Papers.

U.S. National Museum Papers (including papers of Otis T. Mason and Walter Hough).

Smithsonian Institution Archives.

Correspondence of the Assistant Secretary, 1850–1910.

Correspondence of the Secretary, 1846–1910.

Robert Kennicott Papers.

Otis T. Mason's Letters from Europe, 1889.

National Institute Papers.

Richard Rathbun Papers.

William J. Rhees Papers.

Smithsonian Institution Libraries.

Manuscripts of Otis T. Mason and Charles Rau.

Worcester.

American Antiquarian Society.

Samuel F. Haven Papers.

Index